DAVID S. THATCHER

the Growth of a Reputation

Nietzsche in England 1890-1914

UNIVERSITY OF TORONTO PRESS

© University of Toronto Press 1970
Reprinted in 2018
Printed in Canada by
University of Toronto Press
Toronto and Buffalo
ISBN 0-8020-5234-7
ISBN 978-1-4875-7225-9 (paper)

Quotations beginning on pages
20, 21, 61, 157, 161, 162,
251, 252, 257, and 268
are from *The Portable Nietzsche*
translated and edited by
Walter Kaufmann
Copyright 1954 by
The Viking Press, Inc.
Reprinted by permission of
The Viking Press, Inc.

To my parents
LEONARD
and
ANNE THATCHER

PREFACE

Fame, said Rilke, is the sum of misunderstandings that gather about a great name. In Nietzsche's case so great have the misunderstandings been that his fame has been degraded to notoriety, his character debased to caricature, and his philosophy reduced to incendiary tags and catch-phrases. The name of Nietzsche, so often misspelled and mispronounced, seems to release philosophers, authors, and journalists from intellectual responsibility. "I dislike Nietzsche," Bertrand Russell admits in his *History of Western Philosophy*, "because he likes the contemplation of pain, because he erects conceit into a duty, because the men whom he most admires are conquerors, whose glory is cleverness in causing men to die." "We all know," claims Somerset Maugham in *The Summing Up*, "how the philosophy of Nietzsche has affected some parts of the world and few would assert that its influence has been other than disastrous." In 1958 a *Time* reviewer dissociated himself from the prevailing journalistic misconceptions, which he summarized as follows: "Friedrich Nietzsche was a pale, crabby hermit who sat in a cheap Swiss boarding house peering beyond good and evil and demanding, at the top of his apocalyptic voice, the rearing of a daemonically driven breed of superman. Just when the world began to get wind of his prophetic fulminations, he went mad. For the last tragic eleven years of his life, he was a myth – and so he has remained." Quoting this passage in *The House of Intellect*, the brilliant American scholar Jacques Barzun comments: "More dull error could not be compressed into so few words."

Perhaps there was some excuse for these attitudes before Walter Kaufmann began, in *Nietzsche* (1950), his single-handed campaign to convince the English-speaking world that its neglect of Nietzsche was shamefully unjust. His anthology, *The Portable Nietzsche* (1954), his spate of articles and translations, his bibliographies, all testify to the continued energy and dedication with which he has carried out his formidable task. To Kaufmann

I owe my first real orientation in the murky thickets of Nietzschean studies. To those who know his work, his influence will be palpable in the pages that follow; to those who do not, my book can have no better companion than his *Nietzsche*, which, it is encouraging to note, went into a third edition in 1968. There the reader will find a lucid and masterly exegesis of such terms as *Übermensch*, "Eternal Recurrence," and "Will to Power," terms which have so often been distorted by being viewed out of their proper context.

Other intellectual debts should be placed on record. I have, of course, benefited from the findings of critics and historians of literature who have preceded me in the field. Four writers of unpublished dissertations deserve special acknowledgment: Richard P. Benton, of Trinity College, Hartford; T. H. Gibbons, of the University of Western Australia; Milton P. Foster, of Eastern Michigan University; and Wallace Martin, of the University of Toledo.

I am especially grateful to Anthony Ludovici, who allowed me to use unpublished correspondence in his possession. He gave generously of his time and energy to answer my questions about the *New Age* circle, and also wrote to me on matters arising from our discussions. For the opportunity of meeting him and of pursuing research in England I thank the Canada Council, who awarded me a pre-doctoral fellowship in 1966.

W. J. Keith of the University of Toronto has been active in more stages in the progress of the book than he probably cares to remember; his guidance and encouragement have been invaluable. E. W. Mandel of York University helped me work out and utilize methods of organizing my material when its very intractibility was bringing me to the verge of despair.

I am also grateful to those who kindly corresponded with me on various aspects of my work: Ena Collins, Alan Denson, Richard Ellmann, Anneliese Glander, Duncan Grant, Janko Lavrin, Wallace Martin, Katherine Lyon Mix, Margery M. Morgan, Herbert W. Reichert, Lord Bertrand Russell, Ann Saddlemyer, Paul Selver, Frank Swinnerton, Donald Torchiana, Leonard Woolf.

Several colleagues at the University of Victoria read sections of the book while it was in manuscript, and I would like to thank them for detecting errors and suggesting improvements: N. W. Alford, John G. Hayman, Samuel L. Macey, Fred Mayne, Victor A. Neufeldt, Henry Summerfield.

I gladly acknowledge the assistance given by the staffs of the libraries where most of my researches were carried out: the British Museum; Cameron Library, University of Alberta, Edmonton; McMaster University

Library, Hamilton; MacPherson Library, University of Victoria; New York Public Library; University Library, Cambridge. In addition I would like to thank Richard D. Olson, curator of Northwestern University Library, for permission to quote Yeats's annotations to Common's anthology, *Nietzsche as Critic, Philosopher, Poet and Prophet*, and the Henry W. and Albert A. Berg Collection of the New York Public Library, Astor, Lenox and Tilden Foundations, for permission to publish an extract from a letter sent by Lady Gregory to John Quinn.

I would like to thank George Allen and Unwin Ltd. for permission to quote extensively from the eighteen volumes of *The Complete Works of Friedrich Nietzsche*, edited by Dr. Oscar Levy (1909–13); and The Viking Press Inc. for permission to use the translations in Walter Kaufmann's *The Portable Nietzsche* (1954). Although the Levy edition is far from reliable as a translation, it was the means whereby non-German-speaking readers in England gained access to Nietzsche; my use of it, then, is based on historical grounds.

This book has been published with the help of a grant from the Humanities Research Council of Canada, using funds provided by the Canada Council, and with the assistance of a subsidy from the Publications Fund of the University of Toronto Press.

My final acknowledgment is one I make with the keenest sense of pleasure, for without the patience, understanding and unfailing good spirits of my wife, Hedda, to sustain me, this book might never have reached completion. No scholar, I am convinced, could have wished for a more willing and devoted helpmeet. To her I offer a heartfelt tribute of love and gratitude.

Nietzsche's influence in England did not, of course, end with the outbreak of the First World War, and the further history of that influence remains to be documented. To that task I now intend to turn. I shall be grateful for any relevant information with which readers might care to furnish me.

Though Nietzsche's ideas no longer possess the force of novelty – for indeed many of them have passed into the intellectual currency of our age – his work can still give those who read him with care an exhilaration of a rare order. He refreshes, liberates, rids the mind of cant, shows us the way to our own originality. Although this book is written primarily as a contribution to literary history, it would be gratifying if it helped to secure for Nietzsche a wider circle of readers than he now enjoys.

University of Victoria   D.S.T.

DATES OF APPEARANCE

The following table shows at a glance the date of the initial publication of Nietzsche's major works, and the respective dates of the first translations into French and English. *Excerpts* in translation have not been taken into account.

WORK	GERMAN	FRENCH	ENGLISH
The Birth of Tragedy	1872	1901	1909
Thoughts out of Season	1873–6	1907	1909
Richard Wagner in Bayreuth	1876	1877	1909
Human, All-Too-Human	1878	1899	1909
Miscellaneous Opinions and Maxims	1879	1902	1909
The Wanderer and His Shadow	1880	1902	1909
The Dawn of Day	1881	1901	1903
The Gay Science	1882	1901	1910
Thus Spake Zarathustra	1883–5	1898	1896
Beyond Good and Evil	1886	1898	1907
The Genealogy of Morals	1887	1900	1899
The Case of Wagner	1888	1892	1895
The Twilight of the Idols	1889	1899	1896
Nietzsche contra Wagner	1895	1899	1896
The Antichrist	1895	1899	1896
Poems	1895–8	1909	1899
The Will to Power	1899–1902	1903	1909–10
Ecce Homo	1908	1909	1911

CONTENTS

Preface	vii
Dates of appearance	x
I Introduction	3
II The English translations of Nietzsche	17
III John Davidson	53
IV Havelock Ellis	93
V Nietzsche and the literary mind	121
VI William Butler Yeats	139
VII George Bernard Shaw	175
VIII A. R. Orage	219
IX Conclusion	269
Abbreviations	278
Notes	279
Selected bibliography	307
Addenda to the International Nietzsche Bibliography	321
Index	325

Nietzsche
in England
1890-1914

INTRODUCTION

It is frequently claimed, in works of literary history, that Nietzsche's impact on England during the last seventy or eighty years has been very great indeed. Bernard Bergonzi regards Nietzsche as "the dominant intellectual figure of the *fin de siècle*," since his work "embodies all its various strands."[1] Michael Hamburger suggests that Nietzsche's impact on England, though never as strong and immediate as his influence on the rest of Europe, was, if not an earthquake, a tremor in the atmosphere which "can be felt in the works of W. B. Yeats, James Joyce, T. E. Hulme, and Wyndham Lewis, in the circle around A. R. Orage and other groups representative of 'advanced' opinion up to the 'thirties."[2] And a critic of fiction hazards a guess that hardly a mind of any calibre, from the beginning of the twentieth century, has not been influenced to some extent by the teachings of Nietzsche.[3] Such assessments are rarely supported by any evidence, and these are no exception, especially since this important topic has never received the detailed and comprehensive treatment it surely warrants. Roland N. Stromberg's *Realism, Naturalism, and Symbolism: Modes of Thought and Expression in Europe, 1848–1914* (1968) is too general a survey to offer any specific insights into Nietzsche's influence on England. W. Y. Tindall's *Forces in Modern British Literature, 1885–1956* (1956) passes over Nietzsche with a brief word or two, as do the most recent works on the period under present discussion, Samuel Hynes' *The Edwardian Turn of Mind* (1968) and John A. Lester's *Journey Through Despair, 1880–1914: Transformations in British Literary Culture* (1968). This was, Lester maintains, a time of confusion and bewilderment, of disillusion and malaise; the transition from materialistic determinism to a world of chance and change involved "the urgent and pained necessity of a 'transvaluation of values,' to keep man's imaginative life alive under conditions which seemed unlivable." Though he invokes Nietzsche's name to illustrate this crisis, the invocation is never thorough or central – Nietzsche has to queue up in the parade of witnesses summoned before Lester's court of enquiry, and has to say his piece quickly before being summarily dismissed from the stand.* Only one study, a doctoral dissertation on the literary and intellectual milieu between 1880 and 1914, makes a real attempt to substantiate Nietzsche's influence:

> It would not be too much to claim that Nietzsche, in a large variety of ways which reflects his own extreme multiplicity, was the most important single influence upon English thought during the latter half of the period with which we are concerned. ... Nietzsche's optimistically "existentialist" challenge to current forms of scientific determinism appears to have constituted a basic attraction for the period. His later works found admirers in England not only for their advocacy of the Superman, but for their hostility to Liberalism, Romanticism, "decadence," and asceticism.[4]

Nietzsche, this writer continues, was one of the prime factors in the abrupt change of tone in literary discussion between 1905 and 1914: "The introversion and quietism of Pater, one might say, were replaced by the 'hardness,' extraversion, energy and stridency of Nietzsche."[5] But in spite of some admirable perceptions his study does not attempt to give a total picture of Nietzsche's impact on England. The purpose of the present work is to examine Nietzsche's impact on English intellectual life in the years preceding 1914, in the hope that the accumulated data will provide a firmer basis for historical judgment than has existed hitherto. Since it is descriptive rather than critical, synthetic rather than analytic, it should make a greater appeal to cultural historians than to students more interested in the nature of Nietzsche's thought and less in the ways it was appropriated by others.

The investigation of Nietzsche's English reputation was initially undertaken not by English but by German scholars.[6] In 1929, a year after her study of Nietzsche's influence on John Davidson, Gertrud von Petzold published an account of Nietzsche's reputation in England and America up to 1918. In compiling material for her monumental study, she was able to draw on first-hand information cordially supplied by Dr. Levy, the editor of the later English translations. The result, in spite of several minor

---

* *Journey Through Despair, 1880–1914* (Princeton, 1968), xxiii. Much more extensive use could have been made of Nietzsche in dealing with the themes Lester discusses – modern man, death of God, decadence, nihilism, taste for paradox. In the chapter, "The Mask," Nietzsche hardly appears. (Incidentally, the section on "the art of walking" at the beginning of that chapter must surely be the funniest example of unconscious humour in any work of sober scholarship.)

inaccuracies and false attributions, remains a most useful source which modern bibliographies of Nietzsche have not entirely superseded. Comment provoked by Nietzsche's work is gleaned largely from newspapers, periodicals, and books of the war years. Reviews of the Levy translation are cited throughout its progress from 1909 to 1913, but there is a regrettable failure to provide equivalent coverage for the translations which appeared before 1909. Indeed, the whole treatment of these early years is rather perfunctory, and Miss Petzold's bibliographical resourcefulness seems to have deserted her. The result is that her picture of the 1890s is disappointingly dim: the work of Common, *The Eagle and the Serpent* and Pringle-Pattison is given scant mention, and there is no reference at all to the respectful criticism accorded to Nietzsche by such diverse interpreters as Havelock Ellis, Ernest Newman, and J. M. Robertson; bulking largest in this gallery of omissions is the lack of any reference to Max Nordau's *Degeneration* (1895) which, as will be shown, effectively short-circuited any chance the English reading public might have had of looking at Nietzsche with unprejudiced eyes. All too frequently crucial statements and conclusions are given no documentary support: one example of this will serve. She asserts that in the years preceding the first English translations of Nietzsche (i.e. before 1896) the English public, ignorant of German, was obliged to fall back on newspaper and periodical articles for its knowledge of the philosopher; in fact these articles were so few in number and so spreadeagled in different parts of the press that ignorance concerning Nietzsche could not appreciably have been dissipated by them. The most serious drawback of Miss Petzold's study from the point of view of the English reader is her failure to estimate, or even attempt to estimate, Nietzsche's impact on English literature. Reference is made to John Davidson, but only in passing, as he had been the subject of a separate enquiry; of other authors only Bernard Shaw, Edwin Muir, and G. K. Chesterton are considered at all. Chesterton's suspicion of Nietzsche is taken to be typical, not only of his fellow writers, but of the English public as a whole; and the conclusion is that as far as English literature was concerned Nietzsche was accorded little notice, let alone adequate appreciation. The vexed problem of influence is neatly side-stepped by an appeal to "indirect influence" when "direct influence" cannot be shown to exist: in this way Miss Petzold disposes of the genesis of the Shavian Life Force by assuring us it is hardly thinkable without Nietzsche's "at least indirect" influence. To such "indirect influence" is also ascribed a preoccupation with a transvaluation of values in ethics and a deepening concern with psychology in the contemporary English novel.

A second German estimate of Nietzsche's reputation in England, by Dr. Paul Hultsch, appeared in 1938. Hultsch's intention was to take Miss Petzold's "fruitful theme" and examine it exhaustively in the context of the 1920s and 1930s. At once a summary and continuation of Miss Petzold's work, Hultsch's study is informed by a sharper intellectual strictness, a more logical cohesiveness and, most important, by a keener awareness of the difficulties involved in tracing influence, especially when the source of influence is a writer like Nietzsche. Hultsch describes Nietzsche's impact in the *fin de siècle* years as "enormous," and suggests that Nietzsche was greeted rapturously as a comrade-in-arms in the fight against the torpid Philistinism of Victorian culture. Though accepting certain of Nietzsche's doctrines, Hultsch cautions, the English tended instinctively to reject his radical individualism and his gospel of master-morality. He finds no grounds for accepting Shaw's professed kinship to Nietzsche, although he admits that the Shavian view of women underwent a profound change as a result of *Zarathustra*, and that no major English writer owed more to Nietzsche than Shaw. Shaw, he declares, constantly attenuates or trivializes Nietzsche's ideas, as in the case of the superman concept which is stripped of its ethical garb and decked out in borrowed eugenical robes. Other apparently Nietzschean motifs in Shaw's work, such as that of the Life Force, are more directly traceable to other sources, such as Butler and Schopenhauer. Inexplicably, Hultsch seems unaware that Shaw frequently protested against allegations that he was a disciple of Nietzsche. As for Nietzsche's impact on John Davidson, this Hultsch regards as profound but untypical; the more representative English reaction of distrust is found in philosophers like F. C. S. Schiller. Passing cursorily over the war period, which Petzold had thoroughly documented, Hultsch notes that the 1930s marked a rediscovery of Nietzsche, in particular his greatness as a psychologist. This accentuation is apparent in the work of William McDougall, the sociologist, and in the novels of D. H. Lawrence, who is discussed at some length. Lawrence, declares Hultsch, was instinctively akin to Nietzsche; he was one of the few Englishmen to appreciate Nietzsche's true stature and importance.* The conclusion is that the English, by virtue

---

* Hultsch indicates many Nietzschean allusions in Lawrence's work. For this see also H. Steinhauer, "Eros and Psyche: a Nietzschean Motif in Anglo-American literature," *Modern Language Notes*, LXIV (April, 1949), 217–28; Laurence Lerner, *The Truthtellers* (New York, 1967), 288–91; W. H. G. Armytage, *Yesterday's Tomorrows* (Toronto, 1968), 106–8. The seven chapter of Armytage's book, "Superman and the System," also traces Nietzschean motifs in the work of Wells, Shaw, and Yeats.

of their temperament and common-sense mentality, would probably continue to find in Nietzsche something alien and uncongenial unless the national character underwent some radical transformation. A brief outline of Nietzsche's views on the English is given to show that suspicion was reciprocal. Of less value bibliographically, Hultsch's article is critically far more searching than Petzold's pioneering study: Petzold's laborious paraphrases are eschewed in favour of a discerning effort of interpretation.

Hultsch and Petzold are united in their admiration for Nietzsche; both stress how he was distrusted and misunderstood in England; their attitude towards the English wavers between gentle condescension and downright contempt. The general feeling among Nietzsche's countrymen seems to have been that his influence – though great in Germany, France, and Italy – was remarkably small and sporadic in England: "His passionate radicalism and superstyle probably could not appeal to the temper, the common sense, and the political wisdom of the English race. I know only one very fascinating exception, T. E. Lawrence whose passionate soul was as ambitious and ascetic, ruthless and scrupulous, austere and refined, triumphant and desperate, as that of Nietzsche."* The major shortcoming of this German scholarship is that no coherent or detailed picture is presented of how Nietzsche affected English literary life as a whole. Accounts are given of the presumed peaks of the iceberg – John Davidson, Bernard Shaw, G. K. Chesterton, Edwin Muir, D. H. Lawrence – but not of the submerged mass of diverse literary opinion; the enquirer anxious to discover how H. G. Wells, John Galsworthy, W. B. Yeats, or James Joyce reacted to Nietzsche is given nothing to assuage his curiosity. Nor, if we except empty appeals to the sobriety of English common-sense and the essential alienness of the English temper, is any precise explanation offered of how Nietzsche failed to take England by storm. The limited accessibility of the German interpretations has severely curtailed their wider dissemination and usefulness.

English and American scholars, on the other hand, have been extremely reluctant to handle the theme at all. Secondary sources do, of course, exist, but generally in the form of random parentheses and incidental observations in related projects. Not until 1957, when John Lester broke ground with his exemplary monograph on John Davidson, was there any work exclusively devoted to tracing Nietzsche's impact on an English author.

---

* Karl Loewith, "Friedrich Nietzsche," *Church History*, XIII (1944), 164. Loewith goes on: "Among the choice books which Lawrence kept at his cottage were Nietzsche's *The Joyful Wisdom, The Twilight of the Idols, The Antichrist* and *Zarathustra*." The last work Lawrence regarded as one of "the five titanic books" of the world.

This was followed in 1958 by the first general account of "Nietzsche and the Nineties,"[7] a short essay which singled out Davidson, Pringle-Pattison, and Havelock Ellis as the major writers on Nietzsche during this period. In 1961 Miss Nancy Snider wrote a doctoral dissertation called "An Annotated Bibliography of English Works on Friedrich Nietzsche," realizing that there existed "no comprehensive treatment of his reputation in England and America, or of the considerable influence he has exerted on English and American men of letters."[8] Intending originally to write this chapter in the history of ideas herself, Miss Snider was confronted with the unavailability of basic materials for such an investigation. She thereupon set herself the task of supplying them, apparently unaware that two renowned Nietzsche scholars, Herbert Reichert and Karl Schlechta, were simultaneously compiling, with immeasurably greater resources, a Nietzsche bibliography under the auspices of the University of North Carolina. Their *International Nietzsche Bibliography* is dated 1960, but the earliest reviews of it do not appear until the spring of 1962, by which time Miss Snider's dissertation had been submitted and duly approved. Inevitably there is much reduplication: the *International Nietzsche Bibliography* contains 4000 items in 28 languages, 569 of them in English. By her own unaided efforts, Miss Snider has assembled about 400 of these, together with about 200, mostly reviews, not included in the *Bibliography*.

With the appearance of these two bibliographies, the main task of excavation has been achieved, and the present study, based as it is on primary materials, owes a great debt to them. But neither bibliography is wholly reliable in its details* or really intelligible as a guide to Nietzsche's reputation. Both suffer from grave omissions: Miss Snider, for example, omits important articles by John Davidson and Edward Garnett, books by Phyllis Bottome and Jacques Barzun, many numbers of Margaret Anderson's *Little Review* and Orage's *New Age*, and Jack Lindsay's *London Aphrodite*, the Nietzschean magazine of the twenties, in its entirety. There is a disturbing lack of discrimination in the items Miss Snider selects for annotation, and they are often misleading in emphasis: Desmond MacCarthy's views are summarized but not those of Nordau, Tille, Pringle-Pattison, Schiller, Holbrook Jackson and Orage, all of whom were far more influential than MacCarthy. Some of the annotations themselves are misleading: Miss Snider fails to realize, for example, that Davidson's early articles on Nietzsche

---

* A list I have prepared of the more glaring errors in the English section of the *International Nietzsche Bibliography* will appear in *Notes and Queries* in the spring of 1971.

were unalloyed French importations. The present study cannot hope to be free from errors of its own: but its aim, justification, and even principles of organization arise from an effort to overcome the fragmentary incoherence of the bibliographical method by anchoring factual data so firmly in the immediate cultural and social context that an intelligible picture can gradually be seen to emerge. Heaps of raw data are daunting things to make sense of: it is rather like trying to fit together a giant jigsaw-puzzle with no clue as to which pieces make up the outer edge, and certainly with no preconceived notion of the picture which will eventually appear; but when it does begin to emerge, most of the pieces, even those that one could have sworn belonged to a different puzzle, slot cleanly into place.

The bibliography for the present study, unlike the two Nietzsche bibliographies, was not compiled mainly from previous bibliographies, newspaper and periodical indexes, publishers' lists and similar sources. An effort has been made to work *towards* Nietzsche rather than *from* him. Every major writer (and a host of minor ones) has been checked as thoroughly as possible, not only in his own creative or critical work, but also in his private diaries, notes, and correspondence, if available. Such a procedure involves a constant sifting and cross-checking of all sources to which some lead, however slight, has been found. But even when a search has proved disconcertingly unproductive, the energy expended on it is not entirely wasted: in charting an author's reputation and influence, even negative evidence, as long as it is the result of careful investigation and not the product of negligence, can be of some significance in the total pattern. The positive gains of such a method, in the shape of real information about George Moore, Yeats, Galsworthy, Hulme, none of whom are mentioned at all in bibliographies of Nietzsche, are more than sufficient to offset the recurrent disappointment of finding oneself empty-handed at the end of a deceptively promising trail.

Both Nietzsche bibliographies list American and English items together; it is not always abundantly clear whether a writer was American or English by nationality, or whether the journal in which an item appeared was published in America or England or simultaneously in both. This makes it practically impossible for the student primarily interested in one of the literatures to tell at a glance what Nietzsche's impact on it was. Thanks to two excellent doctoral dissertations,[9] the student of American literature is now able to learn of Nietzsche's influence on a number of American writers; the present study complements those works, since there is evidence to show that each country took an interest in how the other was reacting to Nietzsche's ideas. But the Nietzsche bibliographies create even worse confusion by including items, with no strong period demarcations, right up to the date of their compilation. Yet there are good grounds for believing that 1914 marks a turning point: not only does it signal the completion of Nietzsche's works into English, but it also brings to a close the phase of international Nietzsche scholarship which underwent, particularly in England, startling changes of perspective as a result of the 1914–1918 war. Whereas Nietzsche had, until 1914, been seen primarily against a background of thought and culture we associate with Schopenhauer, Darwin, Ibsen, and Wagner, after 1914 he was seen to have strong connections with the psychological and philosophical thinking of a set of writers then coming into vogue: Freud, Bergson, Dostoievsky, and Kierkegaard. Emphasis on the more sensational and destructive aspects of his work gradually gave place to a more sober assessment of his positive contributions to thought. This change of perspective is most dramatic in the Nietzsche criticism of F. C. S. Schiller, but it was most of all the work of young men in their early twenties, men like Herbert Read and Edwin Muir, the first generation of Englishmen to reach maturity with a complete English translation of Nietzsche at their elbow. More informed, responsible, and self-conscious comment began the task of dismantling the image of "the mad philosopher" which had been so acceptable to an Edwardian age unacquainted with the mind-lacerating horrors of modern warfare. However diverse their interpretations, writers like T. E. Hulme, T. S. Eliot, Wyndham Lewis, D. H. Lawrence, Herbert Read, Edwin Muir, J. Middleton Murry, Jack Lindsay, Robert Graves, Aldous Huxley, and John Cowper Powys, to mention only some of the luminaries, were in a position to have more first-hand knowledge of Nietzsche than any of their predecessors in the previous generation. Yet it was this earlier generation which discovered Nietzsche and which witnessed a fierce controversy over his work, finally paving the way for a better understanding of it. The period between 1890 and 1914 has thus a character all of its own, and it is the period chosen for our enquiry; to have extended investigations beyond 1914 would have drastically limited the opportunities for thoroughly detailed exposition, besides presenting quite unmanageable problems of organization if the same degree of detail was to be maintained.

The Nietzsche bibliographies, in order to avoid appearing cumbersome, have turned a blind eye to all the possible ramifications of cross-reference.*

---

* The revised and expanded edition of the *International Nietzsche Bibliography* (1968), published when this book was virtually completed, does, unlike the first edition of 1960, provide indexes and cross references. For a list of items not recorded in the *INB*, see the Addenda, below, p. 321.

An attempt has been made to remedy this by insisting on interrelationships wherever they were perceived to exist, and by emphasizing the degree to which Nietzsche was accessible at any given time. The entire first chapter, therefore, is devoted to a synoptic and chronological account of the English translations of Nietzsche, and to the reviews of those translations up to 1914. Such an arrangement partly offsets the alphabetical arrangement of the bibliographies, which certainly facilitates speedy reference but which precludes a focused understanding of the progressive development of Nietzsche's influence. In five of the six following chapters the strictly chronological approach is abandoned in favour of centring the discussion upon one author in turn; in this way it is hoped to achieve focus and concentration without detracting too much from the woven line of argument which runs from the first chapter to the last.

The five authors selected for discussion are John Davidson (1857–1909), Havelock Ellis (1859–1939), W. B. Yeats (1865–1939), George Bernard Shaw (1856–1950) and A. R. Orage (1873–1934). They have been chosen because they all belonged to the same generation (four of them being born within nine years of each other), all had written or heard of Nietzsche before the turn of the century, and all are major figures whose names have been persistently mentioned in connection with Nietzsche. The order in which they appear is governed partly by chronological considerations, and partly by a desire to stress that Nietzsche, at first the discovery of a small band of artists, was gradually taken over by those whose aim was more broadly political: from Davidson to Orage interpretations of Nietzsche gain enormously in sophistication. The supposed debts of Davidson and Shaw to Nietzsche have often been debated, but there is, perhaps not surprisingly, still no large measure of agreement; as for Ellis and Orage, the importance of their contributions to the dissemination of Nietzsche's ideas has not yet been fully recognized; in the case of Yeats, it is assumed sometimes that he owed little to Nietzsche or disagreed with him, sometimes that he knew him rather intimately; no attempt has yet been made to deal exclusively with the Yeats-Nietzsche relationship. Other authors, such as H. G. Wells and G. K. Chesterton, are also discussed, but only if their views of Nietzsche began to take shape before the complete English translation became available. Borderline cases like that of D. H. Lawrence, whose attitude to Nietzsche is already fairly well known, are omitted for the sake of balance (their adequate explication would demand extra chapters) and because they would not alter the substance of the argument. However, for the sake of completeness, brief accounts of how attitudes to Nietzsche developed after 1914 are included as long as they have some kind of bearing; even post-1914 material has been used when it reflects pre-1914 attitudes. In each chapter, material only tenuously related to the title figure has been included if it broadens the scope of a particular enquiry.

To achieve some standard of comparative judgment in assessing Nietzsche's impact on the texture of English culture, it has been decided to trace this impact, not only broadly in relation to Nietzsche's work as a whole, but to one of his main positive concepts, the concept of the "superman" or *Übermensch*. Although this concept appears under several guises throughout Nietzsche's work, the only complete expression of it occurs in *Thus Spake Zarathustra*, one of the first works to be translated and therefore accessible to non-German-speaking readers. Messianic hero-worship, of course, was a typically nineteenth-century phenomenon – one thinks immediately of Byron, Beddoes, and Carlyle in England, Renan and Comte in France and Ibsen (*adelmenneske*) in Norway; a faith in evolutionary progress can be traced in the work of Bulwer-Lytton, Tennyson, Browning, and Meredith.[10] Something very close to Nietzsche's call for the superman is visible, too, in the nature-mystic Richard Jefferies, who had certainly not heard of Nietzsche by 1887, the year he died: "It is necessary that some far-seeing master-mind, some giant intellect, should arise, and sketch out in bold, unmistakable outlines the grand and noble future which the human race should labour for."[11] Yet after 1895 the term *Übermensch*, or "overman" or "superman" was sufficiently distinctive to be associated, in the minds of those that used and heard it, with the work of Nietzsche. If Nietzsche never defined unequivocally what he meant by the term (and one scholar, Bélart, has discovered eight different uses of it), the account given of it in *Zarathustra* has a hard enough core of suggestive richness to be regarded as the crystallization of his entire philosophy, the nucleus of a seemingly anarchic and amorphous body of moral, aesthetic, and political ideas: it is therefore, in spite of its subsequent vulgarization, a representative concept, a touchstone by which response to Nietzsche as a whole can be gauged fairly accurately.

Finally, a word about the concept of "influence." *Quellenkunde*, as a branch of academic study, has been so much under fire recently that theorists of comparative literature have been active in redefining its aims, scope, and methodology.[12] Perhaps it is too early to say whether they have succeeded in re-instating its importance and dignity and whether they have begun to whittle away the scepticism of those who still regard "source-hunting" in the same way Kant is supposed to have regarded a certain species of philosophical activity, that is, as the attempt of one man to milk a he-goat while another holds a sieve. After all, the sceptics will say, a man's ideas become influential because they are already in the air; Shaw remarked that books which have mind-changing properties, such as Buckle's *History of Civilization*, Marx's *Kapital*, and Ruskin's *Modern Painters*, were persuasive because the world was already coming round to a new way of looking at things. Again, Shaw insisted that the revolt of the Life Force against ready-made morality in the nineteenth century was not the work of "a Norwegian microbe," but would have found expression in English literature if Ibsen had never existed. A man's ideas, we might say, can accelerate a process of change already under way, because the soil into which they fall is congenial. But if we try to be more positivistic, we shall find that the search for influence is apt to promise more than it delivers, and is beset with prickly dangers not always easy to avoid. Many studies of the influence of one writer on another illustrate only too painfully an unconscious surrender to the *post hoc ergo propter hoc* fallacy: the slightest resemblance or analogy is falsely assumed to indicate a direct, rather than a common, source, and any observable affinity of minds is taken to be a proof of influence. It is not always remembered that an expression of open hostility may mask a secret affinity. Nietzsche's own ambivalent attitude to Socrates is familiar, but he exercised the same guarded admiration in regard to other writers. Here he is writing to George Brandes about Dostoievsky: "I esteem him ... as the most valuable psychological material I know – I am grateful to him in an extraordinary way, however antagonistic he may be to my deepest instincts. Much the same as my relation to Pascal, whom I almost love, since he has taught me such an infinite amount: the only *logical* Christian."[13]

As a literary phenomenon influence undoubtedly exists, ranging from a casual debt to something so deep and lasting that one encounter is sometimes sufficient to stop a writer dead in his tracks and open up for him a totally new area of experience for artistic exploration. There is surely a *prima facie* case for a statement such as this; the difficulties begin when one tries to estimate, on an empirical basis of frequently insufficient and sometimes misleading data, the precise *degree* and *kind* of influence in any one particular case. For example, obvious and conspicuous influences are not always the deepest ones: an obvious influence may be obvious for the very reason that it has not been fully adapted and incorporated into another writer's mode of thinking, whereas the indiscernible influence may have been assimilated beyond all recognition, in much the same way as food changes into blood, muscle, bone, and energy in the process of digestion. The location of sources is not enough in itself: it must be shown how a writer uses his sources, how they fertilize his originality and help the reader to understand the workings of the imaginative process. In the present study no attempt has been made to establish incontrovertible proof or denial of influence, but it should be possible to draw from the assembled evidence some conclusions which, even though they may be tentative, are of more value than speculative shots in the dark. Recent work in the theory of comparative literature has prompted these questions: how well was a given writer acquainted with Nietzsche's work, what did he see in it, what did he accept and what did he reject (and why), what elements of it did he absorb into his own work and what degree of integration was achieved? The answers to these questions, it is hoped, will be rewarding. Although the work of a foreign author tends to produce "acquaintance and curiosity without the real permeation that is influence,"[14] its general diffusion may see it making a lasting imprint on isolated individuals: "A foreign influence is a stimulant which has the advantage of exoticism, hence of enhanced magic, and often an authorization for a young writer to accomplish what he was too timid to achieve by himself against a cramping environment or a dulled national tradition."[15] It has been pointed out that, since generations tend to be rivals of each other (an idea much insisted on by writers as disparate as T. S. Eliot and D. H. Lawrence), the influences of authors of the same language and nationality on each other tend to be negative ones: "On the contrary, the education of a writer can be dramatically shaped by foreign authors, first because there is no longer a question of rivalry, and particularly as the reading of foreign literature is done generally at a more mature age when one may be more aware of the need for models and direction."[16]

A frank openness to the influence of contemporary (and often *avant-garde*) foreign authors has surely been the distinguishing mark of English literature in the modern period – it was certainly a marked feature of the literary scene of the 1890s, the point of departure of the present work.*
No longer was it possible to rest in a single cultural tradition, as even so intense a nationalist as Yeats was confessing by 1904: "If Ireland is about to produce literature that is important to her, it must be the result of the influences that flow in upon the mind of an educated Irishman to-day, and in a greater degree, of what came into the world with himself. Gaelic can

---

* Cf. a review of Holbrook Jackson's *The Eighteen Nineties*: "Probably ... these years will be remembered best as the decade when foreign influences were at their highest. In fact, there seems to have been a conscious and deliberate search for new models from abroad. ... The total extent to which the great European writers succeeded in permeating our own productions is incalculable. Nietzsche alone has exerted an extraordinary influence." *Athenaeum* (November 1, 1913), 490.

hardly fail to do a portion of the work, but one cannot say whether it may not be some French or German writer who will do most to make him an articulate man."[17] Yeats himself took the lead in showing what could be achieved by yielding oneself to the life-giving spirit of literary cosmopolitanism.

Real influence is something deeper than mere imitation. As Eliot said: "We do not imitate, we are changed; and our work is the work of a changed man; we have not borrowed, we have been quickened and we become bearers of a tradition."[18] Even so, creative writers have been known to resent the imputation that they have been influenced by another writer's work, wishing for reasons of pride, guilt or (in the case of the alleged influence of a foreign writer) misplaced patriotism to preserve their own originality *virgo intacta*. Davidson and Shaw hotly contested the suggestion that their ideas derived from Nietzsche; so did André Gide. Grouping Blake, Nietzsche, Browning, and Dostoievsky (all non-French authors be it noted) together as a constellation the light of whose combined genius was like a revelation, Guide insisted that these writers were not the source of his ideas so much as the *agents provocateurs* of his own latent talent:

If those in whom I recognize my thought had not been there, I doubt whether it would have been much hampered – but its expression would perhaps have been different. It is useless to go back over what has been well said by others. – Nothing is so absurd as that accusation of *influence* (in which certain critics excel every time they note a resemblance). – How many things, on the contrary, I *have not said* because I later discovered them in others! Nietzsche's influence on me? ... I was already writing *L'Immoraliste* when I discovered him. Who could say how much he got in my way ... ? How my book was shorn of all I disliked to *repeat*.[19]

In the writing of *L'Immoraliste*, Gide declares, Nietzsche did help him to purge the book of its initial theoretic bias, but on the whole Nietzsche was less an instigation than a hindrance. He continues: "Had I not encountered Dostoyevsky, Nietzsche, Blake, or Browning, I cannot believe that my work would have been any different. At the most they helped me to disentangle my thought. And even then, I took pleasure in hailing those in whom I recognized my thought. But that thought was mine, and it is not to them that I owe it. Otherwise it would be valueless."[20] Gide serves on the critic some very salutary reminders.

The question of "influence" inevitably leads to the question of "reputation" or "fortune." Although some scholars have chosen to regard these three terms as practically synonymous, there is a distinction between them based largely, one might say, on the superior degree of tact and discrimination which the tracing of "influence" demands. Yet the interconnections between the two tend to make them coalesce into a single phenomenon: "The reception of foreign authors in a particular literature and time forms a direct and integral part of the literary taste and hence the shaping of an audience for a native author, as well as the native author's own artistic and critical consciousness."[21] This study tries to show the various modes of Nietzsche's influence by repeated and documented reference to his "reputation," that is, to views of him current between the years 1890 and 1914; the basic search is not for "influence," but for a significant pattern of the way Nietzsche affected English literary and social conscience. In Nietzsche's case it was a slow process, for it was not until about 1908 that his vogue can be said to begin. Writing in that year, Desmond MacCarthy referred to Nietzsche's growing popularity, and offered almost the only analysis we shall find of how it had arisen:

The influence of a philosopher upon literature and morals is mainly indirect. His books are comparatively little read at any time, but they influence authors who are read, and so at last, through the agency of critics and the acknowledgments of disciples, the philosopher becomes recognised as the fountain-head of certain current tendencies and ideas. When this stage has been reached he becomes a journalist's philosopher. He will be mentioned every day in newspapers and reviews; he will be referred to as explaining the latest art or the latest propaganda; his name will serve as a cockshy to some and as a banner to others, until the public are sick of the sight of it.[22]

The task lying before us is to confirm and give substance to the bare bones of this analysis.

THE ENGLISH TRANSLATIONS OF NIETZSCHE

1 Nietzsche professed to scorn discipleship. The astonishing originality of his work failed, at least until the year of his break-down, to gain him readers even in his native Germany. A few of his books were reviewed in the German press at the time they appeared, but he had to wait until 1888 for a critical appraisal of his work as a whole. He keenly resented this lack of appreciation; from time to time he would take a few of his intimates into his confidence, and confess a real human need for words of encouragement in his self-imposed tasks. His bitterness and frustration only exacerbated his growing megalomania: public neglect he tried to transform, in characteristic fashion, into a source of personal strength. Having no readers, he was able to choose those whom ideally he would wish to have: "A few readers," as he wrote to George Brandes, "whom one honours and beyond them no readers at all – that is really what I desire."[1] The credentials he demanded of his readers, posterity perforce for one "born posthumously" like himself, were rigorous and exacting:

One must be honest in matters of the spirit to the point of hardness before one can even endure my seriousness and my passion. One must be skilled in living on mountains – seeing the wretched ephemeral babble of politics and national self-seeking *beneath* oneself. One must have become indifferent; one must never ask if the truth is useful or if it may prove our undoing. The predilection of strength for questions for which no one today has the courage; the courage for the *forbidden*; the predestination to the labyrinth. An experience of seven solitudes. New ears for new music. New eyes for what is most distant. A new conscience for truths that have so far remained mute. *And* the will to the economy of the great style: keeping our strength, our *enthusiasm* in harness. Reverence for oneself; love of oneself; unconditional freedom before oneself.*

---

* *The Portable Nietzsche*, ed. Walter Kaufmann (New York, 1958), 568–9. For the most part I have preferred to use Kaufmann's translations of *Thus Spoke Zarathustra*, *The Twilight of the Idols*, and *The Antichrist* because of their superiority to those in Levy's complete edition.

Only these, Nietzsche consoled himself, were to be his right and predestined readers. But they were slow in coming forward. Complimentary copies of *Beyond Good and Evil* were sent to distinguished European men of letters, in the hope that the world would awake to his presence. Nietzsche hugged close the warm gratification of receiving letters of appreciation from Taine in France and Brandes in Denmark. Brandes was so impressed with what he read of Nietzsche that he delivered, in the spring of 1888, a course of lectures on his philosophy at Copenhagen University. By all accounts these lectures were enthusiastically received, and Brandes quickly apprised Nietzsche of the success he was enjoying in Scandinavia. It was through Brandes that Nietzsche was introduced to a genius as formidable and strange as himself – August Strindberg. Before long Nietzsche and Strindberg began to correspond.

Nietzsche's letters to Strindberg reveal his pathetic concern to achieve recognition in the world. It had always been his ardent ambition to have readers in France, a country whose culture – particularly that of the sixteenth and seventeenth centuries – was much more to his taste than that of his native Germany. As he confesses to Strindberg:

Being, as I am, the most independent and perhaps the strongest spirit in our world to-day, one doomed to the fulfilment of a stupendous task, it is impossible that I should allow myself to be constrained from greeting the few persons willing to listen to me, by the barriers which an abominable dynastic national policy has erected between the peoples. And I gladly acknowledge that above all I seek such persons in France. I am well acquainted with all that transpires in the intellectual world of France. I am told that my manner of writing is really French, even though in my *Zarathustra* I have attained a perfection in the German language unequaled hitherto by any other German.[2]

The tone of this letter bears a strong similarity to the overtly paranoiac strains of *Ecce Homo*, but we cannot fail to notice the desperate urgency with which the appeal is made. Nietzsche informs Strindberg that, in expectation of the opening of his "little Panama Canal" to France, he has postponed indefinitely the publication of his latest writings so that he can arrange to have *Beyond Good and Evil* and *The Twilight of the Idols* translated into French. He notes that he is already known as far afield as Vienna, St. Petersburg, Stockholm, New York – everywhere but in Germany and, by implication, England. His plans for *Ecce Homo* are that it should appear simultaneously in German, French, and English; he inquires whether Strindberg would contemplate doing the French translation, and also whether he has any suggestions to make concerning the English one. How, muses Nietzsche, would an anti-German book like *Ecce Homo* be received in England? In his reply Strindberg expresses a willingness to undertake the French translation or, if Nietzsche cannot afford to pay him for doing it, to suggest some reliable translator in his stead. Strindberg continues:

With regard to England I have really nothing to say, for there we have to deal with a puritanical land, delivered into the hands of women – which signifies the same thing as having fallen into a state of absolute decadence. English morality – you know what that means, my dear sir! Subscription libraries for the young person – Currer Bell, Miss Braddon and the rest! I advise you to keep clear of all that! In French you will penetrate even to the world of the blackamoors and you may snap your fingers at England.[3]

We shall never know how Nietzsche reacted to this, for his last two letters to Strindberg are brief cryptic utterances which indicate, all too painfully, the insidious approach of the paralytic stroke which brought about his final mental collapse in the early days of 1889. But the parallels between Nietzsche and Strindberg are interesting. Both knew that France, of all countries, would be most hospitable to their work, and so it proved. Edmund Gosse, referring to Strindberg in 1898 as "the most remarkable creative talent started by the philosophy of Nietzsche," pointed out that writers like Turgenev and Tolstoy were known in France long before they were even heard of in England: "To-day English readers are totally unacquainted with the extraordinary Swedish novelist, dramatist, alchemist and atheist, August Strindberg, yet in France not only has he a large following, but he exercises a positive influence."[4] This was equally true of Nietzsche, as were the reasons for the slow headway Strindberg made in England: lack of adequate and complete translation, the strongly autobiographical element in his work, the suspicions of misogyny and the imputations of madness, and English distaste at being seen as a nation of high-minded Podsnaps and puritanical frumps. Nietzsche's attitude to England and English culture was somewhat similar.

Nietzsche had a youthful enthusiasm for Byron, whose Manfred he called a "superman"; he was respectful towards Shakespeare, but the respect was cool, far from the ardour of the German romantics; the only English writer whose style appealed to him was Landor, whom he ranked as one of the four great prose-writers of the nineteenth century. Thomas Common has pointed out his kinship with Hobbes, Mandeville, and Lord Bolingbroke, and has suggested that Bolingbroke's *Letters on the Study and Use of History* might be compared with Nietzsche's *On the Use and Abuse of History*. Closest of all to Nietzsche, Common believes, was Walter Bagehot, whose *Physics and Politics* (1872) was "very carefully studied by Nietzsche, who quotes it with approval."[5] For English philosophy, by which he understood empiricism, utilitarianism (John Stuart Mill was one of his "impossibilities") and Darwinism, Nietzsche had nothing but contempt. English philosophy, he thought, was laboriously excogitated by mediocre minds – it was respectable, dull, unoriginal, hypocritical, totally lacking in profundity of insight and power of expression. For scientific discoveries like those of Darwin, the specifically English qualities of aridity, narrowness of vision, and indefatigable assiduity were invaluable. There exist truths, Nietzsche suggests, which are best perceived by mediocre minds, and the English, with their unenviable gift for mediocrity, have performed useful donkey work in this field; but the continental influence of the English has been disastrous, for it has lured the best minds of France and Germany to become enmeshed in the "mechanical stultification of the world" which English philosophy sets as a trap for the unwary. What Nietzsche calls the "diabolical Anglomania of modern ideas" has twice been responsible for a general depression of European intelligence: "The European *noblesse* – of sentiment, taste, and manners, taking the word in every high sense, – is the work and invention of *France*; the European ignobleness, the plebeianism of modern ideas – is *England's* work and invention."* He sees it as characteristic of a time-serving and unphilosophical race like the English to hold firmly on to Christianity for the sake of moral guidance and support, even when they have effectually ceased to give it intellectual credence: in this respect, Carlyle's attitude to religion, like George Eliot's, may be taken as representative of a craving for a strong faith and the feeling of incapacity for it. And yet Carlyle is admired in England precisely for his honesty: "Well, that is English; and in view of the fact that the English are the people of consummate cant, it is even as it should be, and not only comprehensible. At bottom, Carlyle is an English atheist who makes it a point of honor not to be one."[6] Nor is Nietzsche much taken by the English temperament. Being more headstrong, gloomy, sensual, and brutal than the German, the Englishman is the baser of the two, and also the more pious – he has a greater need of Christianity, which he uses as an antidote to his inborn melancholy, proneness to dyspepsia, and overfondness for alcohol. What offends Nietzsche most, however, is the Englishman's lack of the

---

* *The Complete Works of Friedrich Nietzsche*, ed. Dr. Oscar Levy (London and Edinburgh, 1909–13), XII, 213. It is mainly from aphorisms 228, 252, and 253 of this work, *Beyond Good and Evil*, that Nietzsche's views on England are drawn. For a fuller account than is given here see Raymond Furness, "Nietzsche's Views on the English and His Concept of a European Community," *German Life and Letters*, XVII (1964), 319–25; and Ernst Sandvoss "Nietzsche's Kritik an den Angelsachsen," *Zeitschrift für Religions- und Geistegeschichte*, XVII (1965), 147–61.

prime quality in life and art – music: "He has neither rhythm nor dance in the movements of his soul and body; indeed, not even the desire for rhythm and dance, for 'music.' Listen to him speaking; look at the most beautiful Englishwomen *walking* – in no country on earth are there more beautiful doves and swans; finally, listen to them singing!"[7] This is no vulgarian's jeer. Nietzsche wrote that "ugliness, in itself an objection, is among the Greeks almost a refutation."[8] So it was to him.

Rilke was no lover of the English either, and it may be that his Anglophobia, like Nietzsche's, was strengthened, if not initiated, by that of a common friend – Lou Andreas-Salomé. One of Nietzsche's most admired exemplars, Heinrich Heine, was also anti-British. Fundamentally, perhaps, Nietzsche was opposed to England because it did not seem to fit into his concept of "good Europeanism." Like Strindberg, he noted among the English a virulent puritanical strain in "all their scientific tinkering with morals," and, in their sociological thinking, an unhealthy absorption with societies in a state of decadence or decline. He despised the democratic spirit latent in English ethical thought, with its small-minded ideals of herd-happiness and the easy, push-button obliteration of any distinction of rank between one man and another. Nietzsche wanted philosophy to concern itself with morals "in a dangerous, captious, and ensnaring manner," and for him nothing could be further from speculative audacity than English utilitarian philosophy. In spite of all his vehement denials of influence, Nietzsche probably learnt more from Mill, Spencer, and Darwin than he was ever prepared to admit, since his reaction against these thinkers helped him to clarify his own position.

Whether Nietzsche following Strindberg's recommendation, really did "snap his fingers at England" as far as his attempt to find an English translator was concerned, is a matter for conjecture. He must have known that English translations were necessary before his work could win any degree of world-wide recognition. One of the few English people to have known him personally was Helen Zimmern who, like so many of Nietzsche's friends and admirers, was Jewish by birth.[9] She was the author of a work on Schopenhauer, a study of Italy, and a paraphrase of a Persian epic called the *Epic of Kings* which her friend Robert Browning had used as a source for "Ferishtah's Fancies." Nietzsche met her for the first time at Bayreuth in 1876, and in a letter to Peter Gast, dated December 9, 1888, he puts forward her name as a possible translator – she had introduced Schopenhauer to the English, he pointed out, why not himself, Schopenhauer's antithesis? As it turned out, few of those who were to translate Nietzsche's work were of English birth – they consisted of Scots, Irishmen, Dutch, Americans, and Germans. How, we must now enquire, was the task of translating Nietzsche's work into English initiated?

2 In May, 1889, Helen Watterson translated twelve brief aphorisms for the New York *Century Magazine* under the heading "Paragraphs from the German of Friedrich Netzsche [sic]." Two years later John Davidson incorporated into an article for the *Speaker* a number of aphorisms from *Human, All-Too-Human* which he had retranslated from a French rendering: some of these aphorisms reappeared in his *Sentences and Paragraphs* (1893). Not until 1894 did someone come forward who saw the necessity of undertaking a complete translation of Nietzsche's works – Thomas Common (1850–1919). Little is known about Common, bar the fact that he was of Scottish birth and abandoned his intention to enter the ministry in order to devote himself to the propagation of Nietzsche's philosophy. He interpreted Nietzsche in terms of Darwin, and believed that Nietzsche would appeal to thinkers and scientists of a Darwinist persuasion. One of these, he hoped, would be Thomas Henry Huxley, who replied to Common's letter of recommendation with disappointing coolness: "I will look up Nietzsche's works, though I must confess that the profit I obtain from German authors on speculative questions is not usually great. As men of research in positive science they are magnificently laborious and accurate. But most of them have no notion of style, and seem to compose their books with a pitchfork."[10] Huxley seems not to have honoured this promise. Undeterred, Common sought out collaborators. He found the first in the American scholar, W. A. Haussmann. Common and Haussmann made arrangements with Nietzsche's German publishers, Naumann of Leipzig, for the translation of Nietzsche's writings. Naumann agreed to allow them to translate *Zarathustra*. Knowing that Nietzsche had Miss Zimmern in view as a possible translator for his work, Common hastened to seek her out. Other supposedly competent translators were assembled; it only remained to find a publisher to issue the translations, and a responsible person capable of editing them.

In 1895, Naumann and Dr. Richard Oehler (Nietzsche's cousin who acted on behalf of his mother) arranged with the newly formed London firm of Henry & Co. to publish the English edition of Nietzsche's principal works: this was specially to include the authorized translations of Haussmann and Common, who, nevertheless, disapproved of the arrangement. They believed that Henry & Co. were too much of an "upstart" firm, and had offered far too generous terms to Naumann and Oehler. The firm was composed mostly of Dutchmen, the leading spirits being L. Simons and

J. T. Grein.* Grein had founded the Independent Theatre, which had staged Ibsen's *Ghosts* in 1891 and, by so doing, had created an immense public outrage. In January, 1896, Grein issued the first number of his monthly review, *To-morrow*. Although this review was mainly concerned with the theatre, it encouraged free discussion of the latest philosophical trends. It gave advance notice of the publication of four volumes of Nietzsche translations, of which only two, *Thus Spake Zarathustra* and *The Case of Wagner* (which also included *Nietzsche contra Wagner*, *The Twilight of the Idols*, and *The Antichrist*), appeared on schedule in 1896. *The Genealogy of Morals* was published in 1899, but its companion work, *Beyond Good and Evil*, was not issued until 1907. In April, 1896, Grein quoted the trade magazine *Bookselling* as saying: "We are of opinion that the publication of Nietzsche's works in England and in the English language will have a most important influence on our literary, political, and moral opinions."[11] But a year later Grein's self-congratulations turned sour when he found that his publishing firm had gone bankrupt, thus making it impossible to continue the translations. He had been forced to price them very high by current standards – *Zarathustra* sold at seventeen shillings and *The Case of Wagner* at ten and sixpence, prices which put them quite out of reach of the average book-buyer. He attempted to publicize them by frequent advertisements in *To-morrow*, sometimes in the form of lengthy extracts.[12] The idea, put into circulation by Dr. Levy, that no English publisher could be induced to take up Nietzsche after the collapse of Henry & Co., is false. Several publishers showed a definite interest in continuing the work of translation: the reasons why nothing came of their readiness will become evident in due course.

Alexander Tille (1866–1912) was appointed editor of the Nietzsche translations in 1895, probably because he already had publications on Nietzsche to his credit, and had lectured on "Friedrich Nietzsche, the Herald of Modern Germany" to the Glasgow Goethe Society at the end of 1894. His fellow Germans at Glasgow University were bringing Nietzsche to the attention of their colleagues by 1887; but not until Tille arrived on the scene hotfoot from Leipzig did Nietzsche, according to a reputable scholar, find enthusiastic disciples:

Tille – so report ran – represented the very last word in modes and moods fashionable with youngest Germany. He was understood to be the Alexander Lauenstein

---

* For further information about Grein see Michael Orme, *J.T. Grein: The Story of a Pioneer, 1862–1935* (London, 1936); and N. H. G. Schoonderwoerd, *J. T. Grein: Ambassador of the Theatre, 1862–1935* (Assen, 1963).

of the *Magazin für Literatur* of the eighties, the Kurt Grottewitz of *Neues Leben* and reputed to have had some conspicuous hand in a novel, *Vor zu Laufgang*, scandalous enough to have earned suppression even in Germany. I never could get a sight of this book; but, in any case, Tille appears to have kicked over the traces with shocking effect upon the Saxon *Philister*. He turned out to be a furious Nietzschean, his *Von Darwin bis Nietzsche* rumbling in his head already.*

In *Von Darwin bis Nietzsche* (1895), Tille considers Nietzsche, as Common was doing, as a spokesman for the Darwinist position; but as this work was never translated, it probably found few English readers. Much the same can be said for his anthology of German lyrics, *German Songs of Today* (1896), which contains ten poems by Nietzsche as well as an introduction – written in English and addressed to American readers – in which Nietzsche's influence on the young generation of German writers is discussed. It was in his introductions to the Nietzsche translations he edited that Tille first gained the hearing of the English public.

In his introduction to the first of the translated volumes, *The Case of Wagner*, Tille observes that philosophy, having the task of uniting various departments of learning into an uncontradictory whole, can no longer neglect the discoveries of natural science, in particular of Darwin's *Origin of Species* (1859), a work which had revolutionized ideas about man's position in the universe, his descent and his relationship to the lower animals: "Darwinism has for ever put an end to that concept of a moral order in a universe of peace. It is now generally admitted that a severe struggle for existence rages everywhere, and that all higher development is due to the effects of that struggle."[13] Foremost among the modern independent thinkers who have assumed the mantle of Darwin is Friedrich Nietzsche. A single theme pervades all four works assembled in *The Case of Wagner* volume – physiology: "Physiology as the criterion of value of whatever is human, whether called art, culture, or religion! Physiology as the sole arbiter on what is great and what is small, what is good und [*sic*] what is bad! Physiology as the sole standard by which the facts of history and the phenomena of our time can be tried, and by which they have to be tried and to receive the verdict on the great issue: decline, or ascent?"[14] Tille

---

* R.M. Wenley, "Nietzsche – Traffics and Discoveries," *Monist*, xxxi (January, 1921), 136. Tille's later career can briefly be summarized. When a lectureship in German was instituted at Glasgow University in 1899, Tille was appointed to it, but was forced to resign the post after a short period of tenure owing to his outspoken pro-Boer sympathies. He returned to Germany and obtained a lucrative secretarial position with a German business firm, taking no further interest in the English Nietzsche movement. He died in 1912.

concludes his introduction by describing the genesis and arrangement of the four works, and by making a rather ill-judged reference to Nietzsche's mental condition: "In the middle of the winter of 1888/9 he succumbed to a serious nervous disturbance which led to hopeless insanity and a temporary confinement in a lunatic asylum."[15] For those readers who found Nietzsche febrile and repellent, forewarned was forearmed.

The Case of Wagner had been translated by Thomas Common, the title-work having appeared one year in advance of the others in the *Fortnightly Review*.[16] Tille himself undertook the translation of *Zarathustra*, the second work of Nietzsche's to appear in English, although this work had already been promised to Common. Calling it Nietzsche's "astounding prose-poem," Tille compared it to "the Three Baskets of Buddhism, the Tripatka," and, with more immediate illumination, to *Piers the Ploughman* and *The Pilgrim's Progress*, which, he thought, showed the same allegorical structure, the same aspiring idealism, and an equal wealth of moral wisdom. Tille goes on to find further analogues in Eastern and German literature. One wonders what profit an English reader would have derived from reading that Nietzsche's Zarathustra "is neither of the family of Spitama nor is he the husband of Frahaoshtra's daughter Huogvî, nor yet the father-in-law of Jâmâspa, who had married Pourusishta, Zarathustra's daughter,"[17] and much more learned preamble in a similar vein, only to be told finally that Zarathustra was neither a historical nor a mythical figure, but "an ideal reflected in a human image."[18] Tille confesses that *Zarathustra*, being an anthology of nineteenth-century wisdom, "gives a person who is well read in the German literature of the present century quite a peculiar pleasure in reading the book."[19] Analogues to *Zarathustra* are assiduously located in the antireligious, individualist movement associated with Goethe and Heine and the anarchist proclamations of Stirner and Bakunin. But, Tille claims, the core of *Zarathustra* is evolutionary idealism. Goethe had called his Faust an *Übermensch* or (in Tille's translation) a Beyond-Man, and Wilhelm Jordan, in his *Demiurgus* (1854), had dimly foreseen the possibilities of controlled, eugenic breeding:

He connected it with patriarchal matrimonial institutions, and made it the point of view from which his heroes select wives for their sons. Although clearly pronounced in at least twenty passages of the epic, it failed to attract public sympathy for a considerable time, and only after Nietzsche, (who follows Jordan closely in all details) had taken up the idea and made it almost the leading motive of his *Zarathustra*, did it impress itself upon large circles of the educated youth.[20]

A brief paragraph follows in which Tille relates the chronology of the composition of *Zarathustra,* but he says nothing about its allegorical significance (bar identifying the "evil wizard" as Wagner), nor does he offer the reader any advice as to the spirit in which the book should be read. He seems unaware that the work would present enormous difficulties, particularly in translation; indeed, on the latter question he sounds almost naïve: "The aim of the present translation has been to give the meaning of the German text as exactly as could be done. Where several interpretations of words or sentences were possible, as is rather frequently the case, that interpretation was chosen which seemed to agree best with the context, although the decision of this question is in many cases quite arbitrary."[21] The problem of how to surmount Nietzsche's fertile literary inventiveness, his wilful iconoclasm and parody, is not even debated, let alone resolved.

Finally, in his introduction to Haussmann's translation of *A Genealogy of Morals,* Tille states that the chasm existing everywhere in civilized Europe between theory and practice, more especially between current social theories and actual social conditions, is felt nowhere less than in Great Britain: "By intoxicating themselves with phrases like altruism, charity, social justice, equality before the law, freedom and right to labour and happiness, the majority of English speaking people do not feel that they live in a world in which these things are by no means self-evident or fundamental to society."[22] Egotism, Tille insists, characterizes everyone in the business of actual life; English people, far from adhering to "the principles of Christian-democratic neighbour-morality," abide by a firm faith – at least in the upper classes – in the aristocratic virtues which the word "gentleman" has long been known to represent: "It involves all those qualities of personal honour, truthfulness, discretion, sincerity, trustworthiness, honesty, and besides that command of the forms of educated intercourse, and that education, culture and freedom from violent eruptions of feeling which are indispensable for anybody who claims to belong to good society."[23] This aristocratic code does not conflict with the Jewish one at all points, but does demand "unspeakably more" than the ten commandments have laid down. In actual life the relationship of the two codes is simple: "The true Englishman speaks more of the Jewish-Christian code, but he acts more upon the Germanic-aristocratic code which survives in his gentleman-morality."[24] The distinction between the two codes is what *A Genealogy of Morals* seeks to explore, and Tille points out, as Shaw was to do later, that Stuart Glennie also "derives the most important facts of civilization from the opposition of a fair and higher and a dark and lower race living in the same country, the former being the ruling, the latter the serving race."[25] Nietzsche's theories concerning bad conscience are at one with those of Glennie, and his views on punishment were anticipated by F. H. Bradley. Tille gives a brief summary of each of three essays comprising *A Genealogy of Morals* – he is most attracted to the essay on ascetic ideals, as it fits in neatly with his physiological interpretation of Nietzsche's work.

3 Many reviewers, as we shall see, took issue with Tille's presentation of Nietzsche's ideas. They usually did it from the standpoint of Max Nordau, whose *Degeneration* had appeared in English in February, 1895, two years later than the German original, *Entartung*. A virulent and sometimes hysterical attack on *fin de siècle* decadence in art and literature, it enjoyed an immense popularity. This popularity was guaranteed, no doubt, by the nature of its subject-matter, but was boosted considerably by the fact that the book coincided with the trials of Oscar Wilde. Wilde himself is one of Nordau's targets, but he finds himself in the distinguished company of the Pre-Raphaelites, Whitman, Gautier, Baudelaire, Maeterlinck, Tolstoy, Ibsen, Wagner, Zola, Nietzsche, and almost everybody of artistic account in the late nineteenth century, the writers, in fact, whom Havelock Ellis had praised in *The New Spirit* (1890). Nordau classifies Wagner and Nietzsche as "egomaniacs," and denounces them with all the vitriolic spite he can muster, especially for what he took to be their anti-Semitism. Nordau, a Jew, cannot forgive George Brandes, a fellow Jew, for numbering himself among Nietzsche's apostles (as had, to Nordau's consternation had he known, many other intelligent Jews during Nietzsche's lifetime): "We know, indeed, that this ingenious person winds himself around every human phenomenon in whom he scents a possible prima-donna, in order to draw from her profit for himself as the impresario of her fame."[26] As for Nietzsche himself, Nordau concentrates on four works, *The Genealogy of Morals, Beyond Good and Evil, Zarathustra* and *The Twilight of the Idols*. He ridicules their "crack-brained" titles as the work of a madman (Nordau knew that Nietzsche was confined in the lunatic asylum at Jena): "From the first to the last page of Nietzsche's writings the careful reader seems to hear a madman, with flashing eyes, wild gestures, and foaming mouth, spouting forth deafening bombast; and through it all, now breaking out into frenzied laughter, now sputtering expressions of filthy abuse and invective, now skipping about in a giddily agile dance, and now bursting upon the auditors with threatening mien and clenched fists."[27]

He criticizes Nietzsche's obsession with etymology, with puns, with images of depth, laughter, dancing, and flying, and his literary exuberance in general. Nietzsche's claim to be a psychologist he dismisses as "ridiculous"; nor is Nordau attracted by "such railway-bookstall humour and such tea-table wit."[28] As for Nietzsche's ideas, they are beneath contempt, being violently dictatorial, self-contradictory and, where they are not commonplace, bellowingly insane. In his ethical theories concerning the superman and master-morality, Nietzsche betrays not only his intellectual sadism but also his "misanthropy, or anthropophobia, megalomania, and mysticism."[29] Nietzsche does not argue or debate, he merely asserts. His books lack system and coherence: "They are a succession of disconnected sallies, prose and doggerel mixed, without beginning or ending. Rarely is a thought developed to any extent; rarely are a few consecutive pages connected by any unity of purpose or logical argument."[30] Nietzsche's recurrent attacks of nervous instability, while establishing his insanity, cannot extenuate the way his books were composed: "Nietzsche evidently had the habit of throwing on paper with feverish haste all that passed through his head, and when he had collected a heap of snippings he sent them to the printer, and there was a book. These sweepings of ideas he himself proudly terms 'aphorisms,' and the very incoherence of his language is regarded by his admirers as a special merit."[31] This polemic continues in the same strain for nearly sixty pages, by far the largest amount of space granted to any of Nordau's victims. Between them, Wagner and Nietzsche occupy one-sixth of the entire book.

First issued in February, 1895, *Degeneration* achieved such immediate success that seven new impressions were called for before the year was out; further editions appeared in 1898, 1913, and 1920. As far as Nietzsche's English reputation was concerned, Nordau's stigmatization of him as a "colossal egoist," a lunatic, a brutal sadist, a *soi-disant* philosopher who lacked system, reason, and basic human decency was disastrous. A learned medical journal took Nietzsche as "a study in mental pathology," showing how he became progressively insane and dismissing the bulk of his writings as "refuse."[*] Nordau's diagnosis, pronounced with such professional authority, was parroted in many sections of the conservative press. *Blackwood's Magazine*, after calling Nietzsche a "German imbecile," wrote: "*Degeneration* is worth reading if only to learn of what very inferior clay are fashioned the idols whom modern 'culture' worships."[32] Most of the reviewers of *Degeneration* were sensible enough to take account of Nor-

---

[*] William Ireland, "Friedrich Nietzsche: A Study in Mental Pathology," *Journal of Mental Science*, XLVII (January, 1901), 1–28. That Nietzsche's insanity resulted from protracted eyestrain was the opinion of G. M. Gould, "The Origins of the Ill-Health of Nietzsche," *Biographic Clinics*, II (1904), 285–322.

dau's violent over-emphasis, but still thought he had a strong case, particularly against Nietzsche.

4 In 1896, then, it was rare to find literary critics, and even less philosophers, who were prepared to be open-minded about Nietzsche. One of the few was the Oxford don, William Wallace, who insisted on the need for a translation of Nietzsche's works:

Report of Nietzsche on this side of the Channel has been heard now and again; but of knowledge, as distinct from notoriety, there is no great amount. Perhaps the majority of such English readers as take interest in these matters have gained their acquaintance with him, and their estimate of his ideas, from the chapter devoted to him in Max Nordau's *Degeneration*. But Nordau's account of literary heretics of the nineteenth century, though a fairly clever piece of journalistic work, is not inspired by the sympathy or intelligence which are indispensable if critical sketches of remarkable persons are to rise above the level of caricatures.[33]

Yet the *Saturday Review* branded Nietzsche as a "frantic street-corner preacher" who resembled Nordau in deriving inspiration from Darwin:

It is rare that two such men as Nordau and Nietzsche have the luck to be so interesting as their circumstances make this pair. They are both essentially commonplace persons, or rather they polarize the commonplace. Nordau – to handle him with the familiar frankness of his own criticisms – is unimaginative, self-assertive, overbearing, profoundly convinced of his own extraordinary reasonableness – a type of man you may find fisting the table in the bar parlour of any English country public of a winter's evening; while Nietzsche is a non-Teutonic type, a flighty conceited creature, bitten by the Great Teacher mania, until at last he has actually attained the martyrdom of the madhouse.[34]

As we shall see later, Bernard Shaw, in his two reviews of Nietzsche for the *Saturday Review*, placed Nietzsche higher than Nordau. But the general view was that Nordau and Nietzsche were two of a kind: both were possessed with the idea of decadence and degeneration, and the similarity did not by any means end there:

Both Nietzsche and Nordau pride themselves on being physiological and psychological, although their "science" is clearly only second-hand, not to say pseudoscientific. Both excel in vituperation and constantly substitute abuse for argument; in this respect, however, Nietzsche is *facile princeps* – chiefly on account of his greater range. Both are anti-religious, because they have no appreciation of the spiritual side of man, and so cannot understand that in the descendents of brutes a certain repression of animality is essential for full sanity of soul. Both are deficient in humor and grotesquely ignorant of the real condition of the English-speaking world, although their criticisms of Germany seem often to strike home. Lastly, to mention a point suggested by the title of the present volume, both have won notoriety by attacks upon the music of Wagner, which they unite in regarding as the incarnation of the morbid tendencies of the age."[35]

As for Tille's preface to the volume under review, *The Case of Wagner*, it was ludicrous of him to suppose that Darwin would have ignored, as Nietzsche did, the moral, intellectual, and social qualities in the make-up of fitness. There was no index, this reviewer complained, "and for the translation not much can be said; it generally fails to reach a fluent and idiomatic English rendering, it not infrequently becomes unintelligible, and sometimes blunders." While conceding that the translations were "more or less satisfactory," the *Spectator* thought that in some respects they were "decidedly inadequate" – admittedly, Nietzsche was a difficult writer to translate: "For Nietzsche's writings have no claim whatsoever to rank as literary productions; a more execrable style it would be difficult to invent or imagine. There is no continuity of style any more than of thought. ... So far as form and method are concerned, they do not constitute a philosophy, but are a series of chaotic and often quite incoherent jottings noted down by a man whose feelings altogether outrun his capacity for thinking."[36] The remainder of the review is given over to a professedly "obvious" refutation of Nietzsche's materialism and antihumanitarianism. Some of Nietzsche's subsidiary ideas, however, were felt to be stimulating and comparatively sound: "It is true that the present decadent movement in literature and life is profoundly unhealthy, though we may be unable to see in Wagner, for instance, as Nietzsche sees in him, a leading representative of disease. But the literature of the age is sombre, and we agree that firm and elastic fibre and a joyous spirit must always attach to a great productive era."

William Wallace, writing in the *Academy*, was more aware of the difficulties facing the translator of Nietzsche, who, he observed, was not easy reading even in German. Common's translation of *The Case of Wagner*, Wallace thought, was careful and laudably idiomatic, but Tille's version of *Zarathustra*, however, was not so creditable: "Something may, no doubt, be allowed for insufficient intimacy with English idiom; but in places the result actually achieved suggests a beginner wrestling with the tools provided by a very elementary dictionary, and often worsted by them."[37] The English "lust" is not, Wallace points out, the true equivalent of the German *Lust*, nor is "kin" equivalent to *Art* nor "perceive" to *erkennen*. It is a strange anatomy which turns *Bauch* into "womb" and *Leib* into "stomach." Indeed, considered as a translation, *Thus Spake Zarathustra* was attacked even more harshly than *The Case of Wagner*. The *Saturday*

Review complained of Nietzsche: "He writes in fables set in the mouth of Zarathustra, in grotesque parody of the gospel form. Dr. Tille, translating, is constrained to pepper "doth" and "hath" in his pages – albeit these words do not belong to modern English prose. It is a quite inappropriate style and form."[38]

The *National Observer*, likening Nietzsche's name to a sneeze, thought that "a more extremely absurd, and at the same time pretentious and offensive volume it has never been our lot to meet."[39] *Zarathustra* was the craziest stuff since Whitman: "Not the maddest of poets combined with the maddest of publishers could have set forth these ravings unless a mad age had prepared the way for it. Before such outpourings reason – and Max Nordau – stand aghast." The *Manchester Guardian* noted a contradiction between the gospel of the superman and Nietzsche's antifeminism; the occasional clumsiness of the translation was excusable in the case of a style as unique and original as Nietzsche's, but the decision to publish Nietzsche's last works was apt to lead to confusion.[40] *The Times*, relying – as John Davidson had done – on Theodor de Wyzewa's account of Nietzsche, reprinted in *Écrivains Étrangers* (1896), called *Zarathustra* "a masterpiece of pessimistic philosophy"; Zarathustra has only one belief, a belief in the coming of the superman, and it is this which he expounds to a chosen band of disciples: "Not very many English readers, we suspect, will enrol themselves in that inner circle; but for all that there will be more than few who will feel the curious spell of this book, as sincere as it is strange, and who will recognize the peculiar beauty of Nietzsche's style, even in the form of a translation."[41]

The Times, the bastion of English conservatism, added with a trace of approval that, although few knew of Nietzsche in England, he was being welcomed in Germany as the "champion of individualism against the invading doctrines of the Socialist, not less than as the destroyer of many received opinions in Church and State." The *Athenaeum* was shocked that an enemy of civilized decency like Nietzsche should have obtained anything that could be called a reputation, for his philosophy, or what passed for it, was one of greed, lust, violence, and rapacity, in which physical strength was the only test of virtue:

Morality is a fraudulent invasion of the rights of vigour, a rebellion of the weak multitude against the few who have overpowered them. Justice, sympathy, self-control, and all the so-called virtues are nothing but so many arbitrary restraints on the indefeasible right of every man to do what he pleases, where and when he can. Under morality, religion, civilization, the race has decayed, and man as he is must give way to man as he might be if he had his way – the Ueber-

mensch, the superhuman. Nothing is true, everything is permissible: "Nichts ist wahr, Alles ist erlaubt."[42]

Zarathustra presents this gospel of the *Übermensch*, "who is to test all things by physiological methods." The attack switches to Tille who had claimed that *Zarathustra* was a kind of intellectual summary of the nineteenth century when in fact it was only "a heterogeneous medley of the offscourings of its literature and science, its wildest dreams, and its many failures." The references Tille had made to some outstanding minds of the nineteenth century unjustifiably suggested that "because some of their ideas are to be found in an adulterated form in Nietzsche, that writer is, therefore, entitled to be put on an intellectual level with them." To compare *Zarathustra* with *Piers the Ploughman* and *The Pilgrim's Progress*, as Tille had done with apparent sincerity, argued a strange insensitivity to the qualities which make these works good literature.

In contrast to those who found *Zarathustra* an easy target for abuse and summary judgment, William Wallace preferred to restrict himself to a sober exposition of its contents:

Nietzsche is at least always honest, pure, and thorough. One of his faults is a natural perversity, if one may so style it, which positively refuses easy and flattering solutions of problems, and would always seek its rest on the hardest and barest of rocks, with inveterate suspicion of any suggestion that happiness and truth can lie down together. Another is a fatal facility to follow the track of epigram, and to wander in the pleasant but devious mazes of verbal conceits.[43]

It should not be overlooked that the English public had another means of access to *Zarathustra* – a musical one. In 1897 Richard Strauss's *Also sprach Zarathustra* was performed at Crystal Palace. In a private letter to Ernest Newman, Sir George Grove expressed, in Newman's view, "what was probably the opinion of most of the people who sat it out": "What can have happened to drag down music from the high level of beauty, interest, sense, force, grace, coherence, and any other good quality, which it rises to in Beethoven and also (not so high) in Mendelssohn, down to the low level of ugliness and want of interest that we had in Strauss's absurd farrago ... ? *Noise* and *effect* seems to be so much the aim now."* Ernest Newman, however, differed:

---

* Quoted by Ernest Newman, *Musical Studies* (London, 1905), 249. Strauss's tone-poem had its première in November, 1896, with the composer conducting. The actual subtitle of the work was *"frei nach Nietzsche,"* but Strauss said he would have preferred the description "symphonic optimism in *fin-de-siècle* form dedicated to the Twentieth Century." Such a quantity of Nietzsche was found indigestible by many of the conservative-minded music critics of the day.

Now what we have to recognise in the case of Richard Strauss is that he is the destroyer – or at any rate, the symbol of destruction – of all previous values, as Nietzsche would say, and the creator at once of a new expression and a new form. ... Certainly *Also sprach Zarathustra* is a marvellous work; no such overwhelming picture of man and the universe has ever before been unfolded to our eyes in music; it almost makes the world-philosophy of Wagner seem, in comparison, like the bleat of evangelical orthodoxy.[44]

Despite the advocacy of Newman, the English public did not care to be serenaded into an appreciation of Nietzsche.

By 1899, when *A Genealogy of Morals* appeared, the climate of opinion had not changed. With the death in 1897, of William Wallace, England lost Nietzsche's sole academic champion.* His place on the staff of the *Academy* was taken by a reviewer who categorically dismissed Nietzsche as a "backwater," a philosopher who was a disconcerting sign of modern trends. Openly disagreeing with Havelock Ellis's judgment that Nietzsche was one of the greatest spiritual forces to appear since Goethe, this reviewer felt grateful that "in England, with the exception of a few lectures and magazine articles, singularly little direct attention has been paid to Nietzsche."[45] The *Pall Mall Gazette* thought that *A Genealogy of Morals* would "sound strange, fantastic, mad and perhaps impious to English ears," but reminded its readers that no error exists in pure undiluted form: "Nietzsche has failed, but his failure has been that of an intellectual Titan who fell scorched and crushed in one of the most sublimely audacious attacks that was ever made on the very citadel of Olympus; but he leaves behind a work of vast bulk, a sort of Pelion and Ossa that will long testify to the vigour of his assaults."[46] But this paper contested Nietzsche's view that Christianity was responsible for the fall of Rome, holding it was caused by the decay of civic spirit: "It was the 'res publica' at Rome and the 'polis' with its fierce civil life in Greece that bred the men that Nietzsche admires. Democracy should be able in its turn to produce a similar élite. If not, democracy will prove the doom of every modern State into which it enters."[47] This is the line of thought, as we shall see, which was to occupy the energies of Wells and Shaw. But the view that Nietzsche was an atheist, an anarchist, a disrupter of civilized society, a harbinger of the "blond beast" (an expression which peppers these early reviews) scavenging in

---

* The first chapter of what was to have been a detailed criticism of Nietzsche, left incomplete at Wallace's death, appeared as "Nietzsche's Criticism of Morality" in *Lectures and Essays on Natural Theology and Ethics*, ed. Edward Caird (Oxford, 1898), 511–29. Had Wallace lived, he might have become a major English interpreter of Nietzsche's work.

search of prey, persisted. Politically the jingoism prompted by the Boer War was deplored as a menacing echo of the Nietzsche-inspired glorification of aggression in Germany.

Typical of the general attitude to Nietzsche until 1899 were two influential articles by the Edinburgh professor Andrew Seth Pringle-Pattison. Noting that the "crass diatribes" of *Degeneration* doubtless helped to introduce this "bizarre genius" to English readers, he claimed that his articles were an attempt to give a precise account of Nietzsche in the belief that "however preposterous Nietzsche's theories may be, his conclusions and the steps by which he reached them form an instructive chapter in the history of ideas."[48] After all, he observed, Nietzsche was becoming something of a European phenomenon, and the "sober occupants of philosophical chairs complain that he is at present the philosopher *à la mode*."[49] As a Christian theist, Pringle-Pattison shared the distaste of his continental colleagues. In his eyes Zarathustra stands convicted of the cardinal sin of pride:

His maniacal pride of will finds, perhaps, unmatched expression when he places the following syllogism before his disciples: "To lay bare to you, friends, my inmost heart; *if* there were gods, how should I bear it not to be a god? *Therefore* there are no gods." In this logical gem it can hardly be doubted that Nietzsche has revealed, half defiantly, half involuntarily, the guiding motive of all his thought, the intense and boundless egotism which eventually shattered him to pieces.[50]

While denying that *Zarathustra* is in any sense an artistic whole, he readily understands why it was hailed as a masterpiece of style: "In Germany, the home of invertebrate prose, the work was indeed a striking apparition."[51] Nietzsche is a *littérateur* rather than a philosopher: "He is not a systematic thinker, but as a moralist in the old sense, a student of human nature, and as a critic of literature and art, he is constantly fresh and suggestive. The style has the virtues of transparent clearness and assured ease, heightened from time to time by a piquant phrase and by epigrammatic sallies that recall Heine by their wit and malice."[52]

But as philosophy he can make little of *Zarathustra*, and is appalled by the "colossal egotism and self-assurance, characteristic of Nietzsche from the first," which becomes even more apparent in the later work: "Denunciation degenerates into foul-mouthed abuse; and the hysterical violence with which he dashes himself against the greatest names and ideals of human history seems to resemble nothing more than the impotent fury of a naughty child."[53] It is to these later works that Pringle-Pattison's attack is largely directed. Nietzsche's "wild beast theory of ethics," with its corollary that "nothing is true, everything permitted," could only lead to "the complete disintegration both of morality and of knowledge."[54] There is nothing original in Nietzsche's teaching: it had all been anticipated, and refuted, by Plato long ago. Contempt is expressed for Tille's physiological interpretation of Nietzsche, and for Common's insistence that ethical principles must now be derived from Darwin, not from Christ.

Pringle-Pattison's articles are much more detailed than these brief excerpts can hope to suggest. His view of Nietzsche gained wide currency in academic circles, and successive writers like George Saintsbury, William Sorley, S. Patton, and Herbert L. Stewart, all owed a debt to what one of them called his "luminous" exposition.* Thomas Common, fearing the influence it might have, quickly undertook an extensive point-by-point refutation of the professor's verdict that "Nietzsche's paradoxes and epigrams are hardly likely to take an important or permanent place in the movement of modern thought."[55] Not only, Common complained, did the professor's articles exhibit "a bitter animosity" against Nietzsche, but they furnished "on the whole a gross caricature and misrepresentation of his most important principles."[56] This, Common charged, was perhaps only to be expected from the champion of the Philistine class, which represented "a vast conspiracy for the purpose of coining and circulating a counterfeit moral currency."[57] Common dissociates himself from the "extraordinary emphasis" which Tille had given to physiology as the characteristic element in Nietzsche's mature teaching, adding that William Wallace, whose criticism of Nietzsche was in "remarkable contrast" to that of the Edinburgh professor," also thought this was a misunderstanding on Tille's part.

Nietzsche's death in August, 1900, passed almost unnoticed, and this fact gave the *London Quarterly Review* cause for self-congratulation: "In this country, despite the efforts of certain devotees, he is but little known, and the practical English mind has small inclination to extract the grain of value from the chaff of speculations which, if ever they came to be generally acted upon, would dissolve society as we understand it and bring us back to the 'dragons of the prime.'"[58] In one of the rare obituary notices, T. Bailey Saunders, well-known translator of Schopenhauer, felt that there

---

* George Saintsbury, *A History of Criticism and Literary Taste in Europe* (London, 1900–4), III, 581–6; and *Periods of European Literature* (New York, 1907), XII, 239–48; William Sorley, *Recent Tendencies in Ethics* (London, 1904); S. Patton, "Nietzsche and His Influence," *Princeton Theological Review*, VI (June, 1908), 392–436; Herbert L. Stewart, "Some Criticisms on the Nietzsche Revival," *International Journal of Ethics*, XIX (July, 1909), 427–43, 'The Cult of Nietzsche," *Questions of the Day in Philosophy and Psychology* (London, 1912), 254–81, and *Nietzsche and the Ideals of Modern Germany* (London, 1915).

was no real call for criticism of Nietzsche's achievements. It was a compliment to modern thought that, on the whole, it had not been disposed to take Nietzsche seriously. Nietzsche was an anarchist: "Civilization was the greatest obstacle to progress, and Christianity the greatest blot on civilization. The hopes of the future lay with the 'Uebermensch,' the man of force, nay, of violence, determined to make his own personal will prevail, and irrespective of others and regardless of their interests, to succeed in the 'struggle for life.' "[59]

Nietzsche's reputation, such as it was in England, was a growth only of the previous decade, and the translations of his work, Saunders assumes, were stopped owing to lack of public support: "He was the subject of a few stray essays in magazines; his writings supplied material to aspiring members of literary societies, or formed the theme of lectures in clubs and institutions anxious to be known as advanced. His philosophy became for a moment at dinner-parties a fashionable substitute for political or theological scandal. But of any serious or abiding interest in him, any deep impression that he had seen truth in a new aspect, there was little trace."

There was, indeed, little "serious and abiding interest" in Nietzsche in the press reports up to 1900. One of the reasons was that until 1903 only three volumes of the works were available in English. Yet under Tille's editorship several translations of individual works had been made which were destined to remain in MS for many years. In 1901 Common drew on them for his *Nietzsche as Critic, Philosopher, Poet and Prophet*, an anthology of extracts which was prompted by the pressing need to give some indication of the great range of Nietzsche's work, a task which Common had begun by his contributions to *The Eagle and the Serpent* (1898–1903), a Nietzschean journal later to be discussed in detail. Common also distributed circulars to distinguished men of letters calling for subscribers for further volumes of the Nietzsche translation, which English publishing houses seemed loath to accept. These circulars, although they netted William Archer, Edmund Gosse, Havelock Ellis, Edward Garnett, and Bernard Shaw as potential subscribers, elicited little public response. When, after a delay of four years, *The Dawn of Day* was finally issued in 1903, probably to test public reaction, the *Academy* was one of the few weeklies to take notice of it. The review, probably by Edward Garnett, begins on a resigned note:

From a combination of causes, it is extremely unlikely that Nietzsche will ever receive his due in England. To begin with, the practical English mind has little taste and less talent for comprehending philosophical speculations almost wholly unorthodox in their teaching; and, in the second place, Nietzsche's brilliantly biased psychology, aristocratic individualism, and poetic violence confuse and repel grave men of science, letters, religion, law, and all the students of exact research.[60]

In place of Nordau's saturation bombing we find a real perceptiveness, a willingness to distinguish, in Nietzsche, between appearance and reality. Nietzsche, this reviewer warns, is not to be taken as the hot-gospeller of brute force and egomania:

Nietzsche, in fact, was a thinker of a singularly pure, noble, and lofty mind, and the misanthropy, egotism, and insane pride of his Zarathustra were in fact but the walls of resistance his indomitable spirit raised to shield itself under the ravages of cruel pain. Those who will not bend must break. ... More, perhaps, than any modern writer he needs to be read with a delicate discrimination of the inner meaning as opposed to the outer or obvious meaning. He is, therefore, not a writer for people who want gospels, text-books, or for "specialists" who are so occupied in tilling their well-ordered fields that they are impatient of raising their eyes to the wide horizon beyond. For Nietzsche, though a thinker of great significance, is above all things a poet.

Beatrice Marshall noted, in a postscript to this review two weeks later, that much of the misunderstanding surrounding Nietzsche had been caused by the order in which his works had been translated: it would have been less erratic to begin with a work like *The Birth of Tragedy*.[61] Arthur Symons, in an anonymous review, hoped that the appearance of *The Dawn of Day* would augur well for the future: "Three more volumes, it appears, are ready for the press, awaiting only a little encouragement on the part of the public, which has hitherto shown an amazing lack of interest." In his opinion, *The Dawn of Day*, or *The Birth of Tragedy*, would have made a better, because less startling, beginning for the translation venture than the volumes which were actually chosen:

The Dawn of Day is one of the ripest and least extravagant of Nietzsche's books, while it is thoroughly characteristic of his mind and method. The translation, by Johanna Volz, is fairly adequate, though lacking in distinction, and from time to time not quite idiomatic. Words like "enamorous" and "labyrinthal," constructions like "different *than*," "a match to," "know to find," "the only preference of the Germans above other nations," seem to indicate a not quite perfect acquaintance with English. But a translator of Nietzsche has no easy task in the rendering of that vivid and gesticulating style, with its nervous starts, its flickering meanings.[62]

To know Nietzsche thoroughly, Symons declares, the English need *The Birth of Tragedy*, *The Gay Science* and *Beyond Good and Evil*. It would be a pity if the translation series had to be suspended through the indifference of the public:

A series of translations issued in France by the *Mercure de France*, under the editorship of M. Henri Albert, has already reached its tenth volume, and of these volumes four are in a fifth and three in a fourth edition. Have English readers, then, so much less curiosity than French readers in regard to what we need call no more than the actualities of thought? Nietzsche, for good or evil, has spoken to his end of the century with a formidable voice. He may be fought, he cannot be disregarded.

Yet after the publication of *The Dawn of Day*, there was a gap of four years before the next volume, *Beyond Good and Evil*, appeared.

It should now be clear what factors were operative in the poor degree of response to Nietzsche in England. One, perhaps the most important, was the preconditioning influence of Max Nordau and, to a lesser extent, Alexander Tille; another was the high price of the individual volumes, and a third was the disapproval they met with at the hands of the press. This disapproval stemmed partly from the fact that Nietzsche's later works had been thrown on the public without the key the earlier ones would have provided, partly from the low standard of translation (by persons whose mother tongue was not English) which obscured Nietzsche's meaning. Difficulties abounded. When the translation venture was taken over by Fisher Unwin in 1899, a scheme to publicize the completed volumes in twenty leading journals was abandoned for lack of funds; mistakes in the new Nietzsche list, such as the misspelling of his name and the description of his works as "novels," were fortunately corrected before the list was circulated. Thòmas Common admitted that the whole venture had not been too well managed, and that "the printing of the books in Germany after a final revision at the Nietzsche Archiv (where imperfect English was too often substituted when an alteration was made) has no doubt been prejudicial to the undertaking."[63] In 1906 an editorial in the New York *Nation* declared that the neglect of Nietzsche was "a terrible reproach" to the civilization of the English-speaking world, and suggested the establishment of a government-subsidized press "to shake the publishers and the public out of the vicious rut into which they have insensibly slipped."[64] This editorial gave rise to some interesting correspondence from the American publishers of Nietzsche, Macmillan, and from Thomas Common, who wrote:

No doubt the cold reception which Nietzsche has met with in England and America has been in some degree owing to the unfavourable auspices under which his books have been presented to the public, but it is partly, also, owing to the character of the Anglo-Saxon peoples, who are less ripe for the best thought than the French. The fact that most of Nietzsche's voluminous writings are already accessible to French readers, and are eagerly purchased by them, confirms the truth of Nietzsche's estimate of France as the home of the highest culture, where people are most receptive of new modes of thought.[65]

England, Common added, does have endowed institutions, such as the Clarendon Press and the Royal Society of Literature, which publish work of a non-commercial nature, but neither of them will have anything to do with Nietzsche: "His originality frightens the narrow-minded delegates and trustees who have the management of these institutions; and instead of helping, they only tantalize those who are in advance of them in the foremost files of time." Common preferred to rely on the resources of those who believed in the need for Nietzsche in English rather than on endowments to publishers or public appeals for funds. Among eminent Englishmen who could vouch for Nietzsche's importance Common listed S. Alexander, W. Archer, S. H. Butcher, Ellis, Garnett, Symons, Shaw, Gosse, and J. G. Robertson.

In reply to Common, the Oxford professor F. C. S. Schiller, with some show of belligerence, took up the cudgels on behalf of the "incriminated" English public. After all, Schiller asserted, the translations were recognized to be bad, and, in the case of Zarathustra, grotesque. Might not the English public, he queried, have also detected that Nietzsche was mad, and "have stupidly regarded this as a drawback to the serious study of his works?"[66] It was surely quite permissible to believe that Nietzsche's more theatrical ideas, such as those of the superman, slave-morality, and the "Blonde Wild Beast," were just as nonsensical as they seemed to the Anglo-Saxon Philistine.

Since Schiller's view was the prevalent one, the years between 1899 and 1907, even allowing for the momentary flicker of hope raised by the publication of *The Dawn of Day* in 1903, were lean ones for those interested in advancing Nietzsche's cause. The dearth and inadequacy of English translations forced some readers of Nietzsche to a dependence on French versions. Davidson's first encounter with Nietzsche was through a French source, and Ellis probably learnt much from reading the established Paris reviews, especially the *Revue des Deux Mondes*. Arthur Symons first read *The Birth of Tragedy* in 1902, but in French, as the English version did not appear until 1909, and Arnold Bennett preferred to read *Zarathustra* in French rather than navigate a passage through the treacherous waters of Tille's translation. There were no books in English to equal Henri Lichtenberger's *La Philosophie de Nietzsche* (1898) or Émile Faguet's *En lisant*

Nietzsche (1904), the first of which had gone into fourteen editions by 1910. The tide began to turn in 1907, when Dr. Oscar Levy appeared on the scene, anxious to apply his energies and financial resources to rescuing the English translation of Nietzsche from apathy and unconcern.

5   Oscar Levy (1867–1946) took his doctoral degree at Freiburg University in 1891, and then settled in London, where he gained the English diplomas of MRCS and LRCP in 1895. His interest in Nietzsche began in 1893. During the 1890s he seems to have tried to persuade Ernest Rhys to publish *Zarathustra*, but this proposal came to nothing on account of copyright difficulties. In 1907 he undertook, at his own risk, to finance the publication of *Beyond Good and Evil*, which, as he said, "had never seen, and was never expected to see, the light of publicity":

It turned out to be a success – a half-hearted success perhaps, but one that at last told the few inmates of the Nietzschean ark that the waters of democracy had diminished, and that at last some higher peaks of humanity were free from the appalling deluge. The success encouraged them once more to take up their old project of the publication of the complete works. New arrangements were made with the Nietzsche-Archiv, whose authorities were found most willing to come to another agreement for a fresh edition. In May 1909 the first four volumes of this, the present translation, left the press and were favourably received, though yet by a small and none too enthusiastic public.[67]

The publication of *Beyond Good and Evil* in 1907 coincided with the appointment of A. R. Orage to the editorship of the *New Age*, which soon became under his guidance the most stimulating weekly of its time. Orage had already written two important books on Nietzsche; he now used the *New Age* to prepare public opinion for Levy's new translation venture. Many of Levy's translators, as we shall see in a later chapter, were regular contributors to the *New Age*, as was Levy himself; the "inmates" (as Levy rather infelicitously called them) of the Nietzschean ark could now command the attention of an educated audience, and by 1909, when a complete translation of Nietzsche had begun, those sections of the press which had formerly denounced Nietzsche were having second thoughts. Brandes and Taine, the two men who had first reached out welcoming hands to Nietzsche, wrote the *Times Literary Supplement* in its first leading article on Nietzsche, were "men of genius and perspicacity, real torch-bearers":

We wonder anxiously what is the use of our colleges, universities, reviews, and critical journals, if they only serve to appreciate and extol what is already appreciated and sufficiently extolled. ... Surely a prudent State should ... constitute a company of watchers with a mission to descry and succour the struggles of sinking genius. They would be wise perhaps to associate in their endeavour some specialist in mental disorders, for the madman of to-day (as in Nietzsche's case) is often the prophet of tomorrow.[68]

The *Saturday Review*, too, welcomed the new venture: "English readers could not have the work of Nietzsche presented in a better form. One of the amusements of reading it is that one traces the brutalities and cynicisms and paradoxes of the German in some of our brilliant English writers whose *métier* is to shock our religious, political and social opinions and prejudices."[69] The *Westminster Gazette*, a Christian paper, wrote: "We have no grudge against the publication of Nietzsche's works in full in this country. To read enough of him is to provide yourself with the appropriate remedies for his doctrine. He leads so obviously to incoherence and chaos. But he stirs and startles, by the way, and is a good tonic for those who are tempted to accept conventions without questioning them. Whatever else he may be, he is at war with frivolity and the mere craving for pleasure and ease which infects the modern world."[70] The *Spectator*, calling Nietzsche "clearly a kind of universal classic," praised the translations but not the introductions, most of which, with the exception of Ludovici's "really valuable" commentary on *Zarathustra*, were held to lack acumen and perspective: "The fact is that Nietzsche is in one sense too easy. Any unbalanced mind can grasp a few of his shibboleths and expound a half-baked gospel. Hence most of the recent writings on Nietzsche have been sad rubbish, and even when the writer has something to say he is apt to work himself into a Dionysian frenzy and say it badly."[71]

The critical study of Nietzsche could hardly be said to have begun since students were either furious devotees or furious antagonists. J. M. Kennedy's *The Quintessence of Nietzsche* (1909) and M. A. Muegge's *Friedrich Nietzsche: His Life and Work* (1908), though serviceable introductions to their subject, suffered from the occupational disease of most Nietzschean expositors – they lacked a sense of humour and proportion. The *Nation* went so far as to say that it was mainly because of his English disciples that Nietzsche had not been taken seriously in England:

In this country he has fallen into the hands of a knot of enthusiasts, who have praised the "master" without stint or discrimination, and have accepted or exaggerated all his inconsistencies. Without possessing his supreme felicity of style they have imitated his dogmatism and violence, and have rendered their pages unpleasant by furious abuse of such things – the Christian religion, for instance – as Nietzsche did not happen to like. And the English Nietzschean is often of opinion that he faithfully carries out the teacher's precepts by representing himself as a devil of a fellow, dancing gaily and supermannishly over all the established moralities. This attitude, even if it may be tolerated in the case of a man of genius, becomes offensive and wearisome when affected by the minor literary person.[72]

Levy's preface to A. M. Ludovici's *Who Is to Be Master of the World?* (1909) as well as the book itself, are cited as a case in point. In his preface to the final volume Levy took account of these criticisms of the way the Nietzscheans conducted their campaign:

Our publications have been very loud, our lectures aggressive, our conversations "conceited." I myself have openly indulged in sneers and sarcasms of a most hearty calibre, as the Preface to this very edition and all the prefaces I wrote to the books of my friends will prove. ... The reason for all this extraordinary behaviour is only too plain: we were an insignificant minority in a state of war with a vast majority, whose arrows, as the Persian ambassador once upon a time said to the Spartans, would well have been able to darken the sun.[73]

The questionable thing here is not Levy's diagnosis but the nature of remedy he sought to apply – nobody can really be instructed by being deliberately antagonized, and Levy might have assisted his cause more by restraining his frothy outbursts against the English nation. It is all the more creditable that by 1909 reviewers were prepared to overlook, not only Nietzsche's diatribes against the English in *Beyond Good and Evil*, but also the more tasteless excesses of zeal on the part of Levy and his collaborators.

Nietzsche, then, was the philosopher *à la mode* in England between 1909 and 1913. The philosophical journals began to give his work a more thorough scrutiny, and leading literary organs, like the *English Review*, followed the lead of the *New Age* by taking Nietzsche seriously. Land once occupied by Nietzsche's hostile critics was patiently reclaimed by those no longer intimidated by the power of the opposition or encumbered by the embarrassing antics of more zealous allies. Yet it is not surprising that pockets of resistance, and ignorance, remained. At the end of a performance of Delius' *Mass of Life* (based on *Zarathustra*) in the summer of 1909, the conductor, Thomas Beecham, ushered the chorus master forward and overheard a young girl in the front row ask her gentleman companion who it was: "The librettist," he replied. If young people were taking an interest in Nietzsche, wrote an observer in 1910, it was as yet of a superficial nature: "The student of London life who cares to visit in the evening those clubs and societies where intellectual young men and women debate, and evermore debate, life, literature, philosophy, politics, will be struck by a curious phenomenon. Alarming and dangerous theories of conduct are propounded by pensive youths and studious maidens, who lead the most innocent and inoffensive lives."[74]

Stanley Houghton's play, *The Younger Generation* (1910), which shows a group of young people in boisterous revolt against their authoritarian and puritan father, provoked the comment that "a truer picture of the 1910 attitudes would show us earnest youngsters at home, reading and discussing Nietzsche, rudely interrupted by the boring return of the parents bursting with hilarious reminiscences of Mr. George Robey from the local music-hall."[75] Horace B. Samuel, who had retranslated *The Genealogy of Morals* for Levy's edition, referred in 1911 to the dangers attendant on the Nietzsche vogue: "With the present boom no doubt Nietzscheanism may become a craze (in Germany, of course, it is already *passé* and has become academic and respectable), like the aesthetic of the Wilde period, and grow liable to equal if dissimilar perversions. Yet none the less, if taken very broadly and very sanely, Nietzsche is capable of constituting a valuable modern bible for the twentieth-century man who proposes to live vastly and to play for grand stakes."[76]

In 1912 the *Times Literary Supplement* devoted its second leading article to Nietzsche. Written anonymously by T. W. Rolleston, it censured Nietzsche's "colossal egotism," his "false and narrow" concept of the superman, his anti-Christian "evangel of Power" and his hatred of democracy, regarding Whitman as the right democratic antidote to Nietzsche's partial views. And yet:

Whatever may be said about Nietzsche – and perhaps the last word may not be said for many a day to come – there can be no doubt that he stands, a big and decidedly menacing figure, on the pathway of the modern pilgrim, and will not let us by till we do battle with him. ... Nietzsche was unquestionably a man of genius; a man who expressed with power and insight something that demanded expression in our age and that found in him not its only, but certainly its most potent voice.[77]

Levy had confessed that Nietzsche's philosophy had come to him "as to the traveller in the desert, an enchanting vision, a beautiful *fata Morgana* rising on the horizon of the future, a fertile and promising Canaan of a new creed";[78] to those who could not share this vision Nietzsche was at least a worthy foe, a formidable Apollyon, and they congratulated Levy on the "monumental" translation he had accomplished in the face of so many setbacks and difficulties. The *Observer* called the translation "a benefit to the community," and the publisher, T. N. Foulis of London, saw fit to include in the endpapers of the final volume, not only a complete review of all "Nietzschean literature" then available in English, but also an announcement of his own:

> As this Nietzsche translation is now completed, the publisher begs to suggest to that part of the public which takes the lead in matters of taste and intellect, that these volumes should not be wanting in the library of any cultured person. The antagonism to Nietzsche's teaching, which first took the form of icy silence and afterwards that of violent contradiction, has considerably diminished since his real meaning has become generally known through this translation. *The opinion is now gaining ground that in Nietzsche's life-work a totally new standpoint in matters of politics, art, literature, and theology is to be found.* Even his enemies now readily acknowledge that Nietzsche at least wrote in an extraordinarily vigorous and bracing style – a style which distinguishes him from all dry-as-dust philosophers, especially those of German origin.

The mistakes made by the first translation venture were not repeated. Each translation was more carefully prepared than its predecessors, and more closely checked in the proof-reading. The introductions, although some reviewers protested against their attitude of uncritical veneration, were on the whole much better than those Tille had written, and more obviously directed to an English audience – the notes to *Zarathustra* were found particularly useful to an understanding of that work. This time the prices were within the reach of the average book-buyer – *Zarathustra*, priced at seventeen shillings in 1896, now sold for six shillings (no volume cost more than this), and some volumes, including *The Birth of Tragedy*, sold for as little as two shillings and sixpence. Lastly, the whole corpus of Nietzsche's work now being accessible, readers could see it in perspective, and follow Nietzsche's advice that his philosophy, however incomprehensible it might seem at first, would become clearer after a painstaking study of his earlier writings. Foulis, in another note to his Nietzsche list, warned that *Zarathustra*, hitherto the book by which Nietzsche had been known and judged in England, "should not be approached until after a perusal of the other volumes." By the spring of 1914, Nietzsche was selling at the rate of five hundred copies a month, and the outbreak of war, the "Anglo-Nietzschean war" as it was dubbed, saw yet a further demand for his works.

England, Levy believed, was probably the most important country of all to conquer for Nietzschean thought, not only on account of her ubiquitous language, but also because if a hearing could not be obtained for Nietzsche there, his philosophy might be lost for ever to the world, "a world that would then quickly be darkened over again by the ever-threatening clouds of obscurantism and barbarism."[79] Nietzsche, of course, had been translated into all the major languages of the world, but Levy thought that conditions in England were very different from those on the continent, particularly in the matter of religion, and this made Nietzschean thought more likely to be understood in England than in any other country of Europe: "For in England, and only in England, can it still be seen that Nietzsche was right in describing Christianity as the religion of the lower classes, while on the Continent his whole attack seems to be without significance, his whole philosophy based upon assumption."[80] Although France, a country "much more Nietzschean" than England where the translation of Nietzsche had been subsidized by the government, might appear to offer a better breeding-ground for Nietzschean ideas, this was, in fact, not the case. French free thought could not be depended upon when it came to turning in earnest against an old religion: "It must never be forgotten that Catholicism, unlike Protestantism, has really entered into the hearts of its believers; that the head of a Latin may be as free-thinking and daring as possible, but that his heart will shrink nevertheless from drawing the final conclusions of his intellectual persuasion."[81] Catholicism, Levy contends, is an admirable system, well adapted to the psychological requirements of southerners. Where Catholicism prevails, it has not led to the intolerable conditions which Nietzsche constantly atttacks. In Latin countries there is still a large measure of patriarchy both in domestic and business life, and thus the state has not had to take into its care those too weak to look after themselves; in these countries the authority of the father is not quite abolished, nor the status of the family as yet totally undermined, women being content with the place allotted to them. The situation, Levy declares, is not such a happy one in England, where Protestantism, the chief object of Nietzsche's attack, has helped weak and worthless people to survive, "nay, to pullulate as freely as possible."[82]

It thus took twelve years for a complete English translation to get off the ground. Levy has recounted the difficulties of those years in two separate essays on the Nietzsche movement in England. He explains that three obstacles stood in the way of his Nietzsche crusade. First, the abuse Nietzsche constantly levels at the English race; secondly, the feudal conservatism of a nation which, although the cradle of democratic institutions, has never, unlike France, felt their ravages, and therefore never needed the "counterbalancing influence" of a Nietzschean reaction; and thirdly, the fact that unlike Germany or France, England lacked any literary genius who might have paved the way for Nietzsche's teachings. After alluding to the disappointing reception given to the early translations, and to the bankruptcy brought on their publisher, Levy writes: "In the next six years – from 1897 to 1903 – in spite of various endeavours by some indefatigable defenders of the faith, it was found absolutely impossible to get a hearing for Nietzsche either with the public, the Press, or the publishers."[83] And yet, at times, Levy does seem to exaggerate the magnitude of his task to make its fulfilment all the more praiseworthy: "One might have thought that some solitaries, a few of the independent thinkers, or some of the literary celebrities of modern England would have come to our rescue; but, apart from a misunderstanding of our cause and a very private and secret encouragement, not a soul stirred, not a mouth opened, not a finger was moved in our favour. Add to this that we were really a beaten crew, that England had stated before she would have nothing to do with Nietzsche."[84]

It is difficult to reconcile this account with Common's version of what happened. In 1913 Common hinted at some dark reason why the translation of Nietzsche had been delayed a dozen years: "It was certainly not the indifference of the public, the press, and the publishers which was the main cause of this long delay."[85] From the beginning Common had campaigned by means of personal intervention, articles, letters and in his quarterly *The Good European Point of View* (1903–16), to interest public and publishers alike in Nietzsche. In two issues of his quarterly in 1914 and 1915 he published his own account of the Nietzsche movement, which is to some extent at variance with that of Levy. After Henry & Co. had given up business, Common wrote in his first article, no publisher could be found to continue the translations at the exorbitant terms which that firm had agreed to, especially at a time when exclusive copyrights to Nietzsche's remaining principal volumes had lapsed. But it was not true that no publisher was interested in Nietzsche. Since 1895, Heinemann (publisher of Nordau's *Degeneration*) had shown an anxiety to get hold of Nietzsche's works; in 1898 or 1899 Swan Sonnenschein was on the point of making an arrangement, but negotiations were unexpectedly broken off, owing to "stubbornness" on the part of Nietzsche's representatives; Edward Garnett also made representations to Fisher Unwin and Duckworth – both of these firms were keen to exploit the latent public demand for Nietzsche. What prevented them from making an arrangement with Nietzsche's representatives? Simply the obstinacy of Nietzsche's sister, Elisabeth Förster-Nietzsche, who had taken over the management of her brother's profitable affairs on the death of their mother in 1897. Irritated that, owing to the lapse of exclusive copyright, she had lost the right of authorization over the unpublished principal works, she insisted that previous arrangements concerning the English translation had become invalid as a result of Messrs. Henry's breach of contract:

> Instead of arranging for the continuation of Messrs. Henry's edition, as she ought to have done and could easily have done, she hit upon a brand-new project. To obviate the loss of copyright of most of the principal works, she resolved to concoct a hodge-podge edition of Nietzsche's writings, to which she spuriously attempted to give full authorisation by mixing in chronological order *some* of the still copyrighted posthumous writings with the lapsed principal works – according to the biblical principle that "a little leaven leaveneth the whole lump." This is at least one special purpose of the German "Pocket edition," which, in spite of the altered title, is practically the basis of Dr. Levy's English edition of Nietzsche's works.[86]

Common notes with disgust that this Pocket Edition, which Frau Förster-Nietzsche wished to sell to the publishers of the English translations in 1901, was not issued in the original until 1906! Finding no English publisher willing to purchase this "conglomerate edition," as Common calls it, the "pythoness of Weimar" did her best to prevent Fisher Unwin from publishing any of their translations already prepared for Henry & Co.:

> Here then was a fine situation! The Nietzsche translation in England and America was delayed ten or a dozen years, owing to the caprice and stubbornness of a lady who has not greatly improved the reputation of the Nietzsche family either for disinterestedness, for uprightness of character, or for soundness of mind! Many publishers were only too anxious to continue the publication of Nietzsche's works on reasonable terms, but owing to her complication of the affair, and her perversion of obvious facts, she made it impossible for any publisher to come to terms with her; at the same time her conduct enervated our independent efforts to get Nietzsche's principal works published – otherwise we should have been successful much sooner.

To overcome this obstructiveness, Common and his collaborators, as he explains in his second article, decided to adopt the expedient of publishing a new and properly revised translation of *Zarathustra* in 1906: this was the first step towards a complete translation of Nietzsche. At this point Dr. Levy came forward. Common allowed him to help finance *Beyond Good and Evil*, and even to make arrangements with the Nietzsche-Archiv, but only "on the tacit understanding that he would act in a thoroughly upright manner":

> He went to Weimar and made some arrangement with Mrs. Förster Nietzsche for the publication of the English translation of Nietzsche's works. He made us believe that he had acquired the sole and exclusive rights to publish translations of Nietzsche's works in English, and that he was going to publish a complete

edition of Nietzsche's works. With a tacit belief in his uprightness we allowed him to get into his hands our originally authorised translation of *Zarathustra* ... and Dr. Haussmann, also, with a tacit belief in his uprightness, allowed him to get his genuinely authorised translation of *The Birth of Tragedy*.[87]

After exclusively appropriating *Beyond Good and Evil*, although he had only financed it in part, Levy went on, according to Common, to exhibit further "moral perversion" by trying to de-authorize the original copyright-preserving translations of *The Case of Wagner* and *The Genealogy of Morals*; this he did by substituting for them the "inferior," "careless" and "questionable" versions of his own "claim-jumpers." Common charges Levy with trying to humiliate Johanna Volz by replacing her translation of *The Dawn of Day* with another one: "It cast all the more dishonour on the Nietzsche Archive, because Miss Volz had rendered the greatest service to Mrs. Foerster-Nietzsche by her great labour in seeing almost all the volumes of the 'Pocket Edition' through the Press in the original German." Neither was it honourable of Levy to refuse Miss Zimmern the liberty of translating *Ecce Homo* when Nietzsche himself had wished her to translate it, when the Nietzsche-Archiv had therefore sought her out as a translator, and when she had specially desired Levy to allow her to undertake the work; it was also humiliating for her to be deprived of the opportunity of translating only one part of *Human, All-Too-Human* when both parts had originally been assigned to her. Common's sense of injury pierces deep: "We cannot but think, also, that Dr. Levy dishonourably laid a great surplus task upon us, by making us among other things thoroughly revise two volumes of other persons' translations when passing through the Press. He seems to have thought that we, the original translators of Nietzsche, were only fit to be drudges to supersmart claim-jumping Neo-Nietzscheans."*

It would be easy to dismiss Common's accusations as a clear case of "sour grapes." But nothing in his account is at variance with the facts as far as it has been possible to ascertain them at this later date, and a recent refusal of the Nietzsche-Archiv to allow access to their English correspondence files, in spite of their preparedness to co-operate in other aspects of Nietzsche scholarship, tends to suggest that Common's indictment is not

---

* "Uprightness or Unscrupulousness," *Good European Point of View*, no. 12 (Winter, 1915), 118. Levy, charged with a failure – in his essay on the Nietzsche movement in England – to pay tribute to the early efforts of Thomas Common, rectified the omission in "Dr. Oscar Levy and Nietzsche Pioneers," *TPW*, XXI (May 30, 1913), 694.

wholly without foundation.* It is certainly more substantial than the various explanations which have been given, then and since, for the tardiness of the English in awakening to Nietzsche's significance. Some pious genuflections in the direction of English practicality, English common sense, and English insularity border on the picturesque. Less self-deceptive was the realization that language instruction in English schools was of a woefully poor standard – this was the view of J. M. Kennedy, one of the more hard-headed Nietzscheans. The advent of Levy's complete translation, however, sometimes gave rise to national self-flagellation: "It is a sign both of mental apathy and of moral cowardice that the works of Nietzsche have, in England, been as yet so little studied and discussed."[88] English philosophers, this reviewer ingeniously argued, were in a conspiracy to ignore Nietzsche, and their hostility had a dampening effect on English publishers. Plausible as these conjectures are, they cannot suffice as satisfactory explanations now that it seems clear that the Nietzsche-Archiv must bear much of the blame.

6 In the seventeen years from 1896, when two volumes of Nietzsche appeared in English, to 1913, which saw the publication of the eighteenth and final volume of the complete translation, Nietzsche's ideas gained an ever-increasing currency. Although by 1913, as F. C. S. Schiller writes, "the invasion of England by a new German prophet" was "an accomplished fact," the painful slowness of that invasion showed that the insulation of British thought was still something to be reckoned with. This insulation, if not inherent, might have been due to a backward-looking educational system; whatever its cause, Nietzsche had penetrated it. Schiller continues:

Nietzsche has at last crossed the Channel, and will doubtless be read more extensively and understandingly than his precursors Kant and Hegel, who have never become more than caste-marks to enable the academically trained philosophers to mystify the common herd. Nietzsche's writing, on the other hand, is forcible and direct; he can be read and even understood without the study of a lifetime, and his ideas may even have an influence on conduct. It will not do therefore to pooh-pooh the ideas he stands for as the vapourings of a megalomaniac, while the lapse of time has rendered it possible to estimate his work with some degree of historical perspective, and to trace its relations to the native developments of British thought.[89]

* A number of letters from L. Simons and Elisabeth Förster-Nietzsche to Fisher Unwin (now in the possession of the New York Public Library) fully corroborate Common's statements.

It was Schiller's opinion that no work on Nietzsche had been able to solve the riddle of his personality, but that enough was known about him for one to make allowance for the extravagances of his thought and the excess of his self-esteem: "When all deductions have been made, there remains in his work not a little which is strong, novel, and important, and has been shown to be fertile and prophetic of further developments."[90] What marks Schiller's remarkable change of heart over Nietzsche is his discovery of *The Will to Power*, in which he finds that the aphoristic style characteristic of Nietzsche's earlier work has become less a psychological necessity involving paradox and exaggeration than a literary device used to work out ideas more systematically. Schiller concludes from this that Nietzsche's thought is more coherent than it appears to be, or than many readers, himself included, had ever suspected. He wishes now to regard Nietzsche, not as a literary stylist or a fashionable prophet, but as a philosopher whose theories of ethics and knowledge deserve serious consideration. Nietzsche's ethical theories, he admits, are more striking, sensational, and famous, but at the same time they are less solid and less immune to vulgarization. He credits Nietzsche with the discovery of the "transvaluation of values," and regards the problem of values as one which it was the distinction of the nineteenth century to have located and defined. Nietzsche's contribution was only partially worked out, being inconsistent and often confused, but his place in the history of philosophy is assured by his epistemological theories which Schiller, drawing exclusively on the relevant sections of *The Will to Power*, describes. Nietzsche's epistemology is traced back to Hume, Kant, and Schopenhauer, and confirmation is found for it in the independent researches of Bergson and Vaihinger. Its relation to pragmatism is emphasized. As Schiller himself was a pragmatist it is easy to see why he suddenly began to give Nietzsche serious attention, although he regarded Nietzsche merely as a precursor of the pragmatist position. Schiller's article concludes with this generous tribute: "In his theory of knowledge, as in his theory of morals, Nietzsche is immensely suggestive, and stimulates to further progress by his very errors. His work is everywhere incomplete and sometimes crude; but it is brilliant and intensely alive; and his career was cut short just as his powers were maturing."[91]

In the same year, 1913, a writer who all along had been in close contact with the Nietzsche movement, Holbrook Jackson, congratulated Levy and his collaborators on their "splendid monument to the genius of the deepest and the highest thinker of our time." Jackson notes that, of the eighteen volumes, seven were in a second, and three in a third, edition:

That would indicate the existence of a public seriously interested in Friedrich Nietzsche, for it may be surmised with some certainty that the light interest aroused by journalistic exploitation of the challenge of his thought, and the tragedy of his life, has long since been surfeited, and those who skim over the surface of philosophic fashions are engaged elsewhere. There are, as a matter of fact, a great many people who feel, rightly or wrongly, that Nietzsche has a message for them; and their number is still respectable after it has been written down by the subtraction of those (and they are still many) who misuse or misunderstand him, drawn as they have been to his work by his apparent, but apparent only to the dull-witted, advocacy of moral license, and his childish and often irritating insistence on a desire to write only for the elect. To say you write for the elect is the surest way of attracting the mediocre. But whatever the status of Nietzsche's public there is little doubt that his thought and ideas are at length receiving something like acceptance in this country, or rather, we are at length in the heyday of surprise at the daring of the great German psychologist, although long after he has ceased to startle our continental neighbours. But up to the present his direct influence has been small, what real influence he has had on English writers has been indirect, coming through French, German and Italian authors who have written under his spell. It may be indeed that Nietzsche will not affect us as he has affected others, for we have become inured to the flaming aphorism of revolt in this country by the genius of Mr. Bernard Shaw, a thinker bearing many superficial resemblances to Nietzsche, though fundamentally opposed to him.[92]

Nietzsche's genuine influence did take some time to make itself felt. As J. G. Robertson wrote in 1898 concerning Nietzsche's influence in Germany:

We may have to wait until the new century to see a real Nietzschian literature in Germany. In the meantime, the relation in which his thought stands to the popular literature of the day shows how difficult it is for a philosophy to adapt itself to the purposes of literature, without first undergoing dilution. The thoughts that fall fresh from the brain of a great and original thinker are too new, too strange; they must undergo a certain popularisation, perhaps even degeneration, before they can become the yeast of imaginative literature.[93]

A consideration of John Davidson will make it possible, in the first instance, to gauge the accuracy of this forecast as it might be applied to England, and also to make, in the context of one man's work, an initial amplification of some of the preliminary findings of the foregoing chapter.

JOHN DAVIDSON

1 One of the first signs of the eventual break-up of nineteenth-century liberalism was the emergence, both in Europe and America, of the gospel of individualism. John Davidson is the chief English representative of this movement: beginning as a poet of strong socialist tendencies, who could write the compassionate and much-praised "Thirty Bob a Week," he developed into a writer of plays and "testaments" which espouse a belief in the virtues of unmitigated egoism.* Discussions of egoism and altruism were a staple of philosophic thinking in the last years of the century, and it was in this context that Nietzsche's ideas began to be noticed.

Two of the first references to Nietzsche occur in George Egerton's *Keynotes* (1893), and *Discords* (1894). Their author had derived her knowledge of Nietzsche from living and working in Scandinavia, where Nietzsche's gospel of individualism was having an impact on such writers as Strindberg, Knut Hamsun, and Ola Hansson. George Egerton wrote: "I translated an almost unobtainable little book of Ola Hansson's *Young Ofeg's Ditties*, little extraordinary word-pictures expressing in parables Nietzsche's exposition of the Ego theory. Difficult, and to me a work of love."[1] This translation came out in 1895, and was excoriated by a conservative reviewer: "The 'triumphant doctrine of the ego,' which Miss George Egerton finds so comforting, appears to be the theory of a German imbecile who, after several temporary detentions, was permanently confined in a lunatic asylum. His writings being thoroughly hysterical and abnormal, he naturally had a crowd of foolish disciples who considered him a very great philosopher."[2] This attitude derived mainly from Nordau,

---

* Not unnaturally, responsibility for this has been laid at Nietzsche's door; but it should be remembered that egoism was only a part of Zarathustra's message, whereas it was the whole of Max Stirner's, whose *Der Einzige und sein Eigentum* (1844) is known to have influenced Nietzsche considerably.

and persisted until the appearance of the biography of Nietzsche by his sister, a work "as remarkable for its literary grace as for its sincere feeling," as one reviewer put it. But behind Nietzsche's "lofty and gentle spirit" was found to lurk a boundless egotism:

Instead of curbing his natural egotism, he erected it into a religion; and it is the law of the mind that no man can remain sane in the perpetual contemplation of himself. In Ibsen's symbolic play the moment when Peer Gynt apprehends himself as the centre of the universe is that when he is crowned ruler in Bedlam over a kingdom of fools.

The moral of the whole situation is that, as all roads led to Rome, so all philosophical systems of the day inevitably lead back to the Christian synthesis.[3]

For Davidson, however, there was no going back. The root of his egomania lies in an urge to discount the past and all its achievements, and to start afresh: "The world is only beginning. We have done nothing, said nothing, sung nothing."[4] Again: "To me it is strange that men should still suppose, because they can speak and write, that therefore they can say what they think and feel. ... It is probable that the whole literature of the world is a lie."[5] The hero of an autobiographical poem, "A Ballad in Blank Verse of the Making of a Poet" (from *Ballads and Songs*, London, 1894), attacks the literature of the past for being "hag-ridden by ideas"; refusing to commit himself to any creed, he sets himself up as a suffering Prometheus, the emblem of defiance:

Henceforth I shall be God; for consciousness
Is God: I suffer: I am God: this Self,
That all the universe combines to quell,
Is greater than the universe; and *I*
Am that I am. To think and not be God? –
It cannot be!

A parallel to this is found in Nietzsche's parable in *The Gay Science*, where the madman, after declaring that men have killed God, concludes that men themselves must become gods to be worthy of such a tremendous deed. To anticipate a little, the worship of the heroic potential in man – in Carlyle, Wagner, Nietzsche – was a natural response to loss of religious faith. Davidson, however, did not yet possess the courage of his new convictions, and goes on, in the same poem, to renounce these ideas since they constitute another "new religion, bringing new offence, / Setting the child against the father still." But as early as 1898 Davidson is proclaiming: "I am the measure of the universe. I would cut my throat, if I, a thinking being, were ever compelled to doubt my own infallibility."[6] A character in one of his plays echoes Zarathustra's injunctions to love oneself:

Oh, learn to love yourself!
Consider how the silent sun is rapt
In self-devotion! All things work for good
To them that love themselves.[7]

And by 1904 Davidson could write:

                Above, beneath,
About me, or within, nothing is great:
I only, I am great: greater than thought.
Spirit and flesh, my casual qualities:
But I, the individual, I am more
Than soul and body: insubmissive me. ...
I am the only individual, I:
The Truth itself is nothing: to believe
The highest Truth would be to abdicate
The individual: all things disappear
Before the sovereign Me.[8]

Authority is no longer vested in Christianity, political institutions, or tradition: "Authority is inherent only in him who says, 'I, of myself, announce this.' "[9] As it stands such a profession of egoism is more reminiscent of Max Stirner than it is of Nietzsche: and Davidson's extension of egoism to the religious plane – materialism – and to the political one – imperialism – is equally foreign to both. More will be said later of this aspect of Davidson's thought. It was Davidson's creed of egoism which attracted the editor of *The Eagle and the Serpent* (1898–1903), about which an account must now be given.

Of the many journals of the nineties which espoused the cause of social reform, *The Eagle and the Serpent* is still one of the most readable. Dubbed after Zarathustra's two loyal companions it bore the subtitle "A Journal of Egoistic Philosophy and Sociology." It proclaimed a dedication "to the Philosophy of Life Enunciated by Nietzsche, Emerson, Stirner, Thoreau, and Goethe," labouring "for the Recognition of New Ideals in Politics and Sociology, in Ethics and Philosophy, in Literature and Art." While Nietzsche is clearly the inspirational force behind the venture, Emerson, Stirner, and Thoreau are only three of many writers whose works were zealously ransacked for material, usually in aphoristic form, to support the editorial creed of egoism; Goethe, on the other hand, is not mentioned at all. A common device was to juxtapose sayings by Nietzsche with those of another writer, most frequently Emerson. *The Eagle and the Serpent*, it was originally hoped, would appear at ever-decreasing intervals, but a lack of adequate financial backing resulted in rather intermittent publication: a total of nineteen numbers appeared between February, 1898, and early 1903 at intervals ranging from one to eight months. The eight-month hiatus was undoubtedly caused by difficulties in securing a new publisher; in its later career the paper changed its publisher as regularly as Beethoven moved house, and for the same reasons.

The first issue contained a fiery editorial manifesto:

A race of altruists is necessarily a race of slaves. A race of freemen is necessarily a race of egoists. Freedom cannot be granted. It must be taken. To convert the exploiters to altruism is a fatuous programme – a maniac's dream. The only remedy for social injustice is this: the exploited must save themselves by enlightened self-interest. ... Egoism spells justice and freedom as surely as altruism spells charity and slavery. Three thousand years of sorrowful experience make the foregoing propositions too evident to us. The object of THE EAGLE AND THE SERPENT is to make them equally evident to all mankind.[10]

The editor doubts whether the "exponents of orthodox Nietzscheism" have sufficiently recognized the parasitic growth of "those twin assassins of the race, rent and interest"; but he adds he does not profess to follow Nietzsche in his economics: "We do not identify Nietzscheism with the cause of anti-exploitation, we identify Egoism with that cause. But Nietzsche is, perhaps, the greatest prophet of Egoism the world has ever seen."[11] As such Nietzsche is "the dying gladiator of our cause" whose courageous example gives heart to those eager to see reform: "The reformer's loneliness, forsakenness, his Gethsemane, his sense of being a dedicated one, a doomed one, his exultation in that feeling, verily never man spake of these things as Zarathustra spake – never man spake with such tenderness, love, insight."[12]

The new journal promised to be bright, provocative, and possibly influential. It won the warm encouragement of certain sections of the liberal or socialist press which pursued similar policies of public enlightenment and radical reform, for example, the *University Magazine and Free Review*, *Adult*, *Clarion*, and *Labour Prophet*. This explains why so many of Nietzsche's earliest readers were of a socialist persuasion. The conservative *Academy* gave it a condescending notice,[13] and fears were expressed in other quarters that Nietzsche's poignant idealism, his hatred of the mean and mediocre, and "his inspiring and sublime faith in the Coming Race" were being shabbily misapplied: "This strange teacher of misty egoism has an elevation that makes a thoughtful reader wonder with what sort of contempt he would have reviewed those of his followers who seek to translate his egoism to petty purposes."* Thomas Common, as the official spokesman for the Nietzschean point of view, also had his doubts. While finding it "quite a pleasant surprise" to learn of a paper devoted to the promulgation of Nietzsche's philosophy, he gently reminded the editor that, in Nietzsche's view, social reform consisted not in the institution of the welfare state but in the realization of a higher type of human being, the superman. Nietzsche's teaching, being aristocratic and esoteric in bias, could never achieve popular acceptance. Nietzsche was not opposed to altruism, since he valued altruism and egoism alike according to the doer and the consequences of his deed; it would be more acceptable to regard Nietzsche, not as the apostle of egoism in opposition to altruism, but as the apostle of a true aristocracy in opposition to democracy. Alfred Russel Wallace, the biologist who had anticipated Darwin's evolutionary findings, praised the paper for its initiative and drive, and its determination to exterminate the evils of exploitation; but he objected strongly to Common's view about aristocracy on the grounds that such an ideal was unworkable and violated the ethical canons of equality and justice. In the long debate that followed, Common held staunchly to the view that rent and interest cease to be an issue when socialism and commercialism are considered unsatisfactory forms of social organization.

Of other individual comments solicited by the journal, Shaw's plea for a Nietzsche society (given in full on page 187 below) is the most interesting. Kropotkin, the Russian exile and anarchist who figures prominently in London literary life of the 1890s, replied that he had no time to comment on the aims of the journal, having no patience (as he remarked elsewhere) with what he called *individualismus Nietzscheanum*: "It is the individualism of the bourgeois who can exist only on condition of the oppression of the masses and of lackeyism, of servility towards tradition, of the obliteration of individuality in the oppressor himself, as well as in the oppressed mass. The 'beautiful blond beast' is, fundamentally, a slave – a slave to his kind, to the priest, to the law, to tradition – a cipher without individuality in the exploiting herd."[14] Nietzsche, he added, was a "philosopher in carpet slippers," even "the first Philistine." Pressure of work was also the excuse

---

* William Platt, "Egoism, and the 'Eagle and the Serpent,'" *University Magazine and Free Review*, x (April, 1898), 96. The same author upbraided the editor of the *Reformer* for a failure, two years later, to mention the passing of "this brilliant but erratic genius" who "in truth or error ... wrote starkly, without stint and without fear; he has earned his place among the heroes." *Reformer*, iv (November 15, 1900), 680, 681.

of Herbert Spencer, whose impersonal lithographed letter was eagerly seized on by the editor as a striking example of the "esoteric egoism" which even such a distinguished altruist as Spencer was forced to practise in the daily economy of life. R. B. Cunninghame Graham pleaded exemption on the grounds that he was insufficiently conversant with Nietzsche's philosophy. Ernest Newman, although he was busily defending Wagner against Nietzsche's attacks, hoped that "a paper devoted to Egoism" would prosper, a view seconded by Edward Carpenter. Benjamin Kidd pointed out that the eighth chapter of his *Social Evolution* (1894) bore a resemblance to some aspects of Nietzsche's ethical doctrines, and agreed that if Christian morality was not obsolete, the propertied classes were more likely to adopt a policy of egoism than altruism: "Your effort to spread the influence of Nietzsche's ideas in England is itself evidence in support of this view – although unexpected; for one does not expect opinions of the kind to reach the propaganda stage however firmly they may be held in private."[15] W. H. Mallock discounted the subversive implications of the egoistic position, but took account of Nietzsche's aristocratism in *Aristocracy and Evolution* (1898) and *The Veil of the Temple* (1904). Other correspondents included Havelock Ellis, John M. Robertson, and Hubert Bland.

Not until the third number had been reached in June, 1898, did the editor of *The Eagle and the Serpent* see fit to disclose his identity, and then only in the form of a pseudonym, "Erwin McCall." His real name was J. B. Barnhill; the paper was his own brainchild, and he ran it, as he once reminded critics, to please himself. One suspects that many of the contributions, under such pen-names as "Volcano" and "Melpomene," were in fact the editor's work.[16] Although the paper was launched with a bang, it ended in a whimper. The theme of egoism, although it was throughout the subject of articles and discussions, proved not to be inexhaustible; after two years of existence the paper showed signs of floundering for lack of direction and purpose. Sensing this decline, the editor beat a hasty retreat behind a smokescreen of great names, and began to publish what he called "memorial issues" to commemorate by mention and sometimes by quotation the "immortal free spirits born in the month." This was a makeshift tactic and was soon abandoned. As in the beginning generous quotations were still made from Nietzsche's works, but this apparent continuity could not conceal the fact that the paper as a whole was becoming increasingly scrappy and disorganized. The contributions began to read like the work of eccentrics, and much advertising space was allocated to charlatans and their dietetic secrets.

It was this last aspect of the paper which gave particular offence to John

Davidson. Davidson had refused to respond to a promise that, if he wrote a letter to the journal, space would be found to reprint some of his writings. He described such tactics as "a modified form of bribery and corruption." The journal persisted in its attempt to elicit correspondence from him; Davidson attacked it by saying that all group-activity was un-Nietzschean, and that the journal itself was "an abominable trick-periodical" whose members – "these nauseous people" – were "a small kind of petty devils bent on the degradation of everything better" than themselves: "I had no idea they were so vile, they advertise quack medicines, quack diet, and sexual condiments – in the name of Nietzsche and Emerson. Let us forget them."[17] Barnhill, realizing that Davidson's obduracy would not easily be broken down, went ahead and published, in the eighteenth issue of the paper, extracts from two of Davidson's *Testaments* and his play *Self's the Man* as a stirring poetic endorsement of the creed of egoism. Quite possibly Davidson's dislike of the paper was increased by its partiality for the aphoristic mode, of which he disapproved: "Epigrams are the resource of weak minds, as meat extract is of weak stomachs. ... They say vegetarians are great makers of epigrams."* Snappy phrase-making was no substitute for the slow poeticization of belief, even when the phrases were Nietzsche's own: "Nietzsche is the most divulsive force in the history of letters. But there is no need why we should concern ourselves about his philosophy, or about Mr. Herbert Spencer's. A new Philosophy – it will not be called an Evolutionary Philosophy when it arrives, and will be neither aphoristic nor synthetic – is an attempt to forestall posterity. The new mood and matter must pass through the fire of poetry before it can become a system; and that will take hundreds of years."[18]

Yet there is no doubt that certain aspects of the journal bear a close affinity to Davidson's own thinking. On one occasion a number of passages in praise of war are cited from the work of Nietzsche, Emerson, Thoreau, Stevenson, and Ruskin, and they preface a letter "fervently praying for universal war." The editor writes of his correspondent: "He believes that the psychological moment has arrived for that bloody earth-wide struggle which Channing, Carlyle, Ruskin, and Lincoln affirmed to be necessary to sweep away the present gold-damned social status. He states that he contemplates with unutterable joy and hope this universal cataclysm, this cleansing of the race's Augean stables, this engulfing of parasitic aristoc-

---

* *A Rosary* (London, 1903), 78. This barb was probably directed at Shaw, who had taken Davidson to task for his adaptation of François Coppée's *Pour la Couronne* in 1896.

racies, this long-deferred advent of the Lord's vengeance – infernal in its methods and divine in its consequences."[19] This mood, naïve as it sounds after the holocaust of two destructive world wars, was widely prevalent. As Jacques Barzun has written: "No one who has not waded through some sizable part of the literature of the period 1870–1914 has any conception of the extent to which it is one long call for blood, nor of the variety of parties, classes, nations, and races whose blood was separately and contradictorily clamored for by the enlightened citizens of the ancient civilization of Europe."[20] Barzun traces this mood to the effects of social Darwinism, and Nietzsche, although he can be quoted to suggest he is in favour of universal disruption, did himself predict that disruption would occur if Darwinistic doctrines took further hold on the human mind. Prudent enough to remember that revolution could have limited success while the workers were still unarmed, Barnhill rejects the incendiary revolutionism of his correspondent, preferring the milder course of effective strike action. But he affirms that a war would sweep away a good deal "with advantage to a future race of laughing lions," and his disgust with democracy, "this God-soaked, Christ-soaked, servile rabble," later reaches such a pitch that he looks forward to "a few preliminary wars" as a means of eradicating it. Only invasion by a hostile power, suggests a later contributor, can revitalize and purify an England which is rapidly falling into decline and decay.

Davidson, after resisting the chauvinism of Kipling and Henley for a while, abandoned all pretence to neutrality on the issue of imperialism and threw in his lot with the militant nationalism of his friend J. A. Cramb, whose *Origins and Destiny of Imperial Britain* (1900) impressed him as "the ablest, freshest, most imaginative and therefore most intelligent statement of British imperialism."[21] Cramb, like Davidson, welcomes war as a phase in the life-effort of the State towards complete self-fulfilment; it answers to the egoism of the individual in his search for personal self-realization. The divine sanction of war is repudiated in favour of its Darwinistic significance:

We recognize at last
   That war is not of God.
Wherefore we now uplift
   Our new unhallowed song:
The race is to the swift,
   The battle to the strong.[22]

The imperialist ambition of Urban, in *Self's the Man*, is quite undisguised: "My lords, it is with nations as with men:/ One must be first."[23] No figure like Urban, believed Davidson, would be possible in America, which is the decadence of Europe: "Our splendid robbers, Clive, Hastings, Rhodes, degenerate there into the pickpockets of the Trusts."[24] In poem after poem Davidson extolled England's Ocean state:

The armed and equal mate
Of power and liberty,
Has this for doom and fate –
To set the peoples free.[25]

He devoted one of the longest of his *Testaments* to the empire-builder, the man in whom "the authentic mandate of imperial doom" silences "the drowsy lullaby of love."[26] In the empire-builder's vision of heaven and hell, heaven is occupied by the warriors:

There were the warriors, they who knew that war
Can deify disgrace, project and change
Ignoble causes into golden grounds,
Who sought their foes instinctively, as bees
With fervid song in search of honey roam,
Whose daily business was the battlefield,
Their hour of rest, the tedious interval
Between two victories, who upset the world
And deluged earth with blood.[27]

We are reminded of Zarathustra: "You say it is the good cause that hallows even war? I say unto you: it is the good war that hallows any cause. War and courage have accomplished more great things than love of the neighbor."[28] Quoting this passage in a 1902 review of Davidson's work, William Archer, after confessing he was no Nietzschean – "my morality, such as it is, is that of the Slaves, not of the Masters" – expresses surprise that the Germans fail to recognize in Chamberlain the ideal overman of Nietzsche's description: "How does the German Nietzschean contrive to reconcile his philosophy with his Anglophobia? I know of one case, at any rate, in which a prominent Nietzschean is also an aggressive Anglophobe; and this case is doubtless typical rather than exceptional."* But Davidson, as Archer saw, was not faced with this dilemma; Davidson saw in the English a chosen race in which the Scots were the higher order and the Celts the lower. As such it was their destiny to extend English sovereignty to all parts of the world. During the last stages of the Boer War *The Eagle*

---

* "Study and Stage: Zarathustra-Davidson," *Morning Leader* (May 24, 1902), 4. The "prominent Nietzschean" Archer had in mind was almost certainly Alexander Tille, who was forced to leave Britain on account of his outspokenly pro-Boer sympathies. See above, p. 24n.

and the Serpent held a symposium on the topic "Is the British Policy in South Africa a consistent exemplification of Nietzsche's Social Philosophy?" The participants, Peter Gast, Henri Lichtenberger, Thomas Common, W. A. Haussmann, all agreed that it was not: the "good war" to Nietzsche was a war of ideas and ideals, not of commercial exploitation. Havelock Ellis, though pronouncing himself "a little sceptical as to 'good wars,'" seconded this view.

The Eagle and the Serpent sought a variety of opinions on Nietzsche. Common, by then regarded as the leading English pundit, was a frequent contributor – not only was he responsible for the bulk of the Nietzsche translations, but he also took it upon himself to translate part of John Henry Mackay's book, *Max Stirner: sein Leben und sein Werk* (1898), although out of sympathy with Stirner's anarchism and egalitarianism. In a letter to the journal, Mackay (a German with a Scottish name) wrote:

No one can admire more than I do Nietzsche's defiant courage, his proud contempt of all established authority, and the occasional power of his language; but to seek to compare this eternally-vacillating, repeatedly-self-contradicting and confused mind, which staggers in an almost helpless manner from truth to error, with the deep, clear, calm and superior genius of Stirner is an absurdity unworthy of serious refutation. ... The fever of the Nietzsche sickness is already lessening. One day even the "overman" will have been shattered by the uniqueness of the Ego.[29]

In the same issue dissenting opinions were canvassed for. Invited to confirm his condemnation of Nietzsche in *Degeneration*, Max Nordau wrote: "It is a shame that anyone in his senses should have taken the incoherent outbursts of a poor lunatic seriously and considered his wild drivel as 'philosophy.'" Nordau's accusation that Nietzsche was insane was followed by some Christian whooping in the same issue of the journal from Robert Buchanan in his poem "New Rome":

"Jupiter's gutter-snipe! A shrill-tongued thing
   Running beside the blood-stain'd chariot wheels,
  Crying, 'Hosannah to the pitiless King,
   The ravening Strength that neither spares nor feels!'

"A slave that glorified the yoke and goad,
   Cast mud into the well of human tears,
  Gibed at the Weak who perish on the road,
   Slain by the Law which neither heeds nor hears!

    .   .   .   .   .

"Poor gutter-snipe! Answer'd with his own prayer,
   Back to primeval darkness he has gone:

> Only one living soul can help him there,
>   The gentle human god he spat upon."

A "curious and entertaining little paper," as Holbrook Jackson described it in *The Eighteen Nineties*, *The Eagle and the Serpent* created quite a stir, and performed the useful function of bringing Nietzsche's work to the notice of a wide range and class of people.* It did this in three ways. First, by founding a lending library of "egoistic" literature to assist those deprived of books on account of their high price (the early Nietzsche translations were, as has been shown, exorbitantly expensive). Secondly, by publishing translations of Nietzsche to offset "the masterly inactivity" of those officially entrusted with the task – numbers 5, 8, and 9 are partly or wholly devoted to Common's English version of the first part of *Zarathustra*, and almost every number contains extracts from Nietzsche, many of them from works not yet available in English translation. Thirdly, by providing a forum for well-known expositors of Nietzsche's work and of books and articles dealing with it, so that interested readers were kept abreast of the Nietzsche movement in England. The editor's persistent identification of Nietzsche with the cause of egoism (in the very last issue he describes the recently translated *Dawn of Day* as "the most egoistic of Nietzsche's works which are accessible in English") did not mean that readers were invited to view him exclusively in that light, although many readers, and some sections of the press, undoubtedly did so. Thomas Common, although he had taken full advantage of the opportunity to make Nietzsche more widely known, could never associate himself, or Nietzsche, with the cause of egoism; when the paper ceased publication Common put his proselytizing energies into his own *Good European Point of View*, a brief series of pamphlets which lasted from 1903 to 1916, thus continuing the work *The Eagle and the Serpent* had begun in 1898.

---

* As late as 1914 there existed "The Society of Social Aristocrats and Conscious Egoists" which had, as its president, Barrihill's co-editor on *The Eagle and the Serpent*, Malfew Seklew. He claimed no small part in bringing Nietzsche to the people: "Through the medium of the *Truthseeker*, a monthly journal published in Bradford, I introduced the public to flashes of lightning from the pen of Nietzsche. In most of the large centres of England and Scotland I introduced the gospel of the Superman and Social Aristocracy, ably assisted by Mr. Thomas Common. In the coffee taverns, where debates are held, the same thing was done. The Cogers Society of London, where the cranks of the Metropolis used to congregate; Lester's Coffee House of Nottingham, which Robert Owen used to frequent; Laycock's Coffee Tavern of Bradford, the Talking Shop of Yorkshire, where all sorts of saints and sinners have assembled for forty years to discuss the Desires of Demos, have all been scenes of wordy warfare in the introduction of the Gospel of Nietzsche. In the County Forum of Manchester, also, I was the first to introduce this strange philosophy." "Was Nietzsche to Blame?" *TPW*, XXIV (November 21, 1914), 560.

Yet John Davidson had discovered Nietzsche as early as 1891. How he reacted to this discovery, and what was the future course of his reading in Nietzsche, are questions to which we must now turn.

2 It is now widely recognized that the distinction of being the first British man of letters to take note of Nietzsche's work belongs to John Davidson; many studies have appeared relating the work of the two men, the most exhaustive of which is an article by John A. Lester Jr., "Friedrich Nietzsche and John Davidson: A Study in Influence";[30] the following account of Davidson's indebtedness, while owing much to Lester, seeks to revise and supplement his findings rather than repeat them.

Davidson may have heard of Nietzsche before he left Scotland in 1890 to take up residence in London. That was the year that Alexander Tille returned from Germany, and began to overawe impressionable students at Glasgow University with his literary notoriety and with the sensational character of the Nietzschean ideas – such as that of the "blond beast" – which he sought to purvey. Awareness of Nietzsche's growing reputation in Germany had spread from Glasgow to Edinburgh by 1894, and it is not surprising that so many of the earlier writers on Nietzsche – Tille, Common, Pringle-Pattison, Saintsbury, and Sarolea – might have heard of him simply by living and teaching in Scotland. However, leaving Scotland as early as 1890, Davidson probably never heard of Tille until he read his introductions to the English translations; these introductions, as we have seen, accentuated – as Davidson himself was to do – the more violent aspects of Nietzsche's work. Davidson originally came across Nietzsche, as George Egerton had done and Havelock Ellis was to do, through the work of continental critics and writers, in his case through Theodor de Wyzewa, a Polish-born critic who had written on Nietzsche in the first of a series of articles in which foreign celebrities were introduced to French readers. Davidson, with his knowledge of French, was able to translate sections of this article into English, and the result appeared in 1891 as an unsigned essay of Davidson's in the *Speaker* under the title "The New Sophist." The article begins:

> Although his reputation is widespread in Germany, Sweden, Russia, Holland, Denmark, and Italy, Frederick Nietsche [misspelt throughout], except to a few specialists, is hardly known even by name in France and England. The most notable of Swedish writers, August Strindberg, bases his novels and dramas on Nietsche's ideas, and George Brandes, the first of European critics, spent a whole winter lecturing on his philosophy. In Germany Nietsche's influence over

the rising generation of authors and artists is said to be as powerful as that which was formerly exercised in this country by Carlyle or Ruskin.[31]

A short review of Nietzsche's life is followed by a section of condensed criticism:

No German writer is less German than Nietzsche. His style is that of a Frenchman – he has a profound horror of dissertation. All his writings are collections of aphorisms; and all ideas disgust him when he has considered them for a short time. His writing is a succession of imagery of the most concrete order, but always with a symbolic value. There is no trace of sentiment – everywhere a morbid sense of reality, incapable of satisfying itself with any thought of man's heart. His irony is altogether different from the ordinary German humour – dry, bitter, cruel, and as perfectly under control as that of Swift. To insure a solid basis in his search after truth, he examined every subject with which man occupies his intellect. He would have been satisfied had he found one certainty. ... He is the Nihilist of philosophy.[32]

De Wyzewa, although widely acquainted with Nietzsche's work, draws for the purpose of his article on what he regarded as Nietzsche's most typical book, *Human, All-Too-Human*; this may explain his lapse in asserting that all Nietzsche's writings are "collections of aphorisms," an error repeated by Davidson. Davidson incorporates many of the aphorisms quoted by de Wyzewa into his own essay, without making it clear, as de Wyzewa had done, that they were translations, rather than interpretations, of the original. More seriously, Davidson is often at fault as a translator: compare one sentence in the foregoing extract with its original in de Wyzewa: "Nulle trace de sentimentalisme; mais au contraire un sens constant de la réalité, un sens qu'on divine maladif, tant il est subtil, incapable de se satisfaire aux plus spécieuses illusions."[33] Clearly Davidson is guilty of gross distortion, and it is characteristic of his essay in general that it over-simplifies and vulgarizes de Wyzewa's delicate and sensitive handling of Nietzsche's philosophy. De Wyzewa's final judgment is taken over by Davidson:

Nietsche's is the most unphilosophical mind that ever attempted philosophy. He is a great poet seeking a system instead of taking things on trust. He starts from nothing and ends in nothing. He proves and disproves, believes and disbelieves, everything. ...

Nietsche's Nihilism, although accepted as final by many, was always regarded by himself as a preface to a positive doctrine. But he failed to unlearn the habit of doubt. He tried hard, and published a book entitled *Thus saith Zarathustra*, in which, although the ideas were obscure and fantastic, it was possible to perceive an attempt at reconstruction. At last he succeeded, when he went mad, and discovered that "without a doubt it was he who had created the world."³⁴

De Wyzewa, in a passage not translated by Davidson, expresses great pity for Nietzsche's fate, and quotes Nietzsche to the effect that modern civilization, by multiplying the objects of knowledge, would throw the human nervous system off balance to such an extent that men would not be able to enjoy the benefits of social progress because they would all be mad. "Personne, d'ailleurs," writes de Wyzewa, "n'a autant exalté la folie, personne ne l'a aussi constamment invoquée, comme le seul refuge contre la terrible vision du néant universel."³⁵ Davidson's own judgment, elaborated solely from what he had read in de Wyzewa, was less generous:

> Probably his insanity is the best criticism of his sophistry. Confinement in a dark cell with toads and vermin for companions will drive the strongest mad; and that is exactly what Nietsche's Nihilism amounts to. He shut himself up in the dungeon of egotism, where love becomes lust; ambition, greed; and religion, vainglory. Or, in another figure – following his own method – he kept digging at roots and pinching skeletons, instead of gathering the rosebuds, and studying "the beauty of the world, the paragon of animals." ... After all, Nietsche's Nihilism is little more than a recrudescence of *Sturm und Drang*. Goethe went through it, and came out serene; and Shakespeare did not turn mad after *Hamlet* and *King Lear*, but lived to write *The Tempest!*³⁶

As an assessment of Nietzsche, this is ill-informed and oratorical, plagiarism on wings; as a prophecy of Davidson's own development, it is devastatingly accurate.

Untroubled by the question of plagiarism, Davidson was soon rifling de Wyzewa's article again. In 1893 appeared a much expanded reworking of de Wyzewa, including Nietzsche's opinions on selfishness, pity, women, politics and aesthetics – the disparaging remarks on artists and men of genius must have pained Davidson considerably. He repeats de Wyzewa's verdict verbatim: "The conclusion of this philosophy is – nothing. Not anything *is*; there never has been anything; and there never will be anything. It has all been said before by Solomon, by Euripides, by Helvetius, by Stendhal, by Schopenhauer. Nietsche's originality is not in the invention of his ideas, but in that he has reduced them to a complete system, and has kept fronting negation as no man ever did before: the result to himself, madness."³⁷ Davidson has tightened up his translation, but he omits any reference to de Wyzewa, and his only individual contribution is the final dismissive sentence: "Any man who has work to do in the world, any man who has children, any man who enjoys ordinary health is furnished with an answer to Nietsche."³⁸

Later in the same year (1893) Davidson, not content to leave well alone, reprinted extracts from his *Speaker* essay of 1891 in *Sentences and Paragraphs*, but without significant change. He did, however, add one more invidious comparison: "Goethe felt and suffered as much as Nietsche, but being stronger, saw through the Brocken spectre of self which interrupted Nietsche's view wherever he turned."[39] This book had the worst reception and smallest sale of all Davidson's works, and could hardly have encouraged its handful of readers to take up Nietzsche on their own account. There is no evidence to suggest anything seminal about what Davidson wrote about Nietzsche between 1891 and 1893. Lester rates de Wyzewa "well qualified" to write on Nietzsche on the strength of his knowledge of German and his two visits to the philosopher; but de Wyzewa himself disclaimed such authority, insisting at the outset that he was only writing prefatory notes: "Je n'ai ni la préparation ni la compétence qu'il faudrait pour des études plus approfondies. Les renseignements que je donnerai seront autant que possible exacts; je ne puis promettre qu'ils seront complets. Et pour toute appréciation je m'en tiendrai à mes impressions personelles, méthode qui ne peut aboutir, comme on sait, qu'à des résultats bien précaires."[40] De Wyzewa, as Lester rightly says, was enthusiastic about his new discovery, but to assume that Davidson read his French source "with eager interest" and that he "was powerfully struck by the explosive force he found in Nietzsche" is not warranted by the evidence. Davidson never sought to extend his knowledge beyond what he learnt from de Wyzewa: had he done so he might have learned to rectify a persistent misspelling of Nietzsche's name, mistakes of biographical fact, and a one-sided critical approach. He chooses to ignore those passages in de Wyzewa which speak highly of certain aspects of Nietzsche's work, his observations on music and literary style, for example. As a journalist who depended on his writing for a living, Davidson was obliged to turn out articles regularly, irrespective of his own personal likes and dislikes; for him Nietzsche was less an "explosive force" than a lucky scoop, and because Nietzsche was a new name de Wyzewa's article could be flagrantly plagiarized with almost no risk of exposure. Davidson saw no inconsistency in announcing Nietzsche's continental fame and then dismissing his Nihilism as a mere recrudescence of German romanticism. The fact that Nietzsche's influence took another five or six years to make itself felt is attributable, not to Davidson's stated reservations, but to the fact that he approached the task of translating de Wyzewa in the spirit of a Grub Street hack.

There are, of course, other reasons why Nietzsche, on this first encounter, failed to register a strong impression. Chief among these is Davidson's own literary activity during the mid-nineties. Full of creative self-confidence, highly regarded as a poet by a number of his colleagues, successful in the sales of his books, Davidson was too preoccupied in his own work to pay much attention to another man's philosophy, especially when that philosophy seemed so out of tune with his optimistic mood. But after 1896 his popularity began to wane, and it is at this time that he sadly confesses to Yeats, a fellow member of the Rhymers' Club, that "the fires are out ... and I must hammer the cold iron."[41] Reviewers began to take note of his fading inspiration, and, to add to his despair, Davidson was cowed by the giant spectre of poverty. He sought relief in philosophy: "When a Scotsman finds himself at cross purposes with life, what course does he follow? ... He invariably does one of two things. He either sits down and drinks deeply, thoughtfully, systematically, of the amber spirit of his country, or he reads philosophy."[42] Davidson spent the winters of 1896-7 and 1897-8 away from London in a retreat on the Sussex coast, where he immersed himself in philosophy in an attempt to come to grips with his despair.

It is highly probable that among the books he read at this time were the two translations of Nietzsche which appeared in 1896, and also, at a later date, the volume which appeared in 1899. In 1902 Davidson wrote that a year or two previously he knew by heart the three published volumes of the English translation of Nietzsche. Once Davidson had freed himself from the restrictive view of Nietzsche as a *Sturm und Drang* Nihilist by reading Nietzsche at first hand, the door was open for the rapid transmission of Nietzschean ideas into his own work. These begin to be apparent from 1898 on, and from this time until his death in 1909 references to Nietzsche are common in reviews of his work. Davidson himself violently repudiated any suggestion of discipleship. "No two minds understand in the same way the simplest idea," he wrote, and went on to castigate the idea of discipleship in general: "It is always something entirely different from what their masters meant that disciples understand. Neo-Platonism, Neo-Catholicism, Neo-Hegelism! Hell! Let no man be another's disciple."[43] Stung by the "tiresome tattle about Ibsen or Nietzsche"[44] which his books invariably provoked, he was moved to make a public protest, declaring that it was a mistake to identify him with the speakers in his *Testaments*, and expressing his bewilderment that any "intelligent being" should be the disciple of anyone: "I should be glad if you would allow me to point out that I am not a disciple of Nietzsche. The gist of Nietzsche, so far as I know him, will be found in my play, *Smith: A Tragic Farce*, written in 1886, long before I had heard even the name of Nietzsche. It is true that in the conversation of the beasts in the *Testament of an Empire-Builder*, the Hackney quotes directly from 'that insane belov'd philosopher' (*The Genealogy of Morals*, if I remember rightly); but it will be observed that it is the Hackney who does so."[45]

The Hackney's rather long-winded and repetitious speech is a versifying of part of the second essay of *The Genealogy of Morals*, which deals with the acquisition of conscience through self-inflicted pain:

Mnemonics and a discipline adept
In conscience-rearing, Man, the traitor, wrought
With grisly human craft upon Himself.
The thing that never ceases to corrode –
That makes a memory: anguish is the soil,
The root, the stem of conscience and the flower. ...
In baths of agony and seas of blood,
Impalements, flayings, faggots, caldrons, wheels,
Man thrust and branded, seethed and carved in Man
A memory and a conscience.[46]

Davidson also agreed with Nietzsche that a sense of sin is the result of instincts which, when denied external discharge, take a disastrous inner direction: a plea for the uninhibited play of the instincts is one of the main themes of his two Mammon plays. Lester has shown how Davidson took Nietzsche's language to express his repudiation of all past philosophies and ethical systems, in particular the word "immoralist," which Nietzsche uses about himself in *The Case of Wagner*. For Davidson, Robert Burns, indeed all great poets, are great immoralists: "I exclude poets from the class of men of letters. Men of letters are humane, moral, civilized, cultured, sceptical; whereas poets are inhuman, immoral, barbaric, imaginative, and trustful."[47] This stress on the primitive, elemental and barbaric – something new in Davidson's later work – is embodied in Davidson's definition of poetry as "Matter become vocal, a blind force without judgment,"[48] and of his view of the poet as essentially indestructible and invincible:

The great poet is always a man apart, separated out by his genius, and by some tragic circumstance. ... He is always great, always an imperial person; he may be neglected and despised in his lifetime, but his will is always to live, his will is always set on power, his empire remains. That is the great poet; and his great poetry is the affirmation of the will to live, the affirmation of the will to power. This imperial passion to be finds expression in such an utterance as Romeo's death-speech ending: –

"Here's to my love! (Drinks.) O true apothecary!
Thy drugs are quick. Thus with a kiss I die."

You are in the presence of the final triumph of the will to live, which every sane suicide must be; despair – really the highest power and sublimation of hope – choosing death rather than resignation; the will to live, the pride of life that cannot *renounce*, the beautiful, the transcendent passion whereby the world survives, destroying itself rather than want its will.[49]

Such a passage contains many clear indications of a close reading of Nietzsche, particularly the insistence on the will to power. Davidson was fond of contrasting Schopenhauer with Nietzsche. A character in one of his dialogues says: "I deny that Schopenhauer has stated the true nature of the world; but you will find one of the most perfect statements of the world I am acquainted with if you complement Schopenhauer with Nietzsche – *Il Penseroso* with *L'Allegro*. Briefly, Schopenhauer says, 'the world is evil and this evil is bad and to be shunned.' Nietzsche says, 'the world is evil and this evil is admirable and to be desired.' The one prays, 'lead us not into temptation'; the other, 'deliver us up to the evil'."[50]

In a more elaborate account of the will to power Davidson wrote:

If a Will to Live is the thing in itself, man is *de trop*, for man is the greatest foe life has. Other animals kill only to satisfy hunger; but man, although for food and for sport he preserves life, yet for sport, for food, for adornment, and to make room for himself, man has destroyed, and continues to destroy, life by whole species, including those of his own kind. No, there is something behind this Will to Live, and that is the Will to Power. A Will to Power accounts for man; man, the tamer of the tide, of the lion and the lightning; and man, the tamer of man.[51]

But here Davidson is setting up Nietzsche's theory only to knock it down. Anyone, he says, can make a metaphysic: "It is a splendid image, that of splitting logs."[52] It could, he declares, just as easily be shown that the world was a Will to Death; he points to his own *Testament of a Vivisector* (1901), where the thing-in-itself is represented as a Will to Know:

It may be Matter in itself is pain,
Sweetened in sexual love that so mankind,
The medium of Matter's consciousness,
May never cease to know – the stolid bent
Of Matter, the infinite vanity
Of the Universe, being evermore
Self-knowledge.[53]

Davidson proclaimed the identity of Spinoza's God, Hegel's Absolute, Fichte's Transcendental Ego, Schopenhauer's Will to Live and Nietzsche's Will to Power – "these all-embracing categories," he declared, "are titles which Man in his madness has conferred on Matter."[54] There is no metaphysical reality, and man is of the same substance as the universe of which he is a part: "Man is Matter; mind and soul are material forces; there is no spiritual world as distinct from the material world; all psychical phenomena are material phenomena, the result of the operation of material forces; hence, I say again, the imagination of man, being a complex of material forces, cannot live in a metaphysical idea or an acknowledged myth, but makes its Heaven and Hell concrete, and itself immortal soul."[55] Again: "I have no system; I have no dogma: it is a new poetry I bring. For me there is nothing immaterial; for me everything matters; for me there is nothing behind phenomena: the very 'thing in itself' is phenomenon; phenomena *are* the Universe."[56] Davidson had a number of possible sources for this gospel of materialism – the cosmologies of Heraclitus and Lucretius, the nebular hypothesis of Laplace and Tyndall, and the evolutionism of Darwin and Haeckel.

It is commonly thought that Nietzsche contributed nothing to this phase of Davidson's thought. Shaw, for example, declared: "Davidson had nothing whatever to do with Nietzsche or his philosophy. His speciality was an attempt to raise modern materialism to the level of high poetry and eclipse Lucretius."[57] In his preface to *Back to Methuselah* Shaw explains the attractions of the materialist view:

Such a picture is dangerously fascinating to thinkers oppressed by the bloody disorders of the living world. Craving for purer subjects of thought, they find in the contemplation of crystals and magnets a happiness more dramatic and less childish than the happiness found by the mathematicians in abstract numbers, because they see in the crystals beauty and movement without the corrupting appetites of fleshly vitality. In such Materialism as that of Lucretius and Tyndall there is a nobility which produces poetry: John Davidson found his highest inspiration in it.[58]

Although Nietzsche tried to construct a metaphysics of his own, he was simultaneously discrediting any suggestion that there was anything behind the phenomena of the world. In *The Genealogy of Morals* he writes: "There is no 'being' behind doing, working, becoming; 'the doer' is a mere appanage to the action. The action is everything."[59] The actual world is the only real world – another kind of reality cannot possibly be established. There is no given moral order, and therefore no possible advance to moral perfection. Occasionally Nietzsche allows his thought to wander very close to an area Davidson developed:

If genius, according to Schopenhauer's observations, lies in the coherent and vivid recollection of our own experience, a striving towards genius in humanity collectively might be deduced from the striving towards knowledge of the whole historic past – which is beginning to mark off the modern age more and more as compared with earlier ages and has for the first time broken down the barriers between nature and spirit, men and animals, morality and physics. A perfectly conceived history would be cosmic self-consciousness.[60]

What Nietzsche entertained as speculation, Davidson converted into dogma, and his materialism, though grounded in Nietzsche's dismissal of a transcendent world, rapidly assumed a non-Nietzschean direction. Nietzsche regarded man as being a bridge to the superman. But Davidson believed that, whereas plants had life and animals had consciousness, man had self-consciousness and was the final triumph of Matter, beyond which no further progress was possible: "I know that there is no future; that there is no past; that time is not; that there is only this eternal, present now."[61] Davidson's superman, as we shall see, is very different from Nietzsche's.

Davidson's rejection of sin and bad conscience, his *Immoralismus*, his materialist elaboration of the Will to Power, all suggest that it was under Nietzsche's guidance that he reached the strongly ultra-moral position of his later plays and poems. Elements of Nietzsche's *amor fati* are discernible in Davidson's thinking about irony, represented by Shakespeare, "which is the soul of things, and of which what are called Good and Evil, Beauty and Ugliness, are attributes."[62] Davidson is surely thinking about that quality in Shakespeare which Keats called "negative capability," but which turns out, in Davidson's reformulation, to be "affirmative capability": "Irony is not a creed. The makers of creeds have always miscalled, denied some part of the world. Irony affirms and delights in the whole. Consciously, it is the deep complacence which contemplates with unalloyed satisfaction Love and Hate, the tiger and the nightingale, the horse and the blow-fly, Messalina and Galahad, the village natural and Napoleon. Unconsciously, it is the soul of the Universe."[63] *Zarathustra* contains a good deal in similar vein, and Davidson was soon to perceive the Nietzschean tinge of this concept of irony: "Irony is perhaps the last word of philosophy, the nearest approach to truth. ... Truth is the reconciliation of antagonisms. Irony integrates good and evil, the constituents of the universe. It is that Beyond-Good-and-Evil, which somebody clamoured for."[64] But, according to Davidson, Nietzsche did not go far enough, and Davidson had to create an Antichrist of his own, Mammon, to show up Nietzsche's shortcomings.

Mammon is the hero of two blank verse plays, *The Triumph of Mammon* (1907) and *Mammon and His Message* (1908), the only completed parts of a projected trilogy. Having slain his father and brother and been crowned king, Mammon receives deputations from the various sects which have sprung up around him. The first of these to seek audience is "the

Will-to-Power Men of the Nietzsche Guild"; on seeing them Mammon exclaims: "Ah! that insane belov'd philosopher!/ Some say he is the spirit of the age./ What think you, Florimond?" To which his interlocutor replies: "I cannot tell:/ My mind was set before his boom began." Mammon then continues:

He posed as Zoroaster, and led us back
To Dionysos: not our mark at all;
The past is past. And, for his prophecy? –
Why, Florimond, this Nietzsche was a Christian;
And that transvaluation of all values
Was neither more nor less than transmutation
Of transubstantiation: – grin, but grasp it: –
His Antichrist is Christ, whose body and blood
And doctrine of miraculous rebirth,
Became the Overman: Back-of-beyond,
Or – what's the phrase? – Outside good-and-evil:
That's his millenium, and we'll none of it.
I want the world to be much more the world;
Men to be men; and women, women – all
Adventure, courage, instinct, passion, power.[65]

Davidson's hostility towards Christianity, evident before he knew of Nietzsche, gains in intensity and vehemence after his reading of Nietzsche's *Antichrist*. In *The Testament of a Man Forbid* (1901), Davidson opposes the Christian need for redemption to a robust, Nietzschean self-affirmation: "It has been said: Ye must be born again./ I say to you: Men must be what they are."[66] A ferocious attack on slave-morality is a common theme of all the *Testaments*. In Davidson's vision of judgment, quite unlike the civilized tomfoolery of the hell scene in Shaw's *Man and Superman*, the meek followers of Christ, whom he calls "apostles, martyrs, votarists, virgins, saints," are accused of having thrown away the inestimable gift of life. They are summarily dispatched to the fires of hell, since they have only shown themselves to be

Deniers, slanderers, fools that turned to scorn
The perfect world I made superb in strength
Unparagoned in beauty.

The true inheritors of heaven are

The kings, the conquerors, the wise, the bold.
The rich, the proud, and all the lusty lives
That took their power and pleasure in the world.[67]

In his drama *The Theatrocrat* (1905) Davidson denounces "the Christendom that hangs in filthy rags / About the eager soul already winged."[68] By the time of the Mammon plays two years later, communists, anarchists, and nihilists are described as "wriggling maggots in the fetid corpse / Of Christendom," and socialists fare no better:

> This socialism is mere misanthropy
> Erected to a creed; the evil smell
> Of Christendom, long dead and rotten, kept
> In salts and sponges to resuscitate
> The hopes of hungry malice; the fishy glow
> Upon the putrid carcass of religion.[69]

And to make his position incontrovertibly clear Davidson has recourse to a prose epilogue:

> It is not a revolution I propose: revolution is nothing. ... Were Socialism a realized ideal to-morrow there would be no actual change: only the dead corpse of Christendom floating up again upon the tide. Socialism, like Christianity, proceeds upon the assumption that men are not what they are. There is little difference between Feudalism and Socialism. Socialism would lay hands upon the earth and its products, upon man and his labour, not heroically, in arms, by superior craft and intellect, as Feudalism did, but unheroically by means of representative government (which is no government), by universal suffrage, bargains with the mob, and the prate of parliamentarians. Socialism is the decadence of Feudalism; that is to say, it is less than nothing. At its very utmost it is only a bad smell; rejoicing in itself very much at present, as bad smells are wont to do: Europe is noisome with it.[70]

The thought here is from Stirner, the heroic stance from Nietzsche: Davidson anticipates a whole host of later "reactionary thinkers," Yeats, Wyndham Lewis, and Eliot among them.

The incidental echoes of Nietzsche in Davidson's work have already been adequately charted by Lester, to whom the reader is referred. They show that Davidson was acquainted, not only with the earlier translations of Nietzsche, but also with *The Dawn of Day* (1903) and *Beyond Good and Evil* (1907). He tended to minimize his indebtedness to Nietzsche, partly because he believed his own philosophy had outstripped Nietzsche's. He acknowledged his admiration for Nietzsche's "triumphant intellect,"[71] and for the man who was "the most potent influence in European thought of our time."[72] In one of his imaginary conversations, between Carlyle and Froude, written in 1899, Carlyle calls Nietzsche "a great man" and "a man of unexampled divulsive power." The conversation ends thus:

> F. I have heard that Nietszche [misspelt throughout], having destroyed the whole world of thought, intended a reconstruction.

c. He did. He meant to restate the world as Lust for Power.
f. Would you recommend Englishmen to read Nietszche?
c. I would indeed. Such a tonic the world of letters has not had for a thousand years. Nietszche set himself, smiling, to dislodge the old earth from its orbit; and – it is something against such odds – the dint of his shoulder will remain for ever.[73]

Shaw, as we have seen, thought that Davidson learnt nothing from Nietzsche: the verdict of Holbrook Jackson, who knew more about Nietzsche than Shaw did, was more judicious:

> Early association with the ideas of Nietzsche had directed Davidson's innate pessimism into channels of creative inquisitiveness and speculation. He learnt more from Nietzsche than did any other poet of his time, but he never became a disciple. He learnt of that philosophical courage which Nietzsche called "hardness," and used it Nietzsche-wise in his continual questioning and re-valuing of accepted ideas. He was imbued also with the German philosopher's reverence for power. But he did not accept the Superman doctrine.[74]

Why was it that Davidson found this doctrine unacceptable?

3 In denying that he was a disciple of Nietzsche, Davidson had claimed that the essence of Nietzsche was to be found in his tragic farce, *Smith* (1888), written before he had even heard of Nietzsche's name. This play is in a direct line of descent from the Spasmodic dramas of Philip Bailey, Sydney Dobell, and Alexander Smith, with their proud, brave rebel-heroes, their extravagance of plot, sentiment, and language, their violence of action and variety of sexual exploit.* Davidson's own heroes in

---

* And, one should add, from Thomas Lovell Beddoes. "Poetic drama has two main directions: (i) the relating of human affairs to the powers beyond, and (ii) the heroic, at the limit the superman, quest. Beddoes alone among our dramatists presents both in juxtaposition. To Adam, says Isbrand [in *Death's Jest-Book* (1826)], life was new and exciting, but to us it has grown dull:

> And man is tired of being merely
>   human;
> And I'll be something more: yet, not by
>   tearing
> This crysalis of psyche ere its hour,
> Will I break through Elysium. There
>   are sometimes,

Even here, the means of being more
   than men ...   (iv.iv.)

He would be 'heavenly in my clay' (iv. iv.). As man is to a beast, so the new man on 'the way to godhead' should be to man as he is, as yet only 'half created.' What is needed is a power to direct the soul as the soul directs the body, a will above the will:

> What shall we add to man,
> To bring him higher? I begin to think
> That's a discovery I soon shall make.
>   (v.i.)"

G. Wilson Knight, *The Golden Labyrinth* (London, 1962), 221. Later in the book Knight discusses Davidson's plays, relating them to Nietzsche.

Smith, Diabolus Amans (1885) and other early plays stand – like the speakers of the *Testaments* and the figure of Mammon – in Promethean isolation from the rest of mankind. Virile in strength, they assert their supremacy, flaunt their unbelief, exert a superhuman will-power to overcome suffering and danger; their heroic vitalism, like their didacticism, is that of Henley and Kipling. They have a mission to mankind, a message to convey at all costs. Smith is fired at the prospect: "One must become / Fanatic – be a wedge – a thunder-bolt, / To smite a passage through the close-grained world."[75] The worship of will is equally pronounced in *Diabolus Amans*, which bears an epigraph from Hawthorne: "A man can transform himself into an angel, if he will only, for a reasonable period of time, undertake an angel's office." The hero of this play – appropriately named Angelus – makes an appeal to Donna to unite on their nuptial bed in what he calls a "passion for the Highest":

But charged each with other's consciousness
Deepening and doubling individual life,
Let us with stronger pinion make for Heaven,
Though it were but the future of mankind.
Only as we are loyal to the light
Within us, shall we love each other.[76]

This flirtation with Darwinism ameliorism was brief – Davidson came to reject the future and its demands, as also the past and its restrictions. Against determinism he set the power of the ego:

Henceforth I shall be God; for consciousness
Is God: I suffer; I am God: this Self,
That all the universe combines to quell,
Is greater than the universe; and *I*
Am that I am. To think and not to be God? –
It cannot be.[77]

This was written in 1894; two years later comes this appeal for self-determination:

                Live at speed;
And call your least caprice the law of God;
Disdain the shows of things, and every love
Whose stamen is not hate; self-centred stand;
Accept no second thought. ...
You are your birthright; let it serve you well:
Be your own star, for strength is from within,
And one against the world will always win![78]

Thus far had Davidson reached before his first serious encounter with Nietzsche in 1896. After this date there is little change in the formula for heroism which Davidson had worked out; but there is, from Urban in *Self's the Man* to Mammon in the last plays a greater intensity, complexity, and ruthlessness. "Urban's philosophy," writes Townsend, "is that of the Henleyan activist grafted to that of the Carlylean hero and the Nietzschean Overman."[79] Great men, Urban learns, should be uncompromising:

To laugh at policy, to over-ride
Wisdom, authority, experience,
To break with the ragged past, and be
The demiurge of order and a time
Stamped with my own image – is to chafe
Mankind, and mark my power and daring ...
Is to read triumph in a storm of hate.[80]

As for Mammon, Davidson's dynamic Antichrist figure, he is "a man apart" whose "deeds shall be unparagoned in time."[81] Like Urban he believes that only one man can rule, there can be no democracy of Napoleonic supermen (as Shaw would wish) because "forthwith would come a greater than Napoleon."[82] Davidson admires men of vitality and power, whether they are rulers, militarists, imperialists, or even industrialists. Perhaps Davidson, like Nietzsche, was driven to exult in cruelty and suffering because his sensitivity to these things made him realize the futility of trying to alleviate them by social or political change. Life was intrinsically terrible, and the right attitude was one of defiant exultation:

> It is ours to make
This farce of fate a splendid tragedy:
Since we must be the sport of circumstance,
We should be sportsmen, and produce a breed
Of gallant creatures, conscious of their doom,
Marching with lofty brows, game to the last.
Oh good and evil, heaven and hell are lies!
But strength is great: there is no other truth:
This is the yea-and-nay that makes men hard.[83]

A system of voluntary euthanasia, had it been practised early enough, would have "weeded humanity" and created "a race of heroes in a golden age."[84] Davidson seeks refuge from the "debris" of Christendom by regarding human suffering as the labour-pangs of a divinity struggling to be born:

So let us think we are the tortured nerves
Of Being in travail with a higher type.

I know that I shall crumble back to dust,
And cease for evermore from sense and thought,
But this contents me well in my distress: —
I, being human, touch the highest reach
Attained by matter, and within me feel
The motion of a loftier than I:
Out of the beast came man; from man comes God.[85]

This is an early (1896) statement of that materialist doctrine which Davidson was to proclaim with ever-increasing excitement. Single-handed, Davidson imagined, he had smashed "the imaginary chrysalis or cocoon of the Other World" in which man had slumbered so long:

Man beholds himself, not now as that fabulous monster, half-god, half-devil, of the Christian era, but as Man, the very form and substance of the universe, the material of eternity, eternity itself, become conscious and self-conscious. This is the greatest thing told since the world began. It means an end of the strangling past; an end of our conceptions of humanity and divinity, of our ideas of good and evil, of our religion, our literature, our art, our polity; it means that which all men have desired in all ages, it means a new beginning; it means that the material forces of mind and imagination can now re-establish the world as if nothing had ever been thought or imagined before; it means that there is nothing greater than man anywhere; it means infinite terror, infinite greatness.[86]

Mammon announces himself as the first of men to be self-conscious, "greater than devil, angel, hero, god."[87] There is a touch of metaphysical conceit in his assurance to his wife that he will beget on her "the whole / Illimitable Universe itself," and that "nothing is greater anywhere than us: / We form the matter of the furthest star."[88]

Davidson's materialist belief, with its conviction that "there cannot be anything higher than man, because man is the whole Universe become conscious and self-conscious," signifies an end to "man's mistaken effort towards an impossible Divinity by way of an impossible Humanity."[89] This rules Nietzsche's superman out of court immediately. What Davidson does is to transpose Nietzsche's futuristic vision to the present, where he can harness it to his support for England as a colonial power, and to his long-held enthusiasm for the rebel-hero; he does not deny having learnt something from Nietzsche's superman theory, insisting merely on its redundancy: "There are signs of a Nietzsche panic in certain quarters; and the word 'overman' is supposed to be an index of evolution in humanity. This seems to me very foolish. Nietzsche has nothing to tell the Englishman of the 'overman'; the Englishman is the 'overman'; in Europe, in Asia, Africa, America, he holds the world in the hollow of his hand. Moreover, he has been stated in our literature again and again, the outstanding instances being these: – Marlowe's *Tamburlaine*, Shakespeare's *Richard III*, Milton's Satan, Carlyle's Cromwell."[90] These ideas are developed in the dedication to his valedictory *Testament of John Davidson* (1908), in which he appeals to the Peers Temporal of Great Britain and Ireland to reassert their ancient authority in the face of effete Christianity, mass government, and democratic institutions. He admits that the lords have lost much of their old power and prestige, yet with the Monarchy they still remain "a most effective estate of the realm, your un-acknowledged veto being our main bulwark against the anarchy of the franchise." Speaking on their behalf, Davidson addresses the working-men of England:

We have made room for you, ample room. But you want to be great: you have heard of the Overman, and you would transcend humanity? Do not be misled by any speciousness of that kind. Let us understand this of the Overman. *Uebermensch*, a word of Goethe's, of the young Goethe's, having a pre-Darwinian half-meaning, was interpreted in an evolutionary sense by Nietzsche, and received its European vogue from him. When the misapprehension of Ibsen in England gave place to a misapprehension of Nietzsche: – Celtic panics, both of these; not English at all; the English care nothing for either Ibsen or Nietzsche: – your absurd neologism, Overman, was accepted by the panic-stricken as an index of evolution in humanity; but not by the English. You must remember that Nietzsche, the fugleman in this business, was a Pole. The Poles being the Celts of Eastern Europe, an inferior race, unable to conquer and unable to be conquered, the idea of a higher type of man than they is natural to them. But such an idea could never occur to an Englishman. The Englishman is the Overman; and the history of England is the history of his evolution. You think we are unjust to Nietzsche, the most powerful mind of recent times? We admit the power: a shattering mind that never spared itself. But an extraordinary individual may spring from any source. ... Nietzsche's notion of Beyond-man was not of the individual; it came of the inferiority of the stock.[91]

Nietzsche's whole theory, according to Davidson, is a psychological compensation for being born of inferior race; he seems unaware that his own much-vaunted championship of power and inequality may have had its root in similar circumstances. Nietzsche, born a German, yearned to be recognized as a Slav; Davidson, born a Scot, tried to conceal his origin and identify himself with the imperial English. It was comforting to a man frustrated by poverty and a growing sense of failure to create men like Mammon who could quell all opposition and turn seeming defeat into victory. When his publisher protested against Davidson's messianic crusade against book-reviewers because of the harm it would cause to sales,

Davidson replied: "I am not afraid of doing an 'undermannish' thing; no overman ever is";[92] and Townsend believes that "most of Davidson's writing after 1895 is the product of a mind egocentric, hypersensitive, and easily unbalanced, intent upon the primary task of justifying a life of disappointment."[93] As for Nietzsche interpreting the superman "in an evolutionary sense," this is as alien to Nietzsche's vision as it was to Davidson, who detested the idea that men were derived from monkeys: "Ugly, loathsome brutes, their horrible caricature of humanity has degraded man in his own eyes, and helped him to a theory of the universe that I, for one, will never accept."[94] Davidson adopted the materialist view of man because it was imaginatively satisfying, and his whole task was to create "a new habitation for the imagination of man."[95] So far he is with Nietzsche. He is also with Nietzsche in his worship of men of genius. He thought genius was "a thing *brut*, not a thing *net*," that it corresponded to instinct in other animals being "a diapason of all the powers of body, mind and soul," and that in the greatest men genius was always accompanied by some nervous disorder or other permanent malady – Caesar and Mahomet were epileptics, Beethoven syphilitic, Schopenhauer and Nietzsche mad: "Genius in the human race is a *lusus naturae*; a tremendous throwback, the atavism of it goes into the remotest past: probably as the human race tends more and more to work out to a net product, genius, which requires the gross sum of the whole nature, not the net sum of the intellectual powers only, will become rarer and rarer in civilized nations."[96]

One of Davidson's lifelong heroes was Napoleon, to whom Nietzsche refers in *The Genealogy of Morals*: "Like a final signpost to other ways, there appeared Napoleon, the most unique and violent anachronism that ever existed, and in him the incarnate problem *of the aristocratic ideal in itself* – consider well what a problem it is: – Napoleon, that synthesis of Monster and Superman."[97] Believing that an extraordinary individual may spring from any source, Davidson wrote: "Napoleon was a Corsican: the smallness, the much meanness of Napoleon was racial: the blood of the pigmies ran in the veins of the giant; and thus it is that Napoleon appears monstrous rather than great."[98] Davidson's reading of Nietzsche made him modify Carlyle's estimate of Napoleon as the only great man, along with Goethe, within living memory.

After Davidson's disappearance in 1909 his son found a manuscript of some unpublished poems containing a list of five poems on the subject of heroic rebels: Cain, Judas, Cesare Borgia, Calvin, and Cromwell. These were listed under the general title of "When God meant God."[99] The superman, Davidson believed, had also been realized in Marlowe's Tamburlaine,

Milton's Satan and Carlyle's Cromwell: but he became very suspicious of Carlylean hero-worship: "Men reject Carlyledom. Willing enough, temporarily, to worship themselves in Mahomet or Cromwell, they find the cult of great men so pursued to end in all unhappiness; which is intolerable. Two men did try to live in Carlyledom – Ruskin and Froude: and the end of them was asphyxiation: Carlyle had exhausted the air: they had only his breath to breathe. Carlyledom is a straight-jacket for the world, and a dusty way to death and to the dull hell of the drill-sergeant and the knout."[100] Carlyle had been one of Davidson's earliest literary admirations, but his brand of hero-worship, like all philosophical systems and all doctrine whether Buddhistic, Christian, or Nietzschean, belonged to "the insane past of mankind,"[101] the nightmare from which the virgin world was struggling to awake. In one of his dialogues Davidson has Carlyle accuse Froude of writing a biography of him which "is the worst disservice literature has ever suffered"; Nietzsche, says Carlyle, though "a man of unexampled divulsive power," was "spoilt for want of a knowledge of my writings."[102] Nietzsche's attacks on Carlyle, Davidson suggests, were based on "that ill-tempered, lugubrious figure" Froude had portrayed. Yet it is not wholly true, as Lester maintains, that "for every Nietzschean derogation of Carlyle, Davidson is ready with a comment or rebuttal,"[103] for Davidson could be highly critical of Carlyle's "insane jealousy" and "his damnable Scotch-peasant's hypocrisy and agonized self-conceit as of a sinless and impotent Holy Willy": "Carlyle's hatred of pleasure – an experience constitutionally impossible to himself; and his dyspeptic, neurasthenic distrust of happiness generally, corrupt all his judgments of men, and especially stultify his opinions of poets and poetry."[104] This is precisely Nietzsche's line of argument.

It is more fruitful to compare Davidson's superman, not with Carlyle's hero-worship, but with the fictional protagonists of some of the novels of H. G. Wells. Wells, like Davidson, was fully aware of subversive implications of Darwinism. In 1897 he wrote: "The tendency of a belief in natural selection as the main factor of human progress, is, in the moral field, towards the glorification of a sort of rampant egotism – of blackguards in fact, – as the New Gospel. You get that in the Gospel of Nietzsche."* As

---

* "Human Evolution," *Natural Science*, x (April, 1897), 244. In assuring Wells that he had misunderstood Nietzsche's position, Thomas Common approximated to Wells's later ideas: "In every well-regulated and progressive society there must necessarily be a system of ranks and castes corresponding approximately to the merit of individuals and families. The best men should rule and the inferior should obey, if things are to go on well; and when inferior men will not obey reasonable rules, they should be coerced." *Natural Science*, x (June, 1897), 393.

in Davidson's case, Nietzchean motifs appear in Wells's work long before Nietzsche was available in English – certainly before his ideas began to make themselves felt. In an 1891 article which set out many of the principles of his work, "The Rediscovery of the Unique," Wells attempted to demolish the validity of logic, mathematics, atomic theory, and conventional morality in a manner familiar to readers of Nietzsche's *Will to Power*. Wells is on common ground with Nietzsche in his repudiation of the notion of original sin, his insistence on the law of change and his premonitions of impending world wars. It has been suggested that *The Island of Dr. Moreau* (1896) reflects Nietzsche's transvaluation of values in Dr. Moreau's abandonment of traditional ethics and his desire to create a new type of man.* Certainly Dr. Moreau places great hope in the Nietzschean idea of sublimating instinctive behaviour: "Very much indeed of what we call moral education is such an artificial modification and perversion of instinct; pugnacity is trained into courageous self-sacrifice, and suppressed sexuality into religious emotion."[105] Davidson was favourably impressed by what he took to be the anti-socialist tendencies of *The War of the Worlds* (1898),[106] in which the Artilleryman describes the *élite* who will lead the struggle against the Martian invaders.

In the novel *When the Sleeper Wakes* (1899), Ostrog's view of democracy is Mammon-like: "The hope of mankind – what is it? That some day the Over-man may come, that some day the inferior, the weak and the bestial may be subdued or eliminated. Subdued if not eliminated. The world is no place for the bad, the stupid, the enervated. Their duty – it's a fine duty too! – is to die. The death of the failure! That is the path by which the beast rose to manhood, by which man goes on to higher things."[107] Ostrog, of course, is the tyrannical ruler of a world-state in which the common man has been stripped of the right to elect a representative government – in Ostrog's eyes parliaments are nothing but "eighteenth-century tomfoolery." The only function of the common man in this world-state is to work – there is no point in emancipating him, for liberty is not a matter of political rights but of wisdom and self-control. If the proletariat succeeded in staging a revolution they would only fall to other masters: "So long as there are sheep Nature will insist on beasts of prey. It would mean but a few hundred years' delay. The coming of the aristocrat is fatal and assured. The end will be the Over-man – for all the mad protests of humanity."[108] The pioneers of this world-state were a mixed bag indeed:

---

* Bernard Bergonzi, *The Early H. G. Wells* (Manchester, 1961), 107. Bergonzi also suggests that the book expresses "something very like Tille's attempt to assimilate Nietzsche and Darwin."

Grant Allen, Le Gallienne, Shelley, Godwin, and Nietzsche. Ostrog, it has been well said, is the supreme realist who "thinks of manipulating the social body rather as Moreau had manipulated the animal body."[109] Both Moreau and Ostrog have a suggestion of caricature about them, but they foreshadow, if grotesquely, Wells's later élitist thinking, in which the elimination of the unfit and the deliberate breeding of the superman is seen to be the only permanently effective remedy for the ills of the world: "In that way," Wells writes, "man has risen from the beasts, and in that way man will rise to be over-men."[110]

Dr. Keppel, a reincarnation of Ostrog in the much later "biological fantasia" of *Star Begotten* (1937), exhibits the revulsion before common humanity which Wells, in his growing disillusionment, was also feeling: "I hate common humanity. This oafish crowd which tramples the ground whence my cloud-capped pinnacles might rise. I am tired of humanity – beyond measure. Take it away. This gaping, stinking, bombing, shooting, throat-slitting, cringing brawl of gawky, under-nourished riff-raff. Clear the earth of them."[111] Keppel's hypothesis is that the coming superman will be stronger-witted, better balanced, and altogether wiser than "this breed of pretentious, self-protective, imbeciles," which is nearly at "the end of its tether." When asked whether he has Nietzsche's supermen in mind, Keppel replies: "He brings in too much oriental bric-à-brac for my taste. And so far as I can make out, he has at least two different meanings for that Übermensch of his. On the one hand is a biologically better sort of man and on the other a sort of aggregate synthetic being like Hobbes's *Leviathan*. You never know how to take him. Let's rule Nietzsche out."[112]

But neither Wells nor Davidson was able to "rule Nietzsche out" so simply.* Wells used Nietzsche as a conscious outlet for his bitter disappointment in the democratic process, whereas Davidson applied him more consistently to dynamite the whole structure of democratic society. Even

---

* In later life however, Wells, who never seems to have studied Nietzsche in any depth, became very suspicious of him indeed: "Literary artistry, erudition, classical pretentiousness, and a dislike for Jews gave his writing its peculiar qualities. He swallowed Persian dualism uncritically and took the side of Satan, because it was the most emphatic way of repudiating the orthodoxies and ungentlemanly beliefs about him. He drew his contrast. God wanted to keep man a naked respectful slave in the Garden of Eden, amidst a great boredom of carnivores and such like frustrated creatures. Satan wanted to get him to eat the tree of knowledge and go out into the great world. Eden meant 'Safety First'; Satan whispered 'Live dangerously.' That was the current of revolt. It was not very original. It followed the drift of the period. There is indeed about one week of clear hard thinking in the whole of the Nietzschean bubble. After that he just blew and blew." *You Can't Be Too Careful: A Sample of Life, 1901–1941* (London, 1941), 282–3.

in the nineties he had looked upon his rebel-heroes, ironically, as exterior to himself: a self-intoxicated autocrat and his Christian mother are dismissed as "bigots – fateful souls that plague / The gentle world."[113] But the closer identification of himself with the heroes of his plays and *Testaments* gradually removed the prop of sanity and perspective: the saving grace of ambivalence. Davidson, who wanted "the meanest man to be great, and to feel great,"[114] projected into his work, particularly in the figure of Mammon, his own personal demand for greatness: "For half a century I have survived in a world unfitted for me, and having known both the Heaven and the Hell thereof, and being without a revenue and an army and navy to compel the nations, I begin definitely in my Testaments and Tragedies to destroy this unfit world and make it over again in my own image."[115] The defiant egomania and megalomania of Mammon drew its sustenance less from Nietzsche's vision of the superman than from his creator's own amoral and apolitical urge to remould the world more to his heart's desire. In obeying this urge Davidson failed to avoid the dangers he had sensed so acutely as far back as 1893: "Neither is man, as was long ago remarked, a naked animal, nor is his soul unclothed: even those who strip it of religion and duty are ready with another garment, if it were only some fantastic new protestantism of Every Man His Own God."[116]

4. Davidson dourly protested that he owed nothing of his philosophy to Nietzsche. In 1902 he wrote: "A year or two ago I knew by heart the three published volumes of the English translation of Nietzsche, and found them as literature very admirable and exciting; but so far as his philosophy goes in these volumes, Nietzsche seems to me to have laid a wind-egg in a mare's nest."[117] Davidson was opposed to philosophy as such, distrusting philosophical activity as too cerebral and too systematizing; metaphysics were "the fossil remains of dead poetries," just as creeds were "the fossil remains of dead religions."[118] The philosopher was a mere onlooker who only abstracted from existence, whereas the poet, always actively involved in reality, could create a total imaginative picture of the world, and formulate what Davidson calls "a statement of the Nature of Things."[119] An insistence on creativity is a keynote of Nietzsche's work, too. Nietzsche liked to regard philosophy as a dynamic activity, more akin to alchemy than to passive scholarship. He writes to Brandes: "These weeks I have employed in 'transvaluing values.' – You understand this trope? – After all, the alchemist is the most deserving kind of man there is! I mean the man who makes of what is base and despised something valuable, even gold. He alone confers wealth, the others merely give change. My problem

this time is rather a curious one: I have asked myself what hitherto has been best hated, feared, despised by mankind – and of that and nothing else I have made my 'gold.' "*

Such a transvaluation is implicit in the distinction Davidson makes between the poet and the philosopher. The poet was superior to the philosopher: "I am not a philosopher; philosophy is the evil conscience of the world, filtering out of power and beauty a sediment of system. I am a poet, poetry being the good conscience of the world, transmuting into power and beauty the utmost evil that can befall the individual and the race. This that I say is not a new philosophy or a new religion: it is more than these; it is the beginning of a new poetry."[120] Yet the poetry Davidson wrote after 1900 seems to depend more and more on a scaffolding of "transvaluations" which critics were quick to see had come from Nietzsche's *chantier*: "The empire-builder, like most of his kind, consciously or unconsciously, is a Nietzschean. He harps on the will to live, and his final note is the sublime 'unmorality' of 'Enlarge your Hell; preserve it in repair;/ Only a splendid Hell keeps Heaven fair.' "[121] Another reviewer observed that *The Testament of an Empire-Builder* dealt largely with the necessity and function of pain in the world:

But it goes further than this. It proclaims that the strong egoist alone is happy, both in this world and the next, and that his happiness is purchased by the sufferings of the weak and altruistic. These were in hell here, and in hell hereafter; and the heaven of the joyful self-seekers is founded on their hell. All splendour and beauty has beneath it a skeleton of pain – the pain of others, not of that which is splendid and beautiful. And what is that will be. It is a terrible gospel, but scarce new – though it may be new in song. For this, surely, is the gospel of Nietzsche; and it might be written, "Nietzsche is great, and Davidson is his prophet."[122]

Francis Thompson's anonymous review, written in the same strain, suggested that Davidson was "a disciple of Nietzsche to his fingertips."[123]

As against those, like William Archer, who saw in Davidson's protagonists "the Olympian egoism of the 'over-man,' "[124] there were critics who thought that Davidson himself imagined he was not only superman, but supergod: "We all know the tag as to the alliance of great wit and madness. The relation of little wit to idiocy is strikingly borne in upon us by this preposterous volume."[125] The volume in question was the valedictory

---

* George Brandes, *Friedrich Nietzsche* (London, 1914), 85. Leter dated May 23, 1888. In *Ecce Homo* Nietzsche defines the "transvaluation of values" as "an emancipation from all moral values, in a saying of yea, and in an attitude of trust, to all that which hitherto has been forbidden, despised, and damned." *CW*, XVII, 92.

Testament of John Davidson. Another view was that Davidson's anarchism was stronger than his megalomaniac pretensions: "Mr. Davidson has no need for the Superman, in fact he rather distrusts him; the Superman might develop a kind of Christian moral sense. ... He is no scientific breeder of a new race, but an apologist for the most unchartered freedom for the individuals of the old one."[126] The view of Davidson as an anarchist was widely held. One critic, writing in 1910, saw Nietzsche and Stirner as the philosophers of anarchic individualism, Ibsen and Shaw as its dramatists, and Whitman and Davidson as its poets: "Whitman proclaimed the sacredness of the body and put forth the dream of the superman. Davidson gave us rather the anarchical phase of Nietzschean philosophy. He is the smasher of things as they are, the pessimist dissatisfied with the present, the optimist dreaming of the larger and nobler tomorrows. His position was the direct result of his temperament, of his own struggles for success in a heedless world, of his wrath and tears over the sufferings of the submerged tenth, of his reading of the advanced thinkers."* One of Davidson's most fervent admirers, James Douglas, rated him with Tolstoy, Ibsen, and Shaw as "the four great anarchists in contemporary literature."[127] But the Nietzschean socialist Orage detected in this anarchism a sign of decadence. Viewing a proposed study of Davidson by Frank Harris, the associate of leading anarchists like Emma Goldman and the creator, in *The Bomb* (1909), of the arch-anarchist Lingg, Orage was visibly taken aback: "A study of such a congeries of moods unhappily gathered in a single consciousness must be a diagnosis of more of our times than of a man; and its name should not be Davidson but Anarchism."[128]

Responsibility for the element of brash argumentativeness now apparent in Davidson's work was increasingly laid at Nietzsche's door: "Metaphysical dialectic is Mr. Davidson's besetting sin. He is a poet let captive by Nietzsche, whose pessimism continually breaks out into songs of joy."[129] The Mammon plays, reviewers complained, were full of "violent absurdi-

---

* Milton Bronner, "John Davidson: Poet of Anarchy," *Forum*, XLIV (1910), 314. The view of Nietzsche as an anarchist in the line of Whitman, Stirner and Kropotkin was expressed with force and consistency by Dr. W. Barry in "The Ideals of Anarchy: Friedrich Nietzsche," *Quarterly Review*, CLXXXIV (October, 1896), 299–328 (later reprinted in *Heralds of Revolt* (London, 1904), 343–78); and in "Anarchy and Culture," *English Illustrated Magazine*, XXVI (November, 1901), 186–92. It is historically false to call the first of these articles, as Crane Brinton does, "the decisive article in English." *Nietzsche* (Cambridge, Mass., 1941), 178. Common and Ludovici continually defended Nietzsche from the impression that he was an anarchist. Cf. the correspondence on this subject in *Outlook*, XXIII (May 22, 1909), 715; XXIII (May 29, 1909), 745–6; XXIII (June 12, 1909), 812–3.

ties" which made for dreary and unprofitable reading. They showed "a steady falling-off in workmanship, an increasing lack of taste or self-control, and an overmastering egoism which would be ridiculous if it were not rather pathetic."[130] The reviewer for the *Times Literary Supplement* read the epilogue to *Mammon and His Message* hoping for a guide to the intractable material that lay before him. It lured him into a confident expectation that he would find something original in the play, whereas in fact he came across Mammon "behaving just as the old-fashioned Uebermensch used to do": "We find him riding lightly over convention and morality, killing his nearest relations when they get in the way, tearing other people's brides from them, and, above all, talking. ... The notion of racking Gottlieb smells of the lamp; pedantry is the besetting danger of the super-man, prepossessed as he is with the fear of doing anything like other people."[131] Davidson only found favour with those who, like Chesterton, were prepared to respond to his poetry by ignoring or playing down its philosophical substance,[132] or by the few who recognized in the Mammon plays, not a "decadence and retrogression, but the true development and culmination of his work."* Far more frequently expressed was a sense of real sorrow that Davidson's exceptional gifts as a poet, even his life itself, had been brought to nothing by an excessive infatuation with narrowly materialist, and particularly Nietzschean, ideas. "He was one of the people who have been ruined by a misunderstanding of Nietzsche," wrote R. A. Scott-James in an angry obituary: "It is not pleasant to reflect on the fatal consequences which may follow the works of a powerful man like Nietzsche. It is not too much to say that he drove the faculty for art out of a finely sensitive artist, and in the long run literally killed him. This tragedy of modern life is strangely like some ancient tale of devil-worship and the uncanny ending of fire and brimstone. One begins to understand the sentiments of the persecutor who suppresses heresy with violence."[133] Nietzsche provided an easy scapegoat for those who wished to seek reasons for Davidson's artistic and personal failure outside Davidson himself.

What of the Nietzscheans? Not unnaturally they claimed Davidson as a fellow-fighter against the "phalanx of priests and professors, politicians and petticoats" which stood in the way of Nietzsche's acceptance. Davidson, wrote Levy, was "a true Nietzschean ..., though one more intoxicated than inspired by Nietzsche," and on Davidson's suicide Levy covetously claimed him as the first martyr of the cause: "The battlefield of thought has its

---

* Filson Young, "The New Poetry," *Fortnightly Review*, LXXXV (January 1, 1909), 145. Young informs the readers of his article – an enthusiastic eulogy – of his difficulties in finding an editor to publish it.

dead, its wounded, and its deserters as well as any other – and only the comfortable citizen who has no idea of what this higher warfare is like will shrug his shoulders at those who come to grief during their noble but dangerous enterprise."[134] J. M. Kennedy praised Davidson for being "the only honest atheist of his time," adding that his atheism, scientific bent, and eventual suicide all had a famous precedent in the figure of Lucretius. Davidson's "profound study" of Nietzsche had convinced him that Christianity was "the enemy of art, of order, and of good government": "Had Davidson realised that Nietzsche's severe criticisms of Christianity were directed against the Protestant rather than the Catholic form of the religion, the effects on his work might have been different. But he was too greatly preoccupied with his scientific investigations to give any attention to this point."[135] Of the five figures – Pater, Wilde, Symons, Gissing, and Davidson – who constitute the main subjects of his enquiry, Kennedy, flying in the face of current literary opinion, claimed that Davidson "probably approached most nearly to the classical ideal": "For a most important trait of the classicist, and one which cannot be overlooked, is his unity, the complete harmony existing between mind and body, his complete self-control and well-developed will power; while the romanticist is equally distinguished by lack of unity, lack of will, and a resultant disharmony of thought."* Another Nietzschean, G. T. Wrench, was appalled by England's failure to give Davidson's later work due recognition; he set it down to the streak of meanness inherent in the English puritanical conscience. It was shameful, he wrote in an article for German readers, that Davidson was now a literary leper in a country noted universally for its devotion to justice, and hoped that Germany, with its great cultural traditions, would not fail to perceive in Davidson a "fearless fighter" who, like Nietzsche, was capable of intellectual audacity, incisive criticism, and captivating powers of expression.[136]

As the earliest English writer to take note of Nietzsche's work, Davidson earned the gratitude of the Nietzscheans; but their approval of his work tended to confirm the popular view that in taking over the more extreme elements in Nietzsche's philosophy – egoism, cruelty, power – Davidson was an accurate and complete reflection of his mentor. Davidson's Mammon

---

* *English Literature, 1890–1905* (London, 1912), 29, 22–3. In one of his dialogues Davidson approaches very close to Nietzsche's theory of "self-conquest," the theory which was to appeal to Yeats so deeply: "Self-control, as I understand it, is the keystone of genius: without it, you may have wonderful ruins, but no lofty bridges triumphantly spanning life. The terrible gifts of brain and blood slay the Titans – Mirabeau, Burns, Byron; the Gods, Shakespeare and Goethe, chain their intellects and temperaments." *A Random Itinerary* (London, 1894), 177.

figure, in particular, gave plausibility to one-sided readings of Nietzsche's superman, such as George Saintsbury's: "There is no God, *He* is dead long ago; actual Humanity is effeminate silliness; what we must strive to produce or develop into is the *Übermensch*, a being with no virtues in the present sense of that word except an infinitely strong will, endurance, and determination to enjoy. Caesar Borgia and a 'fallow wild beast' are the moderate examples tendered; but they are to be much improved upon."[137] It may have been because of Davidson that Richard Garnett and Edmund Gosse could, in 1903, regard Marlowe's Tamburlaine as "the unconscious foreshadowing of Nietzsche's Overman."[138] The "big, blonde beast" wandering in search of prey was the image of the superman which Havelock Ellis, Shaw, Holbrook Jackson, and Orage found it incumbent upon them to destroy.

Later criticism has tended to play down Davidson's direct debt to Nietzsche by pointing out alternative sources and by suggesting that Davidson was a Nietzschean even before he read Nietzsche: "Formal Nietzschean thought merely intensified tendencies that already possessed him."[139] Davidson seemingly accepts all of Nietzsche's cardinal ideas, such as the Will to Power, master morality, *amor fati*, eternal recurrence, the need for pain and suffering:

Yet these numerous likenesses notwithstanding, Davidson can hardly be called a disciple of Nietzsche. In his later work he passes the Nietzschean ideas through a materialistic crucible so that they practically become amplifications of his own point of view: Human beings should indeed, as Nietzsche says, be hard and not hesitate to cause pain, but this time for a new reason, namely, that matter demands this hardness in order to attain self-consciousness. Similarly man is to be a yea-sayer because all is matter and he should be proud of the fact that the entire universe is eager to become man. Finally man is to love the beauty and power of this world because there is no other world and such are the laws of matter.[140]

However, the assimilation of Nietzschean vitalism to a scientific materialism, though it undoubtedly took place,* was never total, and it resulted in strange discrepancies, as one contemporary reviewer observed: "His doctrine of personality, like Nietzsche's, demands a basis wholly different from

---

* Shaw's statement about Davidson having nothing to do with Nietzsche's philosophy is an exaggeration, being less a considered vindication of Davidson's originality than an attempt to establish collateral evidence of English independence of Nietzsche, which Shaw had very personal reasons to proclaim. This statement, too, is an over-simplification: "The foundation of Davidson's structure is scientific materialism; to this Nietzsche contributed nothing." J. Benjamin Townsend, *John Davidson* (New Haven, 1961), 478.

the physiological materialism on which it professedly founds itself."[141] The grafting of the doctrine of the superman, noted a later critic, upon Davidson's "rather weird materialism" resulted in "a philosophic egomania which – to speak plainly – was either insanity, or something on the very verge of it."[142] Davidson tried to synthesize Nietzsche's ideas with materialist ones of his own, and the result is an inconsistency which makes any precise estimate of influence hazardous. What further complicates the issue is that, of all the influences that played upon Davidson, that of Nietzsche is the most apparent, if only "because his demonic ideas, forceful expression, and aphoristic gift would be heard clearly when echoed by any writer."[143] In the face of these complexities it would be difficult to improve upon Lester's cautious summary:

Nietzsche's influence struck hardest, and grew and waned, chiefly in response to a crisis and deep need in Davidson's intellectual development. In 1891 he had made his excited discovery of Nietzsche, partly by chance, partly through an awareness that this sulphurous, anarchic gospel was in some ways similar to his own. ... Through Nietzsche he found a clearer definition of the issues in his battle with the world, new strength with which to defy those who opposed him, and a language in which to express his defiance. The Nietzschean elements in his later thought persisted, though less and less acknowledged as his egomania increased, and hedged about with other elements radically antithetical to Nietzsche's philosophy.[144]

Davidson's life might be seen as a tragic failure to heed his own warnings. Convinced that poetry was superior to philosophy, he realized that "no individual mind and imagination ... can enter a fateful battle in the name of a metaphysic."[145] Davidson did enter that battle, and was defeated. Unlike many later adherents of Nietzsche, he never made a direct comparison between Nietzsche and Blake. Yet his characterization of Blake as a man of powerful and audacious mind, of great originality, and yet of childish petulance and impatience is remarkably close to his view of Nietzsche and, pathetically, to his own later development: "He imprisoned himself in his imagination, and became a mystic and system-monger; with him thought and language grew one with the thing thought and spoken of: figures of speech hardened into articles of faith. ... The mystic will soon be forgotten; not so soon the sweet, keen singer whose songs are dew and light."[146] But the most startling incongruity is that Davidson could so confidently reject the formative power of literature – "The power of the pen has been grossly exaggerated. Napoleon not Goethe made the modern world"[147] – while entertaining messianic ambitions of such proportions that he could believe his own poetry would overturn the old order and effect a revolution in art, politics, and society the like of which the world had never seen. As for the ancillary question of Davidson's indebtedness to Nietzsche, it was a pity, as much for Davidson's peace of mind as for Nietzsche's public reputation, that so few believed his frequent denials of discipleship, or even questioned the basis on which they stood. That Nietzsche was invariably held responsible for Davidson's worse aberrations was a sign that Nietzsche scholarship and appreciation in England had yet to come of age.

HAVELOCK ELLIS

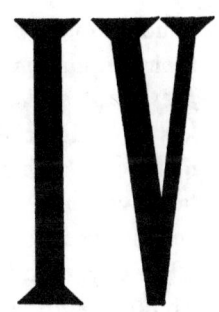

1 John Davidson's reaction to Nietzsche can be best understood against the philosophical controversy which raged during the last decade of the century over the relative virtues of egoism and altruism. This controversy might be regarded as the culmination of discussions, current since the early 1880s, about the distinction between socialism and individualism. Some writers declared that there was no disharmony between the two: this was set forth by Oscar Wilde in 1891: "*Socialism will be of value,*" says Wilde, "*simply because it will lead to Individualism.*"[1] Havelock Ellis agreed that socialism was only a means to an end: "While we are socializing all those things of which all have equal common need, we are more and more tending to leave to the individual the control of those things which in our complex civilization constitute individuality. We socialize what we call our physical life in order that we may attain greater freedom for what we call our spiritual life."[2] The two attitudes are indispensable and interdependent, but each can trespass into a province of human life not properly its own: "No one needs Individualism in his water supply, and no one needs Socialism in his religion."[3] What is more, each can be carried to absurdity: "The individualism of Max Stirner is not far from the ultimate frontier of sanity, and possibly even on the other side of it; while the Socialism of the Oneida Community involved a self-subordination which it would be idle to expect from the majority of men and women."[4] Such a verdict clearly separates Ellis from Davidson's Stirnerite brand of anarchism, as well as from the authoritarian bias of Shaw, who in the appendix to *Man and Superman* alludes to the Oneida Community as a model society for the selective breeding of man.

Ellis's brand of socialism, unlike Shaw's, was not fundamentally economic and political, but moral and cultural. It had a strong spiritual and even spiritualistic tinge: it was widespread enough to result in the formation of a large number of ethical societies, and even to journals specializing in ethical topics.[5] Ellis himself belonged to two of these, and was active in their foundation and administration. In 1882 he helped to found the *Progressive Association*, which was "Established for the Promotion of Intellectual and Social Well-Being"; its principal aim was "to bring about that moral awakening which is itself the occasion of all political and social improvement." A kind of secularized church, the Association retained ecclesiastical form while denying theological substance. Leading socialists of the day, such as William Morris, H. M. Hyndman and Thomas Davidson, would often be invited to deliver an address. Davidson himself, on a visit to London in 1883, introduced to a young audience his ideas about a Vita Nuova, or a Fellowship of the New Life, and several members of the *Progressive Association* – including Ellis, Frank Podmore, Percival Chubb, and the widow of James Hinton (whose *Life in Nature* (1862) had taught Ellis to regard the world not as a dull lifeless mechanism but as an organic whole which permitted of mystic communion) – founded an English Fellowship in October, 1883, at the house of Edward Pease, future secretary and historian of the Fabian Society. The socialism of this group derived less from Marx and Hyndman than from William Morris, Tolstoy, and Kropotkin: its aim was the Goethean one of living resolutely "in the Whole, the Good, and the Beautiful," and it discovered in the works of Whitman, Emerson, and Thoreau a fount of inexhaustible moral idealism. It was a Pantisocratic scheme, similar to that which had tempted Southey and Coleridge in their early days. Shortly after the foundation of the Fellowship of the New Life, Ellis, Chubb, and seven others drafted a short manifesto which read:

Object. – The cultivation of a perfect character in each and all.
Principle. – The subordination of material things to spiritual.
Fellowship. – The sole and essential condition of fellowship shall be a single-
   minded, sincere and strenuous devotion to the object and principle.

Certain members of the New Life, Shaw later remarked, "modestly feeling that the revolution would have to wait an unreasonably long time if postponed until they personally attained perfection,"[6] desired to form a new society on more practical grounds. This was the beginning of the Fabian Society, which soon elected to membership Shaw, Hubert Bland, and Edward Pease. Ellis, unlike Chubb, refused to join the new society, his sympathies remaining with the ambition of the parent body to create, as he wrote to Olive Schreiner, "a kind of atmosphere in which it shall be possible for the outward life to be a true exponent of the inward life."[7] Attempts at community living were made, and a quarterly paper, *Seedtime*, was issued between July, 1889 and February, 1898: Ellis, his wife (whom he had met at the Fellowship), Maurice Adams, and Edward Carpenter were among the contributors. Individualism, both personal and doctrinal, proved in the end to be a source of disunity: experiments in collective living, once they had ventured beyond the stage of outdoor picnics, were a dismal failure, and *Seedtime* was often uneasy and inconsistent in its attitude to manifestations of individualism. Ellis's *The New Spirit*, for example, was warmly reviewed in its pages on its appearance in 1890; this work was no less a paean to individualism than Shaw's lecture to the Fabian Society, "The Quintessence of Ibsenism," castigated in *Seedtime* a few months later as "naked individualism, destructive to household, state, and society," an individualism which represented an adolescent phase of negation and rebellion.[8] Yet some contributors to *Seedtime* were not far from a Shavian, or indeed Nietzschean, heroic vitalism of their own:

The ideal is manifested in all that makes for truest happiness, and this is not to be attained by Algebra, or the Integral Calculus, or even Histology, but by will and energy and purest thoughts.

Our hope must always lie in the noble man – him who immediately, as by instinct, does the deed which wants the doing.[9]

It was about 1885, when Ellis was a medical student, that he came across Nietzsche's *Thoughts out of Season*, and much of what Nietzsche has to say in these pamphlets served to reinforce Ellis's belief that the Fellowship of the New Life was right to reject scientism and concentrate on spiritual development. Later he was to learn of Nietzsche's longing to found "a kind of monastery for free spirits": "He had even found [Ellis wrote] a beautiful old castle in a solitary region of Central Europe which could be had at a reasonable price. With the help of a few friends of like mind, not exclusively men, he resolved to secure this place as a centre for the development of high culture, to work for the progress and liberation of the world. But it was eventually decided that the practical difficulties were too serious."[10]

There is no reference to Nietzsche in *Seedtime*, but several members of the Fellowship, notably Edward Carpenter, Edith Ellis, and Maurice Adams, realized the importance of Nietzsche's "transvaluation of values" and accepted its general direction, if not the specific doctrines resulting from it, as being in harmony with their own moral strivings. Carpenter asserted that the danger of altruism was that it was dull and unexciting:

Against these weaknesses of Christianity Nietzsche was a healthy reaction. It was he [who] insisted on the terms "good" and "bad" being restored to their proper use, as terms of relation – "good" for what? "bad" for what? But his reaction against maudlin altruism and non-resistance led him towards a pitfall in the opposite direction, towards the erection of the worship of Force almost into a formula, Thou *shalt* use Violence, thou *shalt* Resist. His contempt for the feeble and the spooney and knock-kneed and the humbug is very delightful and entertaining, and, as I say, healthy in the sense of reaction; but one does not get a very clear idea what the strength which Nietzsche glorifies is for, or whither it is going to lead. His blonde beasts and his laughing lions may represent the Will to Power; but Nietzsche seems to have felt, himself, that this latter alone would not suffice, and so he passed on to his discovery or invention of the Beyond-man – i.e. of a childlike being who, without argument, *affirms* and creates, and before whom all institutions and conventions dissolve, as it were of their own accord. This was a stroke of genius; but even so it leaves doubtful what the relation of such Beyond-men to each other may be, and whether, if they have no common source of life, their actions will not utterly cancel and destroy each other.[11]

Ellis's own interpretation of the will to power was not as literal as this, but he did share Carpenter's suspicion concerning the superman, and also his feeling that Nietzsche lacked any deep mystical sense of the unity of man with nature.

Ellis's wife, Edith, grouped Carpenter, Hinton, and Nietzsche together in her book *Three Modern Seers* (1910): all three writers, she says, believe in "a striving towards perfection of individual character as the chief factor in social progress," and all plead "for a solidarity working from within outwards."[12] Two-thirds of the book are devoted to Hinton; as the author wrote to her husband: "I've read the new Nietzsche *Life* [by Halévy] and I don't see I can say much more unless I put in another person's thoughts, and in my book Nietzsche is the least important 'seer.' "[13] She notes in the book that the keynote of Nietzsche's moral philosophy is "to look upon suffering and evil as forces to help on towards the over-man," and she approves of Nietzsche's use of asceticism in the original Greek sense of "struggle," "exercise," and "athleticism." Nietzsche's large intellectual ideals and courageous aims make him "a virile warrior of the intellect, a high-priest of culture and self-control." There is no "sedative quality" in Nietzsche – he is more a tonic like quinine: "He braces and fortifies. As a protest against mere philanthropy and sentimental, theoretic love of one's neighbour, his philosophy has its value in an age somewhat given over to forced sacrifices for others as a liberation of one's own soul." Like Carpenter, she criticizes Nietzsche for being devoid of otherworldliness: "The essential wisdom which is childlike in faith and womanly in sympathy is lacking."[14]

A third member of the Fellowship, Maurice Adams, took a special interest in the moral issues of socialism, as his pamphlet, *The Ethics of Social Re-*

form (1887), shows. In a later article he anticipates Ellis's line of thought by taking Tolstoy and Nietzsche as exact antitheses of each other. Nietzsche's acceptance of the passionate side of man's nature, his sane and lofty view of marriage, offset Tolstoy's narrow desire to extirpate the passions: "Perhaps the chief value of Nietzsche's writings is found in the clearness with which he discerns, and the energy with which he repudiates, and combats, the deadly tendency of a morality based solely on the feeling of sympathy, which must finally issue in an asceticism like that of Tolstoy."[15] In *The Birth of Tragedy* Adams finds an acceptable individualism, and even lights on the Goethean adage which the Fellowship had taken as its motto: "Here, in the conception of the tragic man, we find the germ of the *Übermensch*, or Beyond-man. He imagines a generation arising with a fearless glance and 'heroic bent towards the terrible'; and a race of 'dragon-slayers' with bold steps who in their proud daring 'turn their backs upon all the old optimism and its doctrine of feebleness in order to live resolutely in the whole and the full.'" He agrees with Carpenter and Edith Ellis that Nietzsche's attack on sickly sentimentality was long overdue – he even accepts the need for the elimination of the physically weak and the mentally deficient; but he also agrees with them that Nietzsche's philosophy ossifies into a defence of aristocracy and brutal egoism and a repudiation of love and fellowship which is "harmful, false, and evil, and tends only to the disruption of society and the loss of the hard-won gains of evolutionary progress." Adams seeks a *modus vivendi* between the self-negation of Tolstoy and the self-assertion of Nietzsche: "The true good of man – the principle and goal of Ethics, transcending the antithesis of altruism and egotism – is a Common Good realized in a society so organized as to give effect to the equal rights of all its members which belong to them in virtue of their common humanity, whilst affording opportunities for the development of the faculties with which men are so unequally endowed and giving scope for their exercise in the service of the whole."[16]

Of all the members of the Fellowship of the New Life, only Ellis was really able to make Nietzsche harmonize with an adherence to socialist and democratic ideals. How he accomplished this is, in part, the task of the present chapter to explore; but a hint is present in his view that the last third of the nineteenth century was spiritually dominated by two opposing sets of ideals – those of Tolstoy and Nietzsche: "Tolstoy represented the Christian, social, and humanitarian group of ideals, in a form which even the ordinary Christian finds extravagant, while Nietzsche represented the rationalistic, pagan, and individualist group of ideals in a form which, for his part, the ordinary rationalist also finds extravagant. Each of them was a consummate artist in his way, a penetrating psychologist, and a struggling pilgrim along the path of life, painfully seeking to work out his own salvation."[17] Nietzsche's individualism was stimulating and challenging, fortifying to the strong, although dangerous to the weak; as for his proposed solutions to definite problems, they were "scarcely sufficiently precise or sufficiently sound to command general assent."[18] Nietzsche's individualism left gaps which Socialism would have to fill, and a real hope that such an alliance could be achieved by the proper utilization of scientific knowledge lay at the root of Ellis's optimism: "To attain a society in which Individualism and Socialism are each carried to its extreme point would be to attain to the society that lived in the Abbey of Thelema, in the City of the Sun, in Utopia, in the land of Zarathustra, in the Garden of Eden, in the Kingdom of Heaven. ... No Utopia was ever realized; and the ideal is a mirage that must ever elude us or it would cease to be ideal. Yet all our progress, if progress there be, can only lie in setting our faces towards that goal to which Utopias and ideals point."[19]

In 1890 Ellis predicted that the world was standing on the verge of a renaissance of the human spirit, to be brought about by three main factors. These were: a utilization of all the sciences, particularly anthropology and sociology; the further growth and development of democracy; and the emancipation of women. The emancipation of women would bring about "a reinvigoration as complete as any brought by barbarians to an effete and degenerating civilization."[20] The ethical societies to which Ellis belonged offered membership to women on equal terms with men, and Ellis became an ardent supporter of the feminist movement, although his ardour was somewhat dampened by the militant attitude adopted by the suffragettes when, after the Liberal victory in the elections of 1906, seven suffrage bills were summarily rejected by parliament. Ellis never dwelt on Nietzsche's controversial attitude to women; he accepted the view of Nietzsche's sister that Nietzsche, after an early love-affair that never went beyond poetic *Schwärmerei*, thought of women as very fragile, tender little buds: "Nietzsche's attitude [Ellis writes] was not the crude misogyny of Schopenhauer, who knew women chiefly as women of the streets. Nietzsche knew many of the finest women of his time, and he sometimes speaks with insight and sympathy of the world as it appears to women; but there was clearly nothing in him to answer to any appeal to passion, and his attitude is well summed up in an aphorism of his own Zarathustra: 'It is better to fall into the hands of a murderer than into the dreams of an ardent woman.' "[21]

George Egerton, as we noted in the previous chapter, saw in Nietzsche the propounder of a gospel of egoism. This gospel she applied in support of an aggressive feminism, "a feminine '*Umwerthung aller Werthe*,' a new standard of woman's worth,"[22] which was essentially anti-romantic: "When a Strindberg or a Nietzche [*sic*] arises and peers into the recesses of her nature and dissects her ruthlessly, the men shriek out louder than the women, because the truth is at all times unpalatable, and the gods they have set up are dear to them."[23] Here she is attacking, as D. H. Lawrence was to do later, the inveterate masculine habit of imposing a pattern or ideal on women which makes women feel they are being prevented from realizing their true womanhood. Her discussions with her Norwegian friends seem to have revolved around the theme of sexual relations: "Did we not talk about anything? Of course we did. Tolstoi and his doctrine of celibacy. Ibsen's Hedda. Strindberg's view of the female animal. And we agreed that Friedrich Nietzche [*sic*] appealed to us immensely."[24] Taking a more sceptical line, Edith Ellis thought that Nietzsche was "curiously reticent" about women. She quotes Nietzsche's saying in *Zarathustra* that the task of woman is "the recreation of the warrior" and the production of children, commenting: "It is an old-world one, and one far from contemptible – to bear children and to amuse. One is surprised to find, however, that Nietzsche expects from women – who are still cats and birds, he thinks, and the best of us cows – the greatest thing of all, 'Let your hope be "May I bear the over-man," ' he says."[25]

Mrs. Ellis wonders whether the old woman in *Zarathustra* gave the subtlest advice a woman can give a man about her sex when she recommended the carrying of a whip. She notes that Nietzsche found women incapable of friendship, and parasitic in their love. "Wise women," she cautions, read Nietzsche "with an open mind, though, possibly, with the suspicion of a smile."[26] Another woman writer condemned Nietzsche for degrading women by denying them any mission in life except childbearing, and by persistently accusing them of a lack of intellectuality ("When a woman has a taste for science there is generally something wrong in her sexuality"), of honesty and moral scruple: "The piquant part of the whole matter is that he expects, in spite of his uncultured, sexually enslaved, 'pious,' and 'oriental' females, to evolve a superior race of free-thinking, highly-developed, cultured and lordly males."[27] The superman will only come when there is an equality of opportunity, economic as well as political. Yet this writer expresses something of the excitement of Ann Whitefield in Shaw's *Man and Superman* on discovering that her mission is to produce superior progeny: "Nietzsche's dream of an *Uebermensch* is not a dream that women can afford to neglect when working out a philosophy of life."

Nietzsche's remark about the movement for feminine emancipation – "There is a stupidity in this movement, a stupidity almost masculine" – should be taken as a warning rather than a joke: "We must beware that we do not deserve Nietzsche's strictures, by allowing our movement to be identified with a passive acquiescence in aggressive imperialism, capitalism, and militarism." Ellis and Shaw were prepared to grant women full partnership in the societies they envisaged. This was not the case with the Nietzscheans proper, who were more consistent in rating women as the inferior quarter rather than the better half. As feminist agitation grew, Levy and Ludovici, along with Orage, T. E. Hulme and Wyndham Lewis, came to see the emancipation movement as a threat to the male-dominated hierarchical society they all wished to see established.

2 In his autobiography Ellis wrote: "My interest in French, and in modern languages generally, simply as instruments to bring me nearer to contemporary life and contemporary literature and contemporary peoples, has been of inestimable value to my work, as well as a perpetual source of delight and of refreshment."[28] Ellis made good use of his knowledge of French, German, and Italian in his pioneering work as a sexologist and criminologist: it enabled him to keep well abreast of the latest European discoveries, which he later incorporated into his own writings. He was one of the first to recognize the importance of psycho-analysis when Freud's first book appeared in 1896, and in 1898, with Yeats as one of his guinea-pigs, he experimented with mescalin, and wrote about its effects long before Huxley's much-publicized *The Doors of Perception* (1954) attracted attention to the drug. In literary matters, too, Ellis was repeatedly first in the field. In 1888 he wrote the introduction to one of the first English translations of Ibsen; in 1890 appeared *The New Spirit*, a study of literary modernity in the shape of essays on Diderot, Heine, Ibsen, Whitman, and Tolstoy. Most reviewers were shocked by what they took to be a prurient over-emphasis on sex, and accepted Max Nordau's condemnation of Ibsen, Whitman, and Tolstoy as "decadent" writers. Ellis also helped to make current the views of continental literary critics such as Paul Bourget and Rémy de Gourmont, and of continental philosophers such as Vaihinger and Nietzsche. Nietzsche could hardly have hoped for a better expositor. Ellis's eloquent, sympathetic, and judicious handling of his life and works appeared in 1896 in three successive numbers of the *Savoy*,[29] that short-lived but brilliant magazine which served as the rallying point for the most advanced and creative minds of the time. Since 1891 Ellis had shared rooms with the *Savoy*'s editor, Arthur Symons, at Fountain Court in the

Temple, and their common interest in Nietzsche may have begun on one of their annual visits to Paris, where Nietzsche was already the subject of articles in the leading reviews. As we have noted, Ellis had come across *Thoughts out of Season* in the mid-1880s; later he expressed regret at not having written his *Savoy* articles sooner than he did. These articles are quite original, except in the biographical details, which are taken from German and French sources; in a slightly expanded and amended form they were reprinted in *Affirmations* (1898, 1915), and in *Selected Essays* (1936).*

At the outset Ellis states his position with clarity and firmness:

I know of no attempt to deal with Nietzsche from the British point of view, and that is my excuse for trying to define his personality and influence. I do not come forward as the champion of Nietzschianism or of Anti-Nietzschianism. It appears to me that any human individuality that has strongly aroused the love and hatred of men must be far too complex for absolute condemnation or absolute approval. Apart from praise or blame, which seem here alike impertinent, Nietzsche is without doubt an extraordinarily interesting figure. He is the modern incarnation of that image of intellectual pride which Marlowe created in Faustus. A man who has certainly stood at the finest summit of modern culture, who has thence made the most determined effort ever made to destroy modern morals, and who now leads a life as near to death as any life outside the grave can be, must needs be a tragic figure. It is a figure full of significance, for it represents one of the greatest spiritual forces which have appeared since Goethe.[30]

Ellis divides his discussion into three sections, corresponding to the three articles as they had originally appeared in the pages of the *Savoy*. The first of these is primarily biographical. Leaning heavily and rather uncritically on Elisabeth Förster-Nietzsche's highly coloured and idealized portrait of her brother, Ellis is apt to sentimentalize Nietzsche's life, but refrains from moralistic judgment. He notes in Nietzsche a hypertrophied revulsion from the ordinary, the everyday, the mediocre, and, in spite of the importance he attached to sex, a "defective sexuality" which cut him off from true fellowship with men; the delicate subject of Nietzsche's madness he treats with compassionate understanding.

The second section deals with Nietzsche's work, and – as has been customary for many years – Ellis divides it into three periods. To the first of these belong *The Birth of Tragedy* and *Thoughts out of Season*. In *The Birth of Tragedy* (the work which was to tell so powerfully on Symons and

---

* In the account which follows the 1898 edition of *Affirmations* will be used.

Yeats a few years later), Nietzsche makes the origin of tragedy merely a text for the exposition of the philosophy of art he held at that time: "He traces two art impulses in ancient Greece: one, starting in the phenomena of dreaming, which he associates with Apollo; the other, starting in the phenomena of intoxication, associated with Dionysus, and through singing, music and dithyramb leading up to the lyric. The union of these, which both imply a pessimistic view of life, produced folksong and finally tragedy, which is thus the outcome of Dionysiac music fertilized by Apollonian imagery."[31] Although Nietzsche outgrew *The Birth of Tragedy*, says Ellis, it is the prelude to all his work: he always insisted on the primary importance of aesthetic as opposed to intellectual culture, and persistently related modern problems and solutions to those of Hellenic times, in particular to the Greek conception of Dionysus. In his discussion of Nietzsche's essay on David Strauss, Ellis stresses Nietzsche's view of culture as "unity of artistic style in every expression of a people's life," a definition which sustained later readers of Nietzsche in their pursuit of Unity of Being (Yeats), and in their attacks upon cultural "decadence" (Orage). Ellis never lost his admiration for Nietzsche's analysis of German *Kultur*: "He revealed all the elements of narrow provincialism which it held, the latent – when not blatant – vulgarity of its ideals, and its remoteness from all true culture. German scholars, he said, worked in the spirit of agricultural labourers, and German science, so far from making for culture, was possibly making for barbarism. ... It was a forecast which seemed extravagant at the time, but now we may be tempted to regard it as the intuition of genius."[32] By 1915 (when this was written) events had begun to confirm Nietzsche's suspicions. As for Nietzsche's essay on Schopenhauer, Ellis accepts Nietzsche's conception of the philosopher, not as a metaphysician, but as a teacher, a liberator, a guide to fine living.

It is Nietzsche's second period (including *Human, All-Too-Human, The Dawn of Day* and *The Gay Science*) which seems to Ellis "to represent the maturity of his genius": "In form all these volumes belong to *pensée* literature. They deal with art, with religion, with morals and philosophy, with the relation of all these to life. Nietzsche shows himself in these *pensées* above all a freethinker, emancipated from every law save that of sincerity, wide-ranging, serious, penetrative, often impassioned, as yet always able to follow his own ideal of self-restraint."[33] Ellis traces the main currents of Nietzsche's philosophy, and in particular his attitude to religion and morals, which Ellis regards as central. At this point there seems little divergence between Nietzsche's convictions and those of Ellis. Throughout

Ellis stresses that Nietzsche philosophized in the Greek manner, not academically as a matter of books, but vitally, as a matter of a life to be lived; sometimes the self-identification is quite transparent: "He loved travel and movement, he loved scenery, he loved cities and the spectacle of men; above all, he loved solitude."[34] The English (one might almost read "Fabian") obsession with "practical social politics" leaves Nietzsche cold: "He was too much of a philosopher, he had too keen a sense of the vital relation of things, to be content with the policy of tinkering society, wherever it seems to need mending most badly, avoiding any reference to the whole."[35] Ellis gives a résumé of Nietzsche's contemptuous attitude to Darwin, Mill, George Eliot, and other English writers who had "reduced the whole spiritual currency of Europe to a dull plebeian level."[36] Had Nietzsche not been blinded, says Ellis, by the vulgarity of nineteenth-century England, he might have recognized in other writers besides Shakespeare the ardent and heroic qualities he admired so much in sixteenth-century France: "In George Chapman, for instance, at his finest and lucidest moments the typical ethical representative of our greatest literary age, Nietzsche would have found a man after his own heart, not only one who scarcely yielded to himself in generous admiration of the great qualities of the French spirit but a man of 'absolute and full soul' who was almost a precursor of his own 'immoralism,' a lover of freedom, of stoic self-reliance, one who was ever seeking to enlarge the discipline of a fine culture in the direction of moral freedom and dignity."[*]

Nietzsche, says Ellis, did not think of "freedom" in political terms, but in personal ones: "'For,' says Nietzsche, 'whosoever will be free, must make himself free; freedom is no fairy's gift to fall into any man's lap.'"[37] Ellis cites Nietzsche's appeal for a re-assertion of individuality: "At bottom every man well knows that he can only live one single life in the world, and that never again will so strange a chance shake together into unity such singularly varied elements as he holds: he knows that, but he hides it like a bad conscience."[38] "This was," Ellis comments approvingly, "a sane and demo-

---

[*] *Affirmations* (London, 1898), 44–5n., G. Wilson Knight sees in Clermont, Bussy's brother in *The Revenge of Bussy D'Ambois* (c. 1611), a further attempt of Chapman's to create a super-type: "In Clermont, Chapman attempts to blend Renaissance honour and the Sermon on the Mount to create a superman. As a person he is not wholly convincing and structural artistry suffers, but the discursive action must be accepted for its purpose. The insight is exact: were such a Nietzschean fusion of virtue and virility attained it would indeed radiate the powers poetically attributed to Clermont. The thought is working on the frontiers of human destiny." *The Golden Labyrinth* (London, 1962), 96–7.

cratic individualism," but one which in later years "assumed stranger shapes."[39] Ellis is thus inclined to pass lightly over Nietzsche's third period, in which the conception of master-morality, of primary importance as much to Nietzsche's disciples as to his foes, "attained its chief and most rigid emphasis": "This idea of 'master-morality' is in fact a solid fossilised chunk, easy to handle for friendly or unfriendly hands. The earlier and more living work – the work of the man who truly said that it is with thinkers as with snakes: those that cannot shed their skins die – is less obviously tangible. So the 'master-morality' it is that your true Nietzschian is most likely to close his fist over."[40] This is certainly true of Tille and Common; Ellis's refusal to discuss the superman results partly from his associating it with the idea of "master-morality," and partly from his stated preference for Nietzsche's earlier work.

In the third and last part of his study Ellis offers a personal assessment: "To recognise the free and direct but disconnected nature of Nietzsche's many-sided vision of the world is to lessen the force of his own antagonisms as well as of the antagonisms he has excited."[41] Nietzsche's lack of system is seen as a merit, indeed, as his chief claim to distinction, for he taught us that "a man's philosophy, to be real, must be the inevitable outcome of his own psychic constitution,"[42] not of the desire to construct elaborate and self-consistent pictures of the world. Suffering is the final emancipator of the spirit, and it is in regard to the question of pain that Ellis touches briefly on a theory of Nietzsche's whose workings are so amply illustrated in the work of Yeats – the theory of "self-conquest": "A man's real self, as he repeated so often, consists of the things which he has truly digested and assimilated; he must always 'conquer' his opinions; it is only such conquests which he has the right to report to men as his own. His thoughts are born of his pain; he has imparted to them of his own blood, his own pleasure and torment."[43] Nietzsche's "immoralism" is not the laxity of self-indulgence, but the joy of self-mastery: "Every man must be his own saviour, and it is his own blood that must be shed; there is no salvation by proxy. That was expressed in his favourite motto: *Virescit volnere virtus*."[44] To describe the intensity of Nietzsche's own suffering, Ellis coins for him the phrase "the Pascal of Paganism" and comments: "The freethinker, it is true, was more cheerful and hopeful than the believer, but there is the same tragic sincerity, the same restless self-torment, the same sense of the abyss."[45] Ellis admires Nietzsche's "muscular" and "titanic" style, its robustness, vigour and concentration. As he noted elsewhere, Nietzsche was a master of metaphor: "All vivid thinking must be in images ... the thinkers who survive are the thinkers who wrote well and are most nearly poets."[46] In advance of his time Ellis tries to find, by psychological analysis, "some underlying fundamental image of thought" which will help to explain Nietzsche's ideas as a whole – he finds it, not in a formula, but in an image:

As a child, his sister tells us, he had been greatly impressed by a rope-dancer who had performed his feats over the market-place at Naumburg, and throughout his work, as soon as he had attained to real self-expression, we may trace the image of the dancer. "I do not know," he somewhere says, "what the mind of a philosopher need desire more than to be a good dancer. For dancing is his ideal, his art also, indeed his only piety, his 'divine worship.'" In all Nietzsche's best work we are conscious of this ideal of the dancer, strong, supple, vigorous, yet harmonious and well-balanced. It is the dance of the athlete and the acrobat rather than the make-believe of the ball-room, and behind the easy equipoise of such dancing lie patient training and effort. The chief character of good dancing is its union of the maximum of energetic movement with the maximum of well-balanced grace.[47]

It was a departure from this ideal of dancing that caused Nietzsche's later work to become intemperate, reckless, and desperate; but neither the excesses of this third period, Ellis concludes, nor his eventual breakdown will affect Nietzsche's position as an "aboriginal force," for "he remains in the first rank of the distinguished and significant personalities our century has produced."[48]

Despite a certain breathlessness, characteristic of a man eager to be first with the news, Ellis's study still remains an excellent introduction to Nietzsche, and its historical importance can hardly be exaggerated. Of the second issue of the *Savoy*, one daily paper reported: "The article, perhaps, of most interest at the moment is Mr. Havelock Ellis's, on Nietzsche, who it is prophesied is to make the next philosophical invasion of England."[49] The *Academy*, still brandishing Nietzsche as an anarchist who proclaimed the "divine right of selfhood," thought it was difficult to vindicate for him a place among the first men of the time: "But, at least, Mr. Ellis in his elaborate study, succeeds in bringing before us a living image of the man, with his passionate vivacity and decision of ideas, his proud isolation in the world of thought, his mental imaginativeness."[50] While admitting that Nietzsche's influence – on Ibsen's later plays, on the younger Russian school of novelists, on the novels of D'Annunzio – was "widespread and incalculable," it was hopeless for Ellis to seek the sympathy of the British public for Nietzsche's tragic fate: "It is open to question whether in England one in a hundred know anything about Nietzsche beyond his name and the fact that he has gone out of his mind."[51] The *Athenaeum* granted that Ellis's study was an "able exposition," but felt obliged to dissent from the view that Nietzsche was one of the greatest spiritual forces since Goethe – for one thing, Nietzsche lacked originality. This reviewer noted, with some disgust, Ellis's penchant for psychological probings: "He delights to trace literary qualities to their roots in racial and individual temperaments, sometimes even to an origin in physical morbidities."[52]

As for the Nietzscheans, they were of one accord in their praise. Nietzsche's sister wrote Ellis an appreciative letter saying that his views deserved consideration even where she felt bound to withhold agreement. English and American Nietzscheans, like Common and Huneker, were hailing Ellis's study long after its first appearance as still the best available in English, and Tille acclaimed Ellis as "one of the few Englishmen who really feels the greatness of Nietzsche's intellectual achievements."[53] Tille detects Ellis's confusion of the "Higher Men" in *Zarathustra* with the supermen, and also his omission of any reference to the eternal recurrence doctrine. Not unnaturally he regrets that Ellis did less than full justice to *Beyond Good and Evil* and *The Genealogy of Morals*, taking no notice of Ellis's reasons for ignoring them; he regrets, too, that Ellis did not devote the time required for penetrating the secrets of that "most difficult book," *Zarathustra*. J. B. Barnhill liked Ellis's study sufficiently to print generous excerpts from it in the fifth and sixth numbers of *The Eagle and the Serpent* in November, 1898. One of the most important consequences of Ellis's work was that it seems to have encouraged other English critics to write on Nietzsche with a similar degree of sobriety and restraint – the contributions of J. M. Robertson and Oswald Crawfurd are a case in point;[54] Orage's *Friedrich Nietzsche: The Dionysian Spirit of the Age* (1906) is heavily indebted to Ellis for its general ideas as well as for its specific angle of approach. Even as late as 1958 one critic, surveying English work on Nietzsche produced during the 1890s, could write of Ellis's *Savoy* essay: "Keenly critical, well balanced and based on robust common-sense, it might even be used as the basis for a re-assessment of Nietzsche's philosophy."[55] Perhaps "re-assessment" suggests too grandiose a view of it, but it remains, as Crane Brinton ironically says, "an admirable specimen of the aesthetic touch applied to the Master."[56]

In 1903 Ellis wrote an article for the Paris *Weekly Critical Review* which was prompted by the simultaneous publication of the English version of *The Dawn of Day* and the study of the pathological aspects of Nietzsche by Dr. Möbius; it deals in general terms with the connection between insanity and genius, with the specific intention of vindicating Nietzsche from unjust allegations. Ellis sees clearly the dangers to Nietzsche's standing as a philosopher:

During recent years several of Nietzsche's books have been translated into English, but with an enthusiasm which was, to say the least, injudicious. The English publishers exclusively brought forward the latest, the most extravagant, the most insane portions of his work, and it is not surprising that, except among those extravagant persons to whom extravagance naturally appeals, Nietzsche has until lately found few English readers. Now at length one of the sanest and most truly characteristic of his books has appeared in a translation which, if it fails to render the strength and beauty of the original, is at all events careful and correct, and at last, even in England, Nietzsche is beginning to find appreciators and admirers.[57]

Ellis points out that madness is no more common in men of genius than in the population at large, and when it does occur in men of genius it usually has little connection with their highest creative work. Christopher Smart and Rousseau are exceptions to this rule, as is Nietzsche: "His insanity distorted the equipoise of his fine and subtle intellect, but at the same time he owed to the torturing sting of that malady a poignant sensibility, a penetrating impulse to reach the core of things, and an imaginative atmosphere, which, without it, he could never have reached."[58] The thoughts and images fashioned by Nietzsche, Ellis continues, become more and more "the weapons of his personal warfare," of a heroic struggle against disease: "The progress of the struggle is recorded, most as *pensées* strung together at random, in Nietzsche's works. These *pensées* are not of equal value, they are frequently conflicting, sometimes obscure, even outrageous. There are many pearls here, as Dr. Moebius truly remarks, but they are not all pearls. It may be added that as we gaze at them we realise how the beautiful things in the world may sometimes grow around a point of disease."[59]

In 1915 a second edition of *Affirmations* was called for. In a short preface to this edition Ellis states that he has left the book unchanged: if he were to expand it he would concentrate on the chapters on Casanova and Nietzsche. He acknowledges that, owing to the championship of Prussian militarists, Nietzsche's reputation has "now entered a phase, certainly a passing phase, which could scarcely be ignored if I were now publishing this book for the first time." He protests that Nietzsche never shared the German worship of power and war: "The idea of Power and the idea of War both entered into the work – the later work, it is important to remember – of Nietzsche. But in his hands they became spiritualised and transformed. Power was no longer the force of success in this world, and War was no longer a method of overcoming mere human enemies, but both alike belonged to the sphere of the evolving soul. This ought to have been obvious to every reader." To Ellis – as to Shaw, Yeats and Orage after him – this was obvious; but to Carpenter, Wilfred Scawen Blunt, Thomas Hardy, and William Archer,[60] to name only four, it was far from obvious. Ellis did not see fit to alter his earlier study in the light of new political exigencies, since he had written "not of the Nietzsche of the moment but of the essential and significant Nietzsche."

Ellis's final contribution to Nietzschean studies was an article in Hastings' *Encyclopaedia of Religion and Ethics* (1917), written at editorial invitation. The article (and the bibliography appended to it) amply reveals its author's qualifications for the task. Not only has Ellis kept up with the course of Nietzsche scholarship, but he writes with a sense of easy command and firm authority. Well-informed, persuasive, and undogmatic, the article is also, considering the limitations of space, a marvel of lucid compression. In the *Savoy* articles it was disturbingly obvious that he had little to say about *Zarathustra*, or about the theories of the eternal recurrence or the superman. Now he rectifies these omissions:

It is easy to understand the position which *Zarathustra* has attained; it has a certain kind of unity since it is written around a single figure and throughout in the lofty rhythmic style which we commonly regard as Biblical; it is moreover, all are agreed, magnificently writen; it contains pictures and passages of a highly impressive character. Many, however, will agree with so competent a critic as Brandes that it has been over-rated, being too monotonous and lacking in imaginative invention. When we read it carefully, we are made to feel that its imposing surface frequently covers no great depth of thought or truth of insight; it sometimes seems simply a marvellous *tour de force*.[61]

Ellis entertains reservations concerning Nietzsche's "favourite and persistent conceptions" which seem to him to lack fruitfulness, originality, and precision. One of these conceptions is that of the eternal recurrence:

It came to him in 1881, when he was planning *Zarathustra*, and he regarded it as the fundamental underlying doctrine of that work, "the highest formula of affirmation that can possibly be achieved." It seems to have been a revivification of the old Pythagorean idea, stimulated by reading Helmholtz, Riemann, and the earlier writings of Wundt. It can scarcely be said, however, that Nietzsche made any fruitful use of this ancient and outworn formula, however suggestive he may personally have found it; it is, indeed, an idea which, it has been said, seems to place man in the position of a squirrel in a cage, endlessly turning round himself.[62]

The idea of the superman, "Nietzsche's perfected human being," also belonged to the declining years of Nietzsche's life; no precise philosophic or scientific significance can be attached to it, Ellis declares, "however vaguely suggestive in the mouth of the artist and the poet." But Ellis was more in sympathy with Nietzsche's conception than this captious dismissal would suggest. As far as the formula of the eternal recurrence was concerned, Ellis had approached something quite close to it in his introduction to *The New Spirit*: "We marvel at the prodigality of nature, but how marvellous, too, the economy! The old cycles are for ever renewed, and it is no paradox that he who would advance can never cling too close to the past. The thing that has been is the thing that will be again."[63] His attitude to the superman must be looked into more closely.

3 Nietzsche's doctrine of the superman was first brought to public notice by the publication, in the same year (1903), of Shaw's *Man and Superman* and Wells's *Mankind in the Making*. Both writers, it was felt, called for a superman, but Wells's ideas appealed more to English practical sense: "In the one the call remains as a pious aspiration and mere summary of revolt and weariness; in the other there is an attempt to ransack the springs of action, to drive down into fundamentals, to examine how, if at all, it is possible by breeding, by education, by social reconstruction, that the Superman may be attained."[64] Ellis, as a socialist, shared this desire for sweeping social change and reconstruction based on a sound application of evolutionary theory, and found it "a genuine satisfaction to find this question brought into the market-place so vigorously, so sanely, so intelligently."[65] He quotes this as Wells's creed: "We are here to get better births and a better result from the births we get; each one of us is going to set himself immediately to that, using whatever power he finds to his hand."[66] Though not wishing to minimize their prophetic stature or the value of their services to human betterment, Ellis cannot accept the confidence of Wells and Shaw that man will necessarily rise to superhumanity – though an inspiring belief, it is neither self-evident nor supportable by evolutionary argument:

Evolution never proceeds far in a straight line, and while it is undoubtedly true that intelligence is a factor in evolution, it is by no means true that a very high degree of intelligence is specially likely to lead to the evolution of its possessor, it may even hinder it. Many species of ants are highly intelligent and "civilised" – in some respects more so than various human peoples – yet we do not hear of the "super-ant," nor is it likely that we shall. As regards man it might be plausibly maintained that the typical Man reached his fullest and finest all-round development, as the highest zoological species, in the Stone Age some ten thousand years ago, that the Superman really began to arise with the discovery of writing, the growth of tradition and the multiplication of inventions some six or eight thousand years ago, and that we have now reached, not the beginning of the Superman but the beginning of the end of him.*

Man's march is not continually upward – history is a "constant oscillation," and every nation and civilization has a decline and fall, "breaking like a wave on the sands of time."[67] Only when the world is at an end, Ellis seems to be implying, will the peaks of man's achievement be clearly seen.

His second objection to the superman idea is that it lacks substance and reality. Using Nietzsche's and Vaihinger's "fictionalism," he was able to expose the dangers of hypostatization: "When we talk of, for instance, a 'life-force' and its *élan*, or whatever other dainty term we like to apply to it, we are not only summarily mingling together many separate phenomena, but we are running the risk that our conception may be taken for something that really exists."[68] In *Man and Superman*, Shaw had developed certain utterances in *Zarathustra* in order "to analyze the fascination of women as an illusion of which the reality is the future mother's search of a husband for her child."[69] But in his prophecy concerning the superman there is still a vestige of idealistic illusion:

Mr. Shaw has flung away many illusions but only in order to entrench himself more firmly on one remaining illusion, the "Superman." It is a vision that, from the time of Isaiah and earlier, has always floated before the prophet's eyes and has always proved irresistibly attractive to him: the supreme future man, the Messiah who will build up a new Earth, and whose path it is our business to make straight. ... Mr. Shaw will have it that love – and *a fortiori* the virtues ascribed to human institutions – are illusions, while the "Superman" is a piece of solid reality. When the doctrine is so stated, it is necessary to point out that this verity will not resist critical analysis any better than the others, and that it is by no means difficult to flay the "Superman" even before he is born. It is enough to say in passing that, granting to Mr. Shaw that "our only hope is in evolution," the line of evolution has never been straight; in the natural course of things the

---

* *Views and Reviews, First Series: 1884–1919* (London, 1932), 209. The social and ethical superiority of ants to men seems to have been a stock idea of the time. It had been noted by Sir John Lubbock and Herbert Spencer, and by Lafcadio Hearn just after the turn of the century. Hearn, although he had "not the slightest sympathy with most of his ideas," used Nietzsche's term "Beyond Man" to speculate on the, to him, desirable possibility of mankind reaching a moral condition on a par with that of the ants. See "Beyond Man," *Books and Habits* (London, 1922), 134–44. In his introduction to this book, Hearn's editor comments: "Civilization in some later cycle may wonder at our ambition to abandon individual liberty and responsibility and to subside into the social instincts of the ant; and even as it wonders, that far-off civilization may detect in itself ant-like reactions which we cultivated for it." xiii.

successor of man would spring from a form lower than man; but as we have checked the lower forms of life at every point, we have effectually killed the "Superman."[70]

Ellis's strong ties with the Fellowship of the New Life are much in evidence here; yet his objections are hypothetical rather than real, and his arguments so weak that he himself probably remained unconvinced by them. To call ants "intelligent" and "civilised" is a crude begging of the question – no ant can rise to "super-ant" because, unlike man, it lacks actual or potential control of its own evolution. Moreover, to say that we have reached the beginning of the end of the superman is effectively to short-circuit any attempt, whether political or eugenic, to secure some improvement in the human condition – no man was more aware than Ellis of the value of ideals to energize human resources for some great task. Again, the "natural course" of evolution is no longer a relevant term of reference now that man can manipulate evolution artificially; as is clear from the *Savoy* articles, Ellis knew that Nietzsche proposed to substitute, for "the lower forms of life" out of which man's successor might spring, man's own passions and "wickedness," just as Synge suggested that poetry would never become real again until it had learnt to be brutal. As for Shaw's superman, Ellis was entitled (and probably right) to deplore its inhuman contempt of "love"; but while Ellis sees fit to regard love as at once "illusion" and "a solid piece of reality," he gives no reason why the superman should not be regarded in exactly the same way.

In his *Savoy* articles in 1898 Ellis had paid little attention to the superman doctrine, and even confused the superman with the "Higher Men" who gather together, at the end of *Zarathustra*, in the prophet's cave. Nietzsche's ideal man, he says, is a blend of the Stoic ideal – "the laconic, brave, self-contained man, not lusting after expression like the modern idealist" – and that of Epicurus, "the discoverer of the heroically idyllic method of living a philosophy,"[71] a spiritual nomad whose happiness was unending self-discipline. Among Nietzsche's heroes, Ellis notes, can be counted Brutus, Socrates, Goethe, Napoleon, Alcibiades, and Caesar. By 1917, when he referred to the superman as "Nietzsche's perfected human being," Ellis had realized that it was this conception above all which was associated in the popular mind with Nietzsche's name, and he felt called upon to give some account of its genesis and value:

He used the word *Übermensch* first at the age of seventeen, applying it to Byron's heroes, and later to Shakespeare's; as a more abstracted conception, it is probably due, as Brandes has suggested, to Renan. ... When Nietzsche began to use the term seriously, it was rarely or never biologically, as denoting a higher species developed in the Darwinian way, for he regarded Darwinism as an unproved hypothesis, though he accepted evolution and esteemed Darwin. He was acquainted with Galton's work, and it is possible to use many of his sayings concerning the Superman in the eugenic sense, but it is difficult to say how far he so intended them and impossible to regard him as a pioneer of eugenics. More and more, as he spoke of Supermen and declared that "the goal of mankind is in its great Exemplars," he simply had in mind men of genius of the type of Caesar, Napoleon, and Goethe.[72]

Whatever Nietzsche's debt to Darwin, he certainly never professed esteem for him;[73] it is true that he was acquainted with Galton, having read Galton's *Hereditary Genius* (1869) in the last years of his life: a copy of Galton's *Inquiries into Human Faculty and its Development* (1883) was found in his library after his death. Galton, of course, was the founder of Eugenic Science. One of the chief obstacles to the improvement of the human race, he argued in an essay reminiscent of Nietzsche's master- and slave-morality distinction, was "the hereditary taint due to the primeval barbarism of our race," the prevalence of a servile gregariousness now become instinctive:

A really intelligent nation might be held together by far stronger forces than are derived from the purely gregarious instincts. It would not be a mob of slaves, clinging together, incapable of self-government, and begging to be led; but it would consist of vigorous, self-reliant men, knit to one another by innumerable attractions, into a strong, tense, and elastic organization. Our present natural dispositions make it simply impossible for us to attain this ideal standard, and therefore the slavishness of the mass of men, in morals and intellect, must be an admitted fact in all schemes of regenerative policy.[74]

Ellis was very much a disciple of Galton, and he followed up Galton's investigation of great men with his own exhaustive analysis of eminent British men and women from the sixteenth to the end of the nineteenth century in *A Study of British Genius* (1904). Ellis was a strong, if cautious, partisan of eugenics; unlike many of the early adherents of the new science, he never lost sight of the difficulty in reconciling the claims of the race with those of the individual. In the first decade of the century the new science was greeted with enthusiasm: here, at last, was knowledge to change the world, knowledge which made man, for the first time in his history, master of his own fate. As Ellis wrote in 1911: "Galton, during the last years of his life, believed that we are approaching a time when eugenic considerations will become a factor of religion, and when our existing religious considerations will be re-interpreted in the light of a sense of social needs so enlarged as to include the needs of the race which is to come."⁷⁵ Ellis thought that Nietzsche could not be regarded as a pioneer of eugenics. This is puzzling, as in *Affirmations* Ellis had been struck by Nietzsche's observation that science, with its need for sincerity, patience and self-abnegation, demands, even more than poetry does, great nobility in those who practise it. Once we have learnt to trust science, Ellis quotes Nietzsche as saying, it will be possible to teach natural history so that "every one who hears it is inspired to health and gladness as the heir and continuer of humanity."⁷⁶ Nor did Nietzsche lack idealism: "Nietzsche was himself of the stuff of which great religious teachers are made, of the race of apostles,"⁷⁷ but he was also a "realist" confronting the essential facts of life, and regarding man as the *ens realissimum*.

Working on the basis of an identical interpretation of Nietzsche, the Nietzscheans insisted on Nietzsche's connection with eugenics. Levy went so far as to say that "one day it will be known that the greatest and truest advocate of Eugenics was not Sir Francis Galton, but Friedrich Nietzsche";⁷⁸ Wrench thought that man had one saviour – himself: "What of devolution? some one may ask. Well, devolution is a long way off. We are on the upward wave of evolution. We can leave devolution to the wisdom of superman."⁷⁹ If Galton discovered Eugenic Science, wrote Maximilian Muegge, Nietzsche, to his lasting merit, discovered that science's most valuable ally – Eugenic Religion. Eugenic Religion will supply an ideal – the superman – which will appeal to the unknown depths of man's mind and make him a willing participant in biological legislation and experiment: "*The* great thing is the creation of a popular sentiment, a right public opinion. And if this is to become a *permanent* sentiment, if it is to create a *feeling* of responsibility towards the race, a religious atmosphere is needed to preserve that sentiment. The ideal of the Superman will supply this."⁸⁰ Admitting the difficulty of precise definition, Muegge rounds up the scattered suggestions in Nietzsche's work concerning this ideal:

The Superman is a hero and genius, uniting in himself all the partial excellences of former heroes, combining in himself all the scattered units of that archetype that has ever been vaguely discerned in the different objects of man's hero-worship. He is the accumulated, condensed virtue of all ages and nations: an eclectic essence of the boundless love and charity of the Buddhist – pure in body and brave in self-conquest; of the strict sternness and endurance of the Spartan – sound in body and steady in character; of the ethereal aestheticism and loftiness of the Athenian – able in body and acute in intellect; of the rigid rule and citizenship of the Roman – robust in body and regal in will; of the true loyalty and independence of our Teutonic ancestors – grand in body and tender in heart!⁸¹

As another Nietzschean, Georges Chatterton-Hill, put it, the superman finds in the pure creation of his genius a sufficient stimulus to life and a sufficient justification for it – his aim is not Stirnerite individualism, but a religious supra-individualism:

> It is a "religion beyond and above the religions," true; but the ideal of the Super-Man, the worship of beauty, of strength, of courage, of loyalty, of chivalry, all of which were incarnated in this supreme ideal – all this constitutes a religion. Nietzsche placed before us an ideal of transcendent beauty – for Nietzsche is all artist, and everything which Nietzsche wrote was profoundly artistic – and this ideal of beauty was a religion, a religion requiring the sacrifice of the individual in the interests of the race, and having the welfare of the race as an aim.*

Even as late as 1916 the *Eugenics Review* (which published Muegge's article in 1909, its foundation year) carried a contribution entitled "Eugenics and the Doctrine of the Superman,"[82] showing that discussion of Nietzsche in these circles was still common. When the *New Age* took up the question of eugenics and threw it out for debate, Ellis took it upon himself to rebuke Eden Phillpotts, an ardent Nietzschean, for proposing eugenic measures as if they were still a Utopian dream, not realizable for many years.[83]

The reason why Ellis could accept eugenic ideals and still reject the superman was that it erred too far on the side of individualism, just as he thought Stirner's brand of anarchy did. Of Nietzsche's development he writes: "He began by regarding democracy as the standard of righteousness, and ended by asserting that the world only exists for the production of a few great men. It would be foolish to regard either of the termini as the last outpost of wisdom."[84] Ellis notes that Nietzsche was not enamoured of socialism or democracy, and "reasonably enough" would not even admit that democracy had been attained: whatever value Nietzsche ascribed to democracy lay "in its guarantee of individual freedom."[85] Sometimes democracy, as a political and socio-ethical "structure," finds itself in conflict with the aesthetic and spiritual individualism which forms its "function":

> The supreme great men of the race were termed by Carlyle its "heroes," by Emerson its "representative men," but, equally by the less and by the more

---

* *Heredity and Selection in Sociology* (London, 1907), 514–15. For further comment concerning the superman, see the same writer's *The Philosophy of Nietzsche* (London, 1912). Written in 1905, this book follows the "aesthetic" approach of Ellis, Symons, and the French scholar whose work on Nietzsche Ellis so much admired, Henri Lichtenberger.

democratic term, they are always individuals standing apart from society, often in violent opposition to it, though they have always conquered in the end. When any great person has stood alone against the world it has always been the world that lost. The strongest man, as Ibsen argued in his *Enemy of the People*, is the man who stands most alone. "He will be the greatest," says Nietzsche in *Beyond Good and Evil*, "who can be the most solitary, the most concealed, the most divergent."[86]

Increasing degrees of social organization tend to discourage the production of "great and vitally organized persons," and to expose society to destruction at their hands. Individualism and the eugenic guardianship of the race are not a way of arresting social reform, nor of denying the gospel of sympathy: "Nietzsche, indeed, has made a famous assault on sympathy, as he has on conventional morality generally, but his "immoralism" in general and his "hardness" in particular are but new and finer manifestations of those faded virtues he was really seeking to revive."[87] "The secular arm of law or the ecclesiastical arm of theology" are powerless to support morality:

If morality cannot by its own proper virtue hold its opposing immorality in check then there is something wrong with that morality. It runs the risk of encountering a fresh and more vigorous movement of morality. Men begin to think that, if not the whole truth, there is yet a real element of truth in the assertion of Nietzsche: "We believe that severity, violence, slavery, danger in the street and in the heart, secrecy, stoicism, tempter's art and devilry of every kind, everything wicked, tyrannical, predatory and serpentine in man, serves as well for the elevation of the human species as its opposite."[88]

Ellis lists the eugenic measures necessary to realize the dream of poets and prophets concerning "the divine possibilities of Man": "Not until such measures as these, under the controlling influence of a sense of personal responsibility extending to every member of the community, have long been put into practice, can we hope to see man on the earth risen to his full stature, healthy in body, noble in spirit, beautiful in both alike, moving spaciously and harmoniously among his fellows in the great world of Nature, to which he is so subtly adapted because he has himself sprung out of it and is its most exquisite flower."[89] The tone of this echoes the voice of Zarathustra whenever, with baited breath, he speaks of the superman who is to come. It was a vision which haunted Ellis, too. In 1923 he quotes Nietzsche's observation on Leonardo da Vinci: "There is something super-European and silent in him, the characteristic of one who has seen too wide a circle of things good and evil."[90] As a gloss on this Ellis remarks: "When indeed our imagination plays with the idea of a future Over-man, it is Leonardo who comes before us as his forerunner."[91] And eleven years later, in a review of Ortega y Gasset's *The Revolt of the Masses*, he observes that Nietzsche's "potent influence" played a subtle part in corroding the old democratic ideal, although Nietzsche had suggested no definite alternative: "He had a way of probing into things, and somehow, after he had probed, the things never looked quite the same as they had looked before. And then his Over-Man, however fantastic a figure, seemed to make ridiculous any attempt to kow-tow to the mass-man."[92] The superman, Ellis acknowledged, was historically an important idea; although himself in active and even fervent sympathy with what the superman was held to represent and promise, Ellis, with his detestation of everything exaggerated and extreme, could not bring himself to march publicly under the superman banner.

4 If Ellis could not bring himself to accept the "formula" of the superman, he did not let his rejection of it interfere with what he took to be the main points of Nietzsche's originality – his personality, his directness and sincerity, and "his acutely sensitive receptivity to the influences of his time, and his intense energy in reacting to them vitally."[93] He understood how much the superman mattered to Nietzsche: "In the discipline and the joy of a great adventure the philosopher's true reward lies. What he brings home may seem to the public in general – and his fellow-philosophers in particular – only an empty or questionable formula. To the philosopher himself it must always be more than that. It is the symbols of his spiritual adventure. The aspirations, the struggles, the failures, the sudden ecstasies at a new turn in the road – all the things that have depressed and exalted his life are here recalled."[94]

The writers discussed in *The New Spirit* had been selected because their individuality had conferred on them "a typical value," because they had expressed the most intimate feelings of their unique spiritual adventures: "But, in the back of my mind, I was also aware that I had selected special aspects of these selected men, so that it was my own most intimate feelings that I was really setting forth."[95] This was also the avenue of approach to Nietzsche, who self-confessedly had made use of the same technique in his early essays on Wagner and Schopenhauer, talking about himself under cover of their names. Perhaps some writers, such as Yeats, have undergone Nietzschean influence at a greater degree of intensity, but Ellis seems to have found support in Nietzsche for the widest range of intellectual interests, perhaps because his own interests were so unusually multifarious. We meet with Nietzschean allusions and formulations in every field of Ellis's work, from revolutionary views concerning the treatment of criminals to the view of philosophy as disguised autobiography, from the thesis that art is sublimation of suppressed sexual energy to the idea that dreams are not, as Freud believed, the product of wish-fulfilment, but a compensation device for what the waking life denies – a sort of unconscious search for the Yeatsian anti-self.* Ellis's mind was a clearing-house for a wealth of ideas – some of them of startling novelty in their time – which have their source, or at least unmistakable analogues, in the work of Nietzsche. Only three main tributaries can be traced here, each of them forming an eventual part of the mainstream of pre-war literary and aesthetic thinking. These are: the concept of life as an aesthetic phenomenon, the definition of "decadence," and the emphasis on the dance as an image of wholeness. Most of these ideas were derived, at least in part, from Nietzsche's early work which, we recall, Ellis particularly admired: of this work the most seminal influence was *The Birth of Tragedy*.

In F. A. Lange's "epoch-making" *History of Materialism* (1866), Ellis first came across the view, later to be developed by Nietzsche and those who followed in his footsteps, Jules de Gaultier, Hans Vaihinger, Benedetto Croce, that not only art but every creative activity of man – science, philosophy and even mathematics – had an aesthetic motive. As a corollary of this view, Nietzsche's conviction that "only as an aesthetic spectacle can the world be justified" was eagerly accepted by Ellis as an escape from the spiritual aridity and moral confusion of his time. Art was the supreme healer and joy-bringer, and aesthetic values stood paramount. Faced with any moral problem, Nietzsche instinctively sets himself at the standpoint of art, Ellis declares, quoting the lines from Zarathustra about all life being a dispute about taste and tasting: "This gospel of taste is not easy gospel. A man must make himself a work of art, Nietzsche again and again declares, moulded into beauty by suffering, for such art is the highest morality, the morality of the creator."[96] As we shall see in a later chapter, Nietzsche was harshly critical of the proponents of "art for art's sake"; but his view of art, though not granting it full autonomy, appealed to a generation of writers trying to free themselves from the shackles of Victorian moralism. Many writers must have been heartened to read in *Affirmations*:

If we turn to literature, Nietzsche maintains, it is a vast mistake to suppose that, for instance, great tragedies have, or were intended to have, any moral effect. Look at *Macbeth*, at *Tristan und Isolde*, at *Oedipus*. In all these cases it would have been easy to make guilt the pivot of the drama. But the great poet is in love

---

* Cf. Yeats's theories concerning the "anti-self" with what Ellis has to say about Jules de Gaultier's "Bovaryism" in *Views and Reviews, First Series*, 179–86.

with passion. "He calls to us: It is the charm of charms, this exciting, changing, dangerous, gloomy, yet often sun-filled existence! It is an *adventure* to live – take this side or that, it will always be the same!"[97]

This is the constant refrain of Yeats's early essays, and of the critical work of Arthur Symons.

Ellis first defines decadence as a discordant anarchy of atoms in an 1889 review of the work of Paul Bourget. He quotes Bourget's formulation (which probably influenced Nietzsche's): "A style of decadence is one in which the unity of the book is decomposed to give place to the independence of the page, in which the page is decomposed to give place to the independence of the phrase, and the phrase to give place to the independence of the word."[98] In *Affirmations* (in the essay on Huysmans) Ellis distinguishes between the classic and decadent styles: "The first is beautiful because the parts are subordinated to the whole; the second is beautiful because the whole is subordinated to the parts."[99] "All art," says Ellis, "is the rising and falling of the slopes of a rhythmic curve between these two classic and decadent extremes."[100] He emphasizes that decadence is an aesthetic not a moral conception; if our finest admiration is reserved for the classic, that admiration has little worth unless founded on a capacity to appreciate the decadent: "Each has its virtues, each is equally right and necessary."[101] The moralist is naturally suspicious of any sign of "corruption" or decadence: "But as Nietzsche, with his usual acuteness in cutting at the root of vulgar prejudice, has well remarked (in *Die Froehliche Wissenschaft*), even as regards what is called the period of "corruption" in the evolution of societies, we are apt to overlook the fact that the energy which in more primitive times marked the operations of the community as a whole has now simply been transferred to the individuals themselves, and this aggrandisement of the individual really produces an even greater amount of energy."[102] Or, as Nietzsche put it, "culture is indebted most of all to politically weakened periods."[103]

However courageously Ellis supported the distinctive virtues of decadence in literature, his natural bent was to regard art as "a many-sided and active delight in the wholeness of things";[104] he ultimately abandoned an untenable critical dualism in accordance with one of his earliest notes: "The world is full of apparent contradictions, and every highest truth is the union of opposites."[105] Just as Nietzsche contrived to unite what he termed the Apollonian and Dionysian impulses in a synthesis which comprehended them both, so Ellis – fully aware that Nietzsche had dismissed the romantic as ambiguous – tried to bring classic and decadent art together under the rubric of dancing: "Nietzsche regarded the passion for finding antinomies and antitheses as a metaphysical superstition, due to a lack of insight. He ... regards the notion of contradiction as one to be eradicated. He is absolutely sceptical of all antitheses. 'My desire,' he declared, 'is to show the absolute homogeneity of all phenomena,' the differentiations being merely matters of perspective."[106] The image of the dance expresses not only the "classico-mathematical Renaissance" Ellis believed his generation was witnessing, but the universe as a whole – it was no historical accident that Einstein was immediately preceded by the Russian Ballet: "The dance is the rule of number and of rhythm and of measure and of order, of the controlling fluence of form, of the subordination of the parts to the whole. That is what the dance is. And these same properties also make up the classic spirit, not only in life, but, still more clearly and definitely in the Universe itself."[107] Marcus Aurelius and Blake ("I doubt not yet to make a figure in the great Dance of Life that shall amuse the spectators in the sky") were not alone in sharing this belief:

In a later time Nietzsche, from first to last, showed himself possessed by the conception of the art of life as a dance, in which the dancer achieves the rhythmic freedom and harmony of his soul beneath the shadow of a hundred Damoclean swords. He said the same thing of his style, for to him the style and the man were one. "My style," he wrote to his intimate friend Rohde, "is a dance." "Every day I count wasted," he said again, "in which there has been no dancing." The dance lies at the beginning of art, and we find it also at the end. The first creators of civilisation were making the dance, and the philosopher of a later age, hovering over the dark abyss of insanity, with bleeding feet and muscles strained to the breaking point, still seems to himself to be weaving the maze of the dance.[108]

In *The Dance of Life* (1923) Ellis presents thinking, writing, religion, and morals as modes of dancing; for Ellis the dance was an image of the identity of body and soul, life and art, being and becoming, an image all the more powerful because it possessed none of the abstractness of an ideological formula. In the fifteenth phase of *A Vision*, Yeats uses the figure of a dancer to represent Unity of Being, and the dancer and the dance are recurrent images in his verse. The dance came to be symbolic of the perfect non-discursive work of art which, as an amoral artefact, should not "mean" but "be." It might be rewarding for someone to trace Yeats's dramaturgy in relation to this philosophy of the dance, and to such lines as these in *The Birth of Tragedy*: "The essence of nature is now to be expressed symbolically; a new world of symbols is required; for once the entire symbolism of the body, not only the symbolism of the lips, face, and speech, but the whole pantomime of dancing which sets all the members into rhythmical motion."*

Unquestionably *The Dance of Life* represents the high water mark of Nietzschean influence on Ellis's work. So deeply has Ellis integrated the ideas of the German that one senses little palpable sign of indebtedness – it is as if Ellis and Nietzsche were working in collaboration. Nevertheless, Ellis's *Savoy* articles remain his lasting contribution to the Nietzsche movement. His sane and appreciative presentation of the general development of Nietzsche's ideas appealed to the responsive readership of the *Savoy* by complementing these translations of 1896, and providing an aesthetic counterbalance to the fiercely moral and authoritarian tone of Tille's introductions. Ellis's articles, by appearing initially in serial form, were able to generate a feeling of keen interest and expectancy, and the later reprintings (in 1898, 1915, and 1936) bear witness to their durable quality. Ellis's refusal to stand judgment on Nietzsche was a principle which now seems amply justified, and his forbearance was imitated by others. Perhaps the most striking example is that of Vernon Lee, that most formidable of blue-stockings, who – after attacking Nietzsche's unhealthiness in ridiculing the virtues of duty, humility, and compassion – was eventually won round to the belief that his insights might be fruitful – like those of other one-sided philosophers – though his basic position might be unacceptable:

We are beginning to recognize that certain among the philosophic writers who have most influenced us, say Schopenhauer, Carlyle, Emerson, Tolstoi, are not so much thinkers as poets – *lyrists* as my friend Halévy has called one of the greatest of them, Nietzsche – men who have applied passionate temperamental onesidedness to expressing the various modes of spiritual being requisite (all of them) for our complete and balanced emotional and imaginative life.[109]

Ellis could not have wished for a more spectacular conversion than this.

---

* *CW*, I, 32. The famed American dancer, Isadora Duncan, probably had such passages in mind when she referred to *The Birth of Tragedy* as her Bible, and to Nietzsche, together with Rousseau and Whitman, as her only dance masters. Her autobiography is headed by a quotation from *Zarathustra*, a work which, she says, "ravished my being": "If my virtue be a dancer's virtue, and if I have often sprung with both feet into golden-emerald rapture, and if it be my Alpha and Omega that everything heavy shall become light, every body a dancer and every spirit a bird; verily, that is my Alpha and Omega." *My Life* (New York, 1942); cf. pp. 80, 141, 151, 301, 323.

NIETZSCHE AND THE LITERARY MIND

1 It should now be clear that Nietzsche's impact was most strongly felt, not in academic circles, but in artistic ones. Oscar Levy conceded the superfluousness of recommending Nietzsche to artists:

For artists were the first to welcome Nietzsche and have even honoured him with the flattering name of "our philosopher," while, on the other hand, it may safely be predicted that scholars, schoolmasters, and clergymen will be the last to do homage to him – and that for the simple reason that the latter have an easy and the former a difficult life to live. It will be seen that by "artist" here is meant a man who, in whatever direction, has to break new ground, has to create new values, to destroy old errors, and to pay the bill for such daring.[1]

Davidson, certainly, would gladly have answered to this description of the artist as "transvaluer of values," as would Ellis and the writers associated with the *Yellow Book* and the *Savoy*. Symons granted *Savoy* contributors a maximum of artistic licence, and it was thoroughly appropriate that Ellis's articles, by appearing in an *avant-garde* paper, should have excited the enthusiasm of forward-looking young men who, being young, as Yeats said, "delighted in enemies and in everything that had an heroic air."[2] In defending the *Savoy* against its detractors, Yeats argued that literature now demanded the same right to explore everything which passed before the mind's eye as science had to explore everything that passed before its "corporeal" eye: "The critic might well reply that certain of my generation delighted in writing with an unscientific partiality for subjects long forbidden. Yet is it not most important to explore especially what has been long forbidden, and to do this not only 'with the highest moral purpose,' like the followers of Ibsen, but gaily, out of sheer mischief, or sheer delight in that play of the mind?"[3] Yeats desired to recover the "Vision of Evil," but Nietzsche's immoralism, Ellis cautioned, "was far indeed from any rehabilitation of easy vice; it was the justification of neglected and unsanctified virtues."⁴ Nietzsche had never failed to point out that a large sector of life and art falls outside moral jurisdiction: "In an age in which many moralists desire to force morals into every part of life and art – and even assume a certain air of virtue in so doing – the "immoralist" who lawfully vindicates any region for free cultivation is engaged in a proper and wholesome task."⁵ If artists wanted a *carte blanche* for freedom of self-expression, they could have found it in Ellis's Nietzsche essay. Many of them did.

In his introduction to a later edition of *Zarathustra*, Ernest Rhys, a colleague of Ellis's in the Fellowship of the New Life and also Ellis's editor-in-chief in many publishing ventures of the 1890s, took a retrospective look at those years:

Years ago, long years before the war, I remember discussing with Dr. Oscar Levy the doctrine of the *Übermensch* when there was a question of adding *Thus Spake Zarathustra* to the Camelot series, and he urged the book's importance as herald of a new time. For copyright reasons the Camelot volume did not come about; but at that time – in the disruptive nineties – Nietzsche took his place with Wagner, Ibsen, Whitman, William Morris, and Tolstoi as among the rousing revolutionary influences. We did not necessarily accept his ideas, but we felt their powerfully stimulating challenging effect.⁶

The group Rhys is talking about was that which centred on the Rhymers' Club (disbanded in 1894), the *Yellow Book*, and the *Savoy*. Prominent in this group was Aubrey Beardsley, who wrote to the publisher of the *Savoy*, Leonard Smithers, in the autumn of 1896: "Would you be so very kind as to get me everything Henry & Co. have published of Nietzsche – send it here & earn the thanks of Your AB."⁷ The volumes were in his possession the following morning, and, as he reported to John Gray, they were helping to make him feel "quite gay."⁸ Members of the Rhymers who were sooner or later to take an interest in Nietzsche were Rhys himself, John Davidson, Symons, Yeats, and T. W. Rolleston, who participated with Yeats in the Irish movement and who had the advantage of knowing German. Listed as "permanent guests" of the club were John Gray, the Catholic poet-priest who translated Nietzsche's poetry for the 1899 volume and Edward Garnett, who claimed credit for persuading Fisher Unwin to take over the translations when the firm publishing them was forced out of business. The estimate Garnett made of Nietzsche in 1899 is an enthusiastic one, endorsing what Ellis had written three years previously: "To wage war on Sentimentalism, Pity, Christianity, Decadence in all forms, and Feminism, that is the road by which Nietzsche sought to get free of modern tendencies, and set up a new standard of values for the race. ... Poet, philosopher, classicist, scientific critic all in one, Nietzsche undoubtedly was the deepest, though most biassed, psychologist of human institutions that our century has seen."[9]

But, even with artists, Nietzsche was not merely the subject of passive admiration: it induced in those who read him a degree of self-questioning of sometimes painful intensity. Charles Ricketts, stage-designer for Yeats's plays, wrote in his diary on August 27, 1900:

Death of Nietzsche. Years ago when I first read him I was half-frightened to find in print so many things which I felt personally, and to hear them from a mouth I loved so little. ... His end is even more tragic than Heine's – what a temptation for the righteous to rejoice! Where I resemble him is in my estimate of the religious instinct, women, and the crowd, admiration of the Renaissance, belief in the sacredness of laughter: laughter that saves, laughter that kills.[10]

This mingled attitude of resentment and gratitude is well caught in John Payne's poem "Friedrich Nietzsche," the only verse tribute produced by the period:

Nietzsche, I love thee not; thine every page
With insults to my Gods my teeth doth set
On edge and flouts my fondest faiths: and yet,
For all thy querulous quips, thy crackbrain rage
'Gainst many a well-graced actor on Life's stage,
For this at least I own me in thy debt,
That 'gainst Democracy's soul-straightening net
And dragon's maw thou hast armed the maudlin age.
– Ay, and to me thy thought-awakening word
Is as the angel's coming, erst that stirred
Siloam's sluggish tide and brought to life
Its hidden healing virtues. Good or ill,
My soul it floods with fertilising strife
And makes me know myself and what I will.[11]

Payne knew German, and he confessed to having Nietzsche's "seventeen volumes, in German, of course, always at my elbow."[12] Edward Thomas, too, seems to have read Nietzsche avidly, though again with mixed feelings: "Isn't Nietzsche magnificent? & so necessary these days? Yet he damns me to deeper perdition than I had yet bestowed myself." Thomas thought *The Genealogy of Morals* a very great book: "But I kick at his too completely aristocratic view."[13] In his account of the 1909 translations, Thomas asked his readers to take a "dilettante's joy" in Nietzsche: "Perhaps it will make our claim that he is not dangerous more convincing if we point out that he is a poet and prove it by a few delectable quotations. For we in England have special knowledge of the harmlessness of poets. ... Only a poet could have combined in a living unity his profound knowledge of philosophy, history, philology, the arts and life."[14] Thomas perceives that Nietzsche despises "the luxurious 'friend of art,' i.e. the friend of delicate things in an ivory tower," for Nietzsche's vision is heroic: "It is curious to note how this exquisitely sensitive poet and man of culture, greatly desiring beauty, nobility, freshness, and "heady virtues," turns to those who are not "tame house animals, like our cultured people of to-day," and how he sees something after his own heart in the great histories of the Old Testament, where men thought in actions and there is none of the muddy atmosphere that disgusted him in modernity."[15] Noting Nietzsche's description of artistic creation as something inspired, easy and divine, as something closely related to dancing and exuberance, Thomas quotes a statement (from *The Birth of Tragedy*) that "an altogether thoughtless and immoral artist-god" created the world.

2 As *The Birth of Tragedy* was not translated until 1909, it is surprising that so many writers should refer knowingly to the "Dionysian" and the "Apollonian" impulses before that year. Currency may have been given to these terms through the Nietzsche reviews of academic critics, although they tended to disparage the book. George Saintsbury thought the germ of Nietzsche's "farthest and wildest imaginings" might be found in the Dionysian/Apollonian distinction – at least that, he says, is what Nietzsche's "extremer partisans" maintain: "But, for all that, the book contains no very extravagant development or divagation. It is written at the best well, but rather unequally, and does not display the extraordinary vivid, forcible, and flexible style which is the redeeming point of Nietzsche later."[16] Academic philosophers agreed with the critics of Nietzsche's own lifetime that "as an interpretation of Greek art, the *Origin of Tragedy* has no value,"[17] a view, it seems, widely shared among theorists of tragic drama. William Archer, in an article called "Pessimism and Tragedy,"[18] written in 1899, makes no reference to Nietzsche. A quotation from Nietzsche stands as the epigraph to the first chapter of W. L. Courtney's *The Idea of Tragedy in Ancient and Modern Drama* (1900): "Through the influence of music the Apolline element is engrafted on the Dionysiac wildness";* but for all the

---

* J. M. Kennedy, calling this an "admirable book," observed: "Although Mr. Courtney, if a theological expression be permitted, is 'not sound' on Nietzsche as yet, he merits nothing but praise for anything he has written on Greece." *The Quintessence of Nietzsche* (London, 1909), 94.

use made of this insight it might just as well have not been there. A. H. Thorndike, in his *Tragedy* (1908), and C. F. Vaughan, in his *Types of Tragic Drama* (1908), make no reference to Nietzsche at all. In his 1902 lecture on Hegel's theory of tragedy, A. C. Bradley pronounced that since Aristotle's treatment of tragedy "the only philosopher who has treated it in a manner both original and searching is Hegel."[19] Apart from creative writers the first to perceive the originality of Nietzsche's work were the Greek scholars and anthropologists, Jane Harrison in *Prolegomena to the Study of Greek Religion* (1903), and Francis Cornford, who in 1912 called *The Birth of Tragedy* "a work of profound imaginative insight, which left the scholarship of a generation toiling in the rear."[20]

If *The Birth of Tragedy* was received somewhat coolly by the academic, the creative artist was thrilled by its "superb lyricism"; it convinced him of his essential difference from the ordinary run of human beings, and invited him, as one commentator has put it, to glorify in this separation and to "believe in himself as the superman's right-hand man."[21] Beneath the crusty vulgarity of such a view lies a molten core of truth. On writers like Ellis, Symons, Yeats, and Orage the effect of the book was powerful. It even had a hold on writers least likely to interest themselves in Nietzsche – John Galsworthy, for example: "I am always being pulled up by the difficulty of reconciling two opposite laws which seem to govern every problem and thing one looks at. For instance the longer one lives the more one sees, that everything is form, taste, the way a thing is done – and yet at the same time the more one recognises that the only thing that matters is the spirit that moves the man. Cf. Nietzsche. Inscrutably the two must be one."[22]

Orage, who regretted that *The Birth of Tragedy* had not been translated in the 1890s when interest in dramatic theory was at its height, was astonished to find that "the thrice-great Nietzsche's doctrine of Dionysos-Apollo" had been anticipated by Coleridge in his Shakespearean lectures:

Dionysos, he says, "that power which acts without our consciousness in the vital energies of nature – the *vinum mundi* – as Apollo was that of the conscious agency of our intellectual being." What could be clearer, or more pregnant of Nietzsche? The doctrine, definition and all, is there in a few words. Did Nietzsche ever read it? Did the Germans, in short, discover Coleridge? We shall never know. But look again at this passage and tell me it is not Nietzsche: "The Greeks idolized the finite and therefore were the masters of all grace, elegance, proportion, fancy, dignity, majesty. ... The moderns revere the infinite – hence their passions, their obscure hopes and fears, their wanderings through the unknown, their grander moral feelings, their more august conception of man as man, their future rather than their past – in a word their sublimity." Nietzsche might have written it, might he not?[23]

In fact, *The Birth of Tragedy* captivated most of its readers. Scholarship is now beginning to reveal just how seminal a work it was. One study shows that both the comedy of Shaw's *Major Barbara* and the poetic symbolism of Yeats's *The Resurrection* stem from *The Birth of Tragedy*.[24] Another uses it to explain the origin of Eliot's by now notorious idea of the "objective correlative."[25] The work of Robert Graves, particularly in *The White Goddess*, shows strong affinity with it, as does the modern cultivation of myth in general.

3 Irish writers were, on the whole, quicker to recognize Nietzsche's importance than their English counterparts: the names of T. W. Rolleston and Stephen Gwynn, Stephen MacKenna and James Cousins,* Shaw and Yeats immediately come to mind. As a prelude to a detailed discussion of Yeats, a brief account of how Arthur Symons (who prided himself on his Celtic origin), George Moore, James Joyce, and John Eglinton reacted to Nietzsche will first be given.

With the possible exception of Edmund Gosse, Arthur Symons had more points of contact with the artistic life of his time than any other figure. He is chiefly remembered today as the author of *The Symbolist Movement in Literature* (1899), a work to which many writers (especially Eliot and Yeats) were indebted for their knowledge of the experimental poetic techniques being practised in France. Like his close friend, Havelock Ellis, Symons was something of a polyglot, and his prolific output as a cultural intermediary includes translations from several languages, although German does not appear to have been one of them. Like Ellis, he was often the first to introduce continental writers to his English contemporaries. It was certainly through France – by a reading of the advanced reviews or a personal conversation with such men as Taine or de Gourmont – that Symons and Ellis, who first met in 1887, first became aware of Nietzsche's growing reputation.

A reading of the novels of Gabriele D'Annunzio – some of which he translated – probably served as a starting-point for Symons' reception of Nietzsche. D'Annunzio's heroes are patterned partly on the wistful aesthe-

---

* MacKenna, friend, admirer and – by virtue of his translation of Plotinus – inspirer of Yeats, kept a notebook in 1897 in which Nietzsche's views on morality were "very copiously excerpted." *Journal and Letters of Stephen MacKenna*, ed. E. R. Dodds (London, 1959), 20. For James Cousins' interest in *The Birth of Tragedy*, see *A Study in Synthesis* (Madras, 1934), 135–6, 190–208.

ticism of Huysman's Des Esseintes, Pater's Marius, and Poe's Roderick Usher, partly on the more dynamic ideal which D'Annunzio had derived from Nietzsche. In *The Virgins of the Rocks* (English translation 1899), Claudio Cantelmo thinks of himself as an Italian Zarathustra: "I am grateful to my ancestors, an ancient and noble race of warriors, for having given me their rich and fiery blood, for the beautiful wounds and beautiful burnings they inflicted in the past, for the beautiful women they raped, for all their victories, their drunkennesses, their magnificence."[26] He has three aims in life: to bring his own being to a perfect integration of the Latin type, to produce a supreme work of art, and to produce a son and heir who will preserve and surpass his own ideals. The same aims were shared by those struggling for Irish independence and identity, Yeats for example, whose opposition to democracy is paralleled in D'Annunzio: "A State erected on the basis of popular suffrage and equality in voting is not only ignoble, it is precarious. The State should always be no more than an institution for favouring the gradual elevation of a privileged class towards its ideal form of existence."[27]

In an early essay on D'Annunzio, Symons makes only a passing reference to Nietzsche; and in an 1898 essay on Tolstoy, Nietzsche's philosophy is rather curtly dismissed as "a mere bundle of intuitions."[28] The first signs of real enthusiasm are seen in a review of Henri Albert's French translation of *The Birth of Tragedy*, which Symons had read in the *Mercure de France* in the summer of 1902: "I have been reading all that with the delight of one who discovers a new world, which he has seen already in a dream. I never take up Nietzsche without the surprise of finding something familiar. Sometimes it is the answer to a question which I have only asked; sometimes it seems to me that I have guessed at the answer. And, in his restless energy, his hallucinatory vision, the agility of this climbing mind of the mountains, I find that invigoration which only a 'tragic philosopher' can give."[29] He goes on to give a brief outline of Nietzsche's argument, warming to Nietzsche's description of the function of the chorus, the distinction between the Apollonian and Dionysiac spirits, and the attack on Euripides and Socrates as the "instruments of decomposition" who, between them, brought Dionysian tragedy to an end. *The Birth of Tragedy* seems to have provided Symons with a theoretic basis for his dislike (shared by Yeats and Synge) of the realist Ibsenite stage.* Nietzsche's conviction that the

---

* At the end of an essay written in 1906, Symons attacks Ibsen for substantially the same reasons as Nietzsche attacks Euripides in *The Birth of Tragedy*. Earlier in the essay Symons notes that both Ibsen and Nietzsche professed a creed of self-realization; but what in Nietzsche was the pride of individual energy was, in Ibsen,

world could only be justified as an aesthetic phenomenon dovetailed exactly with Symons' own impressionism, and Nietzsche's views on music ("few better things have been said about music") supported Symons' own belief that any attempt to "harness music in the shafts of literature" was based on a false conception of the nature of music. Symons accepts without demur Nietzsche's own explanations of his change of heart about Wagner. Perhaps the most interesting and original of his observations concerns Nietzsche's kinship to Pater:

There are many pages, scattered throughout his work, in which Pater has dealt with some of the Greek problems very much in the spirit of Nietzsche; with that problem, for instance, of the "blitheness and serenity" of the Greek spirit, and of the gulf of horror over which it seems to rest, suspended as on the wings of the condor. That myth of Dionysus Zagreus, "a Bacchus who had been in hell," which is the foundation of the marvellous new myth of "Denys l'Auxerrois," seems always to be in the mind of Nietzsche, though indeed he refers to it but once, and passingly. Pater has shown, as Nietzsche shows in greater detail and with a more rigorous logic, that this "serenity" was but an accepted illusion, and all Olympus itself but "intermediary," an escape, through the aesthetics of religion, from the trouble at the heart of things; art, with its tragic illusions of life, being another form of escape.*

Symons never perceived how greatly Pater and Nietzsche differed, their remarkable similarities notwithstanding. Ellis, and later Yeats, did. Calling *Marius the Epicurean* "one of the most exquisite and significant books of the century," Ellis wrote of the hero of "this serious, sweet, and thoughtful book": "For Marius, life is made up of a few rare and lovely visions. All the rough sorrow and gladness of the world, its Dantesque bitterness or its Rabelaisian joy, only reaches him through a long succession of mirrors, and every strong human impulse as an attentuated echo."³⁰

As in Coleridge and De Quincey, Ellis went on to observe, there is a

---

humility, the sense he had that only through complete self-expression could he produce the finest work. Less courageous than Nietzsche in his profession of egoism, Ibsen could never forsake the duty he owed to society, and this concession to worldly wisdom was a burden which weighed him down. "Henrik Ibsen," *Figures of Several Centuries* (London, 1916), 222-67.

* W. Barry was one of the first to see the Nietzsche-Pater kinship: "For the English reader, probably the speediest way into this fine suggestive essay [*The Birth of Tragedy*], would be through Walter Pater's meditations on 'Dionysus, the spiritual form of fire and dew,' on the 'Bacchanals' of Euripides, the myth of Demeter and Persephone, and the romantic elements – so he terms them – in Hellenic religion." "The Ideals of Anarchy: Friedrich Nietzsche," *Quarterly Review*, CLXXXIV (October, 1896), 308-9.

refined development of the passive sensory sides of the human organism but a corresponding atrophy of the "motor" sides: "It is clearly impossible to go any farther on that road." Pater had not shaken himself altogether free of Christianity – Nietzsche had: "He never sought, as among ourselves Pater sought, the germ of Christianity in things pagan, the undying essence of paganism in things Christian."[31] For Yeats, Nietzsche was the means of liberation from Pater's refracted, nostalgic, and dangerous vision: "It taught us to walk upon a rope, tightly stretched through serene air, and we were left to keep our feet upon a swaying rope in a storm."[32]

It may have been this review of an "awakening" book, or its reprinting in *Plays, Acting and Music* (1903), that Yeats first came across the Apollonian/Dionysian distinction which is referred to in the correspondence of May, 1903. For Symons at least *The Birth of Tragedy* confirmed much of what he had learnt from Pater, as well as many of his own ideas about music. The essay "The World as Ballet" (1898), reprinted in *Studies in Seven Arts* (1906), expresses the Nietzschean view of life as a dance which, as we have seen, was a central figure of Ellis's maturing vision of the world. This same volume contains an essay on Richard Strauss which, though appreciative of Strauss's technical virtuosity, dismisses as futile Strauss's professed aim, in *Also sprach Zarathustra*, "to convey musically an idea of the development of the human race from its origin, through the various phases of development, religious as well as scientific, up to Nietzsche's idea of the Uebermensch." Symons comments: "Nothing so unlike Nietzsche was ever written as the *Also Sprach Zarathustra* of Strauss, which seems to represent the endless agonies of a bad dream. Beethoven's Seventh Symphony might speak in music something of the proud and exultant and laughing and dancing message of Zarathustra; not this straining effort and unheroic carrying of burdens."[33] It was none other than Wagner who once referred to Beethoven's Seventh as "the apotheosis of the dance."

Symons also wrote, anonymously, a laudatory review of *The Dawn of Day* for the *Athenaeum* in March, 1903. He deplored the "amazing lack of interest" shown in Nietzsche by the English public: "No contemporary foreign name is more frequently met with than the name of Nietzsche; it has, indeed, become almost a byword; but English readers seem to be content to take their knowledge of this great modern force at second-hand, and chiefly out of Mr. Havelock Ellis's essay in *Affirmations*, an essay which, though it is the most really interpretative and critical account of Nietzsche to be found in English, was certainly not meant to be a substitute for the work to which it invites readers."[34] There is no page in *The Dawn of Day*, says Symons, which does not provoke thought. He quotes several aphorisms, one concerning "the silent, self-sufficient man in the midst of a general enslavement, who practises self-defence against the outside world, and is constantly living in a state of supreme fortitude." He quotes another aphorism about "the morality of being flexible," a favourite doctrine of a thinker "for whom the supreme image of bodily perfection" was the image of the dancer: "When we begin to understand we grow polite, happy, ingenious; and when we have sufficiently learned and trained our eyes and ears, our souls show greater suppleness and charm." Unlike Emerson, Nietzsche has "a conscious sting in his way of administering truth": "Emerson is sometimes irritatingly suave, and sweeps away your faith or your doubt with the gesture of a gloved hand. Nietzsche is human enough to feel anger against what seem to him lies – contemptuous anger against those who turn their backs on understanding, against the bourgeois, the *dilettante*, the false artist, the teacher of conventions." Symons, alluding to de Gourmont's contrast between Nietzsche, a mind of the mountains, and Tolstoy, a mind of the plains, agrees that the contrast derives from the milieu in which each writer lived and worked: "In the pages of Nietzsche are the intoxication of mountain air, the solitude of Alps, a steadfast glitter, almost dazzling, like that of frozen snow."[35] Yeats, it should be remembered, criticized Emerson for lacking the vision of evil, and thus appearing superficial, and Tolstoy for being "the only joyless man in literature," who, unlike Turgenev, seemed "to describe all things, whether beautiful or ugly, painful or pleasant, with the same impartial, indifferent joylessness."[36]

It seems safe to assume that Symons discussed his *trouvaille* with Yeats, and that they agreed that Blake, of all English writers, was the one whose roots were closest to Nietzsche's. At any rate, Symons chose to introduce his book on Blake, completed by the end of 1906, with an extended comparison between the two writers. Blake's message, he says, has penetrated the world, and is slowly remaking it, but in the process Blake himself has temporarily been forgotten – another prophet has usurped his position: "Thought to-day, wherever it is most individual, owes either force or direction to Nietzsche, and thus we see, on our topmost towers, the Philistine armed and winged and without the love or fear of God or man in his heart, doing battle in Nietzsche's name against the ideas of Nietzsche. No one can think, and escape Nietzsche; but Nietzsche has come after Blake, and will pass before Blake passes."[37]

The Marriage of Heaven and Hell, Symons continues, is an anticipation of Nietzsche's most significant paradoxes, and Blake's ideas on good and evil, sin and punishment, Christianity and asceticism tally with those of Nietzsche. Again, "it is partly in what they helped to destroy that Blake and Nietzsche are at one," but Nietzsche's "strange, scientific distrust of the imagination" and his maddening "sense of divine haunting" precluded him from entrance to the real world whose joys were open to Blake at every moment. Where Blake finds liberty, Nietzsche encounters distrust, hesitation, and despair. Blake's philosophy came like sunlight into his eyes, Nietzsche's was compounded from his suffering, from his nerves:

> No theory ties together or limits his individual intuitions. What we call his philosophy is really no more than the aggregate of these intuitions coming to us through the medium of a remarkable personality. His personality stands to him in the place of a system. Speaking of Kant and Schopenhauer, he says: "Their thoughts do not constitute a passionate history of the soul." His thoughts are the passionate history of his soul. It is for this reason that he is an artist among philosophers rather than a pure philosopher. And remember that he is also not, in the absolute sense, the poet, but the artist. He saw and dreaded the weaknesses of the artist, his side-issues in the pursuit of truth. But in so doing he dreaded one of his own weaknesses.

At first glance this psychological appraisal sounds remarkably discerning. But one should be wary of accrediting too much acuity to Symons' impressionistic sensibility – not only do these observations derive from Ellis, but they are refracted through the peculiar vision of the world which was Pater's. That these same observations are possibly quite valid as far as they go is, of course, another matter. *A New Age* reviewer thought Symons had not pressed the Blake-Nietzsche correspondence hard enough: "For when he opposes Blake's praise and practice of forgiveness to Nietzsche's condemnation of pity he could have added that Blake himself wrote that 'pity would be no more if we did not make somebody poor,' and again that 'pity divides the soul' – the same fruitless, self-satisfying pity which Nietzsche curses."* Symons' approach to Nietzsche, in summary, is the

---

* *NA*, I (October 10, 1907), 378–9. Charles Gardner's *Vision and Vesture: A Study of William Blake in Modern Thought* (1916), written largely before 1914, extends Symons' Blake-Nietzsche correspondence in a discussion of the superman moralities of Shaw and Yeats, and Arthur Ransome, in *Portraits and Speculations* (1913), points out further analogies between Pater and Nietzsche, a subject which has not yet been sufficiently explored. Hans Proesler, in his study of Pater's relationship to Germany, *Walter Pater und sein Verhältnis zur deutschen Literatur* (Freiburg im Breisgau, 1917), seems convinced that Pater was forced to depend almost exclusively on translations for his knowledge of continental writers. He produces no evidence that Pater ever read Nietzsche, although he acknowledges their similarity in certain respects, e.g., in their condemnation of effete mediaeval Christianity. Ruth C. Child notes that Pater first singled out two opposing tendencies in Greek art, which he called the centrifugal and the centripetal, in the 1880 essay, "The Marbles of Aegina"; later he labels these the Dionysian and Apollonian ten-

finest example of purely aesthetic appropriation, unhampered by philosophical or moral objections, that the period covered by this study can show.

George Moore shares with Arthur Symons the distinction of being an important intermediary and ambassador of continental culture. Instinctively averse to his native country, Moore found in France, and in French writers like Balzac, Flaubert, Zola, and Verlaine, and French painters like Manet and Degas, a source of enthusiasm which Ireland denied him. Some of this enthusiasm is transmitted in his retrospective *Confessions of a Young Man* (1888), in which his loathing of Christianity, of democratic education, of pity ("the philanthropist is the Negro of modern times"[38]) and of mass values is strikingly Nietzschean in tone and vehemence. He bewails the new ideals of equality and justice:

All that we deem sublime in the world's history are acts of injustice; and it is certain that if mankind does not relinquish at once, and for ever, its vain, mad, and fatal dream of justice, the world will lapse into barbarism. England was great and glorious, because England was unjust, and England's greatest son was the personification of injustice – Cromwell.

But the old world of heroes is over now. The skies above us are dark with sentimentalism, the sand beneath us is shoaling fast, we are running with streaming canvas upon ruin; all ideals have gone; nothing remains to us for to worship but the Mass, the blind, inchoate, insatiate Mass.[39]

In his 1904 preface to the book Moore commented: "I find not only my Protestant sympathies in the *Confessions* but a proud agnosticism, and an exalted individualism which in certain passages leads the reader to the sundered rocks about the cave of Zarathustra. My book was written before I heard that splendid name, before *Zarathustra* was written; and though

---

dencies, borrowing the terms, according to Miss Child, from Nietzsche, but not using them in Nietzsche's sense. *The Aesthetics of Walter Pater* (New York, 1940), 89. Michael Hamburger detects influence: "Though Pater never mentioned Nietzsche, it is generally agreed that his *A Lecture on Dionysus*, given at the Midland Institute in 1876 and included in his *Greek Studies* (1895) shows an unacknowledged debt to Nietzsche's earlier writings." *From Prophecy to Exorcism* (London, 1965), 29. It would be easier to substantiate a debt to Coleridge, whom Pater is known to have studied. Almost exact contemporaries, Nietzsche and Pater probably never knew of each other: a collation of their attitude to the Greeks, to myth, to personality in philosophy and art, to historical relativism, to style, to an experimentalist dialectic, might be rewarding. It is certainly not true to claim, as Hamburger does, that "at least one English writer, Walter Pater, was among that *élite* whose recognition established Nietzsche as an international figure when he was scarcely read in Germany." Frenchmen and Scandinavians belonged to that *élite*, not Englishmen.

the doctrine was hardly formulated it is in the *Confessions* as Darwin is in Wallace."*

Moore's biographer, J. M. Hone (who not only wrote a number of reviews and articles[40] on Nietzsche but also translated Halévy's French biography), has this to say:

> The reference to Nietzsche is interesting, because Moore, as John Eglinton recalls for me, caught a good deal from the German "impressionist" philosopher of whom he had heard much earlier from Dujardin. I myself remember his admiration for his friend, Daniel Halévy's, *Vie de Nietzsche*; it was in this way that biography should be written, he said. Two of the most successful of his paraphrases resulted from this acquaintance, the one at the close of "Resurgam" (*Memoirs of My Dead Life*) from Nietzsche's poem of the Eternal Return, the other in *Evelyn Innes*, where Ulick Dean bids farewell to the opera singer (the symbol of the two ships which have crossed paths), from Nietzsche's page on "Stellar Friendship."†

Dujardin is, of course, the Édouard Dujardin whose *Les Lauriers sont Coupés* was regarded by Joyce as a novel technical experiment in its use of the so-called "interior monologue." Dujardin was Moore's life-long friend, and it was from him, a co-founder with two other prominent Nietzscheans, T. de Wyzewa and H. S. Chamberlain, of the *Revue Wagnérienne* in 1884, that Moore received his first indoctrination into Nietzsche's philosophy.‡ Perhaps Dujardin's enthusiasm for Nietzsche struck Moore as being rather excessive: Dujardin had a passion for instructing others which was apt to become tiresome, and Moore himself had no great fondness for purely philosophical ideas. There are suggestions in the autobiographical works that Moore submitted with some degree of reluctance to having Nietzsche rammed down his throat. Moore also had long conversa-

---

* *Dana, an Irish Magazine of Independent Thought*, no. 7 (November, 1904), 204. Paul Carus, in his *Nietzsche and Other Exponents of Individualism* (London and Chicago, 1914), devotes a chapter called "Another Nietzsche" to a scathing indictment of Moore's Nietzscheanism in the *Confessions*. Carus's book was strongly attacked by Lascelles Abercrombie, "Genius and Dr. Carus," *New Weekly*, 1 (March 28, 1914), 58.

† *The Life of George Moore* (London, 1936), 257–8. The episode in *Evelyn Innes* referred to occurs in chapter xxxii, and is based like a similar passage in *Hail and Farewell*, on aphorism 279 of Nietzsche's *The Gay Science*; when he wrote it, Nietzsche probably had his own relationship with Wagner in mind.

‡ In *Hail and Farewell* Moore contrasts the favourite topics of Dujardin and Yeats, the first being Schopenhauer and Nietzsche, the second the Rosicrucians and Jacob Boehme, a remark suggesting that Yeats was not one of the earliest discoverers of Nietzsche.

tions about the philosopher with Daniel Halévy, another life-long friend, who had played a large part in bringing Nietzsche to the attention of the French reading public. Yet in spite of this contact with French writers, and later with the fanatical American Nietzschean James Huneker, there is little sign apart from the two appropriations quoted by Hone (both of them, characteristically enough, unacknowledged) that Moore took any real interest in Nietzsche's ideas or that his work as a novelist was in any way affected by them. A letter to John Eglinton reveals that his hatred of Christ and Christianity needed no Nietzsche to buttress it:

Are you aware that Jesus was one of the most terrifying fanatics that ever lived in the world, that he out-Nietzsched Nietzsche in the awful things he says in the Gospel of Luke? Pretty bad occasionally in John, but in Luke he shocked me much more than anything in Nietzsche. His spiritual pride exceeds any words but his own. How splendid his repentance, if I could only write it, not only for saying that he was God but for all his blasphemy against life, human duty and human love. How people have misunderstood this character![41]

Moore once described himself as "rotten with Wagnerism," and certain of his opponents, not charmed by his personal unattractiveness and his much-vaunted amorality, saw fit to think him "rotten with Nietzscheanism" as well. But Moore was not without his staunch defenders: "Moore is not a reptile, in spite of his veneer of Nietzscheism, but an artist of true genius and a man of sincere convictions which he would rather starve than belie."[42] Moore wrote that "there is very little Nietzsche in me,"[43] an ingenuous protest which, in the circumstances, is not lacking in piquancy. One scholar sums the matter up in this way: "Moore had little direct knowledge of Nietzsche and probably did not know that he had once said that 'the misery of the men who struggle painfully through life must be increased to allow a small number of Olympian geniuses to produce works of art.' But the doctrine that the artist is Superman was one that his French tutors had led him to embrace, though in his own dubious and inimitable way."[44] If Moore, as seems probable, never regarded himself as Nietzsche's disciple, he was certainly in a position – by virtue of his close association with Nietzsche's French converts – to have encouraged, even inadvertently, his English and Irish colleagues to discover more about Nietzsche for themselves.

James Joyce's acquaintance with Nietzsche appears to date from 1903 or 1904. His biographer writes:

It was probably upon Nietzsche that Joyce drew when he expounded to his friends a neo-paganism that glorified selfishness, licentiousness, and pitilessness, and denounced gratitude and other "domestic virtues." At heart Joyce can scarcely have been a Nietzschean any more than he was a socialist; his interest was in the ordinary even more than in the extraordinary; but for the moment, in the year's doldrums, his expectations everywhere checked, it was emollient to think of himself as a superman, and he meditated a descent from the mountain to bring his gospel of churchless freedom to the unreceptive rabblement.*

Ellmann goes on to suggest that Nietzsche was the prophet of the omphalos cult in the tower where Joyce lived with Gogarty and other friends for a time. This may be so, but (to anticipate a little) just as Yeats and Shaw tended to assimilate their reading of Nietzsche to what they had learned from Blake and Ibsen respectively, Joyce's temporary rebelliousness might be traced to Rimbaud rather than to Nietzsche. Once, Ellmann reports, he tried to dissuade a pupil from persisting in an enthusiasm for Schopenhauer and Nietzsche by urging that Thomas Aquinas was the greatest philosopher because his reasoning was like a sharp sword. There is no sign that Joyce was conversant with any of Nietzsche's works except *Zarathustra*, although he did read this in the original German. An early draft of what was to become *Stephen Hero* contains suggestions of *Zarathustra*, as does *Ulysses*, but in both cases the references (mostly to the superman) are of a gratuitous and flippant nature. It is in this jocular vein that Joyce writes to George Roberts on July 13, 1904, asking for the loan of a pound, and signing himself "James Overman."

The theme and the hero of "A Painful Case" – one of the stories in *Dubliners* – were possibly derived from suggestions found in *Zarathustra*; a whole article has been devoted to pointing this out.[45] It is difficult to disagree that the theme does, in fact, derive in part from Nietzsche's poem: Zarathustra's observation that women are only capable of love, not of friendship, lies at the basis of Mr. Duffy's realization after he has broken with Mrs. Sinico, that "love between man and man is impossible because there must not be sexual intercourse, and friendship between man and woman is impossible because there must be sexual intercourse." Duffy, like Zarathustra, places a high value on friendship; Mrs. Sinico was "his soul's companion." Her suicide, he felt, had degraded him; it confirmed

---

* Richard Ellmann, *James Joyce* (New York, 1959), 147. Cf. this observation by Harry Slochower: "In bursting the 'natural' bonds of his society, Nietzsche's Superman foreshadows the way of less heroic characters, from Mann's Castorp and Joyce's Daedalus to Kafka's K., who leave their bourgeois plain in quest of 'magical' freedom." *No Voice is Wholly Lost* (London, 1946), 23. As a symbol of soaring aspiration, Stephen's vision in *A Portrait* of the "hawk-like man whose name he bore" may owe something to Nietzsche's vision of the superman.

him in his belief that her physical desire had been a sign of weakness, but later he is overcome by bitter remorse at the thought that he had failed to respond to a genuine offer of love, a thing higher than friendship, and thereby forfeited the only chance he had of ever overcoming "the soul's incurable loneliness." Duffy is led to recognize in despair, though ultimately in gratitude, that he is unable to live according to the high standards he has set himself; he is unable to avert the dangers which are described in the "On the Way of the Creator" chapter in *Zarathustra* as facing the man who wishes to maintain creative solitude.

But it is too much to claim, as this critic does, that Duffy is based on Nietzsche's superman, or even, as he omits to do, that Duffy regards himself as one. Magalaner seems to confuse Zarathustra with Zarathustra's ideal, and Duffy is sometimes equated with Zarathustra and sometimes with the "brother" Zarathustra imagines as his interlocutor; and it is misleading to impose such an incomplete and adventitious view of the superman either on Joyce or on his fictional hero. Self-contradictions abound: Duffy is said to be master of his emotions and yet "emotionally dead"; he leads a "morbidly dreary life" but is supposed to share the superman's heroic exultation. The superman is surely beyond the need for redemption, the rejection of which makes Duffy, if not a tragic, then a pathetic figure; the realization of what he had rejected constitutes Duffy's epiphany – no such epiphany is experienced by the superman, since in a sense he *is* one. Duffy is not even a novice superman, even though he manfully attempts to live a life of superhuman self-sufficiency; "A Painful Case" gives no real clue as to Joyce's reading of Nietzsche, being simply a study in love and loneliness whose central character is portrayed as a man of many weaknesses, which are, indeed "human, all-too-human."

Joyce then, like Moore, went through a period of temporary infatuation with Nietzsche which left no mark of any consequence on his creative work. It is significant that Richard Rowan, Joyce's *alter ego* in his play *Exiles* (1918), should dismiss certain Nietzschean sentiments – "All life is a conquest, the victory of human passion over the commandments of cowardice" – as being the language of his youth.

John Eglinton, described by Yeats as the one philosophical critic Ireland possessed, stood high in the esteem of his Irish contemporaries, and his essay "A Way of Understanding Nietzsche," first published in 1904, was probably influential – at least it was thought important enough to deserve reprinting. Eglinton regards Nietzsche as a dangerous author whose danger is somewhat neutralized by the degree of intelligence required to understand him; Nietzsche is "a caustic and relentless mentor" who strips away the last vestige of comforting illusion from his readers and demands of them "a capacity for 'gaiety' in self-abnegation and self-annihilation."[46] His shrill dogmatism had a basis in pain and privation, and Eglinton emphasizes Nietzsche's insistence on the creative power of suffering by quoting from *Beyond Good and Evil*: "In man CREATURE and CREATOR are united; in man there is not only matter, shred, excess, clay, mire, folly, chaos; but there is also the creator, the sculptor, the hardness of the hammer, the divinity of the spectator, and the seventh day!" Eglinton sees Nietzsche's philosophy as a counterblast to the consolatory, passive pessimism of Schopenhauer:

In the pessimist's affirmation of the ideal, Nietzsche mockingly detects the last resource of hypocritical weakness. He resolves, then, at the point where all the hopes and illusions of chagrined egoism find themselves foiled, to declare himself optimist – a lover of fate, or a "yea-saying man." He denies "the ideal." More courageous and more honest than Schopenhauer, he returns from the dread region of ultimate self-questioning with no deceptive doctrine of resignation, or altruism, or contemplation – seed-grounds of hypocrisy and illusion – but with the frank and "gay" denial of God, freedom, immortality, and, at the same time, with the equally frank and gay avowal of the will-to-live, the desire of power, strength, and activity.

And Eglinton stresses two further points in Nietzsche's philosophy which were to interest Yeats so greatly – the idea of the transvaluation of all values and the need for self-transformation: "Nietzsche stands or falls with his assertion that moral distinctions are not superhuman or superimposed (transcendental) checks and ingredients of human conduct, but the creation, subject to continual transformation from the same source, of humanity itself." Eglinton is rather non-committal in his comments on Nietzsche's distinction between slave- and master-morality, as if he felt uneasy about it but could not locate its weaknesses with any precision. But, believing that civilization does not exist for the few, and that really great men, unlike Caesar, Napoleon and Nietzsche's other heroes, bring nothing but gain to all mankind, Eglinton's verdict on the superman is harshly dismissive: "To the doctrine of the Superman – that 'far-off divine event' to which, according to Nietzsche, humanity moves – a consideration of the 'morality of slaves and masters' naturally leads on; but his conception of the Superman, moulded chiefly by hatred of Christianity and the obsession of his mind by Darwinism, is undoubtedly a little crazy. There is a kind of assumption that those great men who act as 'bridges' to the Superman exist at the expense of the rest of mankind." Such scruples as these were not to bother Yeats.

WILLIAM BUTLER YEATS

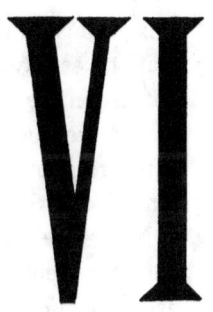

1 Although Yeats must have heard of Nietzsche by 1902, there is no indication that he read him until that year, when John Quinn, his American lawyer friend, visited Britain and persuaded him to look into the writings of the German philosopher.* When Yeats visited the USA on his first lecture tour (November 1903 to March 1904), Quinn lent Yeats Common's anthology of Nietzsche extracts in English translation and a number of annotations which Yeats made in this volume during the tour provide a useful indication of his reaction to Nietzsche. Before looking at those it might be profitable to note the references to Nietzsche in Yeats's published work and correspondence. The first of these occurs towards the end of 1902 (he is writing to Lady Gregory): "I have written to you little and badly of late I am afraid, for the truth is you have a rival in Nietzsche, that strong enchanter. I have read him so much that I have made my eyes bad again. They were getting well it had seemed. Nietzsche completes Blake and has the same roots – I have not read anything with so much excitement since I got to love Morris's stories which have the same curious astringent joy."†

---

* Quinn's biographer, B. L. Reid, writes: "He had talked much to Yeats of Nietzsche, and he sent him now, in mid-September [1902], his own copy of *Thus Spake Zarathustra* and copies of *The Case of Wagner* and *A Genealogy of Morals*. Thus Yeats owed to Quinn his introduction to the writer he later called 'that strong enchanter.' Quinn thought Yeats would find Nietzsche's 'wonderful epigrammatic style' of use in his own writing, though he admitted that he found 'abhorrent' the German's 'so-called philosophy ...of the exaltation of brutality.'" *The Man from New York: John Quinn and His Friends* (New York, 1968), 10. Quinn's interest in Nietzsche is demonstrated by the thirty to forty volumes on or by Nietzsche auctioned – together with the rest of his enormous library – in 1923 and 1924. *The Complete Catalogue of the Library of John Quinn* (New York, 1924), II, item nos. 7247–63, and item no. 11404.

† *The Letters of W. B. Yeats*, ed. Allan Wade (London, 1954), 379. Although Wade dates this letter tentatively as September 26, 1902, there is evidence to show it belongs to a period three months later. See my brief note "A Misdated Yeats Let-

This enthusiasm is first publicly announced early the following year, when Yeats takes advantage of the revisions he is making to some earlier essays to insist on the resemblance between Blake and Nietzsche which had struck him so forcibly: "[Blake had] a strong persuasion that all busy with government are men of darkness and 'something other than human life.' One is reminded of Shelley, who was the next to take up the cry ..., but still more of Nietzsche, whose thought flows always, though with an even more violent current, in the bed Blake's thought has worn."[1] Yeats, of course, had made a close study of Blake in the years 1889–92, and could not fail to notice the similarity between the two writers; it would be instructive to know whether Symons recognized this similarity independently, or owed something of his discussion of it to conversations with Yeats. Richard Ellmann, after pointing out how delighted Yeats was with "the eloquence, psychological acuteness, arrogance, and messianic fervour of the German philosopher," adds that "Yeats rightly perceived that there were few irreconcilable differences between the English poet and the German."[2] Nietzsche and Blake were prophets who issued violent challenges to the conventional habits and morals of their time; both were strident individualists who courted misunderstanding; both possessed an unimpeachable integrity. In many respects they are startlingly close: in their praise of instinctive life as opposed to dry abstract intellectualism, in their search for a life "beyond good and evil," in their cyclic view of history, in their antagonism towards government, constituted authority, church, and priesthood. Blake's antagonism to achieved systems was one of the main links perceived to exist between his work and that of Nietzsche. Blake's command to "put off Holiness / And put on Intellect," to worship God by "honouring his gifts in other men each according to his genius, and loving the greatest men best," and to create original virtue by smashing the ten commandments, was thought to foreshadow Nietzsche's attack on convention and "utilitarian" ethics, as his praise of imagination and detestation of "natural fact" was thought to anticipate Nietzsche's visionary mode of thought and his critique of the realistic method.* In any assessment of the

---

ter on Nietzsche," *Notes and Queries*, xv (August, 1968), 286–7. An unpublished letter in the Berg Collection of the New York Public Library confirms my view, expressed in that note, that *Where There Is Nothing* was written before Yeats had read Nietzsche: "Is not the play splendid? I am glad Y[eats] had finished it before your Niedtsche [sic] (for which he is very grateful) came, for it is the more original." Letter from Lady Gregory to John Quinn, dated October 9, 1902.

* F.A. Lea has suggested that Nietzsche, in choosing the Greek tragedians as his rivals in the power of sustained, inspired creation, was mistaken: "His nearest-of-kin, indubitably, was not Aeschylus, but

Nietzschean aspects of Yeats's work the possibility that Blake's thought may also lie behind them can never be discounted.

An oblique reference to a specific work by Nietzsche, *The Birth of Tragedy*, occurs in a letter dated May 14, 1903: "The close of the last century was full of a strange desire to get out of form, to get to some kind of disembodied beauty, and now it seems to me the contrary impulse has come. I feel about me and in me an impulse to create form, to carry the realization of beauty as far as possible. The Greeks said that the Dionysiac enthusiasm preceded the Appollonic and that the Dionysiac was sad and desirous, but that the Apollonic was joyful and self sufficient."[3] Yeats refers again to these two impulses shortly afterwards in a letter to John Quinn: "Nietzsche, to whom you have been the first to introduce me, calls these the Dionysiac and Apollonic, respectively";[4] there is no reason to doubt Yeats's word that Quinn did, in fact, introduce him to Nietzsche's work.

In the same month (May, 1903) Yeats draws upon Nietzsche in a review of Lady Gregory's *Poets and Dreamers* to support his belief that poets are too full of life to make their work merely a vehicle for moral edification, a form of wisdom "which Nietzsche has called an infirmary for bad poets."[5] Yeats takes exception to the school of criticism "which has decided that *Hamlet* was written for a warning to the irresolute, and *Coriolanus* as a lesson to the proud." He is using Nietzsche to reinforce an ultra-moral approach to literature he had been expressing two years earlier: "It did not occur to the critics that you cannot know a man from his actions because you cannot watch him in every kind of circumstance, and that men are made useless to the State as often by abundance as by emptiness, and that a man's business may at times be revelation, and not reformation."[6]

William Blake; and there is something very Blake-like in the assertion, 'length, the need of a wide-embracing rhythm, is almost the measure of the force of an inspiration.' Isolated though he was, Nietzsche was never driven into total esotericism; *Zarathustra* is more intelligible even than the earliest of the Prophetic Books, and considerably more restrained: his native eloquence, while it reinforced, did nothing to replace, that command of lucid, succinct expression he had acquired by years of training in the aphorism. The affinity, both of style and substance, between *Zarathustra* and *The Marriage of Heaven and Hell* is nonetheless obvious (where else shall we find such a 'clear golden and thoroughly fermented mixture of simplicity, deeply discriminating love, observation and roguishness'?): and it is easy to imagine the delight that Blake might have taken in illustrating Nietzsche's poem." *The Tragic Philosopher* (London, 1957), 180–1.

[6] *Essays and Introductions* (London, 1960), 103. Compare aph. 240 of *The Dawn of Day*, in which Nietzsche discusses *Macbeth* in non-moral terms, with an identical passage in *Samhain* (1904), *Explorations* (London, 1962), 154.

The next reference is contained in a letter to Lady Gregory in 1907: "I don't suppose Synge sympathized with your telling him that you cared most for my work. I really don't think him selfish or egotistical, but he is so absorbed in his own vision of the world that he cares for nothing else. But there is a passage somewhere in Nietzsche which describes this kind of man as if he were the normal man of genius."[6] In an essay on Synge written two years later, Yeats repeats this insight when he remarks that Synge "had that egotism of the man of genius which Nietzsche compares to the egotism of a woman with child."[7] In the same year Yeats mentions Blake's preference for "a happy thoughtless person" to "any man of intellect" – a preference he believes was shared by Nietzsche.[8]

In 1912 Yeats writes *à propos* of Indian families like the Tagore family: "I notice in these men's thoughts a sense of visible beauty and meaning as though they held that doctrine of Nietzsche that we must not believe in the moral or intellectual beauty which does not sooner or later impress itself upon physical things."[9] And in 1918 we find him telling his father: "You should not conclude that if a man does not give his reasons he has none. Remember Zarathustra's 'Am I a barrel of memories that I can give you my reasons?'"[10] This quotation, a favourite of Yeats's, was pressed into service on at least two other occasions.[11]

An allusion to Nietzsche's theory of the eternal recurrence is apparent in Yeat's discussion of modern drawing-room dramas, whose dramatic situations, he says, "are perhaps exhausted – as Nietzsche thought the whole universe would be some day."[12]

Yeats always associated Nietzsche with Italy. In 1930 he wrote to Lady Gregory from Rapallo, one of the Italian resorts where Nietzsche was "waylaid," as he says in *Ecce Homo*, by the idea of *Zarathustra*: "Just outside the gate of the hotel grounds there is a small restaurant and hotel which was once the lodging, or rather tenement house, where Nietzsche lived for some months and boasted to his friends of having found a place where there were eight walks."[13] The only remaining direct references to Nietzsche, apart from occasional allusions to the "transvaluation of all values," are found in Yeats's emergent philosophy of history, which was to find systematic expression in *A Vision*. In the brief poetic exposition of that philosophy, "The Phases of the Moon" (1919), Nietzsche is mentioned as belonging to the twelfth, or heroic, phase: this is a suggestive choice, irrespective of whether Yeats described this phase with Nietzsche in mind, or simply inserted his name as an illustrative afterthought. In *A Vision* itself Yeats once again links the names of Blake and Nietzsche:

Certain men have sought to express the new emotion through the *Creative Mind*, though fit instruments of expression do not yet exist, and so to establish, in the midst of our ever more abundant *primary* information, *antithetical* wisdom; but such men, Blake, Coventry Patmore at moments, Nietzsche, are full of morbid excitement and few in number, unlike those who, from Richardson to Tolstoi, from Hobbes down to Spencer, have grown in number and serenity. They were begotten in the Sistine Chapel and still dream that all can be transformed if they be but emphatic; yet Nietzsche, when the doctrine of the Eternal Recurrence drifts before his eyes, knows for an instant that nothing can be so transformed and is almost of the next gyre.*

This list of direct references to Nietzsche by name is as complete as the regrettable lack of indexing to Yeats's works will allow. They turn out to be few in number, much fewer than Yeats's obsessive allusions to some other writers, such as Blake. It is idle to speculate whether Yeats would have invoked Nietzsche's name more frequently had he discovered him sooner, or had the whole corpus of Nietzsche's work been more readily available; while a knowledge of Blake assisted Yeats to a fluent understanding of Nietzsche, it also detracted from Nietzsche's originality and the impact he exercised. This impact was nonetheless very strong: it resulted, among other things, in the acquisition of at least six books by Nietzsche, and also a biography of him translated from the French by his own biographer, J. M. Hone.† For a more reliable guide to the measure of Yeats's interest in Nietzsche we must make a close examination of his valuable annotations in the anthology edited by Common.

2 Thomas Common's *Nietzsche as Critic, Philosopher, Poet and Prophet* appeared in 1901. In a proselytizing introduction, Common gives an outline of Nietzsche's life and philosophy, fitting the latter, as Tille had done, into a framework of evolutionary thought. Common's adulation is at times excessive: "Besides being a philosopher, Nietzsche is

---

* *A Vision* (New York, 1961), 299. Reference is made in Alexander Raven's *Civilization as Divine Superman* (London, 1932) to the supermen of Nietzsche, Shaw and Wells, and its presentation of a cyclic theory of history offers many interesting parallels to that of *A Vision*.

† Yeats's library contained the following volumes: *A Genealogy of Morals, The Case of Wagner, The Dawn of Day* (inscribed "W. B. Yeats from A[ugusta] G[regory]"), *Thoughts out of Season, The Will to Power, The Birth of Tragedy*, and Daniel Halévy's *Life*. All these books are the English translations; the dates of each edition are not given, as Professor Donald Torchiana – to whom I am indebted for this information – was only able to jot down the titles during a hurried inspection of Yeats's library. He assures me that his inspection was by no means thorough, and that he may have overlooked other Nietzsche titles.

at the same time the most interesting of all writers for cultured men and women to read. In brilliancy of style and originality of thought he is perhaps unequalled. He is not only the most serious and profound of writers, he is also the gayest and most cheerful. There has never been such a master of aphorisms. As a prophetic writer also he stands alone."[14] These rapt, rought-and-ready superlatives are obviously addressed to an audience devoid of first-hand knowledge – in these early years, as an earlier chapter has shown, criticism of Nietzsche, whether in praise or in denigration, tended to err on the side of excess. Common's propaganda is meretricious and simple-minded, but sometimes a real perception of something central in Nietzsche is expressed, as when Common opposes Nietzsche's integrity to the modern tendency to compromise: "Nietzsche's unrelenting rectitude of purpose ... does not hesitate to make the very greatest sacrifices, if by so doing a higher and truer life is realised." While claiming that Nietzsche's philosophy, taken as a whole, forms "an harmonious and original system, which explains the world better than any other system of philosophy," Common concedes that Nietzsche was greatly indebted to Chamfort, Schopenhauer, and other writers – Blake, he says, can be regarded as one of the forerunners preparing the way for Nietzsche's gospel, a remark Yeats would not have disputed.

The value of Common's book lay not in its attitude of prostrate veneration, but in the purpose it served of enabling readers in England to sample Nietzsche's great versatility and range. It might have been more influential, certainly more remunerative, had not the publisher, Grant Richards, become bankrupt shortly after its publication. Its chief interest to students of literature is that it was sponsored by Shaw, whose timely word overcame Richards' initial reluctance to accept it, and that it was recommended to Yeats by John Quinn. It was in Quinn's copy of the book that Yeats was stirred to make a number of marginal annotations, which will now be examined in detail; where appropriate, sections of Nietzsche's text will also be quoted which – to judge by his markings – caught Yeats's special attention.*

As one might expect from the title Common chose for his book, it is divided into four parts. All but one of Yeats's annotations occur in the

---

* Four of these annotations have already appeared in Richard Ellmann's *The Identity of Yeats* (London, 1954), and two of these four in F.A.C. Wilson's *Yeats's Iconography* (London, 1960). All sixteen annotations are given here. My readings of the annotations differ occasionally from those of Ellmann and Wilson: Yeats's handwriting is notoriously illegible. I have transcribed the annotations as Yeats wrote them, adding a minimum of punctuation for the sake of clarity and amending his baffled efforts to spell Nietzsche's name correctly.

second part which is called "Nietzsche as Philosopher," more specifically in the section headed "Ethics." The non-conformist annotation occurs in the last part, "Nietzsche as Prophet," which consists entirely of extracts from *Thus Spake Zarathustra*. It is difficult to account for the heavy concentration of annotation in the middle thirty pages of the book; it could be surmised that Yeats's attention had been drawn to this section, or that he had been expressly invited to write comments at this point. Perhaps he could not restrain himself from scribbling down his reactions. Whatever the reason may have been, the fact remains that there is a good deal in the rest of the book one would have expected him to annotate which seems to have been passed over, if read at all, without comment.

For the section that concerns us, the one headed "Ethics," Common drew on a number of Nietzsche's works, principally *The Genealogy of Morals* and *Beyond Good and Evil* (a work which was not translated in full until 1907), to illustrate Nietzsche's revaluation of morality. A discussion of the origin of morality, its subsequent travesty at the hand of Christians, ascetics, and Jews into "slave-morality" as opposed to "master-morality," the resultant need for a new race of philosopher rulers, all this prepared the ground for Zarathustra's proclamation of the superman and the new commandments he will live by. Yeats's interest is first aroused when Nietzsche speaks of the distinction between slave-morality and master-morality, and the following passage is underlined: "It is obvious that the designations of moral worth everywhere were at first applied to *men*, and were only derivatively and at a later period applied to actions."* An identical line of thought is followed by Yeats in *Samhain* for 1904, when he refers to the subject-matter Irish writers will come to prefer: "We will be more interested in heroic men than in heroic actions, and will have a little distrust for everything that can be called good or bad in itself with a very confident heart."[15] The following passage is also underlined in places, and Yeats scrawls strokes in the margin, presumably to mark his approval:

It is a bad mistake, therefore, when historical moralists start with questions such as – "Why have sympathetic actions been praised?" The noble type of man regards *himself* as the determiner of worth, it is not necessary for him to be approved of, he passes the judgment: "what is injurious to me is injurious in itself"; he recognises that it is he himself only that confers honour on things – he is *a creator of worth*. The type of man in question honours whatever qualities he recognises in himself: his morality is self-glorification. In the foreground there

---

* *Nietzsche as Critic, Philosopher, Poet and Prophet*, ed. Thomas Common (London, 1901), 109. In all quotations from Nietzsche's text the italics are Nietzsche's own.

is the feeling of plentitude and power which seeks to overflow, the happiness of high tension, the consciousness of riches which would fain give and bestow; the noble man also helps the unfortunate, not (or scarcely) out of sympathy, but rather out of an impulse produced by the superabundance of power. The noble man honours the powerful one in himself, and also him who has self-command, who knows how to speak and keep silence, who joyfully exercises strictness and severity over himself, and reverences all that is strict and severe.[16]

Such a passage contains many of the key concepts of the Nietzschean philosophy, and Yeats endorses its central thesis in his 1909 diary: "We require a new statement of moral doctrine, which shall be accepted by the average man, but be at the same time beyond his power in practice. Classical morality in its decay became an instrument in the hands of commonplace energy to overthrow distinguished men. A true system of morals is from the first a weapon in the hands of the most distinguished."[17] Nietzsche goes on to quote from a Scandinavian saga in support of his assertion that the noble man is proud of his lack of sympathy: "He who has not had a hard heart when young, will never have a hard heart."[18] Yeats annotates: "So Oscar's heart, but 'hard' surely in the sense of scorning self-pity." Yeats must have had Oscar Wilde in mind; rightly he sees that Nietzsche's noble man scorns being soft to others, because he would never be soft to himself.

After pointing out that the noble man has "a profound reverence for age and tradition" – an observation underlined by Yeats – Nietzsche adds the stern principle "that one has only obligations to one's equals, that one may act towards beings of a lower rank, and towards all that is foreign to one according to discretion, or 'as the heart desires,' and in any case 'beyond Good and Evil.'"[19] One might expect Yeats to take offence here; after all, what impressed him about Lady Gregory was "her sense of feudal responsibility, not of duty as the word is generally understood, but of burdens laid upon her by her station and her character, a choice constantly renewed in solitude."[20] Indeed his note betrays certain qualms: "Yes, but the necessity of giving remains. When the old heroes praise one another they say 'he never refused any man.' Nietzsche means that the lower cannot create anything, cannot make obligations to the higher." Qualms, certainly, but not outright condemnation as Ellmann, for example, seems to think. We have already been told that "the noble man also helps the unfortunate, not (or scarcely) out of sympathy, but rather out of an impulse produced by the superabundance of power." Helping the unfortunate, then, is not merely an obligation (and it certainly *is* an obligation, as Nietzsche insisted elsewhere), nor is it an expression of sympathy (for certain kinds of pity

Nietzsche had nothing but contempt); it is simply a gesture, a gift. In another note, which Ellmann omits, Yeats reveals the reason for his dissatisfaction with Nietzsche's position: "In the last analysis the 'noble' man will serve or fail the weak as much as the good man, but in the first sense the 'noble' man creates the form of the gift, in the second the weak." It is not, as Ellmann believes, that Yeats rejects Nietzsche's apparent 'hardness,' but rather that he fears that the noble man's powers of discretion may be inadequate to serve the weak in the best way. And this fear was not merely theoretical: from the beginning of their work in the Irish National Theatre, Lady Gregory and Yeats were faced with the choice of whether they should supply what they knew would be popular or give what they thought was good until it became popular – they opted for the second alternative, but not without much self-questioning.

From Nietzsche's distinction between slave-morality, exemplified in the Jews, and master-morality, exemplified in the Romans, Yeats builds up his own picture: "Nietzsche opposes organization from resentment – denial – to organization from power – affirmation." Slave-morality, says Nietzsche, is now triumphant as the assertion of the superior right of the many. The last man to protest against this "will to abasement, to humiliation, to equalising, to the descent and decline of man"[21] was Napoleon, and his attempt to stem the tide, though heroic, was futile. Yeats, also seeing the danger that the noble man might be faced with extinction, makes this comment on Nietzsche: "His system seems to lack some reason why the self must give to the selfless or weak or itself perish or suffer diminution – the self being the end." This is ambiguous: Yeats is either faulting Nietzsche's system for being incomplete, or merely suggesting it needs a tighter rationale; in either case Yeats is not condemning master-morality, but offering a recommendation for its improvement. If the noble man is to retain a chance of survival he must assist others to elevate themselves to his degree of selfhood.

What the "noble" man actually is, as Nietzsche readily admits, is difficult to describe because it is so foreign to modern experience, yet Nietzsche hazards a few strokes of delineation: "The capacity and obligation for prolonged gratitude and prolonged revenge – both only among equals – artfulness in retaliation, refinement of ideas in friendship, certain necessity to have enemies (as outlets for the passions of envy, quarrelsomeness, arrogance – in fact, in order to be a good friend): – these are all typical characteristics of the noble morality."[22] Yeats notes: "This implies that victory achieves its end not by mere overcoming but because the joy of it creates friends – it is a new creation. Victories of mere brute force do not create." Yeats must have been reminded of Blake's animus against those who prolong "corporeal" war at the expense of mental war; Nietzsche's own praise of war is to be taken in a spiritual sense.

Yeats's absorption in Blake and Shelley made him immune to Nietzsche's more extreme statements which, at first sight, seem so outrageous – and so did his acquaintance with the work of the theosophists. For example, Nietzsche's assertion that the slave insurrection in morals began with the Jews might easily be taken as an expression of anti-Semitic feeling, but Yeats comments in the mildest vein: "Swedenborg thought the Jews 'chosen' because the worst – they could not corrupt the spirit having none and would obey." Yeats brings theosophical aspirations to bear on the following passage, in which Nietzsche seeks some remedy for the epidemic of slave-morality which threatens to infest every aspect of modern society:

> We who hold a belief which is different [from that of the democrats, socialists, and anarchists] – we who regard the democratic movement not only as a degenerating form of political organisation, but as equivalent to a degenerating, waning type of man, as involving his mediocrising and depreciation – where have *we* to fix our hopes? *In new philosophers*: there is no other alternative; in minds strong and original enough to introduce opposed estimates of value, to transvalue and subvert 'eternal valuations'; in forerunners, in men of the future, who in the present shall fix the constraints and fasten the knots which will compel the will of milleniums to take *new* paths. To teach man the future of humanity as *volition*, as depending on human will, and to make preparations for vast hazardous enterprises and collective attempts in rearing and educating; in order thereby to put an end to the frightful rule of folly and chance which has hitherto gone by the name of 'history' (the folly of the 'greatest number' is only its last form): for that purpose a new type of philosophers and commanders will be needed some time or other, at the very idea of which everything that has existed in the way of occult, terrible, and benevolent beings might look pale and dwarfed. The image of such leaders hovers before *our* eyes: is it lawful for me to say it aloud, ye free spirits?[23]

Several phrases here are underlined by Yeats, including the last sentence which he annotates thus: "How full he is of esotericism – it is so with all the mystics!" Whether this cryptic remark implies that Yeats regarded Nietzsche as a mystic, or, more reasonably, ascribed to him the esotericism peculiar to mystic writers, is a matter for conjecture; but the emphasis on the need for a new kind of man and for strong authoritarian guidance is theosophical as well as Nietzschean doctrine. As early as 1906 Yeats told Sir Herbert Grierson of his interest in Nietzsche "as a counteractive to the spread of democratic vulgarity,"[24] and his 1909 diary shows his preoccupation with constraint: "No art can conquer the people alone – the people are conquered by an ideal of life upheld by authority. As this ideal is rediscovered, the arts, music and poetry, painting and literature, will draw closer together."[25] The fascination of the Irish National Movement, Yeats goes on to confess, was that it held out promise of such authority; military and political authority, he came to believe late in life, was the only answer to the progressive degeneration of man. In 1924, two years after Mussolini's accession to power, Yeats wrote: "Generations to come will have for their task, not the widening of liberty, but recovery from its errors – the building up of authority, the restoration of discipline, the discovery of a life sufficiently heroic to live without the opium dream."[26] Such statements as this have led some observers to conclude that Yeats's sympathies were decidedly fascist.

Further annotations show that Yeats was being stimulated to work on Nietzsche's ideas and develop them in terms of the Irish search for national identity and cultural unity. In a section headed "The Natural System of Ranks and Castes," which consists of the greater part of section 57 of *The Antichrist*, Nietzsche writes that "such a law-book as that of Manu sums up the experience, sagacity, and experimental morals of long centuries": "At a certain point in the development of a nation, the book with the most penetrative insight pronounces that the experience according to which people are to live – *i.e.* according to which they *can* live – has at last been decided upon."[27] This inspires Yeats to write one of those proud, leonine, resonant phrases which are the hallmark of his best prose: "A sacred book is a work written by a man whose self has been *so* exalted (not by denial but by an intensity like that of the vibrating vanishing string) that it becomes one with the self of the race." And Yeats then comes across Nietzsche's explanation of how social unity is attained: "The authority of the law establishes itself with the theses: God *gave* it; ancestors *obeyed* it. The rationale of such procedure is to oust consciousness step by step from the sphere of life recognised as correct (as *proved* by an immense and carefully sifted experience), so as to attain complete automatism of instinct – the prerequisite for every kind of superiority, for every kind of perfection in the art of living."[28] Yeats's marginal query shows his keenness to develop as well as accept Nietzsche's insights: "Were the bodily functions like that of the pulse once conscious?" One recalls Yeats's admission in the *Autobiography* that his constant endeavour had been to recreate, by a kind of acting, practical instinct in himself; a poem like "Adam's Curse" proclaims that the ousting of conscious effort is an essential factor in the poetic process, whereby everything is made to seem "a moment's thought."

Nietzsche then goes on to discuss the system of castes: "*The arrangement of castes*, the highest, the cardinal law, is only the sanction of a *natural arrangement*, of natural legality of the highest rank, over which no arbitrariness, no 'modern idea' holds sway."[29] This finds an echo in *On the Boiler*, where Yeats voices his fear that "the new-formed democratic parliaments of India will doubtless destroy, if they can, the caste system that has saved Indian intellect."[30] Nietzsche proceeds to argue that every healthy society has three mutually conditioning types: those naturally endowed with intelligence, those endowed with physical strength and those distinguished neither by the one nor the other. Of the highest caste Nietzsche has this to say: "The highest caste – I call them *the fewest* – have, as being the perfect caste, the privileges of the fewest: in this connection it belongs to them to represent happiness, beauty, and goodness on the earth. It is only the most intelligent men who have licence to beauty, to the beautiful; it is only in them that goodness is not weakness."[31] Such men, Nietzsche continues, scorn pessimism and indignation; they regard the world as perfect, they give life the *imprimatur* of their categorical affirmation, and they delight in hardship:

The most intelligent men, as being the *strongest*, find their happiness in that wherein others would find their ruin: in the labyrinth, in severity towards themselves and others, in effort; their delight is self-conquest; with them asceticism becomes nature, requirement, and instinct. The difficult task is regarded by them as a privilege; to play with burdens which crush others to death, as a *recreation*; knowledge – a form of asceticism. – They are the most venerable type of men; that does not, however, prevent them being also the most cheerful, the most amiable men. They rule, not because they want to do so, but because they *are* rulers; they are not at liberty to hold the second place.[32]

Of the last sentence Yeats notes: "Rulers, that is to say, the living, or wholly free, wholly self-moving." The thought here, like the phrasing, is Platonic; to be "wholly self-moving" is, in Nietzschean terminology, to have achieved self-conquest, a phrase which Yeats may have picked up here for the first time. It became a favourite phrase with him; it will later be discussed in detail in connection with Nietzsche's theory of the superman.

What of the two other castes? The second caste, according to Nietzsche, is merely the executive of the first, composed of the guardians of order and security who relieve the rulers "of all that is *coarse* in the work of ruling, their retinue, their right hand, their best disciples."[33] As Yeats put it, the soldiers "obey life." They thus stand higher than the third caste whose members occupy themselves with "handicraft, trade, agriculture, *science*, the main part of art – in a word, the whole compass of business activity,"[34] and whose station Yeats describes with obvious disrelish as "baseness –

the unfree – they serve things, not life." A hatred of the bourgeois middle-class was one of Yeats's most bitter hatreds. Notice how he neatly catalogues Nietzsche's three castes in term of the degree of freedom or life (here almost interchangeable categories) which each possesses.

The four remaining annotations show Yeats making a bold extension of Nietzsche's moral theory to the spiritual sphere, synthesizing the discoveries he has made; two of them are related, the second being an expansion of the first: "The night – knowledge – inaction, in the night dreams, from dreams the day's work afterwards perhaps. The day – power – action." "Night (Socrates/Christ) one god, night, denial of self – the soul turned towards spirit seeking knowledge. Day (Homer) many gods, day – affirmation of self – the soul turned from spirit to be its mask and instrument when it seeks life." F. A. C. Wilson has found in these words "a complete system of world-religions, in which any creed can be found a place";* indeed, the annotation is most suggestive, and its significance in the pattern of Yeats's thought will be examined at a later stage. Suffice it to say here that Yeats began to build on it immediately. As early as 1904 he wrote: "It sometimes seems as if there is a kind of day and night of religion, and that a period when the influences are those that shape the world is followed by a period when the greater power is in influences that would lure the soul out of the world, out of the body."³⁵ Late in life he applies the same dialectic to history: "History is very simple – the rule of the many, then the rule of the few, day and night, night and day for ever."³⁶ The annotation also contains the first reference to the mask in Yeats's work. Although Yeats had a temperamental bias in favour of the second opposition defined here – "Homer is my example and his unchristened heart" – he did not follow Nietzsche's critique of Christianity at every point, as the following note shows: "Did Christianity create commerce by teaching men to live not in the continuous present of self-revelation but to deny self and present for future gain, first heaven and then wealth? But why does Nietzsche think that the night has no stars, nothing but bats and owls and the insane moon?"†

One final annotation remains to be recorded, and it will serve as an appropriate introduction to the discussion on the superman which now follows. It occurs in the fourth part of the book, which consists solely of

---

* *Yeats's Iconography*, 182–3. Wilson's version of the second of these annotations is radically abbreviated.

† Compare the night-scene of one of the dancing-songs in *Thus Spake Zarathustra*: "Here are caves and thickets; we shall get lost. Stop! Stand still! Don't you see owls and bats whirring past?" *PN*, 337.

extracts from *Thus Spake Zarathustra*, where Zarathustra is urging the people to accept the superman: "'The overman is the meaning of the earth. May your will say: the overman *shall be* the meaning of the earth. I conjure you my brethren, *remain true to the earth*, and do not believe those who speak to you of supernatural hopes! They are poisoners, whether they know it or not.' "[37] Yeats notes: "Yet the 'supernatural life' may be but the soul, the earth out of which man leaps again, when the circle is complete." Teasingly cryptic though this is, a certain misgiving is discernible here, as if Yeats had doubts about his own objection. The theory of reincarnation is one which the Irish imagination has no difficulty in accepting; Yeats absorbed it quite naturally, but as early as "Fergus and the Druid" he betrays his uneasiness about the purely passive aspects of the theory. In his youth Mohini Chatterjee had taught him that re-incarnation was a punishment, and that the proper response was quietude; by the time of his valedictory poem "Under Ben Bulben," Yeats regarded re-incarnation as an act of will, and his loyalty to the earth was as fierce and intransigent as that of Zarathustra. Nietzsche's ideas may have played some role in that self-transformation.

3 It is apparent from these annotations that Yeats was fascinated by Nietzsche's distinction between slave- and master-morality, and that his sympathies were almost unreservedly on the side of Nietzsche's noble man. Yeats's socialist sympathies, like Davidson's, were never strong. He had turned socialist in the mid-1880s as a result of reading the lectures, pamphlets, and poems of William Morris. Yeats shunned the study of economics, and Morris's essentially non-economic vision of a harmonious society in *News from Nowhere* (1891) attracted Yeats more than the fastidious "tinkering" of the Fabians, which, Morris warned, would make men lose sight of their common goal by burdening them with "vexatious restrictions and compromises."[38] Yeats confessed that the hostility to religion on the part of so many socialists got on his nerves. During one lecture his anger erupted publicly: "What was the use of talking about some new revolution putting all things right, when the change must come, if come it did, with astronomical slowness, like the cooling of the sun?"[39] Yet only gradually did Yeats give up thinking and planning for some immediate and sudden change for the better. In "Nineteen Hundred and Nineteen," however, he abandons all Utopian hopes:

We pieced our thoughts into philosophy,
And planned to bring the world under a rule,
Who are but weasels fighting in a hole. ...

O but we dreamed to mend
Whatever mischief seemed
To afflict mankind, but now
That winds of winter blow
Learn that we were crack-pated when we dreamed.

Contemporary history was the source of this disillusionment. Yeats had placed so much faith in an Irish Renaissance that the sad condition of modern Ireland threw him into despair. His nostalgia for the heroes of Ireland's past, like Nietzsche's for pre-Socratic Greece, is strongly marked:

One morning we meet them hunting a stag that is "as joyful as the leaves of a tree in summer-time"; and whatever they do, whether they listen to the harp or follow an enchanter oversea, they do for the sake of joy, their joy in one another, or their joy in pride and movement; and even their battles are fought more because of their delight in a good fighter than because of any gain that is in victory. They live always as if they were playing a game; and so far as they have any deliberate purpose at all, it is that they may become great gentlemen and be worthy of the songs of poets. It has been said, and I think the Japanese were the first to say it, that the four essential virtues are to be generous among the weak, and truthful among one's friends, and brave among one's enemies, and courteous at all times.[40]

The Japanese may well have been the first to call these things the four essential virtues, but Yeats is surely echoing a passage in Nietzsche's *The Dawn of Day*, then recently published in English translation: "The Four Virtues. Honest towards ourselves, and to all and everything friendly to us; brave in the face of our enemy; generous towards the vanquished; polite at all times; such do the four cardinal virtues wish us to be."[41] If Yeats recognized and rejected the "brutal implications" – the phrase is Ellmann's – of Nietzsche's ethics, he also fully understood that brutality was no part of Nietzsche's message, as set down, for instance, in *The Genealogy of Morals*: "The knightly-aristocratic 'values' are based on a careful cult of the physical, on a flowering, rich and even effervescing healthiness, that goes considerably beyond what is necessary for maintaining life, on war, adventure, the chase, the dance, the tourney – on everything, in fact, which is contained in strong, free, and joyous action."[42] It is not hard to see that Cuchulain, the noble fighter, the man of joyous spirits, the man who delights in his enemies as much as in his friends, the deliberate seeker of hardship and difficulty, is Yeats's most persistent embodiment of the heroic ideal. It has been thought that the figure of Cuchulain was "drawn probably out of an admiration of Nietzsche's theories,"[43] but this is surely an exaggeration. For the writers of the Irish national movement Cuchulain had already assumed the proportions of a saviour; Lady Gregory's first contribution to the work of national liberation was to translate the Cuchulain stories, and George Russell was urging Irish youth to read them as a revelation of their own potential. Cuchulain rapidly became the Irish Prometheus; Yeats must have known, long before his reading of Nietzsche, of Shelley's description of Prometheus, in the preface to *Prometheus Unbound*, as "the type of the highest perfection of moral and intellectual nature, impelled by the purest and truest motives to the best and noblest ends." Yeats's version of the new hero may have been enhanced by Nietzsche's ideas about master-morality, but it was hardly inspired by them.

Critics have been divided over this question. Alex Zwerdling writes: "The great similarity between Yeats's notion of heroism and that of Nietzsche at first suggests that the influence of the philosopher may have been overwhelming and decisive. In many ways, the Nietzschean 'Uebermensch' compares with the Yeatsian hero."[44] Zwerdling is prepared to support this statement with some cogent argument. But two rather more influential critics, Richard Ellmann and F. A. C. Wilson, have taken a different line. "Yeats never accepted the superman," states Ellman flatly: "His equivalent for Nietzsche's brotherhood of supermen was not a gang of superb Irish roughnecks but an intellectual élite like that of the Duke Ercole in Castiglione's *Courtier*."[45] Granted that Nietzsche never defined the superman in unequivocal terms, it still seems fairly clear that he was no brutal roughneck. Indeed, he was much more an apostle of culture and enlightenment than a cruel monster of depravity and domination – the latter interpretation, current in the early years of the century, and regrettably popularized by the chapter on Nietzsche in Bertrand Russell's *History of Western Philosophy* (1945), is a mere caricature of Nietzsche's meaning.* Ellmann, however, is right in thinking that the superman is "a magnification of the individual," but wrong to assume that Nietzsche was "influenced by meliorist doctrines somewhat at variance with his cyclical theory." Nietzsche expressly rejected Darwin and the Spencerian belief in man's inevitable progress, and the doctrines of the superman and the

---

* Lord Russell comments: "I do not think that Nietzsche ever had any important influence in England. I believe that more people at Oxford than at Cambridge paid attention to him, but they were not the most able people. I should add that I consistently thought ill of Nietzsche, and I may be biased about his influence, which was certainly considerable in Germany." Letter to the writer, dated January 1, 1969.

eternal recurrence are compatible with one another, not inconsistent as is commonly believed. Yeats could accept a good many of the implications in the superman idea without abandoning his cyclical view of history.

F. A. C. Wilson is substantially in agreement with Ellmann concerning Yeat's debt to Nietzsche: "He may have learned something concerning the mask: but *The Unicorn from the Stars*, where the hero is made to turn away from a life of anarchic action to one of mystical contemplation, seems to me a clear sign of his rejection of the superman theory, and was probably written in reaction from it."[46] It is doubtful whether an assessment of this kind can justifiably be made on the basis of one play alone. In any case, *The Unicorn from the Stars* was, on Yeats's repeated admission, largely the work of Lady Gregory, and is therefore extremely suspect as a means of evaluating Yeats's own ideas. What is more, "a life of anarchic action," which Wilson intimates is characteristic of the superman, would surely have been deplored by Nietzsche himself, for he frequently went to great lengths to dissociate himself from anarchist views; the right of the superman to erect his own scale of values is not tantamount to a profession of anarchy. One might even say that Nietzsche would have regarded the change from anarchy to contemplation as a step in the right direction; after all, he saw the superman as a man able to discipline the chaos of his inner life into an harmonious unity, and this discipline belonged to the sphere of individual contemplation, not to anarchic action, which is essentially a political matter.

But such differences of opinion as to what Nietzsche meant will not help us to determine what Yeats understood. For that a close inspection of what Yeats himself wrote on the matter is necessary. Nowhere, we find, does Yeats explicitly repudiate the superman idea. On the contrary, both in his creative work and his correspondence the indications are that he was sympathetic to the theory as he understood it, both as the need for a superior race of human beings and as the worship – if that is not too strong a word – of individual men of genius.

Even before his first reading of Nietzsche, Yeats was opposing pagan hero to Christian martyr very much in the manner of Swinburne or Davidson. In the 1895 revision of *The Wanderings of Oisin* he tells how Manannan, his "dark hall" completed,

          cried to all
The mightier masters of a mightier race;
And at his cry there came no milk-pale face

Under a crown of thorns and dark with blood,
But only exultant faces.

But by 1904 the imagery in which such a race is described is strongly Nietzschean. In *The King's Threshold* Seanchan, in a familiar passage, foresees the coming of "a mightier race than any that has been":

The stars had come so near me that I caught
Their singing. It was praise of that great race
That would be haughty, mirthful, and white-bodied,
With a high head, and open hand, and how,
Laughing, it would take the mastery of the world.*

It is noteworthy that no reference to "a mightier race" occurs in Edwin Ellis's version of the same legend, *Sancan the Bard*, on which Yeats is supposed to have based his own play. Although Yeats is obviously identifying himself with Seanchan as the neglected and dispossessed artist, we must bear in mind that the Nietzschean vision is being exploited for its poetic and dramatic significance, and there is no reason to suppose that Yeats regarded it, at this stage in his life, as anything more than a vague aspiration. Other writers in the Irish movement took it more seriously. F. R. Higgins, for instance, quotes part of a speech from *The King's Threshold* in a note for a lecture which shows how easily notions of race and supermen could be linked to the cause of Irish nationalism: "Let us just sing for that race of men who become immeasurably stronger, wiser, and subtler with the future, their bodies more harmonized, their movements more rhythmic, their voices more musical, when the forms of life become more dynamically dramatic. We may be the predessors [*sic*] of the race of supermen; it is within the conception of human intelligence, aye even Irish intelligence. Therefore 'be you lifted up! and cry to that great race that is to come!' "[47]

Septimus, the protagonist of *The Player Queen* (1922), shares Seanchan's visionary hopes; announcing the end of the Christian era, he declares he will bid the Unicorn "trample mankind to death and beget a new race." But such utterances scattered in Yeats's plays resemble rhetorical gestures more than imaginative structurings of experience. Only when he envisages the imminent collapse of the whole of European civilization does Yeats approximate Nietzsche's sense of urgency, as in a letter to Ethel

---

* In drawing attention to the Nietzschean overtones of this passage Arthur Ransome was the first man, as far as I am aware, to relate Nietzsche to Yeats's work. See *Portraits and Speculations* (London, 1913), 109.

Mannin in 1936: "As a young man I used to repeat to myself Blake's lines 'and he his seventy disciples sent / Against religion and government.' I hate more than you do, for my hatred can have no expression in action. I am a forerunner of that horde that will some day come down the mountains."[48] In aphorism 900 of *The Will to Power*, a copy of which Yeats possessed, Nietzsche distinguishes between the barbarians who come from "down below" and *"another kind of barbarians* who come from the heights." Yeats identified a new race with a new civilization; his vision was not specifically limited to the somewhat narrow aims of Irish nationalism, which he always viewed with a measure of ironic mockery.

And what of the superman as such? Yeats obviously relished the passages concerning the superman which he read in Common's book. Two explicit references to the superman will help us gauge his degree of understanding. The first occurs in 1909, in a diary which is suffused with markedly Nietzschean ideas: "Blake talking to Crabb Robinson said once that he preferred to any man of intellect a happy thoughtless person, or some such phrase. It followed, I suppose, from his praise of life – 'all that lives is holy' – and from his dislike of abstract things. Balzac ... is too much taken up with his worship of the will, which cannot be thoughtless even if it can be happy, to be aware of the preference if he has it. Nietzsche had it doubtless at the moment when he imagined the 'Superman' as a child."[49] The reference, of course, is to the first of Zarathustra's speeches, in which he talks about the three metamorphoses of the spirit. After becoming a camel, then a lion, the spirit becomes a child: "The child is innocence and forgetting, a new beginning, a game, a self-propelled wheel, a first movement, a sacred 'Yes' is needed: the spirit now wills his own will, and he who had been lost to the world now conquers his own world."[50] Here, in compact form, are certain ideas – "affirmative capability," creativity and self-conquest – which will be discussed in the next section in the context of Yeats's work as a whole.

The second explicit reference, again to Balzac, occurs in 1919: "Nietzsche might have taken, and perhaps did take, his conception of the superman in history from his *Catherine de Medici*."[51] Balzac, of course, had been one of the most powerful influences on Yeats in his youth; in 1905 Yeats bought a forty-volume edition of Balzac and in subsequent years read through it systematically, coming to the conclusion that Balzac was "the only modern mind which has made a synthesis comparable to that of Dante."[52] In *Catherine de Medici* (1831–1841) Balzac portrays a woman of superior gifts of character and statesmanship; he describes her as quite free from the weaknesses of her sex, chaste, and a great benefactress of the arts. She was the epitome of nobility: "Catherine had, in the highest degree, the sense of royalty, and she defended it with admirable courage and persistency."[53] Catherine was forced by her predicament to endure terrible sufferings, deprivations, and anxieties – her self-conquest was of heroic proportions. Towards the end of the novel Catherine, long since dead, appears in a lawyer's dream and tries to explain her actions and the harsh misjudgment and misunderstanding that followed in their wake: "The intellect which soars above a nation cannot escape a great misfortune; I mean the misfortune of finding no equals capable of judging it when it succumbs beneath the weight of untoward events. My equals are few; fools are in the majority: that statement explains all."[54] She lived at the time of the Renaissance, which Balzac praises enthusiastically:

At no period of the world's history, in any land, was there ever seen so remarkable, so abundant a collection of men of genius. There were so many, in fact, that even the lesser princes were superior men. Italy was crammed with talent, enterprise, science, poesy, wealth, and gallantry, all the while torn by intestinal warfare and overrun with conquerors struggling for possession of her finest provinces. When men are so strong, they do not fear to admit their weaknesses. Hence, no doubt, this golden age for bastards.[55]

That richness of culture goes hand in hand with political instability is pure Nietzschean doctrine. In the third chapter of another of Balzac's novels, *The Country Doctor* (1833), a detailed account is given of the superman as the Great Statesman, the benevolent dictator.

Nietzsche often felt that men of genius were not supermen, being for him "all-too-human"; but in relation to the mass of mankind they did represent, by approximation, the superman ideal. Great artists and philosophers challenge emulation; they are an earnest of divinity. Yeats prophesied in *A Vision* that after 1927 men would no longer separate the idea of God from that of human genius, human productivity in all its forms. In Yeats's view, it was the task of literature to promulgate all the possibilities of human greatness: "A feeling for the form of life, for the graciousness of life, for the dignity of life, for the moving limbs of life, for the nobleness of life, for all that cannot be written in codes, has always been greatest among the gifts of literature to mankind. Indeed, the Muses being women, all literature is but their love-cries to the manhood of the world."[56]

To ask the question "Did Yeats accept Nietzsche's theory of the superman?" is to state the problem in a way which precludes definitive answer, since the problem has too many variables and is beset with the lurking menace of exclusive definition. To claim, however, that Yeats dismissed the theory outright is surely to misread the sparse evidence available; indeed, he seems to have taken it so seriously at one time that he incurred his father's displeasure. This is the background story: "He quarrelled savagely with his sister over the management of a small hand-press. J. B. Yeats wrote to remonstrate in the name of family affection, but his son replied to the effect that he no longer had need of family affection and quoted Nietzsche whom he had read in 1902 and 1903. The father would have been more sympathetic had he realized that his son's attitude had Maud Gonne rather than Nietzsche at the bottom of it."[57] Here is part of the letter of rebuke which J. B. Yeats wrote in 1906:

As regards the other matter in your letter. As you have dropped affection from the circle of your needs, have you also dropped love between man and woman? Is this the theory of the overman, if so, your demigodship is after all but a doctrinaire demigodship.

Your words are idle – and you are far more human than you think. You would be a philosopher and are really a poet – the contrary of John Morley, who is really a philosopher and wants to be a statesman. Morley is never roused except when some pet synthesis is in jeopardy.

The men whom Nietzsche's theory fits are only great men of a sort, a sort of Yahoo great men. The struggle is how to get rid of them, they belong to the clumsy and brutal side of things.[58]

He also warns his son against "aristocratic illusions, sacerdotalism, and the ferocious absurdity of the Overman."[59] His antagonism to Nietzsche is voiced in another letter to Yeats: "I think the reason you have the popular gift is because your *talent is benign*. That is its essential quality – [word indecipherable] are *malign*; so are aristocracies and pessimists – it is the *whole* of Nietzsche – so are College Dons and *their retinue*; but so were not Shakespeare or Shelley."[60]

There is no evidence that Yeats took his father's strictures to heart. Although J. B. Yeats disliked the superman idea, he had a strong aristocratic bias, and saw it as one of Ireland's chief tasks to "*keep up the supply of great men.*"[61] The same is true of John Eglinton, who, we recall, wrote that Nietzsche's conception of the Superman was "undoubtedly a little crazy," and yet Eglinton was indefatigable in his insistence on the vital part the Anglo-Irish Protestant ascendency would have to play in any cultural regeneration of Ireland. What is more, Yeat's enthusiasm for Nietzsche must have been confirmed by two people he respected and admired – Lady Gregory and Ezra Pound. Of Lady Gregory he writes: "Looking back, *Cuchulain of Muirthemne* and *Gods and Fighting Men* at my side, I can see that they were made possible by her past; semi-feudal Roxborough, her inherited sense of caste, her knowledge of that top of the world where men and women are valued for their manhood and their charm, not for their opinions."[62] And concerning her book *Poets and Dreamers*: "The end of wisdom is sometimes the beginning of heroism, and Lady Gregory's country poets have kept alive the way of thinking of the old heroic poets that did not constrain nature into any plan of civic virtue, but saw man as he is in himself, as an amorous woman has seen her lover from the beginning of the world."[63] It was at Lady Gregory's instigation that Yeats read Castiglione's *The Courtier* in 1907; it was she who suggested to Yeats that the only book he would need on one of his projected trips to Italy would be *Thus Spake Zarathustra*. The possibility of a link between these two recommendations cannot be dismissed.

As for Ezra Pound, he helped Yeats (whom he met in 1908) to ratify a belief in the artist as legislator which Yeats had found in both Shelley and Nietzsche; for Pound the artist was the ultimate authority, the only creator of values in a civilization: "All values ultimately come from our judicial sentences. ... Humanity is malleable mud, and the arts set the moulds it is later cast into."[64] Pound pronounced himself in favour of artistic patronage, of "the deliberate fostering of genius" which alone can bring about a great age in art. Although closely connected with the *New Age* circle of writers, in which Nietzsche's work was a staple of discussion, Pound seems to have taken little interest in Nietzsche,* but he shares many of Nietzsche's most uncompromising ideas about art and culture – these he must have aired frequently during the time he was acting as Yeats's secretary.

In Daniel Halévy's biography of Nietzsche (a copy of which Yeats pos-

---

* According to Pound, Nietzsche was the nineteenth-century maker of "a temporary commotion." *Polite Essays* (London, 1917), 180. "Amid the neo-Nietzschean clatter" of modern civilization, Pound's poetic persona, Mauberley, finds "his sense of graduations, / Quite out of place amid / Resistance to current exacerbations." On occasion Pound makes an incisive point. Citing de Gourmont's belief that "no creed, no dogma, can protect the thinking man from looking at life directly," Pound (probably reminded of Nietzsche's warning, in *Schopenhauer as Educator*, against a man letting "concepts, opinions, things past, and books step between himself and things") writes: "Nietzsche has done no harm in France because France has understood that thought can exist apart from action; that it is perfectly fitting and expedient to think certain things which it is neither fitting nor expedient to 'spoil by action.'" "Remy de Gourmont," *Poetry*, VII (January, 1916), 199. (Nietzsche emphasized that *The Will to Power* was above all "a book for thinking with.") In a letter to the present writer, dated November 4, 1965, Paul Selver, noted translator and frequent contributor to the *New Age*, stated that although he had had occasion to observe Pound at close quarters for several years, he detected nothing that would have placed Pound as a Nietzschean.

sessed), the theories of the superman and the eternal return are casually brushed aside as nothing more than naïve formulae. To Yeats, the theory of the superman was neither crazy nor naïve; it fitted very well with his aristocratic bias, his hope for a great Ireland of the future* and his championship of genius in all its forms. He accepted it as he accepted many other theories he adhered to, that is, mythically, as a symbol of value, as "one of those statements our nature is compelled to make and employ as a truth though there cannot be sufficient evidence."[65] Yet it is the implications of the superman theory, rather than the theory itself, which pervade Yeats's work, and it is to these implications that we must now direct our attention.

4. Reference has already been made to a letter from Yeats's father in which the term "overman" was used, and this was the more common equivalent for Nietzsche's *Übermensch* before Shaw gave popular currency to the word "superman." A recent translator of *Thus Spake Zarathustra*, Walter Kaufmann, has elected to reinstate the older term on the grounds that "it may help to bring out the close relation between Nietzsche's conceptions of the overman and self-overcoming."[66] The idea of self-overcoming, or *Selbst-Überwindung*, is in fact present in Zarathustra's initial presentation of his superman teaching: "I teach you the overman. Man is something that shall be overcome. What have you done to overcome him?"[67] Self-conquest is a literary as well as a moral concept. As Nietzsche put it: "Writing should always indicate a victory, indeed a conquest of oneself which must be communicated to others for their behoof."[68] The concept of self-overcoming is one that Yeats was to make his own. It crops up in many guises throughout his work, and often assertively: "Men are dominated by self-conquest," he writes, and "the act of appreciation of any great thing is an act of self-conquest."[69] Loose and declamatory as they may sound out of context, such statements lie close to Yeat's central preoccupations about life and art.

Nietzsche is quite specific about the purpose and nature of the self-overcoming process. Its end product, he tells us, is the discovery of values

---

* A striking instance of this was the calculating way Yeats invoked the name of Nietzsche in his address (given November 20, 1914) on the centenary of Thomas Davis. The fact that the British hated Nietzsche as the supposed inspirer of German militarism was pretext enough for the Irish to rally round the mention of his name. According to Austin Clarke (who reports the story), placards appeared the following morning bearing the startling caption: "Dublin Audience Cheers Nietzsche." *A Penny in the Clouds* (London, 1968), 13. Yeats's allusion was probably extemporaneous, for it does not occur in the printed version of his speech.

and in particular the discovery of new values and the revaluation of old ones. Such a "transvaluation of values" was even more urgent now, since he believed he was living at a transition point between two civilizations when a new ideal of life was desperately needed to counteract the forces of disruption and anarchy. Yeats felt, with a mixture of terror and joy, that "our civilisation was about to reverse itself, or some new civilisation about to be born from all that our age had rejected,"[70] and this premonition is voiced in such plays as *Where There Is Nothing* (1903) and *The King's Threshold* (1904), and in the visionary poem "The Second Coming" (1919). Such a diagnosis implied that the artist's function as a creator of value was greater than ever. We have already noted how uncompromising Ezra Pound was on this point. What concerns us here is the psychology of valuation, as Nietzsche sees it:

> A tablet of the good hangs over every people. Behold it is the tablet of their overcomings; behold, it is the voice of their will to power.
> Praiseworthy is whatever seems difficult to a people; whatever seems indispensable and difficult is called good; and whatever liberates even out of the deepest need, the rarest, the most difficult — that they call holy.[71]

Valuation, then, is a function of the will to power, and the will to power is primarily the will to overcome oneself, as a later passage makes clear:

> Wherever I found the living, there I heard also the speech on obedience. Whatever lives, obeys.
> And this is the second point: he who cannot obey himself is commanded. That is the nature of the living.
> This, however, is the third point that I heard: that commanding is harder than obeying; and not only because he who commands must carry the burden of all who obey, and because this burden may easily crush him. An experiment and hazard appeared to me to be in all commanding; and whenever the living commands, it hazards itself. Indeed, even when it commands *itself*, it must still pay for its commanding. It must become the judge, the avenger, and the victim of its own law.[72]

This is reminiscent of several passages in his copy of Nietzsche which Yeats singled out for approval, this one in particular: "The most intelligent men, as being the *strongest*, find their happiness in that wherein others find their ruin: in the labyrinth, in severity towards themselves and others, in effort; their delight is self-conquest; with them asceticism becomes nature, requirement, and instinct."[73]

One element in the nature of self-conquest is thus seen to be the deliberate and joyful acceptance of a formidable challenge, the marshalling of one's inner resources against external obstacles. In *The Birth of Tragedy* Nietzsche characterizes the hero of Greek drama as the highest manifestation of the will in the face of some terrible dilemma; and in *The Will to Power* art is still valued as a relief from suffering: "Art is the alleviation of the sufferer, – as the way to states in which pain is willed, is transfigured, is deified, where suffering is a form of great ecstasy."[74] The heroic man, says Nietzsche, is habituated to suffering, even searches for it, and thereby "extols his existence by means of tragedy."[75] The same insight informs Yeats's view that "tragedy is a joy to the man who dies,"[76] this joy being, in Nietzschean terms, the supreme exercise of the will to power. As Yeats's "instructors" in *A Vision* were to confirm, it is the degree of energy roused in the struggle, not ultimate victory, which is important, for "only the greatest obstacle that can be contemplated without despair rouses the will to full intensity."[77] In such passages as the following, Yeats approximates to Nietzsche's *amor fati*, the profoundest expression of life-affirmation consequent upon a belief in the eternal recurrence: "I think it was Heraclitus who said: The Daimon is our destiny. When I think of life as a struggle with the Daimon who would ever set us to the hardest work among those not impossible, I understand why there is a deep enmity between a man and his destiny, and why a man loves nothing but his destiny."* Life as struggle is the very core of Heraclitean doctrine, and Yeats's belief that all creation stems from conflict, in the form of poetry if the conflict is internal and in the form of rhetoric if the conflict is external, may have come to him (if not directly from his father) from Heraclitus. Like Nietzsche, Yeats believed that all aristocracies were founded on a war of conquest, but assented to Nietzsche's view that military battles were not the only ones a man could fight – there was also the "internecine war within the self": "Why should we honour those that die upon the field of battle? A man may show as reckless a courage in entering into the abyss of himself."[78] And again: "I think that all noble things are the result of warfare; great nations and classes, of warfare in the visible world, great poetry and philosophy, of invisible warfare, the division of a mind within itself, a victory, the sacrifice of a man to himself."[79]

This introduces a second element into the process of self-conquest: not only must a man's will to power confront external obstacles, but it must also overcome his own moral and spiritual failings, for they may be his strongest enemy. In *Ecce Homo* Nietzsche proclaims that his humanity

---

* *Mythologies* (London, 1959), 336. A parallel between Nietzsche and Heraclitus was noted quite early by G. Murray, *A History of Ancient Greek Literature* (London, 1897), 156.

is "a perpetual process of self-mastery"[80] and that the writing of *Zarathustra* was an act of spiritual purgation: "The overcoming of morality by itself, through truthfulness, the moralist's overcoming of himself in his opposite – in me – that is what the name Zarathustra means in my mouth."[81] Through his mask or "anti-self" – Zarathustra – Nietzsche tried to purge himself of those merely "reactive" emotions which were so powerful that they threatened to overwhelm him; by purgation Nietzsche meant sublimating the passions, not extirpating them: "We can act as the gardeners of our impulses, and – which few people know – we may cultivate the seeds of anger, pity, vanity, or excessive brooding, and make these things fecund and productive, just as we can train a beautiful plant to grow along trellis-work."[82] Again: "Almost the passions have fallen in disrepute thanks to those who were not strong enough to convert them to their advantage."[83] Self-conquest, as Nietzsche and Yeats see it, means the process of self-discipline a man is forced to undergo if he is ever to come into "the desolation of reality" and realize his full potential self; it involves bitter suffering, "the infinite pain of self-realisation"[84] as Yeats called it. It is the condition of a full creative life: "A poet writes always of his personal life, in his finest work out of its tragedy, whatever it be, remorse, lost love, or mere loneliness."* Torn between two rival perfections, of the life and of the work, Yeats waged his inner war against timidity, remorse and hatred to the end of his life, finding a degree of solace in the thought he was making some advance – he had to make and remake himself as a necessary accompaniment and corollary of making and remaking his poems. Such a poem as "An Acre of Grass" bears witness to the effort, demanded by self-transformation, where vision issues in madness; in this poem Yeats alludes to Timon and Lear and Blake, and Nietzsche's name would not be out of place in this company.

Indeed, Yeats, rejecting the candidature of Pound, uses Nietzsche's name to exemplify the twelfth, or heroic, phase of *A Vision*. Bearing in mind the odd assortment of personages Yeats musters as concrete illustrations to each phase, or incarnation, we might feel wary about attributing too much significance to this choice in itself; but what Yeats tells us about this phase is so unmistakably in keeping with our previous findings about his relationship to Nietzsche that all hesitancies vanish. Of phase twelve Yeats writes:

---

* *Essays and Introductions*, 509. Confessing he was able to remember little of childhood except its pain, Yeats wrote: "I have grown happier with every year of life as though gradually conquering something in myself." *The Autobiography of W. B. Yeats* (New York, 1958), 5.

The nature is conscious of the most extreme degree of *deception*, and is wrought to a frenzy of desire for truth of self. If Phase 9 had the greatest possible "belief in its own desire," there is now the greatest possible belief in all values created by personality. It is therefore before all else the phase of the hero, of the man who overcomes himself, and so no longer needs, like Phase 10, the submission of others, or, like Phase 11, conviction of others to prove his victory. Solitude has been born at last, though solitude invaded, and hard to defend.[85]

Leaving aside the relevance of this extract as a useful gloss on the poem just mentioned, we might recall a Yeats annotation to Nietzsche in which victory was not conceived as mere overcoming but achieved its end by being a new creation – "the joy of it creates friends." The victory of the hero, the self-conqueror (note how Yeats identifies the two), is a victory, not of "mere brute force," but of superior personality, of greater creativeness.

It might be asked, now that the purpose and nature of the self-conquest motif in Yeats's work has been briefly touched upon, what use he made of it. One might begin to explore this question by quoting once again this cryptic annotation: "Night (Socrates/Christ) one god, night – denial of self – the soul turned towards spirit seeking knowledge. Day (Homer) many gods, day – affirmation of self – the soul turned from Spirit to be its mask and instrument when it seeks life." To this succinct formulation Yeats always remained loyal, and many of his poems, such as "Ego Dominus Tuus" and "A Dialogue of Self and Soul," clearly pivot on it. The two attitudes it represents, the first passive ("Being"), religious, mystical, the second active ("Becoming"), secular and dynamic, were later expanded and schematized in the two movements of *A Vision*, the primary and the antithetical antinomies which are symbolically expressed in the form of interpenetrating gyres. The primary movement is towards self-abnegation, self-transcendence; the antithetical movement is towards self-affirmation, self-realization. It is, most simply, the difference between Schopenhauer, for whom the will enslaves, and Nietzsche, for whom the will liberates. There is, of course, no question of choosing one movement in preference to the other, for Yeats envisages both of them as states of consciousness in perpetual conflict, interacting on and with each other, dying each other's life and living each other's death. For Yeats, the two stances, the saintly and the superhuman, exercised an equal fascination; the dialectical tension between them provides not only the pressure behind his work but in many cases the actual thematic substance as well. Although Yeats once confessed that in his lyric poetry, from *The Wanderings* *of Oisin* onwards, the swordsman had repudiated the saint, the repudiation is never final – Yeats preserves a nagging, ironic awareness of the alternative mode of existence. But in the first decade of the century a sharp swing, in this oscillating allegiance, towards the superhuman mode is detectable, and it marks a crisis in Yeats's poetic career. As early as the 1880s Yeats had felt he was writing poetry of longing and complaint, not poetry of insight and knowledge; after reading Nietzsche he redefined his predicament in terms borrowed from *The Birth of Tragedy*; describing as "Dionysiac," which is "sad and desirous," the impulse to transcend form and as "Apollonic," which is "joyful and self sufficient," the impulse to create it. As for his own intentions: "I think I have to some extent got weary of that wild God Dionysus, and I am hoping that the Far-Darter will come in his place."[86] The rather Nietzschean play, *Where There Is Nothing*, might be regarded as a first step towards that "tragic gaiety" which informs much of his last work; it stands as an indictment of Yeats's earlier essays and plays with which, as the correspondence shows, he was becoming increasingly dissatisfied. In *The Land of Heart's Desire* he finds an exaggeration of sentimental beauty which is "unmanly"; *The Countess Cathleen* is no more than "a piece of tapestry" and for a reason which, in the context of the present discussion, is extraordinarily revealing: "The Countess sells her soul, but she is not transformed. If I were to think out that scene today, she would, the moment her hand has signed, burst into *loud laughter*, mock at all she has held holy, horrify the peasants in the midst of their temptations."* Not only is the Countess untouched by her choice, but in making it she bypasses the rigours of self-inquisition; in rewriting the play, Yeats would make that choice a result of a struggle in the soul, and laughter a signal of a triumphant self-conquest; the change which Yeats made to the end of *The King's Threshold*, whereby Seanchan is made to die, is another example of Yeats's desire to embody "athletic joy" in his work. Drama was not only the vehicle for the expression of this desire, but also the means to its achievement: "To me ... drama has been the search for more of manful energy, more of cheerful acceptance of whatever arises out of the logic of events, and for clean outline, instead of those outlines of lyric poetry that are blurred with desire and vague regret."[87]

The need to demolish and recreate his past self, which Yeats saw so clearly, proved easier to formulate programmatically than to put into effect: at the time the above passage was written, for instance, Yeats was

---

* *Autobiography*, 279. My italics. In aphorism 294 of *Beyond Good and Evil* Nietzsche describes laughing at all serious and even holy things as "overman-like."

engaged in the composition of the musicians' songs in *Deirdre*, relapsing once more into that "prevailing decadence" he thought he had successfully overcome. Yet the sheer strenuousness of these tactical manœuvres of self-conquest was a real gain inasmuch as it assisted Yeats to develop a theory of poetry as the expression of the whole man, "blood, imagination, intellect running together," a view which is first coherently set out in *Discoveries* (1906). Yeats's exposition of this theory is conducted almost entirely in terms of the polarities of his Nietzsche annotation. Predictably enough, he still finds it hard to renounce his nostalgia for essences and states of mind, but the more pronounced bias is in favour of "blood," immediacy, actuality and all that makes for unity of being. A letter to Florence Farr probably written in the same year, 1906, makes it apparent that this concern is as much moral as it is literary: "I have myself by the by begun eastern meditations – of your sort, but with the object of trying to lay hands upon some dynamic and substantializing force as distinguished from the eastern quiescent and supersensualizing state of the soul – a movement downwards upon life, not upwards out of life."[88] And in his diary three years later he seeks this new dynamicism by pressing the fruits of personal and theatrical experience into a fresh synthesis: "There is a relation between discipline and the theatrical sense. If we cannot imagine ourselves as different from what we are and assume that second self, we cannot impose a discipline upon ourselves, though we may accept one from others. Active virtue as distinguished from the passive acceptance of a current code is therefore theatrical, consciously dramatic, the wearing of a mask. It is the condition of arduous full life."* Or, in the words of the annotation, "affirmation of self – the soul turned from spirit to be its mask and instrument when it seeks life."

The idea of the mask, of course, is a favourite one with Nietzsche: "If any one long and obstinately desires to *appear* something, he finds it difficult at last to *be* anything else. The profession of almost every individual, even of the artist, begins with hypocrisy, with an imitating from without, with a copying of the effective."[89] And again:

Everything that is profound loves the mask; the profoundest things have a hatred even of figure and likeness. Should not the *contrary* only be the right disguise for the shame of a God to go about in ...? There is not only deceit behind a mask – there is so much goodness in craft. I could imagine that a man with something costly and fragile to conceal, would roll through life clumsily and rotundly like

---

* *Autobiography*, 317. Cf. "No mind can engender till divided into two." 231.

an old, green, heavily-hooped wine-cask: the refinement of his shame requiring it to be so.[90]

For Oscar Wilde the creation of an artificial self was a liberation from his natural one: "Man is least himself when he talks in his own person. Give him a mask and he will tell you the truth." Ellmann, believing Yeats learnt much about the mask from Nietzsche, makes the following observation: "The advantage of the mask of Nietzsche over the 'pose' of Oscar Wilde was that the former was virile and unconnected with estheticism. Yeats, who had been concerned since childhood over the discrepancy between what he was and what others thought him to be, now made 'mask' a favourite term."[91] The doctrine of the mask, as an active and masculine concept, gradually ousted that of the mirror, as a passive and feminine one. In the realm of thought Yeats agreed with Coleridge that the mechanical philosophy of the eighteenth century had turned the human mind into the quicksilver at the back of a mirror, and in the realm of art with Stendhal that a work of realism was "a mirror dawdling down a road." Nietzsche had attacked the "mirroring and eternally self-polishing soul" which "no longer knows how to affirm, no longer how to deny."[92] Shy and awkward as a youth, Yeats set himself "to acquire this technique of seeming" which he had admired in a phrase in Goethe's *Wilhelm Meister*: "The poor are; the rich are enabled also to seem."[93] Goethe, of course, is Nietzsche's principal model of the man who creates himself, who gives style to his life. Such ideas lie behind Yeats's ultimate rejection of Paterism: "Surely the ideal of culture expressed by Pater can only create feminine souls. The soul becomes a mirror not a brazier."[94] In its stead Yeats would seek an approach to the culture of the Renaissance, founded, not on self-knowledge, "but on knowledge of some other self, Christ or Caesar, not on delicate sincerity but on imitative energy."[95] Recalling this view to mind later Yeats wrote: "Some years ago I began to believe that our culture, with its doctrine of sincerity and self-realisation, made us gentle and passive, and that the Middle Ages and the Renaissance were right to found theirs upon the imitation of Christ or of some classic hero. St. Francis and Caesar Borgia made themselves overmastering, creative persons by turning from the mirror to meditation upon a mask."[96] By "self-realisation" Yeats means any effort at self-improvement which involves no personal stake or risk – it is the culture-philistinism Nietzsche assailed in one of his most violent polemics, that on David Strauss.

A tempting over-simplification would be to say that for Yeats the mask was a spur to creativity and for Nietzsche a method to arrive at truth; but this leaves out of account Yeats's struggle to wrest some meaning from the chaos of existence and also Nietzsche's obsession (particularly marked in *Zarathustra*) with creativity. But it is clear that for both writers the adoption of a mask is instrumental in the individual's struggle for self-perfection. This struggle lies at the root of Nietzsche's superman theory. In an early pamphlet, *Schopenhauer as Educator*, he demonstrates that a man can give meaning to his life by a process of unflinching self-discovery. This entails a conscientious meditation on the features of the man he has most admired. For Yeats, as for Nietzsche, we can only learn to "become what we are" by identifying ourselves with the achievements and aspirations of great men, and the work of both men is studied with the names of their chosen progenitors, the "great masters" of ancestral memory and lineage. Yeats's poem "The Statues" has been seen in part as an illustration of what Nietzsche calls "monumental history," one giant calling to another across "the great waste of time," guaranteeing continuity.

And what of the application of this to politics? There is a difference between the hero-worship of Carlyle and other Victorians and that of Nietzsche. For Carlyle, great men make history, and without hero-worship society would degenerate into a condition of anarchy which he deplores. For Nietzsche, on the other hand, the superman is valuable, not on account of any instrumental value he has for the maintenance of society, but because he is the ultimate standard, the ideal to which everyone aspires; society should exist solely for his preservation and development. Yeats sides with Nietzsche:

Science has driven out the legends, stories, superstitions that protected the immature and the ignorant with symbol, and now that the flower has crossed our rooms, science must take their place and demonstrate as philosophy has in all ages, that States are justified, not by multiplying or, as it would seem, comforting those that are inherently miserable, but because sustained by those for whom the hour seems "awful," and by those born out of themselves, the best born of the best.[97]

Although the immediate context here is William Morris's *Sigurd the Volsung*, the passage is redolent of Nietzsche's slave- and master-morality distinction and of that facet of it we are here considering, the idea of self-conquest – "those born out of themselves." Yeats, with his longing for "the old humanity with its unique irreplaceable individuals," and his hatred of democracy and mob-rule which has succeeded a "hierarchial society, where all men are different," and "given Ireland to the incompetent,"[98] is constantly found echoing Nietzsche's asseveration that "the aim of mankind can lie ultimately only in its highest examples."[99] Ireland, Yeats thought, should not be poured into a political system, but moulded on the ablest men the country has. Nietzsche had made an eloquent if desperate appeal for a hundred men to rebuild the Renaissance, and Yeats makes the same appeal for a rebuilding of Ireland: "A hundred men, their creative power wrought to the highest pitch, their will trained but not broken, can do more for the welfare of a people, whether in war or peace, than a million of any lesser sort no matter how expensive their education."[100] The phrase "their will trained but not broken" might easily pass unnoticed, but it reflects Yeats's ever-increasing concern with the virtues of discipline, of strenuousness, of self-exposure – it corresponds to the tough defiance of the typically Nietzschean gesture of "what doesn't kill me, makes me stronger."

It is interesting, at this point, to compare the political idealism of H. G. Wells. In his early work, such as *Anticipations* (1902), Wells had limited membership of his governing *élite* to men of scientific training who would control and restrict the "non-functional" masses under them; but in his influential *A Modern Utopia* (1904), Wells takes more account of men (in Yeats's phrase) of "creative power," who, while conscious of their superiority to other men, govern, not because they relish the exercise of power, but because they are best equipped to further the progress of the race. They are men of great spiritual resources in whom self-discipline is paramount. Wells takes the Japanese samurai as an embodiment of his aristocratic ideal, but it is also exemplified in his fictional characters, of whom Benham in *The Research Magnificent* (1915) is the outstanding representative. Benham protests against democracy, because it hampers individual self-perfection and brings confusion and chaos to society: "Democracy, if it means anything, means the rule of the planless man, the rule of the unkempt mind. It means as a necessary consequence this vast boiling up of collectively meaningless things."* Benham's research into aristocratization is conducted, in the first instance, on the personal level; his aim is to overcome the weaknesses of character which effectively bar him from realizing his ideals – his fear, his self-indulgence, his jealousy, and his prejudice, and the surmounting of these things is very much an act of self-conquest. Ultimately Benham dies out of loyalty to those principles by which he lived: his research is not magnificent in terms of achieved success but in terms of the noble purpose which inspired it. That purpose is instigated by an act of choice:

* *The Research Magnificent* (London, 1915), 107. H. L. Mencken called this book "a poor soup from the dry bones of Nietzsche," in which Wells "smouches an idea from Nietzsche, and then mauls it so badly that one begins to wonder whether he is in favor of it or against it." *Prejudices: First Series* (London, 1921), 24, 33.

We have to choose each one for himself and also each one for the race, whether we will accept the muddle of the common life, whether we ourselves will be muddled, weakly nothings, children of luck, steering our artful courses for mean success and tawdry honours, or whether we will be aristocrats – for that is what it amounts to, each one in the measure of his personal quality an aristocrat, refusing to be restrained by fear, refusing to be restrained by pain, resolved to know and understand up to the hilt of his understanding, resolved to sacrifice all the common stuff of his life to the perfection of his peculiar gift, a purged man, a trained, selected, artificial man, not simply free, but lordly free, filled and sustained by pride.[101]

But here the resemblance with Yeats ends, for Wells came to believe that an ideal society could do without a ruling class altogether, since the inferior types that made government necessary would be eliminated by new discoveries in education and technology. Wells, like Shaw, believed that these would one day transform man's nature, and would make possible a "democracy of supermen"; Yeats, like Nietzsche, thought that such a belief was illusory, and confined his hopes to the emergence of a new caste of leaders which would ensure the stability of a strongly hierachical form of society. Authority and cultural "unity of being" go hand in hand: "No art can conquer the people alone – the people are conquered by an ideal of life upheld by authority. As this ideal is rediscovered, the arts, music and poetry, painting and literature will draw closer together."[102]

Finally, by way of summary, a few words about the role of self-conquest in a sphere to which it is equally applicable – the religious. It has already been stated that Nietzsche's doctrines of the eternal recurrence and the superman are not incompatible with one another. A justification of this view is not hard to seek. A theory of history as the endless repetition of the same cycle (or cycles) of events implies that it has no final purpose, no ultimate goal and no possibility of being redeemed in time by the intervention of a Messiah – history is both meaningless and futile. Familiar with this gloomy view of history from his reading of Indian philosophy and religion before his first encounter with Nietzsche, Yeats seems to have benefited both from Nietzsche's reformulation of it and from the attitude he adopted. One has only to point to the writing of *A Vision* – constructed as "a last defence against the chaos of the world" – and to poems like "Lapis Lazuli," and "The Gyres" where the determination to surmount the problem of a futile and godless world is emblazoned on characters emblematic of "tragic gaiety." For these characters, as for Yeats himself, a capitulation to despair would be, like all surrender, unheroic, for since despair is a merely "reactive" emotion it is sterile and uncreative. Heroic minds strive to conquer despair, and in so doing experience "joy," a word which Yeats uses in a distinctively personal way. By "joy" Yeats means very much what Nietzsche often means when he uses the German word *"Lust"*: not a contented feeling of happiness, which is marked by the absence of pain, but a dynamic exultation in the very face of suffering. This joy is the sign and symptom of the possession of power, and the power is not only over oneself, but also over events themselves, for a knowledge that events must eternally recur confers a power over them: knowledge is power, not in the Baconian sense of power to manipulate, but in the deeper, imaginative sense of spiritual illumination. Such illumination belongs only to the supermen, the self-conquerors. As Nietzsche puts it: "My formula for greatness in man is *amor fati*: the fact that a man wishes nothing to be different, either in front of him or behind him, or for all eternity. Not only must the necessary be borne, and on no account concealed, – all idealism is falsehood in the face of necessity, – but it must also be loved."[103]

Yeats agrees that *amor fati* is a love which eschews pity, which "does not desire to change its object. It is a form of the eternal contemplation of what is."[104] Or, as he indicates in "A Dialogue of Self and Soul," of what must return:

I am content to live it all again
And yet again, if it be life to pitch
Into the frog-spawn of a blind man's ditch. ...

I am content to follow to its source
Every event in action or in thought;
Measure the lot; forgive myself the lot!
When such as I cast out remorse
So great a sweetness flows into the breast
We must laugh and we must sing,
We are blest by everything,
Everything we look upon is blest.

Recalling his meditations on the Capri landscape Yeats wrote: "I murmured, as I have countless times, 'I have been part of it always and there is maybe no escape, forgetting and returning life after life like an insect in the roots of the grass.' But murmured it without terror, in exultation almost."* Contemplation, when pursued against the background of the eternal recurrence and its appropriate psychological counterpart, *amor*

---

* *A Vision* (London, 1925), xiii. Cf. Nietzsche's passage about the demon whispering the eternal recurrence, *CW*, x, 341.

fati, can accept as right and good the destruction of beautiful and valuable things as well as their creation, and so arouses "an energy so noble, so powerful, that we laugh aloud and mock, in the terror or the sweetness of our exaltation, at death and oblivion."[105] In Yeats, as in Nietzsche, "laughter" and "dancing" are the objective correlatives of "joy" and of all the attitudes of which joy is compounded – recklessness, exultation, blessedness, courage, lack of shame, mockery, defiance, all of which originate in fear and the conquest of fear. As Nietzsche wrote: "Every artist first attains the supreme pinnacle of his greatness when he can look *down into* himself and his art, when he can *laugh* at himself."[106]

Man's new-found dignity lies no longer in a passive obedience to divine or human law; it consists in the freedom to "transvalue all values," to destroy all hollow idols and to rehabilitate all that was thought evil or contemptible. This freedom makes man a tragic being, since it is mandatory – man is, in existential terms, condemned to be free; having banished God, he must prove himself worthy of such a deed and create a compensatory greatness in keeping with the revolution he has effected. Sweeping aside all illusions of transcendence, man fashions for himself a new image of immanence which, while remaining human, seeks to be more than merely human. For Nietzsche this new image is the superman; for Yeats it is the joyous heroic man, who represents a "consecrated humanism, the elevation of humanity to near-Godlike status."[107] If Yeats is never found following Nietzsche's thought to the letter, he is clearly very close to its predominant spirit, and it would not be too much of an exaggeration to say of him, as has been said of Rilke, that he is the poet of the world-view of which Nietzsche is the first philosopher.

GEORGE BERNARD SHAW

1   Shaw was generally regarded, even by writers more knowledgeable about Nietzsche's work than himself, as one of the chief popularizers of Nietzsche in England. J. M. Kennedy wrote: "It was chiefly Shaw who made Ibsen, Wagner, Schopenhauer, and Nietzsche familiar to a wide circle, together with many lesser Continental luminaries."[1] Clive writes of Nietzsche in his recent anthology: "His vogue in Anglo-Saxon thought was chiefly connected with the rise of Bernard Shaw and defunct controversies over Social Darwinism."[2] This is a view widely held today, in spite of a growing feeling that Shaw made no thorough study of Nietzsche's work and consequently was justified in being irritated by the persistent charges of plagiarism made against him. Shaw's indebtedness to Nietzsche, the extent of his knowledge, and the manner in which he was responsible for making Nietzsche's name more generally known will be re-examined here, but first it might be useful to see how Shaw and his contemporaries reacted to four figures who contributed largely to the moulding of English opinion on Nietzsche: Ibsen, Wagner, Schopenhauer, and Nordau.

Thanks to the almost single-handed pioneer work of Edmund Gosse in the 1870s and to William Archer's efforts as a translator, Ibsen's status as a writer of European importance was secure by the last decade of the century – "virtually every eminent British critic of current literature in the eighteen-nineties felt it due to himself to register an opinion on Ibsen."[3] He could not be ignored; as early as 1893 Archer had estimated that no less than 40,000 volumes of Ibsen translations, representing, in his view, 100,000 plays, had been sold; and of the twenty plays available in English twelve were staged in London before the turn of the century. Although Nietzsche was never the subject of such heated controversy as blazed around these plays, one might have expected that Ibsen's brand of iconoclasm would have weakened English resistance to Nietzsche's attacks on bourgeois complacency and permitted a cool, circumspect look at the substance of his philosophy undeterred by its forceful but rhetorical top-dressing; but this did not happen. Criticism of Nietzsche was none the less violent for having previously been levelled at Ibsen – if anything, Ibsen's ideas, merely on account of their historical priority, tended to deprive Nietzsche's of urgency and power. George Brandes had found a hearing for Nietzsche in Scandinavia at the end of the 1880s, but his European prestige as a great literary critic seemed to suffer in England from his enthusiasm for "an obscure German iconoclast named Friedrich Nietschke [sic]": "It is difficult to understand how a man of well-balanced brain and logical equipment second to none, can take *au sérieux* a mere philosophical savage who dances a war-dance amid what he conceived to be the ruins of civilization, swings a reckless tomahawk and knocks down everybody and everything that comes in his way. There must lie a long history of disappointment and bitterness behind that endorsement of anarchy pure and simple."4 There is no evidence that Brandes was able to make Nietzsche as familiar to English readers as he had helped to make Ibsen, and if Yeats's impression is any guide his visits to London in the 1890s were not always popular; it was only much later that the publication of his book on Nietzsche confirmed his status as an authority on the philosopher, on whom he was invited to give lectures.* In the Gosse-Brandes correspondence there is no mention of Nietzsche, and although Gosse publicly acknowledged Nietzsche's importance, he was never an activist for him as he had been for Ibsen, and Archer remained a stubborn opponent of Nietzsche all his life. As we have seen, it was the publishing firm of J. T. Grein (the young naturalized Englishman of Dutch birth whose Independent Theatre Group was principally responsible for staging Ibsen's plays) which first issued translations of Nietzsche in 1896. Shaw does not seem to have been a party to this decision to publish Nietzsche, although his failure to find a publisher for his novels must have made him aware of the difficulties involved in trying to put new or unremunerative books on the market. Later in life, however, he was to subsidize the *New Age* out of his own resources and finance a translation of Strindberg from his Nobel Prize money.

Shaw wrote that he first heard of the name of Nietzsche in 1891 from a

---

* Brandes, to Yeats's evident distaste, "was praising all manner of noisy persons." *The Letters of W. B. Yeats* (London, 1954), 268. Brandes delivered a lecture on Nietzsche in the *Times* library in London in November and December, 1913. Julie Norregard, later the wife of Richard Le Gallienne, had attended Brandes' Copenhagen lectures in which he illuminated "the golden thoughts of Niezche [sic], young Germany's ill-fated philosopher." "G. Brandes: A Silhouette," *Yellow Book*, VIII (January, 1896), 166.

German mathematician, a Miss Borchardt. After reading *The Quintessence of Ibsenism* she remarked that he must have read *Beyond Good and Evil* which, Shaw protested, "I had never seen, and could not have read with any comfort, for want of the necessary German, if I had seen it."[5] But he thought the title "promising," –an indication of his willingness to read Nietzsche when translations became available. When they did, Miss Borchardt's remark made immediate sense:

> In fact Nietzsche's criticism of morality and idealism is essentially that demonstrated in my book as at the bottom of Ibsen's plays. His pungency; his power of putting the merest platitudes of his position in rousing, startling paradoxes; his way of getting underneath moral precepts which are so unquestionable to us that common decency seems to compel unhesitating assent to them, and upsetting them with a scornful laugh: all this is easy to a witty man who has once well learnt Schopenhauer's lesson, that the intellect by itself is a mere dead piece of brain machinery, and our ethical and moral systems merely the pierced cards you stick into it when you want it to play a certain tune. So far I am on common ground with Nietzsche.[6]

In a later review Shaw places Nietzsche in a tradition of "Diabolonianism" which began with Blake, was pursued briefly by Swinburne and Mark Twain, and rescued from extinction by Ibsen: "All seemed lost when suddenly the cause found its dramatist in Ibsen, the first leader who really dragged duty, unselfishness, idealism, sacrifice, and the rest of the antidiabolic scheme to the bar at which it had indicted so many excellent Diabolonians,"[7] Shaw sets himself alongside Nietzsche as an iconoclast who carries into philosophy what Ibsen had discovered as a dramatist. For Shaw, the point at which Nietzsche, Ibsen and (as we shall see later) Wagner converge is in their "transvaluation of values," their criticism of current respectability; all three are pioneers in morality who stand for whatever is most advanced. A pioneer such as Ibsen courts unpopularity: "We now see that the pioneer must necessarily provoke such outcry as he repudiates duties, tramples on ideals, profanes what was sacred, sanctifies what was infamous, always driving his plough through gardens of pretty weeds in spite of the laws made against trespassers for the protection of the worms which feed on the roots, always letting in light and air to hasten the putrefaction of decaying matter, and everywhere proclaiming that 'the old beauty is no longer beautiful, the new truth no longer true.'"[8] The change from the "pioneer" in Ibsen to the "superman" of Nietzsche was, for Shaw, a shift in terminology, not in substance, for the Shavian superman is, *par excellence*, the arch-iconoclast. In a 1912 note to *The Quintessence of Ibsenism,* Shaw explicitly identifies the messianism of Ibsen's as that of Nietzsche, however, is the fact that art in general, and music in particular, ought not to be condemned merely in terms of the physical degeneration or abnormality of the artist."[15] After all, Newman points out, abnormality in artists is not unusual – it was Max Nordau's error not to distinguish between physical peculiarities and the artistic work to which they give rise. Shortly after Nietzsche's death in 1900 another Wagnerian, J. F. Runciman, a colleague of Shaw on the staff of the *Saturday Review*, observed that the Wagner-Nietzsche issue was the subject of fiery debate in every European capital except London, where no one was concerned with the attacks of "a great leader of philosophic thought" on "the greatest musician born into the century." For Runciman the real puzzle about Wagner and Nietzsche was not why they quarrelled, but how they ever became friends, Nietzsche being illogical, cerebral, fanatical, bigoted, unpoetic, intolerant and a mere dilettante in music, whereas Wagner was demonstrably the reverse of all these.[16] In a later article Runciman notes with dismay Nietzsche's hold over modern composers such as Delius and Strauss, and over French musicians generally: "The French have never had a music, have not one, and may never have one; and they will certainly not help matters forward by following the Germans and seeking inspiration in the uninspired pages of a mad German pseudo-philosopher."[17]

As for Shaw, he shared Runciman's prejudice against French music, and in both his reviews of the Nietzsche translations made Nietzsche's admiration for Bizet a pretext for condescending exasperation: "Nietzsche had sat at the feet of Wagner, whose hero, Siegfried, was also a good Diabolonian. Unfortunately, after working himself up to the wildest enthusiasm about Wagner's music, Nietzsche rashly went to Bayreuth and heard it – a frightful disillusion for a man barely capable of 'Carmen.'"[18] That Shaw never understood why Nietzsche chose Bizet's music to uphold against Wagner's is clear from this statement: "What can you say to a man who, after pitting his philosophy against Wagner's with refreshing ingenuity and force, proceeds to hold up as the masterpiece of modern dramatic music, blazing with the merits which the Wagnerian music dramas lack – guess what! ... 'Carmen,' no less."[19]

When invited to give his opinion on the Wagner-Nietzsche issue, Shaw restricts himself to a brief and rather lame reply: "As to the question you put to me about Nietzsche contra Wagner, it is of course perfectly idle to discuss whether Nietzsche's sally was 'justified.' But it was inevitable and natural that 'Parsifal,' and the last passages written by Wagner about 'Parsifal' in his Bayreuth leaflets, should have been received with lordly contempt by a young admirer of 'Der Ring des Nibelungen.' "[*] Shaw is not interested in exhaustive critical enquiry – for the whole point, surely, is to discover whether or not Nietzsche's sally *was* justified: Shaw's abdication of intelligence here suggests his main concern was not to dispense justice but to appropriate what he can use. And, indeed, just as he found strong resemblances between Ibsen and Nietzsche, so he finds similarities between Wagner and Nietzsche – whatever substance in Nietzsche he cannot subsume to Ibsen and Wagner he tends to ignore, and the uniqueness of each artist becomes obliterated by being subordinated to a common denominator. Siegfried, as Shaw describes him, bears a strong affinity to Ibsen's pioneer: "A type of the healthy man raised to perfect confidence in his own impulses by an intense and joyous vitality which is above fear, sickliness of conscience, malice, and the makeshifts and moral crutches of law and order which accompany them."[20] After this it is not surprising to read that Siegfried is "a totally unmoral person, a born anarchist, the ideal of Bakoonin, an anticipation of the 'overman' of Nietzsche."[21] It is certainly true that Siegfried was an anticipation of Shaw's superman, if not entirely of Nietzsche's – he is the redeemer of all those enslaved to ideals and laws, which they know to be makeshift and obsolescent, and which they regard with cynicism and ridicule:

No individual Siegfried can rescue them from this bondage and hypocrisy; in fact, the individual Siegfried has come often enough, only to find himself confronted with the alternative of governing those who are not Siegfrieds or risking destruction at their hands. And this dilemma will persist until Wotan's inspiration comes to our governors, and they see that their business is not the devising of laws and institutions to prop up the weaknesses of mobs and secure the survival of the unfittest, but the breeding of men whose wills and intelligence may be depended on to produce spontaneously the social wellbeing our clumsy laws now aim at and miss. The majority of men at present in Europe have no business to be alive; and no serious progress will be made until we address ourselves earnestly and scientifically to the task of producing trustworthy human material for society. In short, it is necessary to breed a race of men in whom the life-giving impulses predominate, before the New Protestantism becomes politically practicable.[22]

Here is the germ of *Man and Superman* and *Back to Methuselah*.

Some writers on the Wagner-Nietzsche controversy, admittedly, did

---

[*] *ES*, no. 3 (June 15, 1898), 37. In due course, it has been suggested, Shaw came to share Nietzsche's wider objections to Wagner. See William Blissett, "Bernard Shaw: Imperfect Wagnerite," *University of Toronto Quarterly*, XVII (1958), 192.

show a deeper understanding and a wider knowledge of the relationship of the two men;* but an interest in Wagner did not automatically lead to an interest in Nietzsche, and the inopportune publication of Nietzsche's anti-Wagnerian works tended to provoke hostility in those circles which might have seen in *The Birth of Tragedy* and *Richard Wagner in Bayreuth* a real tribute to a musician whose genius Nietzsche never denied. Indeed, by one of the more level-headed Wagnerians the latter work was pronounced "an utterance of enthusiastic discipleship and probably the most discerning appreciation of Wagner ever yet published,"[23] and *The Case of Wagner*, although exaggerated in its critical violence, was considered an extremely acute diagnosis of some of Wagner's weaknesses. As a critique, however, it suffered by coming so soon after Nordau's wrongheadedness about Wagner: "That Nordau should have anticipated Nietzsche in this country is a public calamity. The talk about Wagner's degeneracy and decadence had thus passed into tiresome cant, and now that the real source of the only serious anti-Wagnerian criticism makes its appearance the task of disengaging the important side of that criticism seems almost hopeless."[24] A more balanced assessment of Nietzsche's true relationship to Wagner could only be made, and then only with difficulty, by those with sufficient German to read all that Nietzsche wrote about Wagner's art.

The third point of contact between Shaw and Nietzsche is represented by Schopenhauer, whose *Die Welt als Wille und Vorstellung* (1818) was not translated into English until 1883–6, by which time his work had become fairly familiar. Helen Zimmern's biography of Schopenhauer appeared in 1876, and another, by William Wallace, came out in 1890; later admirers of Nietzsche tended to ignore or play down the extent of Nietzsche's indebtedness to Schopenhauer, who was admired, like Nietzsche, for a scintillating brilliance of style quite unprecedented in German philosophy: "Furthermore, Schopenhauer is almost the only German prose-writer (with the exception of the Jewish Heinrich Heine) who possesses what the French call *esprit*, and the present age is always dis-

---

* E.g. Beatrice Marshall, "Friedrich Nietzsche and Richard Wagner," *Fortnightly Review*, LXIII (June, 1898), 885–97; and an anonymous review, "Nietzsche's Criticism of Wagner," *Nation*, VII (July 9, 1910), 533–4. Auden's recent tribute is instructive: "To be worth attacking a book must be worth reading. The greatest critical study of a single figure that I know of, *The Case of Wagner*, is a model of what such an attack should be. Savage as he often is, Nietzsche never allows the reader to forget for one instant that Wagner is an extraordinary genius and that, for all which may be wrong with it, his music is of the highest importance. Indeed it was this book which first taught me to listen to Wagner, about whom I had previously held silly preconceived notions." *The Dyer's Hand* (New York, 1962), 48.

posed to relish, and frequently to overrate, that quality. Hegel is hardly read at all; only students read Kant, but Schopenhauer's works sell by thousands."[25] This was written in 1895. In the same year George Meredith was finding that Schopenhauer's sounding of life was a "most tonic reading, that braces me like an East wind"; but Nietzsche, he thought, was "a wrong-headed madman of morbid tendencies."[26] Five years later supporters of Schopenhauer, partly because many of them were also Wagnerians, took exception to the growing reputation of Nietzsche: "The present furore over Nietzsche (simply a part of the reaction against 'psychological' and 'romantic' literature, and against foolish 'altruism' and foolish 'philanthropy') will probably soon give place to renewed attempts to estimate the magnitude and the breadth of Schopenhauer, an immeasurably greater and infinitely more serious man, to whom Nietzsche long ago acknowledged his indebtedness and to whom, after all, serves but as a kind of king's jester."[27] The verdict of Schopenhauer's principal English translator, T. Bailey Saunders, has already been given in an earlier chapter (pp. 35–6). Saunders believed that Nietzsche's philosophy did not call for extended criticism since it was vitiated by a Darwinistic fallacy about "the survival of the fittest." In his ethical and social theories Nietzsche was an anarchist. Saunders is appalled at the thought that a man "who possessed something of the equipment of genius should have gone so far astray and fared so miserably": "His writings – in general so harsh and chaotic, so full of conflicting ideas, so vehement in tone, but flashing out here and there in luminous aphorism, or striking, as it were by accident, a note of the deepest human sympathy – speak for themselves. Possibly the subject upon which he wrote best was art. With a profounder insight than was displayed in the definition of it as 'a criticism of life,' he proclaimed it as 'the great incentive to life.' On music, too, he said some memorable things."[28]

Many readers of Schopenhauer first learnt of him indirectly through writings on Wagner. One of the works already mentioned, Franz Hueffer's *Richard Wagner and the Music of the Future* (1874), contains an account of Schopenhauer's aesthetic theories, and William Ashton Ellis wrote an article on the use Wagner made of Schopenhauer's ideas,[29] placing both men, as he was doing in *The Meister*, in the context of a reaction against the scientific materialism of Tyndall, Darwin, Huxley, and Spencer. A knowledge of Schopenhauer helped Davidson, Ellis, and Yeats to understand how Nietzsche developed, and in some cases resisted, Schopenhauer's ideas about the dependence of the phenomenal world on the mind, the identity of biological impulse and personal will, and the necessity of pain and suffering in the world. As far as Shaw is concerned, the chief debt is seen to be a belief in the supremacy of will over reason, although Shaw converts Schopenhauer's malevolent *Wille* into a benevolent Life Force. Shaw accepts Schopenhauer's view that sexual relations are to be conducted, not with the aim of achieving personal happiness, but in the interest of the species as a whole: *Man and Superman* is an illustration of this line of thought. On the whole, Shaw's reading of Nietzsche contains traces of transcendentalism which have rubbed off from Schopenhauer.

A final point of contact between Shaw and Nietzsche is represented by Max Nordau's *Degeneration*, a work, as has already been pointed out, which did much to condition the reception of Nietzsche's works in England. In 1895, at the invitation of the editor, Benjamin Tucker, Shaw wrote an open letter (later published as *The Sanity of Art*) to the American anarchist paper *Liberty*, Shaw's task was to discredit Nordau. He devotes much of his article to an extended defence of Ibsen and Wagner against Nordau's criticisms, but the only reference to Nietzsche occurs in a quotation from Nordau's text: it seems reasonable to suppose that in 1895 Shaw did not know enough about Nietzsche to defend him at equal length. But when *The Sanity of Art* was republished in 1907, initially in the *New Age*, Shaw added nothing about Nietzsche either to the text or to the new preface. Of two other books written in reply to Nordau, one does not mention Nietzsche at all and the other merely observes how inconsistent it was of Nordau to quote Nietzsche in order to substantiate his own view that Wagner was a decadent![30] This failure to come to Nietzsche's assistance, whether it arose from ignorance of Nietzsche or lack of concern for his plight, must have been taken as an implicit confirmation that, at least as far as Nietzsche was concerned, Nordau's judgment was correct. The result was that Nordau's version of Nietzsche prevailed even when Nordau's other victims had been rehabilitated, and when Nordau himself was generally discredited. Their two names were linked indissolubly together – as a recent historian of the impact of *Degeneration* on England and America puts it: "Comment on Nordau's *Degeneration* occurs more frequently in twentieth-century studies of Friedrich Nietzsche than in writing on any other of the recipients of Nordau's censure."[31] Shaw came to believe that, single-handed, he had killed Nordau stone-dead: this is belied by the fact that Nordau continued to sell long after Shaw's supposed homicide, and also by this judgment from a Nietzschean who knew what harm Nordau had done: "This criticism having come from an author who was considered profound, and from a publisher, Mr. Heinemann, who was generally believed to possess an extraordinary flair for Continental wisdom, it was readily accepted by English people, and in this way, for ten years, considerably damaged the cause for which I stand."[32]

Why, we might ask, was Nordau able to condition English opinion about Nietzsche on this spectacular scale? To that question his chapter on Nietzsche, ironically enough, provides the answer. There he scoffs at the attempts of Theodor de Wyzewa to convince the French that "Nietzsche is the greatest thinker and most brilliant author produced by Germany in the last generation," for the reason that the French "are not in the position to prove the accuracy of his assertions."[33] Nor, as an earlier chapter has demonstrated, were the English in a position to contest the accuracy of Nordau's assertions about Nietzsche, eight editions of *Degeneration* having been devoured before Nietzsche became available in English; and when translations of *The Antichrist, Zarathustra*, and the Wagner polemics did appear, the English found their preconceptions about Nietzsche, gained from Nordau, abundantly justified. Preconceptions thus became settled convictions, inhibiting further discussion and enquiry. Nietzsche was branded as a lunatic, a sadist, and a writer of meaningless bombast. Voices were raised on the other side, but they were comparatively weak and ineffectual, and it took twelve years to exhaust the first edition of *Zarathustra*.

2 As noted above, Shaw wrote reviews of the first two Nietzsche translations. Nearly half of the first review is a piece of buffoonery, in Shaw's worst facetious vein, about what it means to be a philosopher. The tone hardly changes when Shaw, with apparent reluctance, eventually veers round to his ostensible subject – Nietzsche: "Nietzsche is worse than shocking, he is simply awful: his epigrams are written with phosphorus on brimstone. The only excuse for reading them is that before long you must be prepared either to talk about Nietzsche or else retire from society, especially from aristocratically minded society (not the same thing, by the way, as aristocratic society), since Nietzsche is the champion of privilege, of power, and of inequality."[34] Although Nietzsche has become famous – "he has had a great *succès de scandale* to advertise his penetrating wit" – Shaw declares that he had not heard of him until *Beyond Good and Evil* was mentioned to him in connection with *The Quintessence of Ibsenism*: then the spiritual affinity between Ibsen and Nietzsche became at once apparent. But "never was there a deafer, blinder, socially and politically inepter academician" than Nietzsche: "To him modern Democracy, Pauline Christianity, Socialism, and so on are deliberate plots hatched by malignant philosophers to frustrate the evolution of the human race and mass the stupidity and brute force of the many weak against the beneficial tyranny of the few strong. This is not even a point of view: it is an absolutely fictitious hypothesis."* Appalled at Nietzsche's inordinate love of Bizet, Shaw goes on in the article to find him no more reliable as a critic of art: Nietzsche's idols, the Romans and the men of the Renaissance, Shaw dismisses as "bad artists" and "arrant intellect-mongers." But if Nietzsche is often wrong-headed, his ideas are still striking and suggestive: "In short, his sallies, petulant and impossible as some of them are, are the work of a rare spirit and are pregnant with its vitality. It is notable that Nietzsche does not write in chapters or treatises: he writes leading articles, leaderettes, occasional notes, and epigrams. He recognizes that humanity, having tasted the art of the journalist, will no longer suffer men to inflict books on it."

Shaw's second article on Nietzsche appeared three years later, in 1899. Shaw places Nietzsche in a tradition of Diabolonianism, but has little to say about the works under review, in this case *Zarathustra* and *The Genealogy of Morals* except that *Zarathustra* is "a diffusion of Diabolonian wisdom in the guise of a concentration of it."[35] Shaw later regarded the book as a modern bible, "less comforting to the ill and unhappy than the Psalms; but it is much truer, subtler, and more edifying."[36] It was "the first modern book that can be set above the Psalms of David at every point on their own ground."† Its central thesis he took to heart: "When, as Nietzsche-Zarathustra put it, 'God is dead,' Atheism dies also. Bible-smashing is tedious to people who have smashed their Bibles."[37] *Zarathustra* had first appeared in 1896, and Shaw could assume that it might be known by anyone likely to read his column; but his reluctance to discuss *The Genealogy of Morals* suggests not disfavour but rather an admission of philosophical incompetence.

Shaw was able to extend his knowledge beyond the official English translations by subscribing to *The Eagle and the Serpent*, which began in February, 1898. The editor, regarding Shaw as a possible ally, sent him the proof-sheets of the first number, and Shaw promised to subscribe to further issues: "The journal, as far as I can judge, promises to be sufficiently

---

* Fictitious or not, it was a hypothesis which Shaw later modified into a scheme he adopted so completely that it is invariably associated with his name—the deliberate breeding of a superior race of human beings to replace an inadequate and inefficient process of political and social change.

† "Our Book-shelf," *Fabian News*, xvii (April, 1907), 38. I have not been able to verify it, but I have been told that Shaw's sister Lucy Carr Shaw worked at a translation of *Thus Spake Zarathustra* and even tried to adapt it for the stage.

foolish to make people think: and its quotations are excellent." The editor had requested him to distribute a few dozen copies. Piqued, Shaw replied: "I am not an altruist, and do not distribute papers gratuitously."[38] Shaw's interest in the journal is shown in his letters to the editor, the most important of which deserves to be quoted at length. Believing that Thomas Common's suggestion to form a Nietzsche Society might possibly "prove fruitful," Shaw wrote:

Since the foundation of the Fabian Society in 1884, no organ of a new popular development of social philosophy has been formed among us. It is noteworthy that the Fabian Society was formed by the division of a pre-existing group into two sections; one, the Fabian Society, taking up the political and economic side of the social question; and the other, then called the Fellowship of the New Life, and still in existence as the New Fellowship, taking up the ethical and philosophical side. The result is noteworthy. The Fabian Society has exercised a great influence, and has attained, perhaps, the maximum of success possible to such organisations. The New Fellowship, though composed largely of the same men, has exercised practically no influence at all, because it had no really new ideas. There was nothing to be learned from it that had not already been learned from the best of the Unitarians. Like them, it sought to free social and personal ideals and duties from superstition; but it laid even greater stress on the sacredness of the ideals and duties than the comparatively easy-going superstitious people did. It was not until after 1889, when Ibsen and Nietzsche began to make themselves felt, that the really new idea of challenging the validity of idealism and duty, and bringing Individualism round again on a higher plane, shewed signs of being able to rally to it men beneath the rank of geniuses who had been feeling their way towards it for two centuries. Had the New Fellowship started with any glimmering of this conception, their history might have been different. As it is, it seems to me quite possible that a Nietzsche Society might hit the target that the Fellows of the New Life missed, and might repeat on the ethical plane the success of the Fabian Society on the political one.[39]

Shaw's association with *The Eagle and the Serpent* continued until its demise in 1903.

It was possibly through this association that Shaw made the acquaintance of Thomas Common. In the introduction to his Nietzsche anthology Common extends a special debt of thanks to Shaw "for the interest he has taken in the work, and for the valuable suggestions he has furnished with reference to arrangement and other matters."[40] Common was delighted to enlist the prestige of Shaw's name, but even more to acknowledge the fact of Shaw's active participation: Common states elsewhere that Shaw "read the MS. of the book of Nietzsche extracts with approval, and afterwards carried it himself to the publisher's office, where he recommended that it should be issued."[41] Shaw would hardly have staked his personal reputation with the publisher, Grant Richards, or given support for Common's later attempts to gain support for further Nietzsche translations, had he not believed in Nietzsche's importance.

In the light of this evidence it is odd to find Shaw's biographer declaring that Shaw "could not have read much of the few English translations that were attempted except Thomas Common's book of selections" and that "the German originals he never even attempted to read."[42] As we have seen, Shaw read as much Nietzsche as was available, and even made the admission, which seems to have been universally overlooked, that he had read some Nietzsche in the original.* Even if his advocacy of Nietzsche's work appears rather perfunctory at times, as when he says that works like Nietzsche's *The Gay Science* ought to be read because, after all, Nietzsche might be right,[43] Shaw balances this by certain insights into Nietzsche's work. In 1903, for example, he suggests to Forbes Robertson a revival of *Richard III* along Nietzschean lines:

A really brilliant Nietzschean Richard would be fresh and delightful. I believe I could fill it with the most captivating business for you, and practically get rid of the old-fashioned fight at the end. No actor has ever done the curious recovery by Richard of his old gaiety of heart in the excitement of the battle. It whirls him up out of his vulgar ambition to be a king (which makes the middle acts rather tedious after the fantastic superhumanity of the first), and he is again the ecstatic prince of mischief of the 'Shine out, fair sun, till I have brought a glass' phase which makes the first act so rapturous. All Nietzsche is in the lines:

Conscience is but a word that cowards use
Devised at first to keep the strong in awe.
Our strong arms be our conscience, swords our law!†

---

* "The proverbial bits of Goethe and Wagner and Nietzsche are familiar to me." *WBS*, xviii, 5. In the same note Shaw speaks about his translation of Trebitsch's *Frau Gitta's Sühne*, remarking that he had to spell Gitta "Jitta" in his English version "to avert having her name pronounced with a hard G." Shaw's preference may have been purely aesthetic, since in German all Gs are hard except in some words of foreign derivation.

† Quoted in Hesketh Pearson, *Bernard Shaw: His Life and Personality* (London, 1950), 229. Chesterton quotes the same lines to show that Nietzsche's supposedly revolutionary morality was not new; also, in putting them in the mouth of a half-insane hunchback the day before his inevitable defeat, Shakespeare was only showing how fallacious they were. *The Common Man* (New York, 1950), 23–4. In an unpublished letter to Anthony Ludovici, dated April 9, 1915, Eden Phillpotts wrote: "It was I think Arnold Bennett who said you could find all Nietzsche in Shakespeare's Richard III. It is that sort of silly rot one resents so much, because it simply means the writer has taken other people's opinions and not been at the trouble to read Nietzsche before he started to write about him."

Shaw is aware, too, of the strong autobiographical strain in Nietzsche's writings, comparing them to the "startling confessions and self-revelations"[44] in the epistles of St. Paul. Again, the following estimate of Nietzsche, made in 1905, suggests more than a superficial acquaintance:

Nietzsche's erudition I believe to be all nonsense. I think he was academic in the sense of having a great deal of second-hand book-learning about him, and don't care for him except when he is perfectly original – that is, when he is dealing with matters which a peasant might have dealt with if he had brains enough, and had had the run of a library. You feel how clever and imaginative he is, and how much he has derived from writers of genius and from his own humanity about men and nations; but there is a want of actual contact knowledge about him; he is always the speculative university professor or the solitary philosopher and poet, never quite the worker and man of affairs or the executive artist in solid materials.[45]

Nietzsche's bouts of "professorial folly," which Shaw had impugned in the 1896 review, still remained a source of irritation; but Shaw goes on to complain, as he does in the preface to *Major Barbara* a year later, about the way Nietzsche's ideas are being received: "It annoys me to see English writers absolutely ignoring the work of British thinkers, and swallowing foreign celebrities – whether philosophers or opera-singers – without a grain of salt. It shows an utter want of intellectual self-respect; and the result of it is that Nietzsche's views, instead of being added soberly to the existing body of philosophy, are treated as if they were a sort of music-hall performance."* Shaw may be levelling these charges against *The Eagle and the Serpent*; but, insofar as Shaw's own early review articles tended to make Nietzsche a pretext for flamboyant intellectual display, they might be regarded as conscious self-criticism. By 1907 Shaw was extremely irritated by journalistic perversions of Nietzsche: "It is old-fashioned now to dispute about Wagner and Ibsen; but on Nietzsche folly and ignorance are still busy. The journalists have read in one another's paragraphs a certain sentence about 'the big blonde beast;' and from this misunderstood sample they construct an imaginary Nietzsche of impossible mental and moral inferiority to themselves."[46] But Shaw had begun to take Nietzsche seriously as early as 1901. This is the time of his association with Common, and with the beginning of the composition of *Man and Superman*, the most recognizably "Nietzschean" of all Shaw's works. Shaw's biographer

---

* Archibald Henderson, *George Bernard Shaw: His Life and Works* (London, 1911), 479. Henderson's later biography of Shaw gives "soberly" instead of "solely." I have transposed the word to the earlier text, thinking it makes more sense.

insists that Shaw never made any thorough-going study of the philosophy of Nietzsche and Schopenhauer: "Indeed, Shaw is an unwilling imposter as a pundit in the philosophy of Schopenhauer and Nietzsche. What, for example, could be more foreign to the Shavian philosophy than Nietzsche's repudiation of Socialism, his admiration of the Romans, or his notions about art?"* He reports that Shaw laughingly said to him one day: "If all this talk about Schopenhauer and Nietzsche continues, I really will have to read their works, to discover just what we have in common."[47]

Increasingly Shaw emphasized his right to take an interest in Nietzsche without being regarded as an impeccable authority. He did this in two ways, first by trying to play down his own indebtedness, and secondly by maintaining that Nietzsche himself was not as original as his more fervent supporters believed: "Nietzsche, by the two or three who had come across his writings, was supposed to have been the first man to whom it occurred that mere morality and legality and urbanity lead nowhere, as if Bunyan had never written Badman."[48] Shaw insists again and again that it is not surprising that he should have anticipated Ibsen and Nietzsche: "I mention this fact, not with the ridiculous object of vindicating my 'originality' in nineteenth century fashion, but because I attach great importance to the evidence that the movement voiced by Schopenhauer, Wagner, Ibsen, Nietzsche, and Strindberg, was a world movement, and would have found expression if every one of these writers had perished in his cradle."[49] Everywhere he turned Shaw was met with "nothing but vague cacklings about Ibsen and Nietzsche," and was as irritated by them as Davidson had been. Max Beerbohm, in a satirical cartoon, accuses Shaw of dressing himself up in borrowed plumes – a coat from Schopenhauer, a waistcoat from Ibsen, trousers from Nietzsche; "Ah," replies Shaw, "but look at the patches." Two close associates of Shaw, Wells and Archer, made identical charges. Wells, writing in 1914, is critical of Shaw: "He is an activity, a restless passion for attention. Behind that is a kind of jackdaw's hoard of other people's notions: much from Samuel Butler, scraps of pseudo-philosophical phraseology such as that Life Force phrase he got from Dr. Guest; old Hammersmith economics, worn fragments of Herbert Spencer, some Nietzsche conveyed no doubt from the convenient handbook of Mr. Orage, shreds of theosophy, current superstitions, sweepings of all sorts of 'ad-

---

* Henderson, *Shaw*, 479. A similar statement has been attributed to Shaw himself by R. F. Rattray, *Bernard Shaw: A Chronicle and an Introduction* (London, 1932), 145. Henderson may be giving his own view, but it is also possible that he was paraphrasing a part of the letter he later quotes verbatim: Rattray may have seen the letter, but he is probably guilty of false ascription.

vanced' rubbish but nothing anywhere of which one can say 'Here is the thought of a man.' "⁵⁰ In 1923 Archer bluntly told Shaw that he was "incurably credulous":

Someone comes along and tells you that wool is the only wear; and instantly you go in for woollen boots, which lead, in due time to a course of crutches. Then Wagner comes along, and you are a Wagnerite: Ibsen, and you are an Ibsenite (I never was); Nietzsche, and you are a Nietzschean; Bergson, and you are a Bergsonian. And all the time you are no whit nearer the real secret of things. All these men, I admit, had something to say, though Nietzsche to my mind was only a crack-brained poseur who was vastly overrated in his little day.⁵¹

Speculation about Shaw's debt to Nietzsche has been an attractive pastime for several generations of critics. One regards this influence as an established fact, being most easily identifiable in Shaw's theories of the relativity of good and evil, and his view that marriage should be used for the propagation of a better race.⁵² Such ideas as these, together with the suggestions found in Shaw for trial marriage and easy divorce, are all found in *Zarathustra* – but Shaw could easily have derived them from other sources. J. W. Groshong believes that Shaw was never anything more than a "superficial" student of Nietzsche:

In the first place, through a writing lifetime of roughly seventy years, Shaw published comments on Nietzsche to fill no more than six or eight printed pages, certainly far from enough for positive proof of his erudition. In the second place, Shaw is very positive about Nietzsche in his early reviews, much more doubtful and vague in his later writing. One may therefore suspect that as awareness of Nietzsche grew in England, Shaw may have become less and less disposed to betray his ignorance by positive statements. In the 1896 review, for example, he confidently describes the Nietzschean concept of slave-morality. But ten years later, in the Preface to *Major Barbara*, he implies that he has no first-hand knowledge of Nietzchean ethics: "Nietzsche, *as I gather*, regarded the slave-morality as having been invented and imposed on the world."⁵³

[Groshong's italics]

This, on several counts, is not as plausible as it seems. If Shaw did not make an extended critique of Nietzsche, or examine his system with any thoroughness, it is because he is dealing with Nietzsche as with all the other philosophers he read, that is, sporadically, allusively, illustratively: he did not possess the technical equipment to respond to them in any other way. Again, it is not permissible to conclude that Shaw was a "superficial" student of Nietzsche on the ground that he lacked "erudition": nor is it necessary to accept the implication seen in Shaw's phrase, "as I gather." The Preface to *Major Barbara* sets out to minimize Shaw's alleged debt to

Nietzsche and other continental writers, and in such a context it is in Shaw's interest to make such disclaimers, although this one is so sweeping that one suspects that Shaw is having his own ironic joke. The immediate impact of a work like *Man and Superman* on a public largely ignorant of, or hostile to, Nietzsche was to gain for its author a reputation for Nietzschean scholarship which he had never pretended to, and could never hope to sustain; nevertheless, Shaw's later positive statements, as in his 1907 review of Orage's first book on Nietzsche,* do not sound more doubtful and vague than the earlier ones, and the suggestion that he hesitated to make them for fear of betraying his ignorance is not borne out by the facts. Shaw's verdict on Nietzsche, already given, is considered and firm; his rejection of the idea that Nietzsche's superman is a beast of prey is decisive enough; and an observation on the theory of the Will to Power, currently misconceived as a brutal urge to tyrannize others, is surely far from doubtful and vague: "[Nietzsche] had no difficulty in concluding that the final objective of this Will was power over self, and that the seekers after power over others and material possessions were on a false scent."[54] In Nietzsche Shaw enlisted a powerful ally in the war against nineteenth-century Darwinism and materialism.

Shaw's admiration for Nietzsche is beyond question. Nietzsche, he wrote, was one of the writers "whose peculiar sense of the world I recognize as more or less akin to my own,"[55] and a portrait of Nietzsche was one of the fixtures in Shaw's London apartment. Three aspects of Nietzsche's work seem to have held a particular fascination for him – his iconoclasm, his wit, and his prophetic vision. Immensely gifted as polemicists, both writers were the Socratic gadflies of their age, to awaken its conscience, expose its illusions, and lacerate its hypocrisy. When Shaw writes, "It annoys me to see people comfortable when they ought to be uncomfortable,"[56] his tireless "moral passion" echoes Nietzsche's "to make the individual uncomfortable is my task."[57] "I attack only things that are triumphant," wrote Nietzsche, "if necessary I wait until they become triumphant."[58] Shaw writes: "It is an instinct with me personally to attack every idea which has been full-grown for ten years, especially if it claims to be the foundation of human society."[59] Shaw was attracted by Nietzsche's wit, particularly by its aphoristic form. As the early correspondence shows, Shaw had a fondness for aphoristic expression, sometimes indulging it at the expense of an abnegation of feeling and intelligence. Nietzsche's example showed

---

* "Our Book-shelf," 37. Further extracts from this review are given in the following chapter.

that neatness of expression need not always be a substitute for honesty. It was not merely the substance and the surface brilliance of Nietzsche's epigrams which Shaw (particularly in the maxims of "The Revolutionist's Handbook" in *Man and Superman*) was drawn to emulate, but also their effectiveness as instruments of moral chastisement. As early as *The Quintessence of Ibsenism* Shaw had believed that really revolutionary ideas had to begin as jokes or their proponent would not live to see them realized; later he preferred to regard new ideas organically, as delicate plants which needed careful tending: "Before ideas can blossom into action, they need many years' nurture. They begin as jokes, epigrams, seeming paradoxes, and end as political and religious movements."* "When a thing is funny," says the He-Ancient in *Back to Methuselah*, "search it for a hidden truth." For Shaw Nietzsche was the "epigrammatic Diabolonian" who despised the luxury of righteous indignation and told his truth by assuming the role of buffoon. And as for Nietzsche's prophetic vision, this was the natural obverse of his iconoclasm; once the past was abolished, the future had to be constructed – and the creator of this future was the superman. What, we must now ask, was the kinship, if any, of Shaw's superman to that of Nietzsche?

3 Shaw protested again and again that "the cry for the Superman did not begin with Nietzsche, nor will it end with his vogue."[60] An early veneration for Michelangelo, who chose "Supermen and Superwomen" for his models, had taught Shaw "always to put people of genius into my works. I am always setting a genius over against a commonplace person."[61] Indeed, Michelangelo had embodied the superman "three hundred years before Nietzsche wrote *Also Sprach Zarathustra* and Strauss set it to music."[62] The superman has a long genealogy: "From Prometheus to the Wagnerian Siegfried, some enemy of the gods, unterrified champion of those oppressed by them, has always towered among the heroes of the loftiest poetry. Our newest idol, the Superman, celebrating the death of godhead, may be younger than the hills; but he is as old as the shepherds."[63]

Julian, in Ibsen's *Emperor and Galilean*, had proclaimed the death of

---

* "Was ich der deutschen Kultur verdanke," *Neue Rundschau* (March, 1911), 344. My translation. In this article, destined to be the preface to a German edition of his plays, Shaw complains to his German readers that London theatre critics persist in seeing in him "*ein Papagei und Nachschwätzer von Schopenhauer und Nietzsche*," and indicates that the preface to *Major Barbara* contains a strong rebuttal of these charges.

God, and the need for a new dispensation – his revaluation of values is total: "The old beauty is no longer beautiful, and the new truth is no longer true."[64] Julian repudiates the first empire of simple pagan sensuality, and also the self-abnegating idealism of Christianity, the second empire, which succeeded it. Both Caesar and Christ will succumb, but not perish; they will be incorporated in the new messiah who will be both Emperor and God, Pan and Logos. This synthetic conception is identical with one description Nietzsche gave of the superman – "the Roman Caesar with Christ's soul"[65] – and also with Shaw's description of what would happen when the democratic attitude became yet another expression of romanticism: "When it comes to that, the brute force of the strong-minded Bismarckian man of action, impatient of humbug, will combine with the subtlety and spiritual energy of the man of thought whom shams cannot illude or interest."[66] This messiah is self-begotten in the man who wills, and his empire, in Shaw's words, is "the empire of Man asserting the eternal validity of his own will."[67] *Emperor and Galilean* certainly furnished Shaw with many hints for his theory of the Life Force; but it also helped to shape one aspect of his superman, the aspect we might call the religious or messianic. In this aspect the child is regarded as a fresh attempt to make humanity divine. By 1911 Shaw had worked out the relationship of the Life Force to the superman. In an address on "The Future of Religion" Shaw is reported to have said:

We were ... all experiments in the direction of making God. What God was doing was making Himself, getting from being a mere powerless will or force. This force had implanted into our minds the ideal of God. We were not very successful attempts at God so far, but he believed that if they could drive into the heads of men the full consciousness of moral responsibilities that came to men with the knowledge that there would never be a God unless we made one – that we are the instruments through which that ideal was trying to make itself a reality – they could work towards that ideal until they got to be supermen, and then super-supermen and then a world of organisms who had achieved and realised God. They could then dispense with idolatry, intimidation, stimulants, and the nonsense of civilisation.[68]

The messianic aspect of the superman is most prominent in *Back to Methuselah*.

A second aspect, and one which lent itself more readily to dramatic presentation, was the idea of the superman as the iconoclast, the anarchic individualist. The prototype here was undoubtedly Wagner's Siegfried, whom Shaw, as we have seen, regarded as a "totally unmoral person, a born anarchist, the ideal of Bakoonin, an anticipation of the 'overman' of

Nietzsche." In a note to *Caesar and Cleopatra* Shaw wondered whether he was right to assume "that the way to produce an impression of greatness is by exhibiting a man, not as mortifying his nature by doing his duty ... but as simply doing what he naturally wants to do."[69] In 1907 Shaw is still preoccupied with this problem:

I know no harder practical question than how much selfishness one ought to stand from a gifted person for the sake of his gifts or on the chance of his being right in the long run. The Superman will certainly come like a thief in the night, and be shot at accordingly; but we cannot leave our property wholly undefended on that account. On the other hand, we cannot ask the Superman simply to add a higher set of virtues to current respectable morals; for he is undoubtedly going to empty a good deal of respectable morality out like so much dirty water, and replace it by new and strange customs, shedding old obligations and accepting new and heavier ones. Every step of his progress must horrify conventional people; and if it were possible for even the most superior men to march ahead all the time, every pioneer of the march towards the Superman would be crucified.[70]

Louis Dubedat, in *The Doctor's Dilemma*, protests that he has not the vanity to set up as a superman, but that it remains the ideal towards which he strives: he represents the strain of individualism in Shaw's thinking about the superman.

Shaw's religious and social idealism was inherited from Ibsen and Wagner, and confirmed by Nietzsche. Unlike Tille and Common, Shaw saw in Nietzsche an opponent and not an ally of Darwinism. Of the Darwinian principle of natural selection Shaw wrote: "There is a hideous fatalism about it, a ghastly and damnable reduction of beauty and intelligence, of strength and purpose, of honor and aspiration."[71] Shaw's attitude to Darwinism partly explains a change in his creative career. Towards the turn of the century he was beginning to regard himself more as a thinker and less as "a common dramatist." Saddened by the spectacle of the Boer War, and disgusted by the sordid repercussions of the war in the popular English press, Shaw suffered a severe disillusionment. Before the war Shaw had written in a spirit of calculated provocation: "The majority of men at present in Europe have no business to be alive; and no serious progress will be made until we address ourselves earnestly and scientifically to the task of producing trustworthy human material for society."[72] This was a mood Shaw did his utmost to restrain, but now his impatience with the sluggish progress of democratic society burst all bounds: *Man and Superman* was the immediate result.

In the "Epistle Dedicatory" to the play, Shaw dismisses the third Act as "totally extraneous," a mere "pleasantry" which is not the essence of the drama; later he was to regard it, as well as "The Revolutionist's Handbook," as "the new religion at the centre of the intellectual whirlpool."[73] It is in this act that the superman is introduced:

THE STATUE. And who the deuce is the Superman?
THE DEVIL. Oh, the latest fashion among the Life Force fanatics. Did you not meet in Heaven, among the new arrivals, that German Polish madman? What was his name? Nietzsche?
THE STATUE. Never heard of him.
THE DEVIL. Well, he came here first, before he recovered his wits. I had some hopes for him; but he was a confirmed Life Force worshipper. It was he who raked up the Superman, who is as old as Prometheus; and the 20th century will run after this newest of the old crazes when it gets tired of the world, the flesh, and your humble servant.
THE STATUE. Superman is a good cry; and a good cry is half the battle. I should like to see this Nietzsche.
THE DEVIL. Unfortunately he met Wagner here, and had a quarrel with him.
THE STATUE. Quite right, too. Mozart for me!
THE DEVIL. Oh, it was not about music. Wagner once drifted into Life Force worship, and invented a Superman called Siegfried. But he came to his senses afterwards. So when they met here, Nietzsche denounced him as a renegade; and Wagner wrote a pamphlet to prove that Nietzsche was a Jew; and it ended in Nietzsche's going to heaven in a huff. And good riddance too.

Ann asks where she can find the superman, and on being told that he is not yet created, exclaims: "Not yet created! Then my work is not yet done. I believe in the Life to Come. A father! a father for the Superman!"[74] Perhaps we are no nearer a definition of what Shaw took Nietzsche's superman to be, but in *Man and Superman* it is at least clear that the superman is a thing of the future, and that it is not the military man who is held up as the ideal. As Don Juan says: "I sing not arms and the hero, but the philosophic man: he who seeks in contemplation to discover the inner will of the world, in invention to discover the means of fulfilling that will, and in action to do that will by the so-discovered means. Of all other sorts of men I declare myself tired."*

---

* *WBS*, x, 114. Jacques Barzun wonders why Shaw kept abusing "Romanticism" in his writings while praising its representative figures: "One explanation will not cover the multitude of facts and motives, yet they can be ranged under one analogy: the nineties (Symbolist-Naturalist) were reacting against the Realists as sons against fathers. In so doing they manifested anew some of the traits of their common grandsires the Romantics: individualism, the cult of beauty, an outspokenly social art, passionate expression. But at the same time the original Romanticism of history was still in sight, surviving unpleasantly in second hand formulations that were unbearable; so it too had to be repudiated, ridiculed, and abused,

In his Preface to *Major Barbara* Shaw is anxious to defend Nietzsche as well as himself against prevalent misunderstandings:

> Nietzsche, like Schopenhauer, is the victim in England of a single much quoted sentence containing the phrase "big blonde beast." On the strength of this alliteration it is assumed that Nietzsche gained his European reputation by a senseless glorification of selfish bullying as the rule of life, just as it is assumed, on the strength of the single word Superman (*Uebermensch*) borrowed by me from Nietzsche, that I look for the salvation of society to the despotism of a single Napoleonic Superman, in spite of my careful demonstration of the folly of that outworn infatuation.*

Shaw also found it galling to be accused of preaching "a Final Ethical Superman: no other, in fact, than our old friend the Just Man made Perfect!"[75]

Shaw's positive suggestions about the nature of the superman are no more helpful than these disclaimers; it is as if he senses that too rigid a formulation will detract from the power of the idea over man's imagination. He beats a retreat behind the smokescreen of portentous mysticism: "What is really important in Man is the part of him that we do not yet understand."[76] The true characteristic of the superman will be "that superiority in the unconscious self,"[77] but it is impossible to list specifications: "The proof of the Superman will be in the living; and we shall find out how to produce him by the old method of trial and error, and not by waiting for a completely convincing prescription of his ingredients."[78] This experimentalism underlies Don Juan's own conception of the superman, which is close to the faith Shaw thought a disciple could gain from Wagner's *Ring*: "Are we agreed that Life is a force which has made innumerable experiments in organizing itself; that the mammoth and the man, the mouse and the megatherium, the flies and the fleas and the Fathers of the Church, are all more or less successful attempts to build up that raw force into higher

---

just like Realism. *Man and Superman* contains a proof of this difference within similarity; Shaw's Superman is close to the Byronic Hero – the genius against the world, alone right because fired with an idea and endowed with the will to make it triumph. But in the same play is Mendoza, the caricature of the Byronic hero-as-brigand, ridiculously lovesick and ineffectual. The Byronic symbols have by overuse lost their power and Shaw's neo-Romanticism rightly insists on making its own." *The Energies of Art* (New York, 1956), 256–7.

* CPBS, 117. In a postscript to the Oxford World's Classics edition of *Back to Methuselah* (1945), Shaw sought a compromise between "a Marxist world in which the millenium will be guaranteed by a new Catholicism in which the proletarians of all lands are to unite" and "an idolatry of imaginary Carlylean heroes and bogus Nietzschean supermen."

and higher individuals, the ideal individual being omnipotent, omniscient, infallible, and withal completely, unilludedly self-conscious: in short, a god?"[79] Don Juan believes that life's darling object is brains; he wants to transcend the "greasy commonplaces" of flesh and blood. This emphasis on intellect, rather than on strength or love or beauty, is one which became increasingly marked in Shaw's philosophy of the Life Force. Shaw's astringent puritanism relegated sensual pleasure to a premonitory role: "I valued sexual experience because of its power of producing a celestial flood of emotion and exaltation which, however momentary, gave me a sample of the ecstasy that may one day be the normal condition of conscious intellectual activity."[80] The Ancients of *Back to Methuselah* enjoy an almost infinite life-span, and devote themselves to contemplation free from the distractions of the flesh; they wish to be rid of their bodies completely, to exist as "vortices in pure thought." The Devil in *Man and Superman* had warned, "Beware of the pursuit of the Superhuman; it leads to an indiscriminate contempt for the Human," but Shaw's contempt outpaces these words of caution, and ignores Zarathustra's admonitions to the despisers of the body. It is here that the gulf between Nietzsche's superman and that of Shaw looms widest.

The theoretical basis from which Nietzsche and Shaw are working is strikingly similar: they repudiate the notion of automatic progress, and believe that modern man is, if anything, a creature more bungled and botched than his predecessors. The chief cause of this degeneration is, for Nietzsche, Christianity, and for Shaw, man's intellect itself – "all Man's reason has done for him" (exclaims the Devil in *Man and Superman*) "is to make him beastlier than any beast." But Nietzsche realized that the degeneration is not total: "On the other hand isolated and individual cases are continually succeeding in different places on earth, as the outcome of the most different cultures, and in these a *higher type* certainly manifests itself: something which by the side of mankind in general, represents a kind of superman. Such lucky strokes of great success have always been possible and will perhaps always be possible."[81] Shaw agreed with this, but complained that such a haphazard and random production of superior types had not achieved any lasting success:

Napoleon's military system finally reduced itself to absurdity and forced the dufferdom of Europe to combine and destroy him. Caesar, with immense social talents and moral gifts in addition to moral capacity, bribed the masses into tolerating him, but was killed by a conspiracy of "good" men who killed him on principle as a protest of right against might. So much for the Superman of action! As to the Superman who merely writes and talks, he escapes because nobody understands him. "The triumph of his principles" means their degradation to the common level, the mob accepting his teaching just as a cannibal accepts the teaching of St. John or an Oxford undergraduate the philosophy of Plato or the poetry of Euripides.[82]

Man's inestimable instinct, the play contends, to worship an ideal is thwarted because contemporary ideals are not high enough to generate an effective degree of energy: "He is never without an array of human idols who are all nothing but sham Supermen. That the real Superman will snap his superfingers at all Man's present trumpery ideals of right, duty, honor, justice, religion, even decency, and accept moral obligations beyond present human endurance, is a thing that contemporary Man does not foresee: in fact he does not notice it when our casual Supermen do it in his very face."[83] Like Nietzsche, Shaw wants to remedy this chaotic situation by a process of breeding and willing. The idea of breeding, which occupies much of "The Revolutionist's Handbook," was available to Shaw from other sources before he came across Nietzsche.[84] Shaw certainly differs from Nietzsche in his reasons why a superman should be bred. For Shaw, "the need for the Superman is, in its most imperative aspect, a political one";[85] democracy cannot rise above the level of the voters who maintain it in existence: "The only fundamental and possible Socialism is the socialization of the selective breeding of Man: in other terms, of human evolution. We must eliminate the Yahoo or his vote will wreck the commonwealth."[86] One critic has suggested that the superman was the main link between Shaw's politics and his religion:

Shaw had begun with socialist ethics, according to which you must change society in order to change man. The trouble was that unless you changed man he refused to change society. It was a dilemma. Shaw's way out was not to reverse his earlier decision by staking all on the prior need of inner change. He had begun by asking for change from without; he later asks for change from within, *not instead, but as well*. Shaw said, moreover, that you could not have democracy until everyone is a Superman. He did not say you could not have *socialism* till then.[87]

Nietzsche would not have thought a democracy of supermen possible, or even desirable. Only the best can rule, and they must obviously be the minority. Nations must be guided by their wisest men, and unless the bigotry and fanaticism of narrow nationalism are transcended then more than a single commonwealth is in danger of being wrecked. As Shaw wrote, looking back ruefully at the Great War: "If the Western Powers had selected their allies in the Lamarckian manner intelligently, purposely, and vitally, *ad majorem Dei gloriam*, as what Nietzsche called good Europeans, there would have been a League of Nations and no war."[88]

The major difference between Nietzsche and Shaw is that Shaw employed the superman concept to infuse dynamism into a socialist doctrine endangered by inertia, whereas Nietzsche thought of the superman as an antidote to the nihilism which was bidding fair to engulf the whole of Europe. The scale of Nietzsche's conception is vast compared to Shaw's – Nietzsche's superman is no denizen of democracy. Nietzsche prays for relief from nausea at the sight of modern democratic man: "But from time to time do ye grant me – assuming that 'beyond good and evil' there are goddesses who can grant – one glimpse, grant me but one glimpse only, of something perfect, fully realised, happy, mighty, triumphant, of something that still gives cause for fear! A glimpse of a man that justifies the existence of man, a glimpse of an incarnate human happiness that realises and redeems, for the sake of which one may hold fast to *the belief in man!*"[89] The superman helped Shaw to hold fast to a belief in socialism. In grafting the Nietzschean figure on to a socialist programme, Shaw produces a hybrid – and a loss of vitality, richness, and imaginative appeal. The yoke of Benthamite social thinking weighs heavily on Shaw, and this partly explains his "incorrigible tendency to mentalize, socialize, and domesticate the more dangerous insights of rebel artists and philosophers."[90]

Moreover, the fact that Shaw could refer to Siegfried as an anticipation of Nietzsche's superman indicates that he did not know of Nietzsche's own estimation of Siegfried: "The figure of Siegfried, that very *free man*, who is probably far too free, too hard, too cheerful, too healthy, too *anti-Catholic* for the taste of old and mellow civilised nations."[91] Nietzsche's superman reveres tradition and ancestry, and rejects the ideals of socialism and anarchism which are so prominent a part of Siegfried's make-up. This difference escapes Shaw, who here – as so often – is intent on forging identities in the face of manifest dissimilarity. Shaw's appreciation of nature never descended to the perception of differences, and on one occasion he confessed that one tree looked exactly like another to him. Homogeneity and synonymity were part of a philosophic creed which held that truth was one and indivisible, however multiform the various expressions of it might be, and it is this belief which is responsible for a certain myopia in some of Shaw's strange cultural equations. His passion for tracing an illustrious line of thinkers, those he calls Diabolonian, for example, and then coolly announcing himself as its latest scion blinds him to the real distinctions that might be assumed to exist between Bunyan, Blake,

Nietzsche, Wagner, and Ibsen. This leads him to absurd oversimplifications, such as identifying Bunyan's Justification by Faith and Justification by Works with Schopenhauer's *Wille* and *Vorstellung*. On one occasion, God's Providence, the scientist's phlogiston, Bergson's *Élan Vital*, Kant's Categorical Imperative, even Shakespeare's "divinity that shapes our ends" miraculously coalesce in harmonious unity: "They all come to the same thing: a mysterious drive towards greater power over our circumstances and deeper understanding of Nature, in pursuit of which men and women will risk death as explorers or martyrs, and sacrifice their personal comfort and safety against all prudence, all probability, all common sense."[92]

Shaw's superman is the result of a similar process of superimposition, in which the chief debt to Nietzsche – apart from the name itself – seems to be the part marriage is to play in his production. Not only does Ann Whitefield's cry for a father for the superman and the view of marriage propounded in "The Revolutionist's Handbook" correspond very closely to the section "On Child and Marriage" in *Zarathustra*, but there is a distinct similarity in some points of detail. Shaw writes: "There is no evidence that the best citizens are the offspring of congenial marriages, or that a conflict of temperament is not a highly important part of what breeders call crossing. On the contrary, it is quite sufficiently probable that good results may be obtained from parents who would be extremely unsuitable companions and partners."[93] As an example of uncongenial parents capable of producing superior offspring Shaw adduces the son of "a robust, cheerful, eupeptic British country squire, with the tastes and range of his class, and ... a clever, imaginative, intellectual, highly civilized Jewess";[94] and almost identical parents, with the father a Prussian *Junker* instead of an English squire, are cited by Nietzsche in *Beyond Good and Evil* as good breeding potential.[95] Shaw's proposal that the association of marriage with conjugation should be dissolved is an idea which goes back to Plato, who believed that the institution of the family debased the artistic aim of the state to the level of a mere domestic art. Following Plato Nietzsche wrote: "Woman accordingly means to the State, what *sleep* does to a man. In her nature lies the healing power,"[96] and Zarathustra declares that woman exists for the recreation of the warrior – a woman ministers to the man she loves as she would to her own child; the behaviour of such Shavian heroines as Ann Whitefield and Candida towards their men is closer to the Nietzschean standpoint than to the agitation for female emancipation and equality which was a feature of Shaw's own time.

The sharp particularity of Shaw's revaluation of marriage begins to blur when he turns to the superman the new kind of marriage is intended to produce. It is a hazy and variable concept which eludes precise definition – its meaning changes according to the drift of Shaw's immediate argument; it provides variations for the Life Force theme, a rallying cry for the faithful. It is strange that Shaw, starting with the most ardent humanitarian motives, should arrive at an image of man so dehumanized that it is felt to be demoralizing. Dr. Levy, representing the whole body of Nietzschean opinion, issued a warning that when Shaw and Nietzsche praise the devil or the superman they do not mean the same thing: "Shaw's Superman is only the accentuation of conventional morality, this morality made real (and men therefore unreal, as Shaw's stage proves); while Nietzsche's Superman is a genuine poet's creation, the creation of an artist, who knows that both good and evil are necessary for greatness, that wherever there is light there must be shade, and that whoever objects to shade is in reality afraid of light."[97] What Levy, and other contemporaries, thought about Shaw's "Nietzscheanism" will be the subject of the next section.

4. *Man and Superman* did not usher in a new phase in the English attitude to Nietzsche, although it certainly gave popular currency to certain of Nietzsche's ideas, a currency, as Ernest Rhys remarked, which "the proverb-maker himself might have seen gaining vogue with dismay."[98] A measure of Shaw's hold over younger minds is shown by the way Stephen Graham and his friend MacCallum stole time from their office to see *Major Barbara* and *Man and Superman* at the Royal Court Theatre: "We were impressed almost to the point of brainstorm, new ideas going to our heads like wine. We were very advanced. I sat on MacCallum's desk and read him chosen pages from Nietzsche's *Genealogy of Morals*, which made the first dent in his socialistic creed and the democracy of the many-headed. He heard what Nietzsche called the 'rapturous counter-cry of the privilege of the fewest.' "[99]

But, whatever Shaw's appeal to the young may have been, it is undeniable that *Man and Superman* provoked attacks from every political quarter. As far as the conservative press was concerned, the play only served to reopen old wounds: Shaw was stigmatized as one of "the empty-headed eccentrics who pretend to a knowledge of philosophy and to an 'advanced' state of culture on the strength of a few madhouse smatterings of Nietzsche."[100] *Blackwood's Magazine*, which made this charge, scoffed at *Man and Superman* and its revolutionary antics, calling it a work "which, in the guise of a tediously elaborate joke, shall reform the human race." As for the word "superman": "It, of course, is the mere jargon of a new Methodism, and, despite the advocacy of Mr. Shaw, it will have no influence for good or evil upon our ancient world. This world of ours, in its passage through space, has collected far more wisdom than ever can be acquired by an emancipated 'thinker' who has just discovered Nietzsche."[101] Dreams for the amelioration of mankind, though forgivable and even praiseworthy in a generous, uninstructed youth, were recognized by mature men to be futile and unfeasible. Shaw's idealism, *Blackwood's* insisted, was strained and unrealistic: when Francis Galton had called for a conference to discuss the possibility of such amelioration he did so, unlike Shaw, in a spirit of playful banter. Similar views were held by liberals like G. M. Trevelyan, who rejoiced that writers such as Meredith were returning to masculine ideals. This, he thought, signalled a healthy reaction from mere self-culture, but was liable to abuse: "In a crude form, partly false and wholly unattractive because Mr. Shaw puts the means to stand for the end and despises the love of human beings for one another, it is the theory of the 'Superman.'"[102] Nor were Shaw's fellow-socialists particularly charmed by the direction his thought was taking. Max Beer, writing in 1904 from the Marxist standpoint, saw clearly that the superman doctrine was implicit in the Fabian "expert":

Having no objective guide, no leading principle to go by, Shaw necessarily arrives at hero-worship – at the hankering after a Superman to guide mankind. I have noticed the same mental development in several continental critics like Harden, Bahr, Ernst, etc. They began with Social Democracy, passed through the Ibsen period, worshipped *An Enemy of the People*, finally becoming adherents of Nietzsche in theory and of Bismarck or some other social imperialist in practice. Marxism is the antithesis of all that. It has a body of doctrine; it regards theory as the guide in practical life; and it destroys all heroism in history. In the place of the heroic factor it sets material and economic factors as the motor power of historical development. ... The Revisionists, or Fabians, say: "Socialism is, before all, an administrative problem; it is not a class struggle, but a clever management of public affairs! It is the Superman in local government."[103]

Even middle-of-the-road socialists took exception to "the whole Nietzsche-Shaw-eugenist movement," and proclaimed the need for a "super-society" rather than a "super-man": "The super-man has been the idol of the privileged few, and suggests, like many a penny-in-the-slot panacea, an easy and mechanical settling of the great problem of social happiness and harmony."[104]

The Christian standpoint was that Shaw's ideas lacked coherence and compulsive power, and even originality: "For if a Superman be really needed, Christianity has long insisted on the need for one, or rather for many, for a world of Supermen. It has been accustomed to speak of them as the regenerate, and has taught that they can be produced from our present human nature, if the moral lever be present, so that there is no need of the production of a new and for us inconceivable thing, a physiological Superhumanity."[105] A suggestion was advanced that Christ himself was now "the Spiritual super-man, who has anticipated humanity and reached the goal of its spiritual evolution."[106] Some criticisms of Shaw were overtly satirical. In G. F. Abbott's *The Philosophy of a Don* (1911), a work initially serialized in the *New Age*, Shaw is ruthlessly pilloried as a garrulous iconoclast whose supermania was fast becoming something of a bore; Adam Neave's *Woman and Superwoman* (1914) is a satiric portrayal of the days "when woman rules and the Millenium is at hand," women having risen to the upper echelons of American and English Eugenic Societies; and in Allen Upward's *Paradise Found* (1915), Shaw is made to wake after two hundred years' hypnotically induced sleep to discover that his cherished ideals have been taken seriously by posterity, but survive in a travestied form – when the Viceroy of England, who rules despotically, declares himself a superman, Shaw realizes in horror that he is another Frankenstein and has created a new monster.

Others took Shaw's Nietzscheanism more seriously. Holbrook Jackson, for example, wrote a popular article on the superman, suggesting that although the superman was yet but a name, "an exuberant and tragic ghost pervading the twilight of humanity,"[107] it would perhaps emerge from the infancy of a dream to dominate the imagination of the entire world. In those circles where Shaw's claim to be a philosopher was unquestioned, there was a feeling of indebtedness to him. He had, at long last, made Nietzsche's ideas palatable, not only in a broad sense, but also in points of specific detail: "We did not take kindly to Zarathustra's "Uebermansch" [*sic*] because its literal translation the Overman sounded too much like a Foreman; but Mr. Shaw's inspired hybrid "Superman" has happily solved that difficulty."*

Perhaps the chief service of *Man and Superman* was that it brought forcibly to the attention of the ordinary play-goer a sense of disillusionment with practical democracy which was being voiced by liberals and

---

* George Sampson, "Nietzsche and Another," *Daily Chronicle* (May 14, 1909), 3. Indeed, as one columnist observed, the prefix "super" was in evidence everywhere one looked – not only had the "superwoman" long since made her début, but the fetish extended to such things as "supersoap," Asquith's "supertax," the "super-Dreadnought" and even to "super-tramp." Bernard Lintot, "At Number 1, Grub St.," *TPW* (June 6, 1913), 713.

socialists alike. The rise of imperialism, the spread of political corruption, the popular appeal of yellow journalism, new discoveries in the field of social psychology had combined to produce grave anxieties about the basis, value, and effect of mass enfranchisement. These anxieties were pungently expressed in L. T. Hobhouse's *Democracy and Reaction* (1904) and in a work which was republished six times in the two years after publication, C. F. G. Masterman's *The Condition of England* (1909). In an earlier work, *In Peril of Change* (1905), Masterman had regarded Shaw's superman ideas with a mixture of respect and suspicion: "His cry for the Superman is little more than the cutting of a stick with which to emphasise the ultimate impossibility of the finite life of man. Amidst his world of supermen, undoubtedly one rebel against the common superiority would be Mr. Bernard Shaw, convicted of a horror and loneliness all the more real because there would be less obvious material for his pleasant and bitter discontents."[108] *The Condition of England*, however, is a prolonged and conscientious examination of a problem which Shaw had epitomized in one brief sentence: "The overthrow of the aristocrat has created the necessity for the Superman."[109] Masterman believed that the aristocratic ruling classes were now effete, totally lacking in ideas and creative energy: "If only they had had a little more brains, they would have been halfwitted."[110] He doubts whether England is now breeding men the calibre of those of the England of Elizabeth. The undeniable note of the age is that material advance has far transcended moral progress – economic inequality is full of the elements of danger: "We seem destined to pass from the antithesis of the class war – the rich against the poor – to the antithesis which Nietszche [sic] foresaw many years ago – the Many against the Few; the demands of incapacity to share in the benefits created by the competent."[111] But Masterman rejected the implications of a new superman class – he thought that the world would be saved, not by a stratified system of rulers and ruled, but by an equitable system of partnership and co-operation.

In Nietzschean circles, too, *Man and Superman* met with a mixed reception. Welcoming it as an earnest and faithful version of the master's principles, Thomas Common and Maximilian Muegge in England, and Henry Mencken and James Huneker in America, were quick to appreciate the publicity which Shaw's play had given to Nietzsche's ideas. Shaw, significantly enough, favoured Common with a complimentary copy. Common responded by pronouncing the work a masterpiece, both as drama and philosophy, and by noting the pervasive influence of Nietzsche – nearly half of the first issue of Common's *Notes for Good Europeans*

(Autumn, 1903), was devoted to excerpts from the play. Mencken reported that in Shaw the Nietzschean creed was set forth with great earnestness and fidelity.[112] Huneker, however, pointed out that Shaw's obligations to Nietzsche were perhaps excessive, and that the scene in Hell was a duplication of a similar situation in Grabbe's *Don Juan und Faust*, which also contained the word "superman," borrowed, he surmised, from the second part of Goethe's *Faust*.[113] But the Nietzscheans in Levy's circle rejected Shaw's appropriation of Nietzsche out of hand, since they believed that Nietzsche and socialism would never lie down together: "Everyone knows that Mr Shaw is a socialist, despite the fact that he claims to be in agreement with Nietzsche's attitude towards morality."[114] Shaw was right to perceive that England had reached a critical point in her history, but his socialism was no way to remedy the situation:

> The "hush" which a cultured statesman recently referred to may be the prelude to a fierce world-struggle, when the older European nations, under the influence of socialistic and democratic opium, have sunk into a state of humanitarian torpor, and the united younger races, in whose land Nietzsche was born, begin (as they have done) to put the cruellest side of their Master's teaching into practice. The ideals sought by Mr. Masterman [in *The Condition of England*] and the "new way of life" recommended by Mr. St. Loe Strachey cannot be found – need I say it? – in out-of-date superstition, in reliance upon a higher power ... nor yet can they be found in universal suffrage. State nationalisation of everything, votes for women, or any of the other means recommended in the hoarse Socialistic claptrap shouted ungrammatically into the patient air from thousands of inverted soap-boxes and *Clarion* vans; they can be found only in the thorough grasp of the writings of one of the greatest philosophical geniuses that ever lived: Friedrich Nietzsche.[115]

It was the unanimous verdict of Dr. Levy and his followers that Shaw lacked any thorough grasp of what Nietzsche was trying to say. When Shaw protested that he owed few of his ideas to continental writers Levy took him at his word: "If Shaw had tried to burgle their houses ... he wouldn't have known what to steal from them, and would probably have run away with a worthless brass poker instead of their golden treasures."[116] Levy was convinced that the "gloomy Hebraic Shaw" was temperamentally incapable of appreciating Nietzsche's attachment to Greek and Renaissance culture, and this explains "the enormous abyss" separating the two men: "It was against people like Shaw that Nietzsche wrote his books. Shaw himself in one of his clever aphorisms states that every genuinely religious person is a heretic and therefore a revolutionary. This is exactly the reason why Nietzsche combatted religious people à la Shaw, because he foresaw that all tradition and culture would finally be uprooted by them."[117] Shaw attacks mediocrity and conventionality, whereas Nietzsche scorns to do so; Shaw thunders against the dishonesty and sinfulness of his age, whereas Nietzsche regards the age as the most honest in history and far too weak to commit, in Levy's words, "a good fat sin." Levy's caveat that Shaw's superman was not to be confused with Nietzsche's has already been given, and it was endorsed by a critic in Middleton Murry's *Adelphi*, who criticized Shaw from Nietzsche's point of view:

> Both have that great longing which is a great contempt and both use prevalent biological ideas to express it: to Shaw Evolution is the path to Godhead, and to Nietzsche Man is a bridge to the Superman. But here similarity ceases. To Shaw Godhead is omniscience and omnipotence: to Nietzsche it is innocence. To Shaw the Superman is an Ancient who aspires to become Force without Form: to Nietzsche the Superman is a Child. Shaw's Ancient seeks a heaven where contemplation shall be his only joy: Nietzsche's Child seeks nothing but to stand as man upon the natural earth and be a man with men. But there is still deeper difference. Shaw sees a moment only as a point on an infinite straight line, and imagines the only Life Eternal to be Everlasting Life; but Nietzsche, knowing otherwise, cancelled the Dogma of the Superman by the equal and opposite Dogma of the Eternal Return so that every moment's living should be Eternal Life.[118]

This generation of Nietzscheans followed the view, as expressed by Wells, Harris, and Lawrence, that Shaw was a species of rationalist-eunuch. Those who were to see in Yeats's *A Vision* the most important contribution to philosophy since Nietzsche rejected Shaw's pretence to respect the dignity of ideas, calling him a mere entrepreneur of talent: "Shaw with his impertinent degradation of the Beyond-man in terms of intellectual superhumanity, was the first and worst vulgariser of Nietzsche."[*]

The most sustained attack on Shaw's "Nietzscheanism" came neither from Havelock Ellis, whose critique has been given on pp. 109–11 above, nor from Levy and his circle, but from the Roman Catholic G. K. Chesterton. In 1913 a close associate of Chesterton's, the Belgian professor Charles Sarolea, who had written on Nietzsche as early as 1897, declared: "A searching estimate of Nietzsche in English still remains to be written. And there is only one man that could write it, and that man is Mr. Gilbert K. Chesterton. I confidently prophesy that a study of Nietzsche, if he has the

---

[*] P. R. Stephensen, "The Whirled Around," *London Aphrodite*, no. 5 (April, 1929), 340. This polemic goes on to suggest that Shaw never had an original thought in his life except about the Salvation Army.

courage to undertake it, will be Mr. Chesterton's greatest book. He will find in the German heretic a foe worthy of his steel."[119] As Chesterton never addressed himself to this task, we have to piece together his attitude to Nietzsche from the books he has left us. In his *Autobiography*, for example, Chesterton recalled his impression of certain debating clubs in London where Nietzsche was often a topic of discussion. He found their atmosphere uncongenial, even oppressive: "The Intelligentsia of the artistic and vaguely anarchic clubs was indeed a very strange world. And the strangest thing about it, I fancy, was that, while it thought a great deal about thinking, it did not think. Everything seemed to come at second or third hand: from Nietzsche or Tolstoy or Ibsen or Shaw; and there was a pleasant atmosphere of discussing all these things, without any particular sense of responsibility for coming to any conclusion on them."[120] The obsessive question seemed to be "whether we should love everybody with Tolstoy, or spare nobody with Nietzsche."[121] This state of intellectual confusion he ascribed to the absence of basic moral and metaphysical principles – men struggled to reconcile a fervent altruism with an equally fervent acceptance of Darwinism. No wonder they were thrown into turmoil! "Men who naturally accepted the moral equality of mankind yet did so, in a manner, shrinkingly, under the gigantic shadow of the Superman of Nietzsche and Shaw. Their hearts were in the right place; but their heads were emphatically in the wrong place, being generally poked or plunged into vast volumes of materialism and scepticism, crabbed, barren, servile and without any light of liberty or of hope."[122]

Escaping this confusion by taking his stand on Christianity, Chesterton waged an incessant war against the encroachments of "deleterious" modern ideologies, especially the new science of eugenics, and felt particularly sensitive about the ascendency which Nietzsche seemed to be gaining over the best minds of his time:

This eloquent sophist has an influence upon Shaw and his school which it would require a separate book adequately to study. By descent Nietzsche was a Pole, and probably a Polish noble; and to say that he was a Polish noble is to say that he was a frail, fastidious, and entirely useless anarchist. He has a wonderful poetic wit; and is one of the best rhetoricians of the modern world. He had a remarkable power of saying things that master the reason for a moment by their gigantic unreasonableness; as, for instance, "Your life is intolerable without immortality; but why should not your life be intolerable?" His whole work is shot through with the pangs and fevers of his physical life, which was one of extreme bad health; and in early middle age his brilliant brain broke down into impotence and darkness. All that was true in his teaching was this: that if a man looks fine on a horse it is so far irrelevant to tell him that he would be more economical on a donkey or more humane on a tricycle.[123]

Chesterton notes the widespread worship of will, a fashion he ascribes to Nietzsche's influence – Davidson, Shaw, and Wells have all been ensnared by voluntarism:

Mr. John Davidson, a remarkable poet, is so passionately excited about it that he is obliged to write prose. He publishes a short play with several long prefaces. This is natural enough in Mr. Shaw, for all his plays are prefaces: Mr. Shaw is (I suspect) the only man on earth who has never written any poetry. But that Mr. Davidson (who can write excellent poetry) should write instead laborious metaphysics in defence of this doctrine of will, does show that the doctrine of will has taken hold of men. Even Mr. H. G. Wells has half spoken in its language.[124]

What is more, Nietzsche is the archetype of the modern revolutionist whose infinite scepticism makes all his expressions of revolt ultimately self-defeating, for rebellion ceases to be effective when it is all-embracing. Rebellion, like satire, must presuppose standards and principles if it is to have any significance; Nietzsche's criticism of society lacks a basis of principle, and therefore tends to backfire – Nietzsche himself is more preposterous than anything he denounces. Chesterton believes that Nietzsche was mistaken in thinking he was rebelling against Christianity: in fact, he was only taking issue with certain of its critics, Herbert Spencer for example. Nietzsche also imagined he was rebelling against ancient morality, when he was actually "only rebelling against recent morality, against the half-baked impudence of the utilitarians and the materialists."[125] Admittedly, his hatred of pity was not Christian, but this was the outcome, not of doctrine, but of disease. It was not this morbid attack on Christian mercy that caught Shaw's attention, but the equally un-Christian doctrine of the superman: "Nietzsche might really have done some good if he had taught Bernard Shaw to draw the sword, to drink wine, or even to dance. But he only succeeded in putting into his head a new superstition, which bids fair to be the chief superstition of the dark ages which are possibly in front of us – I mean the superstition of what is called the Superman."[126]

Since for Chesterton, the theory of the superman is Nietzsche's primary intellectual weakness, he sees Shaw's adoption of it as nothing less than sensational: "He who had to all appearance mocked at the faiths in the forgotten past discovered a new god in the unimaginable future. He who had laid all the blame on ideals set up the most impossible of all ideals, the ideal of a new creature."[127] Why, asks Chesterton, should we worry about producing a superman? If he is to come by natural selection there is no need for us to intervene; if he is to come by human selection what kind of superman are we to have? If he is to be more just, more brave and more merciful all we can do is to strive to be these things ourselves. On the other hand: "If he is to be anything else than this, why should we desire him, or what else are we to desire? These questions have been many times asked of the Nietzscheites, and none of the Nietzscheites have even attempted to answer them."[128] To Nietzsche's form of aristocracy, which is merely an aristocracy of weak nerves, Chesterton infinitely prefers that found in a popular fiction series of the time:

Nietzsche and the *Bow Bells Novelettes* have both obviously the same fundamental character; they both worship the tall man with curling mustaches and herculean bodily power, and they both worship him in a manner which is somewhat feminine and hysterical. Even here, however, the *Novelette* easily maintains its philosophical superiority, because it does attribute to the strong man those virtues which do commonly belong to him, such virtues as laziness and kindliness and a rather reckless benevolence, and a great dislike of hurting the weak. Nietzsche, on the other hand, attributes to the strong man that scorn against weakness which only exists among invalids.*

Chesterton's distorted view of Nietzsche has all the mischievous wickedness of wilful caricature, but some of the barbs he launched in Shaw's direction struck firmly home. As a publicist of Nietzsche, Shaw drew on his own head the wrath of the reactionary press, the resentment of Nietzsche partisans who thought him guilty of misrepresentation, and the stupified incredulity of those who found in his futuristic visions nothing but idle fancy or illusory superstition.

5 Shaw's declared purpose in writing *The Quintessence of Ibsenism* was not to demonstrate the aesthetic side of Ibsen's work (his "poetic beauties" as Shaw says) but the social doctrine embedded in it; similarly, in *The Perfect Wagnerite*, Shaw treats *The Ring of the Nibelungs* as an economic allegory. In both cases the imaginative, mythical content is reduced to a programme for social reform: even as a music critic Shaw was driven by his utilitarian bias to find some religious or moral significance in

---

* *Heretics* (London, 1905), 197–8. Chesterton cumbrously versified the same point: "Zarathustra who couldn't take stout,/He made war on the weak and they banged him about." "An Alphabet," *NA* IV (October 29, 1908), 11.

the most abstract compositions. Nietzsche criticized Socrates for reducing literature to the level of didactic Aesopian fable, and Shaw's partiality for Bunyan suggests he, too, would have incurred the censure Nietzsche meted out to Socrates, and to the poet of aesthetic Socratism, Euripides. Euripides, wrote Nietzsche in *The Birth of Tragedy*, substituted cool, paradoxical thoughts for the Apollonian intuitions of classic Greek tragedy, and fiery passions for the earlier Dionysian ecstasies. These thoughts and passions, Nietzsche objects, are copied very realistically, and are in no way suffused with the atmosphere of art: as a poet Euripides echoes his own conscious knowledge. The supervention of rationalistic method, noted by Nietzsche in the Euripidean prologue, is equally apparent in the Shavian preface. Orage attacked Shaw from the Nietzschean point of view as a dramatist, declaring that his attitude to Shaw was exactly that of Aristophanes to Euripides:

Has it occurred to you to ask why Aristophanes preferred Aeschylus and Sophocles? It was not because these latter were better dramatic craftsmen than Euripides. Quite the contrary. Euripides is much superior technically. It was because Euripides was an inferior artist in that he was unable to put a soul into his plays. For a soul he substituted an idea. The descent was rapid. An idea became a political moral notion. Euripides in a decade after Sophocles' death was down among the propagandists. Shaw is there still.[129]

Gilbert Murray, who felt especially drawn to Euripides, wrote of him: "His contemporary public denounced him as dull, because he tortured them with personal problems; as malignant, because he made them see truths they wished not to see; as blasphemous and foul-minded, because he made demands on their religious and spiritual natures which they could neither satisfy nor overlook."[130] Such a comment, it has been suggested, reveals that Murray regarded Euripides as standing in the same relation to the classic age of Greek drama as Shaw and Ibsen stood in relation to the period of Victoria and Edward VII.[131] But Murray's high estimate of Euripides was not shared by Nietzsche or Orage, or by Francis Fergusson, who follows Nietzsche in thinking that Euripides relied upon a common heritage of ritual and myth as much as his predecessors, but only drew upon it for the purposes of parody, satire, and metaphorical illustration. Fergusson writes of Euripides' plays: "The human action he reveals is the extremely modern one of the psyche caught in the categories its reason invents, responding with unmitigated sharpness to the feeling of the moment, but cut off from the deepest level of experience, where the mysterious world is yet felt as real and prior to our inventions, demands, and criticisms."[132]

If Shaw felt this sense of alienation, as he surely did, he did not face up to it. At least Yeats thought so: "Shaw, as I understand him, has no true quarrel with his time, its moon and his almost exactly coincide. He is quite content to exchange Narcissus and his Pool for the signal-box at a railway junction, where goods and travellers pass perpetually upon their logical glittering road."[133] Listening to *Arms and the Man* with mingled admiration and horror, Yeats confessed he stood aghast before its energy: "It seemed to me inorganic, logical straightness and not the crooked road of life. ... Presently I had a nightmare that I was haunted by a sewing machine, that clicked and shone, but the incredible thing was that the machine smiled, smiled perpetually."[134] Whereas Yeats rebelled against his utilitarian inheritance with such fervour that he managed to oust it altogether from his consciousness, Shaw incorporated it into his socialism – after all, Jeremy Bentham was one of the main inspirers of the Fabian movement. But the superman is not a utilitarian concept, and Shaw's representation of it in his plays suffers, as all his characters tend to do, from an excess of social purpose. As Ashley Dukes, in perhaps the most brilliant attack on Shaw, writes:

> He nationalizes his men and women the instant they are created. He expropriates their imagination. He municipalizes their emotion. He confiscates their surplus value. And he renders compensation to each by the gift of a flickering cloud-halo of wit which sometimes illumines, sometimes obscures, the individual figure and the eminently social purpose. ... [Shaw is a Puritan and Puritanism] sets ethics before taste, desiccates illusion, diverts all artistic emotion through the individual to a social end, creates a moral test of pure enjoyment, and offers a bribe of civic self-satisfaction to the artist as surely as Calvinism offers the promise of heaven and the threat of hell.*

Shaw's picture of man is optimistic, for it is based on the ultimate removal of all ills through humanitarian effort and enterprise – as Nietzsche saw, this was a movement which restricted the power in human life of inexorable fate, and hence of material for tragic art; Yeats, on the other hand, is closer to Nietzsche in believing that the better the state is organized, the duller its human products will turn out to be. In terms of Nietzsche's three categories in *The Birth of Tragedy*, Yeats had passed through both the Socratic phase of Shavian Fabianism ("knowledge as virtue and power")

---

* *NA*, vIII (March 23, 1911), 497–8. Dukes was a regular contributor to the *New Age*. Recounting his reading for 1909, he concludes: "By no means lastly, but outstandingly, there was Nietzsche; and I confess that for a while *Thus Spake Zarathustra* and *The Birth of Tragedy*, both read in the lyrical German, were like an Old and New Testament." *The Scene is Changed* (London, 1942), 30.

and the artistic phase of Pater's impressionism ("aesthetic veil of illusion"), to emerge as the Dionysian celebrant of tragedy ("life indestructible"). This difference between Shaw and Yeats is further illustrated in the distinction Nietzsche makes between the "rational" and the "intuitive" man: "Both desire to rule over life; the one by knowing how to meet the most important needs with foresight, prudence, regularity; the other as an 'overjoyous' hero by ignoring those needs and taking that life only as real which simulates appearance and beauty."[135] It is only the "rational" man who believes in Utopias, and Nietzsche has no more patience than Yeats with those who hope that mankind will discover "a final and ideal order of things, and that happiness will then and ever after beam down upon us uniformly, like the rays of the sun in the tropics."[136]

In Nietzsche's mind, this "ideal order of things" was invariably associated with Socrates: "With Socrates *Optimism* begins, an optimism no longer artistic, with teleology and faith in the good god: faith in the enlightened good man. Dissolution of the instincts."[137] But Nietzsche does entertain an idealism about the future: his vision of the future he would have regarded as classical – derived from the strength of his time – and Shaw's as romantic – derived from its weaknesses. The task of promulgating such a vision devolves on the artist, whose *surplus* energies (Shaw would have said his *total* energies) should be directed towards its embodiment. But Nietzsche adds a word of warning, incidentally making clear the point at which his idealism diverges from that of Shaw:

Nor should this be so done as if the poet, like an imaginative political economist, had to anticipate a more favourable national and social state of things and picture their realisation. Rather will he, just as the earlier poets portrayed the images of the Gods, portray the fair images of men. He will divine those cases where, in the midst of our modern world and reality (which will not be shirked or repudiated in the usual poetic fashion), a great, noble soul is still possible, where it may be embodied in harmonious, equable conditions, where it may become permanent, visible, and representative of a type, and so, by the stimulus to imitation and envy, help to create the future.[138]

This might have been written with Shaw in mind, so striking is its aptness. Whereas Shaw thought predominantly in terms of economic man, Nietzsche was thinking in terms of tragic man; for Shaw the archetype of the superman was Prometheus, who defied the gods to bring alleviation to mankind; for Nietzsche the archetype of the superman was Dionysus, whose courage offers mankind the possibility, not of mere alleviation, but of redemption. Nietzsche's superman is much closer to the modern existentialist's hero, Sisyphus, than to the rebellious benefactors of humanity which Shaw admired. For the distinguishing mark about Sisyphus is surely his courage and determination in the face of hopelessness and despair, and courage, as a student of Shaw's heroic vitalism has pointed out, is the one quality his heroes seem to lack: "Shaw's intellectual instruments are those of the comedian, and therefore his picture of man excludes the Dionysian."* It was Chesterton's opinion, be it recalled, that "Nietzsche might really have done some good if he had taught Bernard Shaw to draw the sword, to drink wine, or even to dance." It is a complaint echoed by a recent student of the element of revolt in Shaw's work: "Certainly, the Shavian Superman – stripped of instincts and emotions, and reduced to disembodied mind – is a far cry from the Nietzschean Uebermensch, that wild, ecstatic immoralist whom Nietzsche hoped would galvanize the feeble emotional core of modern life."[139]

In *Man and Superman* and *Back to Methuselah* Shaw intellectualizes Nietzsche's superman beyond recognition – William Archer thought that in *Man and Superman* Schopenhauer's "sullen pessimism" had been transformed into nothing more than "enthusiastic stoicism," and that what life the play had was purely mental: "Every page ... crackles with wit and tingles with cerebral activity, if not always with thought."[140] In his portrayal of the superman Shaw forsakes the hesitant suggestiveness of myth for the brash explicitness of dogma, and the bright resonance of a genuine imaginative prophecy degenerates to the percussive reiteration of a slogan whistled by an opportunist to keep his spirits up. It was not entirely Shaw's fault that in his hands the superman became a journalist's romantic cliché: it was to a large extent conditioned by the limitations of the medium Shaw

---

* Eric Bentley, *The Cult of the Superman* (London, 1947), 174. "Nietzsche says very little about the comic, which apparently did not have much interest for him. He ascribes the source of the comic to a sudden transition from the condition of fear to that of exuberance. In this way, the comic becomes the opposite of the tragic. In Nietzschean psychology the basic emotions are considered in terms of their development during millenia of human experience before man became socialized. For thousands of years, Nietzsche says, 'man was an animal who was susceptible in the highest degree to fear.' His life and security were constantly jeopardized by the *unexpected*. When man became socialized, however, he found himself in a reverse situation. His life, bound by custom and convention, was based almost solely on the *expected*. Hence, if something surprising or unexpected occurs in the presence of the man of society, and he sees that it does not endanger or offer injury to him, he 'becomes exuberant and passes over into the very opposite of fear – the terrified, crouching being shoots upward, stretches itself – man laughs.' It is this transition, says Nietzsche, 'from momentary fear into short-lived exhilaration' that constitutes the comic." Richard Benton, "The Aesthetics of Friedrich Nietzsche," Johns Hopkins University dissertation, 1955, 141. See *Human, All-Too-Human*, aph. 169.

had chosen for himself, the realistic drama, limitations which Yeats outlined as follows: "Except where it is superficial or deliberately argumentative it fills one's soul with a sense of commonness as with dust. It has one mortal ailment. It cannot become impassioned, that is to say, vital, without making somebody gushing and sentimental."[141] There is much of the bluster of pure assertion about Shaw's handling of the superman, which he often uses like a swagger stick which can be struck impressively more or less anywhere.

Worse still, Shaw wriggles out of his dilemmas by vigorously protesting the truth of the homely proverb "where there's a will there's a way," and indulging in the consoling uplift of wishful thinking. Consequently many of Shaw's opponents did not really need to demolish his arguments, but, like Chesterton, only to call his bluff. Bent on clearing the world of lies, Shaw could not avoid perpetrating his own. Nietzsche wrote that "the most common sort of lie is the one uttered to one's self; to lie to others is relatively exceptional,"[142] and the theory of the Life Force – with which the superman was amalgamated – was the lie Shaw told to himself. Nevertheless, there were moments when the imminence of Armageddon threatened to shatter the theory to pieces, as in *Heartbreak House*, written during the bleakest days of Shaw's disillusionment over the First World War. In that play Hector, enraged that the noise of an approaching storm could be mistaken for nothing more than the rumble of a passing goods train, cries out fiercely: "I tell you, one of two things must happen. Either out of that darkness some new creation will come to supplant us as we have supplanted the animals, or the heavens will fall in thunder and destroy us."[143] Mankind, thinks Hector, is now useless, dangerous, out of reach of panaceas, liberal or otherwise. Shaw had reached the same vision of disgust which T. E. Lawrence was to voice several years later: "I think the planet is in a damnable condition, which no change of party, or social reform, will do more than palliate insignificantly. What is wanted is a new master species – birth control for us, to end the human race in 50 years – and then a clear field for some cleaner mammal. I suppose it must be a mammal?"[144]

It was a vision which Shaw had developed in *Man and Superman* and *Back to Methuselah*, but the sense of terror which belongs to such a vision is, in both plays, only intermittent. Such terror, it seems, Shaw was constitutionally unable to understand or sustain, and his feelings of disgust and futility are crushed by his relentless optimism, ceding to the necessity to dedicate himself to the service of a worthy ideal: "This is the true joy in life, the being used for a purpose recognized by yourself as a mighty one;

the being thoroughly worn out before you are thrown on the scrap heap; the being a force of Nature instead of a feverish selfish little clod of ailments and grievances complaining that the world will not devote itself to making you happy."[145] At first sight this may seem no different from Nietzsche's scorn for human happiness and his insistence that man should think of himself as a bridge to the superman. But Nietzsche would have criticized Shaw for succumbing to the allurements of the ideal at the expense of intellectual honesty – convictions can be rightly or wrongly used:

> Great passion makes use of and consumes convictions, it does not submit to them – it knows that it is a sovereign power. Conversely; the need of faith, of anything either absolutely affirmative or negative, Carlylism (if I may be allowed this expression), is the need of *weakness*. The man of beliefs, the "believer" of every sort and condition, is necessarily a dependent man; – he is one who cannot regard *himself* as an aim, who cannot postulate aims from the promptings of his own heart. The "believer" does not belong to himself, he can be only a means, he must be *used up*, he is in need of someone who uses him up. His instinct accords the highest honour to a morality of self-abnegation: everything in him, his prudence, his experience, his vanity, persuade him to adopt this morality. Every sort of belief is in itself an expression of self-denial, or self-estrangement.[146]

The reference to Carlyle here is illuminating, since Nietzsche's attacks on Carlyle were made for reasons which are equally applicable to Shaw. In Nietzsche's view Carlyle was an English atheist who made it a point of honour not to be so (see above, p. 20); he possessed a loquacity which resulted from a sheer delight in noise and confusion of feelings; and he made the fatal error of mistaking the desire for belief for the will to truth. The accusation that Carlyle's hero-worship was merely romantic prostration before Napoleon or any ruler of men who was strong, unjust, and cruel might apply to Shaw's infatuation with Stalin, Hitler, and Mussolini.* Most importantly, both Carlyle and Shaw stress the social instrumentality of their hero-worship, whereas Nietzsche regards the superman in extra-social (or ultra-social) terms as the end and justification of the society in which he lives. As for the histrionic element so apparent in both writers, Nietzsche would have abhorred it, as he came to abhor it in Wagner – he would have regarded all three as the mere play-actors of their own ideals.

In summary, then, it was undeniably through Shaw that many of Nietzsche's ideas – perhaps in defective form – began to infiltrate English so-

---

* It has been suggested that Shaw's veneration for these men, as for Nietzsche's superman, can be explained by "his somewhat sadistic temper." W. Y. Tindall, *Forces in Modern British Literature* (New York, 1947), 102.

ciety. At a time when Nietzsche was almost universally condemned, it was Shaw who granted him a reprieve, or at least, a stay of execution. Shaw acknowledged Nietzsche's importance as a great artist-philosopher, claimed intellectual kinship with him, and probably had a better first-hand acquaintance with Nietzsche's work than he has generally been given credit for or even than he himself, for various reasons, wished to admit. In spite of this, Shaw's work would not have been substantially different had he never heard of Nietzsche, for Nietzsche is mainly used to dress out a philosophy derived from other writers – Ibsen, Wagner, Bergson. Shaw was right in thinking that Nietzsche's superman bore certain affinities to Wagner's Siegfried, but failed to accentuate the real differences between them. Shaw's own superman, whether arch-iconoclast or disembodied mind, is quite distinct from Nietzsche's, who, by being allied to the Shavian Life Force, found himself in sedate quarantine. It is quite wrong to assume, as one critic has done, that in *Back to Methuselah* the influence of Nietzsche is "pervasive" and to make it responsible "for the un-Shavian unpleasantness of several sections of the play."[147] Finally, if Nietzsche's attitude towards Euripides and Carlyle is any guide, Shaw had little genuine understanding of why Nietzsche proclaimed himself the first tragic philosopher of modern times.

A. R. ORAGE

1 Shaw approached Nietzsche by way of a short-cut (or rather detour) through Ibsen and Wagner, but others of his generation found very different, and more improbable, means of access. Critical exegesis of the Bible during the nineteenth century had resulted in a re-emphasis on the mystical and sacramental side of Christianity as opposed to its doctrinal content, and towards the end of the century there was a strong revival of mysticism, spiritualism, and theosophy. Such works as Madame Blavatskys' *The Secret Doctrine* and A. P. Sinnett's *Esoteric Buddhism*, both published in 1888, fascinated those who felt themselves painfully alienated from the institutional Christianity in which they had been nurtured. Yeats, for example, was a founder-member of the Dublin Hermetical Society, and remained a student of the occult for many years afterwards. Yet there is a strong connection between hermetical beliefs and the aspirations one associates with Nietzsche's superman; in one of the rebirth rituals in which Yeats is known to have taken part, the adept was supposed to conjure up for himself an image of idealized selfhood and imaginatively unite himself with it. There are times when Yeats seems to look upon Nietzsche as a mystic who possesses esoteric knowledge and the inestimable gift of joy;* and for Alfred Richard Orage Nietzsche was above all a mystic whose affinities with the mystical tradition were beyond all question. Nietzsche's superman, he believed, had a forbear in Mejnour, the occult superman of Bulwer-Lytton's *Zanoni* (1842):

Mejnour is justifying his sacrifice of thousands of aspirants for the sake of a single success. He is inspired in this, he says, by "the hope to form a mighty and numerous race ... that may proceed in their deathless destinies from stage to stage of

---

* A view, however, not shared by Havelock Ellis: "A mystic Nietzsche certainly was not; he had no moods of joyous resignation. It is chiefly the religious ecstasy of active moral energy that he was at one with." *Affirmations* (London, 1898), 47.

celestial glory, and rank at last among the nearest ministrants and agents gathered round the Throne of Thrones." ... Such an ideal can be paralleled perhaps in the work of a real man, singularly like Mejnour in his apparent chilly isolation, and singularly like him too in his passionate devotion to humanity – Frederic Nietzsche; and the parallel is almost complete when one finds Mejnour saying of himself, "my art is to make man above mankind."[1]

Orage joined the Theosophical Society in 1896, the year of his marriage, and wrote a number of articles for its organ, the *Theosophical Review*. (In 1894 the review was known simply as *Lucifer*, and had contained an article on Nietzsche's *Zarathustra*.) Orage's own writing shows a strain of idealism characteristic of the review. Man, declares Orage in strangely modern terminology, is not yet defined, and his task is to define himself. He appeals for a New Romanticism which will concentrate on the "deliberate vision and creation of the world, not as one thinks it ought to be, but as one thinks it can be."[2] He agrees with Nietzsche about the need for some illusion to make life tolerable: "The question for legislators (I have Plato's guardians in my eye, Horatio), is which of the possible illusions is at once most necessary, most beneficent, and most enduring."[3] During the seven years before 1900 Plato had been, as Nietzsche was to become after that date, Orage's chosen subject of abiding interest and study. His rationalist approach to theosophy made him accentuate its neo-Platonic philosophical side while increasingly leading him to deprecate the weird eccentricities of which, on its occult side, it was not seldom guilty. One of the works Orage almost certainly read at this time was R. D. Bucke's *Cosmic Consciousness* (1901). The leading disciple of Gurdjieff, under whom Orage studied in retirement after resigning his editorship of the *New Age*, had this to say about Bucke's curious book:

All this announces to us the nearness of the NEW HUMANITY. We are building without taking into consideration the fact that a NEW MASTER must come who may not at all like everything that we have built. Our "social sciences," sociology, and so forth, have in view only man, while as I have several times shown before, the concept "man" is a complex one, and includes in itself different categories of men going along different paths. The future belongs not to *man, but to superman*, who is already born, and lives among us.

A higher race is rapidly emerging among humanity, and it is emerging by reason of its quite remarkable understanding of the world and life.

It will be truly a HIGHER RACE – and there will be no possibility of any falsification, any substitution, or any usurpation at all. It will be impossible for anything to be *bought*, or *appropriated* to oneself by deceit or by might. Not only will this race be, but it already is.

The men approaching the transition into a new race begin already to know one another: already are established pass-words and countersigns. And perhaps those social and political questions so sharply put forward in our time may be solved on quite another plane and by quite a different method than we think – may be solved by the entrance into the arena of a new race CONSCIOUS OF ITSELF which will judge the old races.[4]

Such a belief underlies much of what Orage wrote on cultural, literary, political, and economic matters; it is at the basis of the declared policy of the *New Age*, and suggests not only Orage's general agreement with Nietzsche's call for a new aristocracy, but also the points at which he dissents from Nietzsche's scheme. It is clear from three theosophical lectures Orage gave, later published as *Consciousness: Animal, Human, and Superman* (1907), that he was preoccupied with one key problem: "Is it possible for the human to transcend the human? Can man become more than man? May he enter the one ocean of consciousness from which the myriad streams of particular modes of consciousness flow?"[5] Orage was convinced that, by the operation of the Transcendental Self, "the suggestor of human consciousness, the concealed Magician,"[6] these things *are* possible. Like Nietzsche, Orage treats man, not as a goal, but as a bridge; not as possessing freedom, but capable of it.

Orage's enthusiasm for Nietzsche began in 1900, when a chance meeting at a Leeds bookstall acquainted him with Holbrook Jackson, already an avid reader of *The Eagle and the Serpent*. Jackson has left a detailed record of this meeting, and of their impact on one another: "Did we not on that occasion build a bridge from the Orient to the Occident? You left behind you that night, or rather the next day, for we had talked the night away, a translation of the *Bhagavad Gita*; and you carried under your arm my copy of the first English version of *Thus spake Zarathustra*."[7] Although Orage had read a little of Nietzsche in French, as had his wife, his knowledge of Nietzsche was limited to what he had picked up in Ellis's *Affirmations*; apparently his excitement over *Zarathustra*, which he had not read before, was so great that he spent the whole night reading it and returned to see Jackson "with a new light in his eye," rejoicing in his discovery, and eager to discuss it with his new friend. Jackson wrote later that he had been taking Nietzsche in small doses as a stimulant but had found no one to share his taste until he met Orage, who was quite overwhelmed: "That was my fault. Orage went over the top and so did the group. We all developed supermania. He wanted a Nietzsche circle in which Plato and Blavatzky, Fabianism and Hinduism, Shaw and Wells and Edward Carpenter should be blended, with Nietzsche as the catalytic. An exciting brew."⁸ For Orage, at least, it was exciting: for the next seven years an unremitting study of Nietzsche's work was to produce countless lectures to theosophical societies and art groups, two popular expositions of Nietzsche's thought, *Friedrich Nietzsche: The Dionysian Spirit of the Age* (1906) and *Nietzsche in Outline and Aphorism* (1907), as well as a cultural philosophy which was to be the basis of all his literary criticism, particularly of his attacks on literary decadence. While seeing certain connections between his theosophical studies and Nietzsche's moral theories, Orage soon came to regard Nietzsche's ideas as more dynamic and practical than his own earlier belief in the virtue of contemplation on the eastern model, and Nietzsche began to loom large even in Orage's expositions of theosophy. One witness gives what he calls a typical example of theosophist conversation: "The fourth dimension is played out. It's done with. ... Nietzsche goes much further. Have you read Nietzsche? No? I haven't either, but I have heard Orage talk about him. Nietzsche says we can all do what we want. We must dare things. We must be blond beasts. Mary Wollstonecraft and her set, you know. Godwin and those people."⁹

Even if these theosophists were intellectual freaks, "talkers of divine flapdoodle," as this witness describes them, they constituted for Orage an audience of willing listeners. In these early years Orage was learning to take the leading role in discussion, gaining experience which was to stand him in good stead when he became the presiding figure of the *New Age* circle some years later. Certain of his auditors may have thought it sacrilege to mention Nietzsche and theosophy in the same breath. Ralph Shirley, editor of the *Occult Review*, condemned Nietzsche for wishing to evolve the physical and mental aspects of man at the expense of the spiritual and emotional ones – Nietzsche's higher type of man was not higher at all, but lower, since unlike the occult and Christian ideal he was not evolved through suffering and self-sacrifice:

The conception of evolving a higher type of the human race is one which is very familiar to the Occultist, but the methods by which he would attain his end are far indeed removed from those of Nietzsche. What we feel about the Superman is that, even supposing he had been successfully evolved, he would not be the sort of person one would care to encounter alone on a dark night. As a matter of fact, I think we should be justified in assuming that he would be one of those human pests which it would be to the general interest of mankind to exterminate at the earliest possible moment.¹⁰

Theosophy was not the only means of access to Nietzsche; Orage even more improbably, found a way to him through Fabian socialism.* We have already seen how Shaw's socialism gradually assumed a strong Nietzschean tinge; indeed, Fabian interest in Nietzsche was becoming articulate as early as 1898, when Hubert Bland delivered a lecture to the society. Summing up Nietzsche's importance he said: "His value is the value of a sparkling paradox, which is not itself a truth but which suggests a truth. He is a fine antidote to current sentimentality and to the modern tendency to carry morality into every sphere of life. We are all in danger of being done to death by Ethical Societies."[11] Bland was not impressed, any more than Shaw had been, by the ineffectualness of the Fellowship of the New Life, and his suggestion that Nietzsche might be used to counter current sentimentality is reminiscent of Shaw's endorsement of an idea to form a Nietzsche Society.

At first sight socialism and Nietzscheanism appear quite incompatible; Nietzsche believed that socialism, like democracy, was an offshoot of the Christianity he so much despised, and he assailed it constantly in his work. Some socialists, it is true, took stern objection to Nietzsche's ideas about socialism. One writer found them lacking in consistency, since at times they were illuminating, but at others merely ignorant, stupid or misleading – they were grounded, he thought, in Nietzsche's attitude to Prussian Imperialism, and were lifted straight from Bismarck: "Nietzsche chose to be blind with Bismarck's natural blindness, and to see in Socialism something that warred with individuality and difference, instead of something that would infallibly multiply the opportunity and occasion of both."[12] But such an attitude does not seem to have been typical; many socialists were able to discount, as Shaw did, Nietzsche's frontal assault on their political creed, and sought a common basis in the pressing need for change. One of their number wrote: "He knew and preached, as we modern Socialists know and preach, that the majority of existing customs, religions, laws etc., must be demolished before any new system could really have its beginning."[13] Nietzsche's concern for cultural values was another bond: "How much of the distrust of the Socialist movement by the intellectual class," wrote A. J. Penty, the Guild Socialist colleague of Orage, "has been due to Socialists' neglect of art and philosophy!"[14] A common hostility to

---

* In the halcyon days before the war, wrote a *Times Literary Supplement* reviewer in 1920, "public taste decreed that you should attend Fabian summer schools with vegetarians and suffragettes, and sit at the feet of Nietzsche, Ibsen, and Mr. Bernard Shaw." "The Experiments of Youth," *TLS*, November 11, 1920, 729.

Liberalism united socialists and out-and-out Nietzscheans like J. M. Kennedy, who wrote: "Speaking as one who is, on the whole, a Conservative, I have no hesitation in saying that we Tories feel that we have much more in common with the Socialists than with the Liberals."[15] And Florence Farr, reviewing Orage's book on *Consciousness*, wrote: "England has been trembling on the verge of the Socialism that levels down for half a century; and the shade of Nietzsche, more powerful in death than ever in life, overshadows the great reforming movement and informs it with the aristocratic spirit."[16] This makes it sufficiently clear that a *modus vivendi* between Nietzsche and socialism was not only possible, but was actually thought by some to be in the process of being achieved.

"Socialism" was a notoriously vague term, used loosely to cover any of the innumerable aspects of the socialist movement. For many people it was less a political doctrine than a state of mind which reflected the social and political upheavals of the age. Orage himself was both a socialist and a Fabian; he regarded socialism, not as an identifiable set of political beliefs, but as a cult which had strong affiliations, at least for a time, with other movements such as theosophy, arts and crafts, and even vegetarianism and the "simple life." Orage's socialism, like his theosophy, can be traced back to Plato, and Plato provided Orage with a fervent Utopian idealism which seems to have united – not only the various aspects of his own thinking, including those picked up from Nietzsche – but also the various interpretations of socialism current at the time. A series of articles on socialism which Orage wrote for the *New Age* is so Utopian that it might be said to constitute a break with declared Fabian policy. It totally ignores the practical issues which were a continual source of dissension among socialists of different persuasions and tries to establish a philosophy of socialism on an almost metaphysical basis. Acknowledging the basic fact that the socialist movement was so "multiform and variegated" that it could only be said to agree on one idea – that poverty was attributable to private property – Orage saw no need for an organized socialist party. But poverty would not be abolished without Utopian vision – "there is no inspiration in social reform, even of the most radical order, without passion for a remote end."[17] The abolition of poverty was only a beginning: "Abolish poverty for us, and our men of genius will then begin their cyclopean task of building a civilisation worthy of the conquerors of titans."[18] And by "civilisation," Orage made it clear, he did not mean a welfare state: "Civilisation is no more than the possession by a people of individuals, on the one hand, capable of inspiring great enthusiasms and of individuals, on the other hand, capable of being so inspired. The rest is all but leather and prunella."[19] This is pure Nietzsche, and although Orage hardly ever refers to him in his articles on socialism it remains true that they are permeated by a Nietzschean spirit. At one point Orage echoes *The Birth of Tragedy* by declaring that he cannot regard human life even in "its more tragical and serious features as anything more than aesthetic phenomena," insisting with Nietzschean emphasis that man can, and must, be changed: "Liberty as the will of the individual, the nation, mankind, to be responsible for itself; to dispense with every divine purpose; to fix its own ends, within the limits imposed by Nature's own purpose, and all for the sake of experience!"* These paraphrases, and even more explicit statements such as the statement that punishment is inhuman, are easily traceable to Nietzsche.

The National Guild system of socialism which Orage personally adopted had an aristocratic conception of society; it contained, too, a strong if rather reactionary strain of social idealism, and it was not difficult for Orage to fuse this social idealism with the cultural idealism he had now accepted from Nietzsche. In due course a *New Age* reader brought to his attention a passage in Nietzsche which, it was claimed, contained the germ of the guild system:

Concerning the future of the workman. – Workmen should learn to regard their duties as *soldiers* do. They receive emoluments, incomes, but they do not get wages!

There is no relationship between *work done* and money received; the individual should, *according to his kind*, be so placed as to *perform* the *highest* that is compatible with his powers.[20]

Another reader, by presenting parallel extracts from *Past and Present*, tried to show that Nietzsche probably derived these ideas from Carlyle, whom he professed to despise. Orage, for his part, agreed they contained the germ of the guild system: "That an Army and a Guild are not on all fours I am, of course, aware; but their similarities are sufficient to justify the drawing of a proximate parallel. Rent, Interest and Profit, for example, are eliminated from both. So is Wages. There is a common end, subordination is by merit, and the task is national."[21] Even so, Orage had little faith in

---

* "Towards Socialism," *NA*, II (November 7, 1907), 29. Cf. Herbert Read on Nietzsche's attempt to define freedom: "The more he considered it, the more clearly he realized that freedom is not something which one has by natural endowment, or by social contract: it is something which one wins by conquest, by a discipline of the spirit. Freedom is the will to be responsible for one's self." *Anarchy and Order* (London, 1954), 172.

Nietzsche as an economist: "Nietzsche, however, like many of his disciples, was satisfied with glimpses into economic reality and never, to the end, appreciated the importance of half the observations he made. My own view, nevertheless, is that Nietzsche and his specific problems must wait upon the economic problems he affected to despise. Until, in fact, workmen have become 'soldiers,' the military order of society with its grand campaigns of culture and science will never be possible."[22] Just as Nietzsche had succeeded theosophy, a study of "economic reality" was to succeed Nietzsche.

Holbrook Jackson was also a Fabian socialist. This was yet another point of contact between him and Orage. Under the influence of Nietzsche they made plans together for cultural reform, hoping to engineer an aesthetic revolution that would disrupt and ultimately overturn the corrupt social order. Plutocracy, they believed, was the great enemy. Their schemes resulted finally in positive action: the formation, with the help of A. J. Penty, of the Leeds Arts Club, a society which was to be characterized by "its contempt of pedantic philosophy and academic art, and its insistence upon the necessity of applying ideas to life."[23] From the club's inception Jackson was its honorary secretary and Orage its leading spirit, and it was Orage who delivered the very first lecture – on Nietzsche. According to Jackson, the "ostensible but not admitted object" of the club was "to reduce Leeds to Nietzscheism!"[24] The club was a great success: "The local bourgeoisie were flabbergasted when the shocking views of such as Nietzsche, Ibsen, and Shaw were acclaimed in their midst by this heterodox seminary, and advocated with a mixture of aestheticism, moral earnestness, and egoistic flippancy. They went away horrified, and yet returned again unable to withstand the temptation of such outrageousness. There were gala nights, too, when a star like Shaw himself would appear, or G. K. Chesterton, or Edward Carpenter, and set the town talking for weeks."* Although the club's membership never exceeded a hundred, its achievements were so impressive that neighbouring towns, such as Bradford and Hull, formed similar groups of their own. But this joint venture was mean and parochial compared to the enterprises which Orage and Jackson embarked on in the summer of 1907, when they assumed the editorship of that extraordinary weekly review, the *New Age*.

2 One of the major shortcomings of Fabianism, Shaw believed, was its Philistine neglect of art and philosophy, and he attempted to

---

* Quoted in Philip Mairet, *A. R. Orage* (London, 1936), 25. Another guest speaker, according to Jackson, was W. B. Yeats.

stimulate a wider interest in cultural matters by helping to arrange lectures – of which Bland's lecture on Nietzsche was one – on a variety of topical subjects. His concern was shared by several other leading members of the society who deeply resented the growing domination of Sidney Webb, Beatrice Webb, and Edward Pease, whose policies were regarded as being insidiously bureaucratic and "collectivist." Their dissatisfaction came to a head in 1907 with the formation of a splinter group, the purpose of which was to debate the place of the arts under socialism. This new Fabian Arts Group, as it was called, included Shaw, Wells, Lowes Dickinson, Eric Gill (a passionate devotee of *Zarathustra* and designer of the type heading for the *New Age*), and Orage. Holbrook Jackson's experience with the Leeds Art Club was probably instrumental in his election to the position of honorary secretary. Jackson, in moving that such a group should be formed, urged that it would supply a medium for forms of propaganda until then outside the scope of the Fabian Society: "It would make an appeal to minds that remained unmoved by the ordinary Fabian attitude, and it would provide a platform for the discussion of the more subtle relationships of man to society which had been brought to the front in the works of such modern philosopher-artists as Nietzsche, Ibsen, Tolstoy, and Bernard Shaw."[25]

In seconding the motion, Orage pointed out that the arguments both for and against socialism were becoming more philosophic and less related to the immediate application of socialistic measures. A general agreement with this view is shown by the lecture programme that was later worked out, in which prominent place was given to the attitudes of three individualists – Tolstoy, Ibsen, and Nietzsche – towards socialism. Orage's lecture, "Nietzsche *contra* Socialism," was supplemented by a talk by Wells on the Samurai, and one by Lowes Dickinson on Plato's guardians. Dickinson's lecture was given a short notice in the society's paper, the *Fabian News*:

If Nietzsche's race of Supermen were evolved, what sort of equality could the undermen be expected to maintain, unless these Supermen were like the benevolent guardians of the *Republic*? And then they would not be Nietzsche's supermen. He suggested equality of education, which he thought might tend to uniformity of intellectual growth.

Mrs. Herzfeld controverted the lecturer's interpretation of the Nietzschean idea. Man would be surpassed. There could be no undermen, as the race which could produce such would be outgrown. Bernard Shaw thought equality of education would be an impossible thing until every man, in spite of the quality of his work, would receive no more and no less pay than any other man.[26]

Yeats, who was present at the first meeting, promised to give a lecture on

"The Few and the Many," but was unable, presumably through illness, to deliver it. All these lectures were given to crowded audiences, and must have contributed largely to the wider dissemination of Nietzsche's ideas.

But lectures, however useful in their way, were too limited to effect cultural regeneration on an appreciable scale: something more was needed. When a defunct weekly, the *New Age*, was put up for sale, Orage and Jackson immediately recognized an opportunity to procure a platform for the group's ideas. Under Fabian sponsorship they sought financial support, managed to secure £1000 (half of which was contributed by Shaw), and set themselves up as the editors of what was to become, in spite of its comparatively low circulation, the most stimulating and influential weekly of its time. Although the *New Age* was ostensibly a Fabian organ, Orage adopted an editorial policy which was totally non-doctrinal, and the hospitality of his columns was extended to every possible shade of political opinion, socialist and otherwise. Polemical controversy was the very life-blood of the paper. Orage quickly enlisted the participation of some of the most vigorous minds of the time, such as Belloc, Ellis, Bennett, and Galsworthy; he provoked a quarrel between Shaw and Chesterton which survived several issues; and he gathered about him a regular staff of contributors who had little in common apart from a dedication to their work. Since the paper gave little or no remuneration to contributors, it soon earned the nickname "The No Wage." The significance of the *New Age* in the history of Fabian socialism has long been recognized; more recently attention has turned to its significance as a literary review which made an outstanding contribution to the formation of literary taste and the encouragement of original talent; but it is not so generally known that the *New Age* gained for the work of Nietzsche an intellectual respect and recognition which it had been denied in England up to this time.

Subtitled "An Independent Socialist Review of Politics, Literature, and Art," Orage's *New Age* began its career on May 2, 1907 with a statement of its aims which will not sound strange if Orage's theosophical background (or even the Shavian Life Force) is kept in mind: "Believing that the darling object and purpose of the universal will of life is the creation of a race of supremely and progressively intelligent beings, THE NEW AGE will devote itself to the serious endeavour to co-operate with the purposes of life, and to enlist in that noble service the help of serious students of the new contemplative and imaginative order."[27] Interest in "a new contemplative and spiritual order" had been stimulated by the publication of Wells' *A Modern Utopia* (1904), which itself owed much to Plato and to Inazo Nitobé's book *Bushido: The Soul of Japan* (1905), a work which found an appreciative audience as a result of Japan's victory in the Russo-Japanese War of 1904-5. The chivalric code of the ancient Japanese warrior class, the Samurai, made an instantaneous appeal to many English writers, including Wells, Orage and Yeats.* One review, after listing the typical Samurai qualities (rectitude, courage, benevolence, courtesy, loyalty, honour), stressed that these qualities were not the narrowly intellectual ones which school education exclusively insists upon – the appeal of "bushido" was deeper than this: "The great strength that it has to the thinking mind is that it gets beneath the various creeds and dogmas to the fundamental truths necessary to the building up of fine character."[28] Taking their cue equally from *Bushido* and from *A Modern Utopia*, Harold Monro (later the editor of *Poetry and Drama*) and Maurice Browne envisaged an order of modern Samurai dedicated to austerity and high ideals, and pictured their pioneer in this way: "Undeterred by failure, undaunted by opposition, made strong by suffering, and steadfast in his strength, he sets his face to the sunrise and presses gladly forward out into the unknown future with unfaltering footsteps and the light of dawn radiant on his brow."† Looking back on these "Proposals for a Voluntary Nobility" from a distance of some thirty years, Browne was touched by the simplicity and single-mindedness of his youthful idealism – the pamphlet, he wrote, was "jejune and at times highfalutin; [but] it was not ignoble."[29] It derived from authors like Nietzsche, Tolstoy and Shaw, whose writings were the "vital fount" of modern literature; and it was this connection with Nietzsche which Orage seized upon when the pamphlet was reviewed in the pages of the *New Age*: "By forcing the growth of the Samurai idea, analysing its nature, and forecasting its future, it co-ordinates and throws open to discussion what promises to be one of the absorbing questions of the immediate future. There is no doubt that such ideas as that contained in the Samurai, and again in that of the Superman, bear a close relationship, if not with actual politics of to-day, with the near development of the saner political outlook."[30]

* Yeats may have read about it in a review of Nitobé's book which appeared in *Dana* in March, 1905.

† *Proposals for a Voluntary Nobility* (Norwich, 1907), 11. As a youth Browne had known Helen Zimmern, whom he called the "most famous of British Nietzscheans." Her toleration of him, he wrote, turned to affection "when I quoted *Thus Spake Zarathustra*; that great poem had been my bedbook. Incipient affection had become reciprocal friendship when I dared to criticize some of Nietzsche's other writings." *Too Late to Lament* (London, 1955), 172. Of Orage, whom he met around 1904, Browne wrote: "His influence over me was enormous and, as I look back, entirely for good." *New English Weekly*, vi (November 15, 1934), 118.

From its beginning the *New Age* evinced a deep concern with the new science of eugenics; behind this concern, of course, lay a preoccupation with the cultural advancement of man which had obsessed both Orage and Jackson since the days of the Leeds Arts Club. Nietzsche's vision of the superman, a frequent topic of discussion in the *New Age*, was drawn upon to support and embody this preoccupation. Even as late as 1913 a *New Age* correspondent wrote the following about Belloc's *The Servile State* (1912):

No Protestant could have a bleaker vision of the future than has this Catholic. Only Nietzscheanism can lead us out of this impasse. A sound system of eugenics will prevail, free alike from that false "humanitarianism" which is more devastating to the race than all the Tartar invasions, and from the false eugenist theories that preserve the wrong persons. Science, instead of bolstering up an outworn ethical system, will be harnessed to the service of the Superman. Thus Nietzsche's true leaders, the men of strong and beautiful bodies, wills and intellects, will be developed. The elements of Christianity may still be used for the maintenance of which Nietzsche called "herd-morality." But the world of masters will rid itself of the paralysing doctrine of original sin, and find a new Bible in *Thus Spake Zarathustra*.[31]

By 1913 Orage himself had outgrown this youthful intoxication with Nietzsche's ideas, but before becoming editor of the *New Age* the degree of his infatuation had been just as great. What view of Nietzsche, it is time to ask, did Orage bring with him to the *New Age*?

Orage's discovery of Nietzsche, after many years' fruitless search in theosophy for the key of knowledge, might be described in the same words he uses about Nietzsche's discovery of Schopenhauer: "Only one whose fortune brings him, after years of arid solitary thought, suddenly and as if by chance, into a world of thought and of men such as he has dreamed of but never realised, can understand Nietzsche's emotion on first reading Schopenhauer."[32] In his first book, *Friedrich Nietzsche: The Dionysian Spirit of the Age* (1906), Nietzsche is pronounced the greatest immoralist the world has ever seen, the tragedian in the spiritual drama of Mansoul, and the writer of aphorisms as bright as forked lightning. The book has this opening paragraph:

Friedrich Nietzsche is the greatest European event since Goethe. From one end of Europe to the other, wherever his books are read, the discussion in the most intellectual and aristocratically-minded circles turns on the problems raised by him. In Germany and in France his name is the war cry of opposing factions, and before very long his name will be familiar in England. Already half a dozen well-known English writers might be named who owe, if not half their ideas, at least half the courage of their ideas to Nietzsche. Ibsen seems almost mild by the side of him. Emerson, with whom he had much in common, seems strangely cool: William Blake alone among English writers seems to have closely resembled Nietzsche, and he who has read the *Marriage of Heaven and Hell*, and grasped its significance, will have little to learn from the apostle of *Zarathustra*. In other respects, however, Nietzsche is incomparably more encyclopaedic than Blake or Emerson or Ibsen. He stood near the pinnacle of European culture, a scholar among scholars and a thinker among thinkers. His range of subjects is as wide as modern thought. Nobody is more representative of the spirit of the age. In sum, he was his age; he comprehended the mind of Europe.[33]

Among a host of writers who have transcended both the pagan and the Christian standpoints, the "Dionysians" of Nietzsche's usage, Orage includes Whitman, Wilde, Shaw, Wells, and Yeats. The only works Orage discusses are *The Birth of Tragedy, Beyond Good and Evil,* and *Zarathustra,* laying stress in turn on Nietzsche's distinction between Apollo and Dionysus, his revaluation of morality and his theory of the superman; the chapter on *The Birth of Tragedy* is the first extended treatment of this book in English, and Orage was, like Ellis, one of the first to recognize in it not only a basis for a philosophy of art, but also the key to Nietzsche's thought as a whole.

In time this book came to be widely read among those of the *New Age* group – Shaw and Chesterton both reviewed it and it was privately praised by Wells. Shaw praised it as the badly needed work of "a competent Fabian": "His selection from Nietzsche's aphorisms and his statement of Nietzsche's position are just what is needed: that is, they give the characteristic and differential features of Nietzsche's philosophy and influence, and make quite clear those categories of Apollan [sic] and Dionysian which are not only useful as instruments of thought, but indispensable conversationally as the catchwords of Nietzschean controversy."* This, Shaw continues, was no small critical feat, for Nietzsche took over many of the philosophical and aesthetic "delusions" of his age: "I have seldom read ten pages of Nietzsche without coming upon some historic or artistic illustration in which the conventionality and shallowness of the view he accepts is not in striking contrast to his ingenious, original, and suggestive application of it. ... Mr. Orage, more Nietzschean than Nietzsche himself – as he ought to be – shews his competence and his advantage over me-

---

* "Our Book-shelf," *Fabian News*, xvii (April, 1907), 37. In a letter to Florence Farr, dated September 7, 1907, Shaw wrote: "You must get Murray or Orage if you want a lecture on Dionysus." *Florence Farr, Bernard Shaw, W. B. Yeats: Letters,* ed. Clifford Bax (London, 1946), 29.

diocrity by omitting the common form, and giving the distinctive features by which Nietzsche stands out from the mob of Europeans as a man of genius." Chesterton made of Orage's book a pretext to retrace all the "obvious" arguments against Nietzsche, prefacing them with rhetorical resentment: "How can any man with laughter in his soul talk of Neitzsche [sic] just after Christmas?"[34] Ironically enough, an irascible and sarcastic notice of Orage's book appeared in the *New Age* itself before he became editor, expressing contempt for his "moderate estimate" of Nietzsche's value: "Possibly [Nietzsche] has given impassioned utterance to some partial ethical truths, which may, or may not, be adopted, but which certainly flow from Darwin's supreme discovery. But these things can't excuse his rudeness to woman, his rant of whips and warriors, and his contempt for democracies."[35] Nietzsche's real value, Orage believed, was in danger of being obscured, if not entirely neglected, if such prejudiced thinking was allowed to prevail.

Orage's first book, though original and perceptive, was too slight to counteract current misconceptions; but his second book, *Nietzsche in Outline and Aphorism* (1907), the fruit of prolonged reflection, was substantial enough to belie its title. It is no skeleton exposition which reduces ideas to the level of superficiality, but a reliable hand-book of masterly compression, surpassing even Ellis's essay as an introductory guide to Nietzsche's thought. Orage makes reference to the whole corpus of Nietzsche's work. He preserves the framework of the first book—using short aphorisms to illustrate the chapters which accompany them, but the chapters have grown from three to ten. The best of these (those headed "Philosophy," "Man and Woman," and "Willing, Valuing and Creating," for instance) are in no way inferior to, one might almost say different from, modern interpretations of Nietzsche. The first paragraph of the opening chapter is a distinct advance on the first paragraph of the earlier book:

Profound natures who themselves experience the delight as well as the necessity of co-ordinating and tracing to a single root in themselves all their ideas, theories and opinions, thereby exercising themselves in the spirit of wholeness which is true holiness, will not need to be informed that Nietzsche spent a good deal of his intellectual life in the attempt thus to understand himself. But this attempt was bound to result at length in the search for the nature of reality and for the criterion of the true. In so far as Nietzsche in strict pursuit of a personal problem was finally driven to the examination of these problems, he may be said to have been a metaphysician and a philosopher in the accepted sense. But the qualification must instantly be made that his vocabulary as well as his material became always more and more concrete and sensuous in proportion as his metaphysic became abstract and speculative. In his case, as to a certain extent in the case of Plato, and still more in the case of Epictetus, the proof of his superior philosophy was always his increased insight into practical life. In all great natures extremes meet; and readers of Nietzsche must beware of taking his materialism grossly or his metaphysic abstractly.[36]

Orage's training in eastern philosophy made him place special emphasis on Nietzsche's doctrines of becoming, consciousness, will, and reason, the latter being, for Orage as for Nietzsche, man's noblest faculty but also his most dangerous one; and Orage was not alone, among those of a spiritualist persuasion, in noticing in Nietzsche a relativist view of history in which all phenomena were interpreted in terms of the conflict of polarities, a philosophy of man which stressed his role as the noble protagonist in the drama of tragic existence, and a view that nihilism (neatly defined by Orage as the attempt to find reality where, in fact, there is none) was bringing Europe to the verge of anarchy and disruption. What is more, Orage implicitly denies the common accusation that Nietzsche's philosophy was inconsistent and fragmentary, not by merely asserting, as Common had done, that it was systematic, but by making illuminating syntheses of his own. He equates, for example, the Dionysian impulse with masculinity, and both of these with the Nietzschean Will to Power; similarly, the Apollonian impulse is equated with femininity, and both of these with the Schopenhauerian Will to Live. His comments on Nietzsche's superman (to be discussed later in greater detail) also link together various strands in Nietzsche's thought.

Beatrice Hastings wrote an unsigned review of the book in the *New Age*. If Orage was not known to be the champion of Nietzsche, she wrote, he might be thought to be the subtlest of antagonists, for this exposition of Nietzsche, while scrupulously accurate and devoid of bias, had an almost Galilean mildness: "There is no theorising and even little comment. It is that, in some cool, discriminative fashion, the hysterical, destructive howl of the older Nietzsche has been allowed to lose itself on the mountains, and the stiller, smaller voice pipes like a dove on the temple of the true Jerusalem."[37] Even Orage's version of the superman as a child sounded like Christ's injunction that only the childlike shall enter the kingdom of heaven: "The difference seems to lie in that this kingdom of grace was not to be made by tooth or by claw." While this note of calmness was welcome, it was a pity that the "vocabulary of special emphasis which makes Nietzsche so acceptable after epochs of tyrannically-academised philosophy" was lost, even if Orage was making allowances for the tendency of translations to accentuate idiosyncrasies of expression. In a review which stressed and attempted to analyse Nietzsche's fast-growing influence in England, Desmond MacCarthy praised Orage's book, singling out the section dealing with the superman as the most valuable.[38]

Orage's co-editor, Holbrook Jackson, also played his part in assuring *New Age* readers of Nietzsche's importance. Even as early as the 1890s, Jackson believed, Nietzsche had been "a half-felt motive force, in this country at least, behind the tendencies of the times,"[39] although Davidson had been, in his view, the only writer to come directly under Nietzsche's spell. In his "Book Notes" column in the *New Age*, Jackson proclaimed Nietzsche's affinities with Blake, but also with the philosophy of Max Stirner: "Now that Nietzsche has entered the sphere of general discussion it is natural that publishers should find a growing demand for works dealing with the philosophy of Egoism."[40] It was a demand which *The Eagle and the Serpent* had tried to satisfy; Jackson alludes to the "chequered and fitful career" of this paper which, he says, gave many English people their first taste of Nietzsche. In the course of an affectionate tribute, he remarks that it "had eminent readers and a valuable trick of beguiling them into its controversies." It was a trick which the *New Age*, itself a socialist organ pleading for greater social justice, was learning to play. After six months Jackson relinquished his share of the editorship, but remained Orage's friend and contributor for many years afterwards. He later wrote articles about Nietzsche and a review of the complete translation besides finding space for correspondence on the history of the Nietzsche movement in *T.P.'s Weekly*, which he edited from 1910 to 1916.

Orage, like Jackson, was convinced that Nietzsche was still largely misunderstood in England, but that hitherto nothing had been done to rectify this situation. Now, with the reins of the *New Age* firmly in his grasp, he was in a position to disperse the hostility and suspicion surrounding Nietzsche's name, and his task was facilitated by the non-sectarian editorial policy he had adopted. He wasted no time: the third issue of the *New Age* contained a poem by a member of the Fabian Arts Group, Frederick Richardson. Entitled "The New Dionysos" it begins:

Soon will dawn the day of wonder,
When, with many-footed thunder,
Comes the fresh god, trampling under
All the dead and outworn things.[41]

This note of exaltation was soon to be sounded again, this time in English versions of poems from *Zarathustra*.[42] Before the year was out the name of Nietzsche cropped up in the drama criticism of L. Haden Guest, and the music critic appealed to him to rise from the dead and revitalize English music, which was thought to be stagnating in the backwash of German formalism. The same critic is struck by the detached iconoclasm of the music of Richard Strauss, and is not offended by it as Sir George Grove had been in the 1890s: "I really think he must believe God is dead, and that he is himself a reincarnation of Nietzsche. He has all his great countryman's egotism, all his genius for epigram, all his intellectual detachment, all his compelling, magnetic power of attraction, all his great sympathy and pity. And his pity is an aloof pity like Nietzsche's, not the charitable pity of Jesus and the Christian saints."[43]

From May, 1907, until the end of 1913 – a period of five and a half years – Nietzsche's name is hardly absent from the pages of the *New Age*: apart from casual mentions of his name there are some eighty items relating to Nietzsche during this period, ranging in importance from extensive articles and book reviews to readers' comments in the correspondence columns.[44] It is no exaggeration to say that with the advent of Orage's *New Age* a new phase in the English reputation of Nietzsche begins. Of those associated with the *New Age* the most indefatigable campaigners for Nietzsche's cause, besides Orage and Jackson, were Dr. Oscar Levy, J. M. Kennedy, and A. M. Ludovici.

Levy's *The Revival of Aristocracy* (1906) had won for him a reputation as a leading exponent of Nietzsche's philosophy, and it was a common interest in Nietzsche which led to him meeting Orage. One of Orage's earliest associates on the *New Age*, he was an active canvasser for new contributors, and was probably responsible for introducing both Kennedy and Ludovici to Orage. Nietzsche's work was the principal subject of discussion in his Vienna Café coterie, which included a large percentage of Jews, among them Paul Cohn, George Schwartz, H. Samuel, and A. Rappoport. Levy's translation, wrote the editor of the *Jewish Chronicle* in 1909, was an "event of considerable importance," and he felt proud that Jews like Levy and Zimmern had worked to make it possible: "Nietzsche makes a special appeal to Jewish readers, firstly because he had an exalted opinion of our race, and secondly because he assailed the current morality for which he regarded Judaism to be responsible."[45] This group of Jews, given a Gentile leavening by the presence of G. T. Wrench, A. Collins, Kennedy and Ludovici, met regularly from 1908 to the outbreak of war in 1914, and from it came most of the translators of Levy's complete edition of Nietzsche's works, begun in 1909. Levy himself answered to the entire cost of the translation, and also made generous donations to the *New Age* when, as so often happened, its funds started to run low. As an editor he seems to have been fairly lax, relying on his translators to check each other's work. As with any close-knit group bound together in a common cause there was some degree of friction, even disunion; the mystical side of Nietzsche, on which Orage laid so much stress, remained foreign to Levy, who was attracted to what he conceived to be Nietzsche's philo-Semitism. In a letter to Levy in 1927 Ludovici pointed this out: "Whereas Wrench has expressed his Nietzscheism in writing history first aesthetically (*The Mastery of Life*) and then amorally (*The Causes of Peace and War*) and that I should have expressed my Nietzscheism by applying my mind to health problems, politics and feminism, you have expressed your Nietzscheism by vindicating the Jews. ... The few paragraphs strewn over N's works dealing with the Jews constitute for you the quintessence of Nietzscheism. So much so that you say that the disunion in the Nietzsche ranks is due to the fact that no one follows your lead."*

Thomas Common, it will be recalled, believed that Levy had used underhand tactics to sponsor a translation of Nietzsche, and had accepted more than a fair share of credit for a venture which he, Common, had initiated many years earlier. When Ludovici gave a lecture on Nietzsche in Edinburgh in 1909, Common, much to the astonishment of Ludovici's hosts, did not turn up to support him. Clearly, this was intended as an open rebuff to Levy. But, internal dissension apart, Levy was the recognized leader of the Nietzsche circle, and his articles (some of them violent attacks on Shaw and Chesterton for "misreading" Nietzsche) and reviews for the *New Age* were undoubtedly influential. During the First World War Levy was accused of bringing Nietzschean "poison" to England, and even of being a German spy. In October, 1921, he was expelled from England as an "undesirable alien," having been informed that only Germans "of definite benefit to British trade" would be allowed to remain. The editorship of the Nietzsche translation did not count, either in cultural or commercial terms, in Levy's favour and may, as he remarked later, even have contributed to his disgrace.†

J. M. Kennedy, author of *Tory Democracy* (1911) and several expository works on Nietzsche, enjoyed a reputation among the *New Age* circle as a profound scholar and an accomplished linguist: in neither case was this reputation wholly deserved. As an energetic propagandist for Nietzsche

---

* Unpublished letter, dated November 25, 1927. Dr. Melhado, in Ludovici's novel *Mansel Fellowes* (1918), is a portrait of Levy. For further biographical details see Ludovici's obituary notice of Levy in the *New English Weekly*, xxx (November 14, 1946), 49–50.

† See Levy's account of his expulsion in his introduction to the sixth edition of *Zarathustra* (London, 1932), 60–1.

he felt grateful that "the time is past when this Germanico-Polish value-destroyer must be apologised for, veneered, and sugared";[46] but his own attitude to Nietzsche was unfailingly laudatory, and he liked to *épater les bourgeois* by writing popular expositions of Nietzsche's most ruthless ideas.[47] Previously on the staff of the *Daily Telegraph*, Kennedy became the chief *New Age* spokesman on foreign affairs, assuming the Portuguese pseudonym of "S. Verdad." He also wrote, under his own name, many book reviews, and translated articles on Nietzsche which had originally appeared in the German press. At the beginning of the First World War he loyally denied allegations by Austin Harrison, editor of the *English Review*, that Levy was a German spy who should not be allowed to remain in England; but after Kennedy's death in 1918 Orage, at the invitation of Kennedy's mother, went through his papers and discovered in dismay that Kennedy had been acting as a secret service agent whose task had been to supply the government with information about the subversive activities of the *New Age* group – the group had made no secret of its aversion to the war nor of its refusal to hold Nietzsche responsible for it, and obviously gave the impression of being a hotbed of sedition.

It was for Ludovici that Levy felt the warmest affection, and he was entrusted with the largest share of the translation work. Like Kennedy, Ludovici wrote a number of expository works on Nietzsche, several of which began their life as lectures in the University of London. The editor of *The Young Man*, who had heard Ludovici's lectures and read his books, was gratified to find Nietzsche spoken about in a fashion different from "the contemptuous, shocked, incredulous, superior, day-of-judgment manner so dear to Professor Saintsbury, Dr. Barry and Mr. Chesterton," and recommended Ludovici's sane approach to an important philosopher: "No European thinker of the last century of anything like his eminence and influence has been so neglected in England, and when not neglected, so caricatured, denounced and misquoted."[48] Helen Zimmern told Ludovici that his *Who Is to Be Master of the World?* (1909), was "the best book far and away written in English on Nietzsche,"[49] but perhaps *Nietzsche and Art* (1911) will ultimately take its place as the most important. Eden Phillpotts, with whom Ludovici had struck up an intimate friendship, assured him that this work was "a luminous and valuable exposition of this immense genius," adding: "Your translations are conceived in the spirit of the writer and show that his thought and even his style can be turned finely into English. Do you know Orage? I'm always amused that he, who has drunk so deeply at Nietzsche's fount, should be a socialist."[50] Ludovici did indeed know Orage: he had met him in October, 1908, at the time Ludovici was preparing to deliver a series of lectures on Nietzsche at the University of London. They discussed Plato, particularly the *Gorgias*, with reference to Nietzsche's *Will to Power*,[51] and Orage soon became aware of Ludovici's passionate interest in art (not surprising in one who had been Rodin's secretary), eventually appointing him to his staff as art-critic. Ludovici's experience as art-critic for the *New Age* put him in close contact with the contemporary artistic scene, but it also made him enemies: T. E. Hulme, himself a contributor, never forgave Ludovici for daring to criticize a work of Epstein adversely – not only were Ludovici's lectures dull, he declared, but they completely missed the point. Hulme's disapprobation was warmly seconded by Wyndham Lewis, who expressed an earnest hope that "some less ridiculous go-between" for Nietzsche might be found: "His dismal shoddy rubbish is not even amusingly ridiculous. It is the grimest pig-wash vouchsafed at present to a public fed on husks."[52] The target of a good deal of vindictive criticism, Ludovici maintained in the face of it all an exemplary composure and dignity.

Levy, Kennedy, and Ludovici – assisted by such cohorts as Paul Cohn, Judah Benjamin, and Paul Selver – ransacked the English and continental press for any items on Nietzsche which would keep *New Age* readers abreast of important developments. Two examples might be cited. In 1911, anti-Nietzschean sections of the English press had exploited for their own ends a report that volumes of Nietzsche had been found in the possession of two German schoolboys who had committed suicide together. To counter the insinuations that followed, Cohn wrote a letter to the *New Age*, quoting from an article in one of the most respectable and influential German newspapers which emphatically denied the suggestion that Nietzsche exercised an evil hold over the young. In the following year, a leader from an Irish newspaper was quoted to the effect that it deplored the action of the Belfast Library Committee in withdrawing the list of Nietzsche's works from the library catalogue.* The Nietzscheans were able to close their ranks and retaliate when any attack on their master was made, especially if an attack seemed likely to gain any measure of popular acclaim. Ludovici, looking back on their activities nearly half a century

---

* In an address to a Public Morals Conference in 1910, the publisher John Murray stated that in his view the books of Henry George, Karl Marx, and Nietzsche had done and were doing a great deal of harm – he would class them as noxious literature. Samuel Hynes, referring to this episode, comments: "Apparently no one else did, for there is no evidence that books by any of these writers were suppressed." *The Edwardian Turn of Mind* (Princeton, 1968), 301n. But the action of the Belfast Library in banning Nietzsche's works was probably not an isolated case.

later, had this to say: "There was really an air of amateurishness about us all. The fact was, we were rather a friendly côterie of Nietzsche-admirers assembled under the benign patronage of Levy, than a team of scholars bent on giving the world the best possible representation of our Master. There wasn't even unanimity amongst us concerning Nietzsche's views. Levy shied at the doctrine of the Eternal Recurrence ..., and men like Wrench, Collins, Scheffauer etc. were eclectics believing only in the Nietzschean ideas that suited them."[53]

It must be remembered that Levy, not Orage, presided over this Nietzschean phalanx of writers. As editor of a paper backed by Fabians, Orage rarely lost sight of his principal mission, which was to disseminate, not only his own Guild System brand of socialism, but the views of socialists at large. As already noted, it appeared anomalous to many that Nietzsche, whose attitude to socialism was far from conciliatory, should be so much publicized in an organ dedicated to the socialist cause. Keir Hardie, the first socialist elected to Parliament, took violent exception: "The handful of irresponsibles who control the political policy of the *New Age*, most of them disciples of Nietzsche – the neurotic apostle of modern anarchism – who assail the Labour Party, are thereby assailing the canons of classical Socialist doctrine."[54] Orage replied: "It is a mere trifle that not a single member of our staff is a disciple of Nietzsche; it is even a less trifle that Nietzsche is not an apostle of modern Anarchism."[55] Orage's denial can be better understood if it is realized that, even at this time (1909), to admit oneself a disciple of Nietzsche was to brand oneself in the popular imagination as an apostle of cruelty, tyranny, and rapine: the fact that Orage re-issued Shaw's *The Sanity of Art* in 1908 is sufficient evidence that Nordau still needed refuting. Levy, Kennedy, and Ludovici – the hard core of the Nietzschean writers on his staff – all became acquainted with Nietzsche before they met Orage, who appointed them for reasons unconnected with their Nietzscheanism. Not only did Orage refuse point-blank to set on their work a seal of editorial approbation, but even engaged them in lively controversy on his own account: his protracted debates with Ludovici, for example, about the Nietzschean implications of Guild Socialism and modern plutocracy are a case in point. By 1914 Orage's enthusiasm (though not his admiration) for Nietzsche was on the wane, and he conducted his discussions with something less than his old spirit and accuracy: he frequently retreated, under pseudonymous cover, into testy arguments *ad hominem* and flabby generalities, as if he resented being outmanoeuvred by younger men on ground which he had staked out as his own.

Yet Orage's efforts to bring Nietzsche to the attention of the English public were unremitting. The prevailing ignorance of Nietzsche he attributed to the disgraceful lack of translations, a lack which placed the English intellectual at a great disadvantage compared to his French counterpart, or to the few who had the good fortune to know German. As we have seen, many Englishmen were forced to rely on French translations for their knowledge of Nietzsche, including for a while Orage himself. Orage advertised his two books on Nietzsche in the *New Age* during the first week of 1908: "No socialist can afford to leave unconsidered the ideas of Friedrich Nietzsche, the greatest teacher of the aristocratic philosophy." The books were a provisionary stopgap, not a real substitute for a complete translation, and when the interrupted translation of Nietzsche's works was resumed in 1907 with *Beyond Good and Evil*, Orage was jubilant about the promise this held for the future. When the announcement came in March, 1909, that a complete translation was at last under way he was quite elated. While paying tribute to the public spirit and generosity of Levy he observed, with some bitterness, that the extraordinarily unadventurous English reading public hardly deserved, by means of such a gesture, to have Nietzsche made available to them.

When Orage reviewed the second edition of Tille's version of *Zarathustra* in 1908, he pointed out that this work should have been the last, not the first, to appear in England. The publishers had mistakenly ignored advice to publish *The Birth of Tragedy*, a work which, profiting from the interest in dramatic theory at the time, would have sold easily; instead, they issued *Zarathustra* which, although written at the climax of Nietzsche's powers, was "full of the most seemingly extravagant doctrines and paradoxes."[56] Small wonder, then, that the English public, even if it could have afforded the outrageously high price of the book, should have been rather bewildered; besides, Tille's translation left much to be desired, and his introduction was "about as forbidding a foreword for English readers as could well be imagined." Since that inauspicious beginning Nietzsche had found better hands to serve him; not only was *The Birth of Tragedy* one of the works chosen to inaugurate the complete translation, but the individual translations were moderately priced. The project won round even those whose view of Nietzsche had been somewhat soured by the more violent works published in the 1890s. Arnold Bennett, who wrote a weekly column for Orage under the pseudonym of "Jacob Tonson," was one who welcomed this "admirable enterprise": "It is quite useless saying that you do not mean to read Nietzsche. Nietzsche meant to be read, and in the end he will have his way with you."[57] Orage kept his readers informed on the progress of the translation, and even whetted appetites by printing extracts in advance of official publication. Levy's essay on the Nietzsche movement in England was serialized in the *New Age* before appearing as the preface to the final translation volume in 1913.

Elisabeth Förster-Nietzsche, who was finding it profitable to tempt the public with tasty morsels by publishing her brother's work piecemeal, had, in 1905, characteristically referred to *Ecce Homo* as an autobiography by Nietzsche written "expressly for himself and his friends,"[58] but at the same time slyly hinted at possible future publication. When she did decide to release the book for publication in 1908, Kennedy quickly translated excerpts of it for the *New Age*. *Ecce Homo* is, above all, the testament of an artist, and its record of personal suffering is one most likely to appeal to those who know what it is, in Yeats's words, to know the agony of the choice between perfection of the life and perfection of the work. Holbrook Jackson thought *Ecce Homo* one of the most remarkable and inspiring books ever written; Arnold Bennett hazarded the guess that *Ecce Homo*, which he had been reading in French, was the most conceited book ever written; though it was, in his view, a great work "full of great things," it would "assuredly" be laughed at when it got translated into English.[59] Indeed it was. The Nietzscheans' unconcealed delight over *Ecce Homo* touched off more professorial fury: "The soil is unpromising for those foreign gentlemen who are endeavouring to operate upon our minds. We are not impressed by their epigrams and still less by their hysterics about British insularity. The effort to prove that Nietzsche's autobiography was the work not only of a sane but of a supremely gifted and philosophical mind will leave most of us cold."*

Cohn noted a tendency, manifest as late as 1913, to see a touch of madness, not only in Nietzsche's later productions, but in his work as a whole, so that Nietzsche is pitied as "a lunatic with occasional moments of inspiration":

What must always militate against Nietzsche in England is his incurable propensity for seeing things as they are. Your typical Englishman may be privately quite well aware of the truth, but he does not like to see the truth set down in cold print. He wants to be rocked in the cradle of his illusions. And for the indi-

---

* Herbert L. Stewart, *Questions of the Day in Philosophy and Psychology* (London, 1912), 279. A similar view was held by F. C. S. Schiller: "Nietzsche's autobiography is psychologically very disappointing. It throws very little light on the genesis of his character and thought, and exhibits only the prophet's anger at the neglect of an uncomprehending world." "The Philosophy of Friedrich Nietzsche," *Quarterly Review*, ccxviii (January, 1913), 150. The Nietzscheans received further criticism from a *New Age* staff writer, Huntly Carter, in "The Rape of Drama," *The New Freewoman*, I (August 15, 1913), 94–6.

vidual this may perhaps often be a healthy instinct. Ruthless clearness of vision and overpowering sanity may, especially in a delicate organism, finally lead to insanity: with Nietzsche this was certainly the case. It is because the healthy Englishman is a little mad that he remains predominantly sane: it is because Nietzsche was so terribly sane that he finally went mad. But the world must not let itself be robbed of his work on that account.[60]

Nordau's insistence that Nietzsche's books had been written between periods of confinement in a lunatic asylum, wrote Ludovici in a passage already quoted, had for ten years "considerably damaged the cause for which I stand," and he complained that Nordau had not yet had the decency to withdraw his erroneous statement: "Apparently all means are allowable to moral people in waging war upon the first amoral philosopher."[61] One of these means was to revile, not only Nietzsche, but his followers too, who were dismissed as a cult: "It appears fitting to speak of the Nietzschean movement as a cult, for it has but little resemblance to a set of reasoned and considered opinions. If one may adapt a phrase from Max Nordau it is a piece of '*fin-de-siècle* thinking' with a vengeance."[62]

The Nietzscheans may have been enthusiastic, sometimes fanatically so, about the thinker's work, but they were usually more chivalric than their vociferous opponents. It is true that they could not always resist the temptation of making ideological capital out of Nietzsche's philosophy, but their overriding object was to persuade a reluctant British public to show more charity towards it. Even in this latter capacity, the mendicant order of Nietzscheans was unpopular, even detested. They would hardly have gained a hearing for their ideas but for the *New Age* – many sections of the English press would have nothing to do with them, refusing even to print the many letters they wrote defending Nietzsche from abuse and misunderstanding. Ludovici felt impelled to define "Nietzscheism" as the spirit of free enquiry, made up of the following things: "Free-spiritedness, intellectual bravery; the ability to stand alone when every one else has his arm linked in something; the courage to face unpleasant, fatal, and disconcerting truths."[63] The spirit of free enquiry was what the *New Age*, as anyone who has consulted the files of the paper will know, professedly stood for; as Eden Phillpotts wrote to Orage: "The spirit of your paper possesses that fine Nietzschean quality of sending all that is old and crusted, not to say rusted, down the drain."[64] If this is borne in mind, Orage's sympathy for the Nietzschean cause, which was always more publicist than doctrinaire, is understandable, and the anomaly of Nietzsche's persistent appearance in a socialist organ is seen to be more apparent than real. And if, in the pages of the *New Age*, Nietzsche was often little more than a name to conjure with, the vogue he enjoyed, particularly at its height from 1909 to 1913, was a serious and intellectual one; and it was through the mediumship of the *New Age* that the generation of writers and artists after that of Shaw, Yeats and Orage first came in contact with the philosopher whom, in many cases, they regarded as the chief educational influence of their early lives.

3 Orage's hatred of realistic fiction explains why he found meagre support in English fiction, and that only in the first half of the nineteenth century, for such an exalted concept as the superman: "Disraeli and Lytton are in my opinion the two English novelists who aimed highest, though I admit they fell far short in actual achievement. Their heroic characters were at least planned on the grand scale."[65] Disraeli's strong aristocratic bias endeared him to all the Nietzscheans: his racial pride made a particular appeal to Levy, who suggested that Disraeli's novels were the best introduction to Nietzsche for an English reader, and to Kennedy, who saw him as the English counterpart to Bismarck. In his novels, thought Kennedy, Disraeli foresaw the decline of the aristocracy and the need for a new order of men: "It was Disraeli alone who saw that the old system had actually passed away, and that before the new system could be changed the national character itself would have to be entirely altered. Hence his appeals for 'loyalty and reverence,' and his advocacy of the old Tory principles set forth with such force by Bolingbroke and Burke. Hence also his appeal to the imagination instead of the reason, for which, had he lived half a century later, he might have invoked the weighty support of Nietzsche himself."[66] Orage's general view of aristocracy has much in common with that of Disraeli, but it is founded solidly on the mystical aspirations of such a work as Lytton's *Zanoni*. Orage had little respect for the realism of Ibsen – to the discussion of social problems he preferred the visionary quality of such plays as *Emperor and Galilean*, which he called a great pioneering effort "to restore the mystical drama on the scale of Aeschylus, but with modern and non-mythological material,"[67] and Shaw, we recall, had seen in Julian's Third Empire a foreshadowing of Nietzsche's superrace to come.

Orage regarded the superman as Nietzsche's positive doctrine, "the crown and the justification of all his criticism and destruction."[68] His creation will not be left to chance evolution, which does not always lead in the direction of progress; it must be willed or bred. Nietzsche had found it impossible to describe the superman: "He could no more foretell what the Superman would be than the Jews could describe their Messiah. The

Superman and the Messiah are, in fact, very similar, and it is possible that Nietzsche, in this respect, had borrowed his idea from the Polish Messianist, Slowacki. But by means of negatives it was possible for Nietzsche to define what the Superman was not."[69] The superman, in Orage's view, had never existed on earth. The coming philosophers in *Beyond Good and Evil* were Dionysian spirits, but they were not supermen—*Beyond Good and Evil* merely mapped out the distant sphere in which the supermen might dwell. Orage refers to the chapter on the metamorphoses of the spirit in *Zarathustra*, in which the spirit becomes in turn a camel, a lion, and a child. Man, says Orage, is still at the camel stage, the coming philosophers are the "laughing lions," and the superman will be the child: "In his nature all the wild forces of the lion are instinctive. He will not seek wisdom, for he will be wise. Man will have become as a little child. The psychology of these metamorphoses is too profound to be stated here; but nobody who *understands* Nietzsche will doubt that behind all his apparent materialism there was a thoroughly mystical view of the world. As already said, Blake is Nietzsche in English."[70]

Nietzsche, says Orage, is a mystic *malgré lui*, and it is only in mystical terms that the superman can be conceived, let alone undestood: most of the descriptions given of the superman are travesties and caricatures simply because this elementary fact has not been grasped. The change from man to superman involves, not a change of degree as is so often thought, but a change of kind, and this has been the perennial concern of the mystics: "For the main problem of the mystics of all ages has been the problem of how to develop superconsciousness, of how to become superman."[71] Orage regards ordinary human consciousness as animal consciousness folded upon itself, or consciousness in two dimensions: "Following the analogy, then, superman, or, as it is sometimes called, cosmic consciousness, is consciousness in three dimensions, or human consciousness folded upon itself."[72] This permits a standing outside, or *ecstasis*. Orage employs also the image of the embryo: "If we regard human consciousness as, in itself, no more than the antenatal condition of superman, then it is plain that what the mystics call the second birth, the interior birth, is the coming forth within the mind of a being hitherto embryonic. The idea of ecstasy is clearly contained in this image no less than in the former. The mystic child is born within the field of the animal nature, and stands, after birth, outside that field."[73]

Analogous to the idea of second birth is the image of awakening; Orage takes Ibsen's *When We Dead Awaken* as a representation of human consciousness as sleep. The awakening from this sleep might be described as a form of *ecstasis* – Orage was later to find confirmation of this idea in the teachings of Gurdjieff and Ouspensky. Warning his reader that the images he uses are only approximate, Orage makes five observations about the superman mode of consciousness. Firstly, the superman mode of consciousness is, after all, only a mode in which the limitations of human consciousness, not *all* human limitations, are transcended. Secondly, the extension of mental powers will be accompanied "by the formation of definite ecstatic faculties, which in their turn constitute the activity of the superman."[74] Thirdly, the abolition of the subject/object dichotomy means that the superman will regard the interior world of emotion and desire phenomenally, as man now sees nature phenomenally. Fourthly, present human imagination will be the main sense by which the superman contacts nature – "his body would be our mind, and ... therefore, he feels with all that he now only thinks, and identifies his body with all of which he can form an image."[75] Lastly, intuition is characteristic of the state of ecstasy (or super-consciousness) as it is of our present faculties when they are functioning at full stretch – "the ecstatic state of perception is insight, which is a swift-winged judgment; the ecstatic state of reasoning is imagination, which is a swift-winged process of deduction and induction";[76] what is, in human consciousness, a series, becomes in superman consciousness a swift summation. The state of ecstasy can be induced by religion, art, love, nature and great men: "It is the moments of ecstasy which we or the race have experienced that constitute the ground of our faith, and it is the means of ecstasy that constitute our highest and most sacred things."[77] These "means" of ecstasy are the safe and certain ways, but special means doubtless exist: "Perhaps the sure way is to raise, to deepen, and to extend our human faculties; for as man is only an intensified animal, an ecstatic animal, if you will, superman is no more than an intensified man, man made ecstatic. Therefore it is that superman is not the contradiction but the fulfilment of man; and he who hopes to become superman by becoming less human instead of more human, has set his foot on a path that leads into strange places – into the desert where are mirages ringed about with human bones."[78]

This last passage betrays the source of Orage's uneasiness: superman, he says, stands in relation to man as man does to the animals, and he uses the phrase "Shepherd of Men" as an apt illustration of this relationship. The great men of history and legend might be taken to be supermen, although, unlike Christ, they were not always beneficent:

Nor do the darker sides of the traditions destroy the idea; for it is not necessarily to be supposed either that we now see the necessity for much that appears terrible, or, again, that superman implies necessarily benevolence towards humanity. It is unfortunately far from true that man in relation even with domesticated animals is uniformly beneficent. Perhaps in the long run association with man will prove the means of the transformation of animal consciousness, and so be justified. Even so may perhaps the earlier associations of humans with heroes be justified, though in the details the pictures of that association are often painted with blood.[79]

Orage declares his agreement with Nietzsche that the terrible lives of Caesar Borgia, for example, or Napoleon or Cromwell, impress the race with a sense of self-respect which is the indispensable condition of well-being and well-doing: indeed, a sense of self-respect can only be obtained by the witnessing of power. But "nowhere is Nietzsche to be taken less grossly than in his conception of power":

The men of power in his eyes are not the men of sinew and brawn, but men in whom the power of mastery over both themselves and others is greatest. For it is to be observed that the surplus of will that Nietzsche calls spirit cuts as deeply into its own source as into the lives of others. All tragic heroes are self-torturers no less than torturers. It is by power over themselves that they demonstrate their right to power over others. Other power is illegitimately held, and is a mere abortion and simulacrum of power. Again, it is in the will of such men to surpass themselves that their virtue resides. Because they are the finest types of the race their own self-surpassing is a victory for the race as a whole.[80]

This is, of course, the doctrine of "self-conquest" which is implicit in so much of Yeats's work; but Orage, while conceding the benefits of a purely personal domination, is not prepared to accept domination as a social principle. Both kinds of domination are implied by the Nietzscheans, as in Wrench's *The Mastery of Life* and Levy's *The Revival of Aristocracy*. Levy traces Nietzsche back to Goethe: "In *Faust* all the problems of Nietzsche's lifetime are anticipated; there an attempt is made to create a race of sturdier men; the solution of the difficulty is also there, that only danger and fighting can beget happiness and freedom, but not the overrated security of life and property. There Nietzsche's expedients are already forecast, for conferring on men more strength and mirth, namely, through more suffering; that the feeble may go to the wall and the strong find either slaves they can command or opponents worthy of them on whom to steel and test their strength."[81] Orage, however, believed that men prefer "all the horrors of freedom to all the amenities of benevolent slavery."[82] The guild system was aristocratic in so far as it was based on mutual respect of the workers and implied liberation from dehumanizing wage-slavery; but being unstratified, communal and co-operative, it was a far cry from Nietzsche's own hierarchical ideal. Aristocracies, whether hereditary or intellectual, which implied the subordination of one individual to another were anathema to Orage: he pronounced them ridiculous, inhuman, and tyrannical, and he believed it was inconsistent of Nietzsche to prefer Dionysus to Apollo, since this was to prefer the democratic principle to the aristocratic one: "How comes it then that Nietzsche and the Nietzscheans, so seldom in the same boat, pull together in respect of Aristocracy? The question is more interesting than the answer."[83]

Orage did not believe in the superman as the offspring of male and female, but "as self begotten from within the mind of man."* An individual will turn from procreation and sex the more he aspires to perfection: celibacy is the distinguishing mark of culture wherever it appears. The idea that marriage and sex tend to divert creative minds from their true pursuits, and even endanger the cultural life of an entire nation, is a persistent theme in Nietzsche's work: Orage was so preoccupied with it that he devoted his seven "Tales for Men Only," which appeared in the *New Age* between 1911 and 1916, to its examination. In these stories Orage portrays a group of creative spirits, artist-philosophers, who are "intent on creating between them a collective soul or superman,"[84] or "a communal mind which, by its nature and powers, shall constitute a new order of being in the hierarchy of intelligent creation." He shows how an obsession with sex can hinder the attainment of these ideals. But Orage is careful to stress elsewhere the importance of feminine companionship. When Nietzsche's unfortunate affairs with women (particularly with Lou Andreas-Salomé) were being held up as examples of preposterous indiscretion and *gaucherie*, Orage pointed out that this was no reproach to Nietzsche: "That a man of his intellectual value to the human race could not find a woman-servant-pupil-friend is a reproach to women. What would Disraeli have been without such an one? Was Nietzsche only to blame because all Germany failed him?"[85]

Since no one seemed to agree with him that Nietzsche's conceptions of power and aristocracy were not to be taken in a gross, literal sense, Orage's own caveat seems to have back-fired: perhaps, he came to suspect, Nietzsche really meant what he said. Instead of trying to reconcile Nietzschean idealism with Christian mysticism, Orage began to declare an open

---

* "Unedited Opinions: II. – The Superman," *NA*, VIII (December 1, 1910), 107. This exactly fits Ibsen's description, in *Emperor and Galilean*, of how the messiah of the Third Empire is to be created.

breach between the two, and even to renege on convictions about Nietzsche he had tenaciously held for so long. An indication of this change is apparent in a comment on the chapter on power in Æ's *Candle of Vision* (1918):

> Nietzsche died before he began to understand himself. His preoccupation with the problem of power was undoubtedly an occult exercise; and his discovery that spiritual power needs to be exercised "beyond good and evil," was a hint of the progress he had made. Unfortunately for Nietzsche, his *Beyond Good and Evil* was still not clear of the element of egotism; he carried into the occult world the attachment and the desire that emphatically belong to the world of both Good and Evil. In short, he attempted to take Heaven by egoistic storm, and his defeat was a foregone conclusion and a familiar tragedy in occult history. "Æ," like his authorities, is full of warning against the quest of power. ... I commend this chapter to Nietzscheans in particular. They have most to learn from it.[86]

Orage also scornfully rejects the idea, held by the Nietzscheans, that Nietzsche's thought was a unified system: "In pursuit of the will o' the wisp they call his doctrine (strictly a non-entity, for Nietzsche never lived to express it), they twist and distort and misread his various opinions as if, somehow or other, Nietzsche would be disgraced if they did not make them all fit."[87] To see such statements a complete *volte-face* would be a superficial judgment. Orage remained, as firmly as any of the Nietzscheans, convinced of Nietzsche's importance, but became increasingly impatient with what he took to be their uncritical stance of wide-eyed idolatry and naïve enthusiasm. This, he thought, could only alienate those still sceptical of Nietzsche who needed to be persuaded by rational argument. He knew that Nietzsche was a trap for the unwary:

> Nietzsche is full of ambiguities, and he riddled like an Adelphian. Not being a man of action, and, therefore, never being compelled to make up his mind upon any point, he could afford (or he allowed himself) to express contradictory judgments upon almost every problem that occurred to him. You can find in Nietzsche anything you choose to look for; the most extreme form of Christianity, the most extreme of paganism, gentleness and brutality, praise and denunciation of force, the same of the virtues, and the same of various kinds of social life. He was, as he said, an interrogation mark; and every attempt to define him in more accurate terms must end in an interrogation.[88]

Knowing this, Orage opposed the Nietzschean camp-followers as a tactical move to promote more critical attitudes, and he took full advantage of this new freedom to express his own doubts and reservations. But from the time of an early article on education, in which he proposed transforming the elementary schools into nurseries of aristocracy,[89] to his later mystical adumbrations of the superman, Orage's basic position is the Nietzschean one he had outlined in one of his books: "Of all creatures Man is the most promising, just because of all creatures he is the most adventurous, experimental, and self-torturing. All the tragical history of man would be nothing better than a meaningless comedy were it not that such a history can be regarded as the pre-natal condition of a superior and justifying species."[90] And this history is guided by those who give it value, meaning, and direction, in short, the artists. How Orage, and his colleagues, made use of Nietzsche's philosophy of art is a problem to which we must now turn.

4. Much of Orage's writing for the *New Age* was in the field of literary criticism. Several collections of his critical work have already been issued, and it has also been the subject of a recent doctoral dissertation (see p. 304, n. 94). But Orage's importance as a critic is still not generally recognized, although readily conceded by his peers. Herbert Read, for example, wrote to him: "I am convinced that when the literary history of the period between 1907 and 1922 comes to be written your influence will be found to have run deep and far."[91] Later critics, like T. S. Eliot and John Holloway, are drawn to Orage by his concern for problems of moral wholeness. Eliot wrote: "To say that he was a moralist is not to say that he was a moralist *instead* of being a critic of literature. He was that necessary and rare person, the moralist in criticism ..., the critic who perceives the morals of literature, and who recognizes that intellectual dishonesty, laziness and confusion are cardinal sins in literature. ... He saw that any real change for the better meant a spiritual revolution; and he saw that no spiritual revolution was of any use unless you had a practical economic scheme."[92] More recently John Holloway has placed him in the tradition of Arnold, Ruskin, Patmore, and Leslie Stephen, all of whom believed that the values of life and art were ultimately one: "Orage's work seems to radiate out almost equally towards Arnold, Eliot, and Leavis. When his work is better known, Orage may prove to be one of the decisive figures in the continuity of criticism over the last century."* This is not the place to review Orage's critical achievement in detail, but in view of his un-

---

* "The Literary Scene," *The Modern Age* (Harmondsworth, 1961), 89. Cf. Ludovici: "No one seems to feel nowadays that a picture, like a sonnet, like a sonata, and like a statue, if it claim attention at all, should claim the attention of all those who are most deeply concerned with the problems of Life, Humanity, and the Future; and that every breath of Art comes from the lungs of Life herself, and is full of indications as to her condition." *Nietzsche and Art* (London, 1911), 34.

doubted significance it is necessary to point out that Orage was considerably assisted by Nietzsche in the working out of his philosophy of art. His position parallels that of Ludovici and Kennedy, both of whom applied Nietzsche's ideas to artistic criticism, Ludovici in his art column and in *Nietzsche and Art* (1911) – praised by Edward Garnett as "a vigorous, stimulating, and ably written book"[93] – and Kennedy in his book reviewing and in his *English Literature, 1880–1905* (1912). Taken as a whole, the work of Orage, Ludovici, and Kennedy underscores, and even anticipates, the classic revival for which, more than any other, T. E. Hulme is generally credited for being responsible: "If he has been viewed as a solitary figure in the history of twentieth century English thought, this is only because his writings have not been related to the context in which they appeared."[94] This context was the *New Age*, and the *New Age* was a hotbed of Nietzschean ideas. In what follows an attempt will be made briefly to suggest some of the points of contact between Nietzsche and Orage on the one hand, and between Nietzsche and Hulme on the other – reference will be made to Ludovici and Kennedy as the need arises.

What binds together the whole of Orage's criticism is a conviction that art can not be regarded in isolation from the society which created it. The *New Age* itself endeavoured to give equal weight to every aspect of contemporary civilized life. As Orage put it: "The sooner the whole of THE NEW AGE is regarded as more important than any of its parts the better."[*] This conception of society as an organic whole, in which no part can flourish at the expense of any other part, was more a hope for the future than an interpretation of the age itself, which Orage believed to be in a stage of transition; he therefore, like Nietzsche, places great stress on the function of art to mould the future, appealing for a new epic strain in literature which, like the *Mahabharata*, will lead men on to a higher life: "Nobody will deny that what my colleague, Mr. Ludovici, calls 'a great order of society' is lacking in most men's minds today. ... Our writers do not *think* from a settled background either of fact or imagination. Actually either variety would serve the purpose of literature and art; the order of society that exists (if only it would stand still for five minutes) or an order of Utopia. But on neither have our writers any hold, and in consequence they flounder about alternately howling like dragons or wailing like

---

[*] *NA*, XVI (January 21, 1915), 313. On this point he was unswerving: "It will be found, if we all live long enough, that every part of THE NEW AGE hangs together; and that the literature we despise is associated with the economics we hate as the literature we love is associated with the form of society we would assist in creating." *NA*, XIV (November 13, 1913), 51.

babes."⁹⁵ In the absence of "a settled background," which was last enjoyed in the eighteenth century, Orage believes that creative energies should be harnessed to the formation of a new order of society: this is the long-term purpose. What is more, the short-term view of aesthetics as applied physiology is one which is constantly found in Nietzsche: "The essential feature in art is its power of perfecting existence, its production of perfection and plenitude; art is essentially the affirmation, the blessing, and the deification of existence."⁹⁶ Orage once defined art as "the imaginative perfecting of nature; or the intuitive perception and representation of reality in actuality."⁹⁷ The first of these, he says, divines the potential reality behind existence by a process of transfiguration, and the second, through an extension of the first, divines the intention behind existence by discovering universal truths. Such an idealization, as Nietzsche warns, does not consist, as is commonly held, in ignoring or discounting the trivial and inconsequential: "What is decisive is rather a tremendous drive to bring out the main features so that the others disappear in the process. ... One enriches everything out of one's own fullness: whatever one sees, whatever one wills, is seen swelled, taut, strong, overloaded with strength. A man in this state transforms things until they mirror his power – until they are reflections of his perfection. This *having* to transform into perfection is – art. Even everything that he is not yet, becomes for him an occasion of joy in himself; in art man enjoys himself as perfection."⁹⁸

The core of Orage's attack on the realistic novel is contained in another passage from Nietzsche: "Nature, estimated artistically, is no model. It exaggerates, it distorts, it leaves gaps. Nature is *chance*. To study 'from nature' seems to me to be a bad sign: it betrays submission, weakness, fatalism; this lying in the dust before *petits faits* is unworthy of a *whole* artist. To see *what* is – that is the mark of another kind of spirit, the anti-artistic, the factual. One must know *who* one is."⁹⁹ A passage like this helps us to understand what Orage meant when he referred to "the Nietzscheanism of Wilde."* But Orage never accepted, any more than Nietzsche did, the gospel of "art for art's sake," which Nietzsche opposes in no uncertain terms:

* NA, xii (June 13, 1913), 177. There is no evidence that Wilde ever read Nietzsche. Gide wrote: "Nietzsche astonished me less, later on, becaue I had heard Wilde say: 'Above all, not happiness. Pleasure! We must always want the most tragic ...'" *Oscar Wilde* (New York, 1949), 15. But my impression is that Wilde and Nietzsche were vastly different. Janko Lavrin, a *New Age* contributor and author of *Nietzsche and Modern Consciousness* (1922), put it this way: "In spite of his coquettish individualism and his shower of paradoxes, which makes one think of Nietzsche, Oscar Wilde is the very antipodes of the philosopher of superman.

The fight against purpose in art is always a fight against the moralizing tendency in art, against its subordination to morality. *L'art pour l'art* means, "The devil take morality!" But even this hostility still betrays the overpowering force of the prejudice. When the purpose of moral preaching and of improving man has been excluded from art, it still does not follow by any means that art is altogether purposeless, aimless, senseless – in short, *l'art pour l'art*, a worm chewing its own tail. "Rather no purpose at all than a moral purpose!" – that is the talk of mere passion. A psychologist, on the other hand, asks: what does all art do? does it not praise? glorify? choose? prefer? With all this it strengthens or weakens certain valuations. ... Art is the great stimulus to life.[100]

Not only is this passage, and many of Nietzsche's other ideas about art, paraphrased in Orage's *Nietzsche in Outline and Aphorism*, but it forms the basis of his thinking – as late as 1920 Orage wrote: "Literature has come that we might have life and have it more abundantly; and the test of literature is whether it gives and intensifies life or takes away and diminishes life."[101] This will depend on the temperament and character of the writer. At this point we come upon a cardinal distinction on which Orage, Ludovici, and Kennedy all base their critical credo. It occurs in *Nietzsche contra Wagner*: "Every art and every philosophy may be regarded either as a cure or as a stimulant to ascending or declining life: they always presuppose suffering and sufferers. But there are two kinds of sufferers: – those that suffer from *overflowing vitality*, who need Dionysian art and require a tragic insight into, and a tragic outlook upon, the phenomenon life, – and there are those who suffer from *reduced* vitality, and who crave for repose, quietness, calm seas, or else the intoxication, the spasm, the bewilderment which art and philosophy provide."*

Ludovici distinguishes between "Ruler" art, which is associated with inner riches, the function of giving, and an aristocratic society, and "democratic" art, which is associated with inner poverty and a slavish "re-active" dependence on environment which means that it is beneath reality (in-

---

Nietzsche wrote in order to fight and overcome his inner tragedy; Wilde – in order to avoid it. He was deliberately anti-tragic. From art he demanded as aesthetic shelter; and from life, hardly anything more than pleasantly arranged appearances, coupled with an Epicurean chase after new sensations for their own sake." *Aspects of Modernism* (London, 1935), 17. (*Aspects of Modernism* is dedicated to Orage.) For a different view, see Thomas Mann, *Last Essays* (New York, 1959), 157–8, 172; and Norbert Loeser, *Nietzsche en Wilde en andere essays* (Amsterdam, 1960).

* *CW*, vIII, 65–6. Nietzsche continues: "In regard to all artists of what kind soever, I shall now avail myself of this radical distinction: does the creative power in this case arise from a loathing of life, or from an excessive *plenitude* of life? In Goethe, for instance, an overflow of vitality was creative, in Flaubert – hate."

competence), on a level with reality (realism), or fantastically different from reality (romanticism).[102] What Ludovici calls "Ruler" art is no more than classicism in a Nietzschean guise – Kennedy, in a review of *The Works of Charles and Mary Lamb*, makes this explicit:

> Books must henceforth be judged by a new standard, a new table of values ... a period of strength, expansion, and conquest in a nation is, generally speaking, followed by a period of weakness, shrinkage, and degeneration. This law holds good in the realm of literature – the strong, expansive, healthy period of classicism is followed by a flaccid, shrinking, degenerative period of romanticism. Classicism, it is true, may tend to over-develop and become pedantry, just as romanticism usually degenerates into spasmodicism and hysteria; but these latter facts hardly bear upon the point at issue – the place of Charles Lamb as judged by a new literary standard. The prime test is a man's strength – his will to power – does he command, or does he obey?[103]

And another note by Ludovici shows that the ruler-artist is very much the artist-superman, the creator – as Yeats would say – of a nation's sacred book: "He is either the maker or the highest product of an aspiring and an ascending people. In him their highest values find their most splendid bloom. In him their highest values find their strongest spokesman. And in his work they find the symbol of their loftiest hopes."[104]

Ludovici, like Kennedy and Orage, regarded himself as the heir of Arnold, and much of his book *Nietzsche and Art* is a continuation of the principles Arnold had enunciated in *Culture and Anarchy*. He quotes Worringer and other German aestheticians to the effect that art is not imitation but the expression of life-need, man's only way of emancipating himself from the accidental and chaotic character of reality; but the ideas in the following passage are Arnoldian: "The highest Art, Ruler Art, and therefore the highest beauty, – in which culture is opposed to natural rudeness, selection to natural chaos, and simplicity to natural complexity, – can be the flower and product only of an aristocratic society which, in its traditions and its active life, has observed, and continues to observe, the three aristocratic principles, – culture, selection, and simplicity."[105]

Orage, also taking Arnold as a guide, had been quick to criticize the "Weirdsley" decadence of the 1890s, but the attacks on decadence he made later seem to owe a good deal to Nietzsche's example in *The Twilight of the Idols* and, in particular, *The Case of Wagner* and its appendages – both these works had been available to English readers since 1896, but the lessons they held were only now being learned. Misled by the vehemence of Nietzsche's tone into thinking that his attack on Wagner was the outcome of vindictive spite and personal envy, readers failed to acknowledge that Wagner was the prism through which a concerted critique of romanticism as a whole was to be refracted. Wagner, whom Nietzsche labelled the Cagliostro of modernity, the rhetorician in music, was taken to be the inspirer and exemplar of all that was worst in the romantic artist: his desire for expressiveness at all costs, his yearnings for the infinite and the unattainable, his hatred of the logical and the precise. Decadence in Wagner's music, just as in literature, shows itself in an abandonment of stylistic and moral wholeness:

How is *decadence* in literature characterised? By the fact that in it life no longer animates the whole. Words become predominant and leap right out of the sentence to which they belong, the sentences themselves trespass beyond their bounds, and obscure the sense of the whole page, and the page in its turn gains in vigour at the cost of the whole, – the whole is no longer a whole. But this is the formula for every decadent style: there is always anarchy among the atoms, disaggregation of the will, – in moral terms: "freedom of the individual," – extended into a political theory: "*equal* rights for all." Life, equal vitality, all the vibration and exuberance of life, driven back into the smallest structure, and the remainder left almost lifeless. Everywhere paralysis, distress, and numbness, or hostility and chaos: both striking one with ever increasing force the higher the forms of organisation are into which one ascends. The whole no longer lives at all: it is composed, reckoned up, artificial, a fictitious thing.[106]

"Decadence," wrote Orage, "I have often defined as the substitution of the part for the whole,"[107] and he contended that moral decadence could be discovered in style itself, "in the very construction of a man's sentences, in his rhythm, in his syntax": "Decadence ... is at once a moral and an aesthetic term. ... Decadence, for me as a critic, is absence of a mission, of a purpose, of a co-ordination of powers; and its sign manual in style is the diffuse sentence, the partial treatment, the inchoate vocabulary, the mixed principles."[108] Pound, Orage believed, should relinquish all pretence to be a cultural messiah until he had put his own house in order: "Mr. Pound's own English style is a pastiche of colloquy, slang, journalism, and pedantry. Of culture in Nietzsche's sense of the word – a unity of style – it bears no sign."[109] One way of combatting the rise of decadence in literature is the application of "brilliant common sense": "What we mean by brilliant common sense is, in the sphere of literature in particular, a happy union of simplicity with complexity – of simplicity of form (which includes everything definable) with complexity of meaning (which includes everything spiritual and indefinable)."[110] Just after the outbreak of hostilities in 1914 Orage was optimistic enough to look forward "to a classical revival after the war, and to the return of the spirit of the masculine eighteenth century."[111]

His optimism derives, at least in part, from the attention then being paid to the classical theories of T. E. Hulme, whom Orage regarded as one of the most promising minds of his generation. Hulme was a frequent contributor to the *New Age*, his articles – many of them introductions to the thought of Bergson – appearing between 1909 and 1916. He was killed in action in 1917.

It is now generally acknowledged that Hulme was a seminal thinker, but not an original one: most of his ideas are derived from such continental thinkers as Pascal, Sorel, Worringer, Husserl, and Bergson, and Hulme's effort to reconcile diverse points of view often results in serious shortcomings in coherence and consistency. But Hulme deserves credit for introducing these ideas to his contemporaries, on whom their impact would not have been so great but for his mediation. To what extent Hulme was personally acquainted with Nietzsche's work is hard to establish; his knowledge of the language permitted access to the German original, but he never makes Nietzsche the focal point of any of his philosophizing – all his references to Nietzsche are in the nature of asides. What severely complicates the issue is that several continental writers to whom he is especially indebted in his observations on romanticism and literary theory (for example, Scheler, Sorel, Lasserre, de Gourmont) were themselves deeply influenced by Nietzsche.

What is certain is that Hulme's attacks on romanticism, Rousseau, and liberalism can all be paralleled in *The Twilight of the Idols*; perhaps more significantly, Kennedy's *Tory Democracy* appeared in serial form in the *New Age* before Hulme's better-known articles in the same weekly, and Kennedy and Hulme are at one in the condemnation of liberalism. Liberalism in politics was seen by Hulme to correspond to romanticism in literature: "Conversely, Classicism, which was taken to imply 'the correct subordination of the parts to the whole in works of art,' was equated with the concept of a feudalistic or hierarchical society in which the social parts or classes would be "correctly' subordinated to the interests of the whole society."[112] Nietzscheanism, wrote Kennedy, ran quite counter to liberalism: "It is simply a new trend of thought, which will have for its most proximate effect, not the abolition of class distinctions, which it may rather accentuate, but the abolition of class wars and the definite fixing of a social hierarchy."[113] According to Hulme, the classical view of man sees him as "an extraordinarily fixed and limited animal whose nature is absolutely constant," but who can be "disciplined by order and tradition to something fairly decent"; whereas the romantic or liberal view sees him as "intrinsically good, spoilt by circumstance,"[114] a being potentially in reach of perfection. Kennedy writes that permanence and liberalism are diametrically opposed:

> The Liberal cannot tolerate anything that descends from generation to generation; for he looks upon the innate and inherited forces of man as being susceptible of change from day to day and from year to year. He is not concerned with man in his fixed and permanent state, but with some idealistic human being who is in a constant condition of transition from a state of "evil" into a state of "good" the definition of what is good and what is evil naturally varying with every fresh twist given to Liberal philosophy. The Liberal, in short, cannot understand the influence of tradition, and the place tradition occupies, and ought to occupy, in politics, art, literature, or sociology.[115]

The romantic or liberal view goes back to Rousseau, and both Hulme and Kennedy (in agreement with Nietzsche) make him responsible for the intellectual maladies of the age, characterized by Hulme as "Romanticism in literature, Relativism in ethics, Idealism in politics, and Modernism in religion."[116] The antidote to Rousseau, it is agreed, is Machiavelli, but Hulme goes further than Nietzsche in tracing romanticism back beyond Rousseau to classical antiquity and the Renaissance and their ideals of self-knowledge, self-culture and the free growth of personality. These ideals, says Hulme, have dominated western thought for too long, and we are due for a classical revival based on the doctrine of original sin. Such a revival will assert cardinal religious values; if these values are neglected, as romanticists and rationalists have neglected them, man's natural instincts will find a perverted outlet: "You don't believe in a God, so you begin to believe that man is a god. You don't believe in Heaven, so you begin to believe in a heaven on earth."[117]

Nietzsche's repudiation of original sin, his worship of Greek and Renaissance ideals, and his appeals for a new race of supermen would seem to class him, in Hulme's definition, as a romantic. Hulme does, in fact, classify him in this way. Like Nietzsche, Hulme perceived that the humanist tradition, with its religious and moral values, was a tradition in decline, but he could not accept Nietzsche's proposed remedy: "There are people who, disgusted with romanticism, wish for us to go back to the classical period, or who, like Nietzsche, wish us to admire the Renaissance. But such partial reactions will always fail, for they are only half measures – it is no good returning to humanism, for that will itself degenerate into romanticism."[118] More subtly, Nietzsche regarded romanticism, not as the inevitable outcome of humanism, but as a movement which distorted the older values: "It is true that both humanism and rationalism have brought antiquity into the field as an ally; and it is therefore quite comprehensible that the opponents of humanism should direct their attacks against antiquity also. Antiquity, however, has been misunderstood and falsified by humanism: it must rather be considered as a testimony against humanism, against the benign nature of man, etc. The opponents of humanism are wrong to combat antiquity as well; for in antiquity they have a strong ally."[119]

Hulme admits that Nietzsche is a despiser of romanticism, but considers him a romantic even though most people (according to Hulme) habitually associate Nietzsche with classical views:

It is true that they do occur in him, but he made them so frightfully vulgar that no classic would acknowledge them. In him you have the spectacle of a romantic seizing on the classic point of view because it attracted him purely as a theory, and who, being a romantic, in taking up this theory, passed his slimy fingers over every detail of it. Everything loses its value. The same idea of the necessary hierarchy of classes, with their varying capaciites and duties, gets turned into the romantic nonsense of the two kinds of morality, the slave and the master morality, and every other element of the classic position gets transmuted in a similar way into something ridiculous.[120]

It is illustrative of Nietzsche's reputation that Hulme, like so many of his contemporaries, tries to play down a fundamental agreement by taking such precautions to preserve the pristine purity of the classical viewpoint from Nietzschean contamination. Even if Nietzsche were only a classical *poseur*, his diatribes against Rousseau and his avowed hatred of romanticism do at least have the merit of force and consistency. Generally speaking, Nietzsche views the distinction between romanticism and classicism very much as Goethe did: it is the difference between sickness and health, between adolescence and maturity, exuberance and restraint. Nietzsche declares, time and time again, his preference for the classic,[121] and his praise of Horace sounds like a prescription for imagist poetry: "This mosaic of words, in which every word – as sound, as place, as concept – pours out its strength right and left and over the whole, this *minimum* in the extent and number of the signs, and the maximum thereby attained in the energy of the signs – all that is Roman and, if one will believe me, *noble* par excellence. All the rest of poetry becomes, in contrast, something too popular – a mere garrulity of feelings."[122] Hulme denies that a distinction in terms of restraint and exuberance is a sufficient one, the reason for this being that he wishes to claim Shakespeare, equally with Racine, as a classical poet. To perform this acrobatic he asserts that there are two kinds of classicism, the static and the dynamic, a distinction he claims, quite baselessly, to have found in Nietzsche;* he then places Shakespeare in the dynamic category. Nietzsche, more consistently, rates Sophocles above Shakespeare, on the grounds that Sophocles is more classical.

Hulme's rejection of Nietzsche as a proponent of classicism cannot mask a striking similarity in their attitudes. They both protested against the expression of violent feeling in art, and both accepted the need for a convention of form which obliges the artist to overcome self-imposed restrictions. The strict obedience of the French classical dramatists to certain laws, such as that of the three unities, Nietzsche sees as a counterpart to the discipline of fugue in the development of music, and these limitations can be justified: "Such a restriction may appear absurd; nevertheless there is no means of getting out of naturalism except by confining ourselves at first to the strongest (perhaps most arbitrary) means. Thus we gradually learn to walk gracefully on the narrow paths that bridge giddy abysses, and acquire great suppleness of movement as a result, as the history of music proves to our living eyes. Here we see how, step by step, the fetters get looser, until at last they may appear to be altogether thrown off; this *appearance* is the highest achievement of a necessary development in art."[123] Restrictions are now considered senseless, and art achieves "liberation" by reverting to the incompleteness, the boldness, and the excess of its early beginnings: the cosmopolitan mingling of different styles prevents the slow growth and maturation of any single organic style, so that "all poets *must* become experimenting imitators, daring copyists, however great their primary strength may be."[124] Art, to Nietzsche, is self-discipline, not self-indulgence: "Every artist knows how different from the state of letting himself go, is his 'most natural' condition, the free arranging, locating, disposing and constructing in the moments of 'inspiration' – and how strictly and delicately he then obeys a thousand laws, which, by their very rigidity and precision, defy all formulation by means of ideas."[125]

Hulme, likewise, resists any movement towards irresponsible originality and the search for novelty for novelty's sake; he calls for self-discipline, "this struggle against the ingrained habit of the technique."[126] In Hulme's well-known description, classical poems are dry, hard, clear and sophisticated; Nietzsche, who admired Bizet's work for its dryness of atmosphere, its *limpidezza*, thinks likewise: "We must understand how a certain modi-

---

* There *is*, to my knowledge, no such distinction in Nietzsche. Hulme's attribution here may be based on a faulty reading or recall of aphorism 370 of The *Gay Science*, an attack on German romanticism, where a similar distinction is made.

cum of coldness, lucidity, and hardness is inseparable from all classical taste: above all consistency, happy intellectuality, 'the three unities,' concentration, hatred of all feeling, of all sentimentality, of all spirit, hatred of all multiformity, of all uncertainty, evasiveness, and of all nebulosity, as also of all brevity, finicking, prettiness, and good nature."[127]

Nietzsche also notes that, owing to centuries of exaggerated feeling, "all words have become vague and inflated," and as a remedy recommends "careful reflection, conciseness, coldness, plainness, even carried intentionally to the farthest limits."[128] Hulme agrees that such antiseptic measures are necessary, but they should not be carried to extremes – language must be perpetually revivified by the introduction of fresh imagery. The need of language for metaphorical infusions is now a commonplace of criticism which owes much of its familiarity to the example and precept of Eliot. Nietzsche has little to say about the poetic use of metaphor, but does write metaphorically much of the time: *Zarathustra* is the most obvious example that springs to mind, but Nietzsche was also a lyric poet of no mean achievement. Hulme had a great respect for this kind of writing; indeed, according to Herbert Read, Hulme intended to cast the final version of his philosophy in allegorical form, "perhaps analogous to Nietzsche's *Zarathustra*."[129] Hulme had no patience with the insubstantial meanderings of idealist philosophy, even defending Nietzsche against one of its typical representatives, Haldane: "The abstract philosopher has a great contempt for the visual one. Hence the steadfast refusal to recognise that Nietzsche made any contribution to metaphysics."[130] Here, Hulme indirectly defends Nietzsche's use of a metaphorical language against abstract logic.

Indeed, Hulme thought that the metaphysical part of Nietzsche, generally neglected, was the root of Nietzsche's philosophy, and that Nietzsche was groping in a rhapsodical way towards insights which Bergson was later to express with greater clearness: his praise for Nietzsche's metaphorical method was no mere genuflection, for he, too, as Herbert Read points out, "preferred to see things in the emotional light of metaphor rather than to reach reality through scientific analysis."[131] This was probably the result of a scepticism concerning language which he shared with Nietzsche. One object of the Hulmean philosophy is to destroy the idea that anything can be described in words; Nietzsche regards language as basically metaphorical, since we cannot perceive things directly, but only through metaphorical conceptions which place reality perpetually at one remove or more from ourselves – such conceptions, when they have solidified to a state where they are powerless to affect the senses, are a constant source of error and illusion. Nietzsche's observations concerning language amount, at least in part, to an implicit endorsement of some of the major tenets of Imagism.[132]

Hulme probably learnt more from Nietzsche the philosopher of art than from Nietzsche the moralist or even (his above statement notwithstanding) Nietzsche the metaphysician.[*] In a projected book on modern theories of art he planned to discuss Nietzsche in regard to the question "Is art independent or subordinate to human activities and needs?"[133] But it is difficult to assess Hulme's indebtedness accurately because his attitude to Nietzsche is so often patently dismissive or polemically unfair. For example, Hulme affirmed his belief that a really scientific philosophy is possible, but cautioned his readers: "I do not mean what Nietzsche meant when he said, 'Do not speculate as to whether what a philosopher says is true, but ask how he came to think it true.' This form of scepticism I hold to be just fashionable rubbish. Pure philosophy ought to be, and may be, entirely objective and scientific."[134] The allusion to Nietzsche here is purely gratuitous. In making out a case for scientific philosophy Hulme chooses to ignore his own statements elsewhere that a personal philosophy (following Husserl and Dilthey he calls it a *Weltanschauung*) is quite allowable; moreover, in one of his articles he actually quotes with approval Nietzsche's dictum that "philosophy is autobiography" in order to explain the necessity of defending his ideas about romanticism and original sin by showing how he arrived at them.[135] Eclectic opportunism can go no further.

Like Orage, Hulme never aligned himself with the Nietzscheans on the staff of the *New Age*, but some of their ideas may have been powerful enough to have squeezed through the barricade of his contempt and lodged themselves in the mind of a man who is still credited with revolutionizing the course of English poetry almost single-handed. The work of Orage, Hulme, Ludovici, and Kennedy is too homogeneous to rule out the

---

[*] So did T. S. Eliot. In a review of A. Wolf's *The Philosophy of Nietzsche* in 1916, Eliot (newly returned to London from Germany and clearly tutored by Hulme) described Nietzsche as "one of those writers whose philosophy evaporates when detached from its literary qualities," and whose work therefore appeals to "the large semi-philosophical public, who are spared the austere effort of criticism required by either metaphysics or literature"; but he regretted Wolf's failure to discuss Nietzsche's views on art, particularly the "interesting pessimism" with respect to the future of art shown in *Human, All-Too-Human*. *International Journal of Ethics*, XXVI (April, 1916), 425–6. As Hulme was doing, Eliot compares Nietzsche unfavourably with Bergson; Holbrook Jackson suggested that intellectual snobbery may have had something to do with the preference. For a Nietzschean view, see Anthony Ludovici, "Nietzsche and Bergson: A Comparison," *TPW*, XX (October, 1912), 457, 495, 529–30.

possibility that Nietzsche's writing may have played some part in twentieth-century English neo-classicism.

5   Neither the *New Age*, nor Orage, have received the attention they deserve. The *New Age* is not even mentioned in the standard work on the little magazine, and other authorities allude to it only in the skimpiest fashion.[136] Yet all available testimony points to the overwhelming formative influence, not only of the *New Age*, but of its editor as well. In their autobiographies Edwin Muir and Herbert Read admit that the *New Age*, over a period of many years, was their chief mentor in matters of contemporary literature, politics and economics; and more recently Margaret Cole has written: "The *New Age*, particularly just before and in the early part of the first World War, was *the* left-wing paper, which everybody who was anybody read."* As for Orage's own personal influence, that, too, is beyond question. Maurice Browne, in a remark already quoted, wrote that "his influence over me was enormous and, as I look back, entirely for good." Storm Jameson had this to say: "On the 'young generation' of 1912 he had, I suppose, more influence than any other single person and it was an unmitigatedly good influence, working for an intellectual integrity and honesty."[137]

Orage's books on Nietzsche, particularly *Nietzsche in Outline and Aphorism*, were widely read in their day. Holbrook Jackson, writing in 1914, suggested they "really prepared the way for such acceptance as Nietzsche has had in Great Britain."[138] To suggest that they were written "with more enthusiasm than judgment"[139] is severely to underrate their value, for Orage's work was both cause and effect of changing attitudes towards Nietzsche. Orage's efforts to gain Nietzsche a hearing were eventually successful, and Nietzsche, according to Augustus John, "appeared on the scene with the impact of a home-made bomb, scattering everybody and forcing even Dostoievsky to a secure but secondary eminence."[140] No

---

* Letter to *New Statesman*, LVIII (December 29, 1959), 912. The paper's reputation gives point to an amusing incident which connects it with John Davidson. In 1909 Davidson submitted a poem to the *New Age*, accompanied by a letter in which he assured the editor that for several weeks he had been reading the paper with pleasure and profit; on discovering that the *New Age* was a socialist organ he flew into a rage, and declared that had he known what advanced views the paper supported he would never have submitted the poem in the first place. A contemporary witness reported: "Further correspondence did not allay his anger although it was gently hinted to him that in all probability Mr. John Davidson was the only man in Great Britain who could read the *New Age* for weeks on end and not discover its political views." "Concilio et Labore," *Manchester Courier* (March 29, 1909), 6.

longer could Nietzsche be regarded as an anarchist – his was the voice of prophecy, poetry and parable which would have to be heeded: "Nietzsche ... is taken seriously in Germany; and, though handicapped by the advocacy of certain of his prophets in this country, will have to be taken seriously here."[141] Since the readers of the *New Age* were men of creative talent, imagination and potential influence in the field of letters – Hulme, Eliot, Ezra Pound, John Middleton Murry, Richard Aldington, Wyndham Lewis, D. H. Lawrence, Herbert Read, Edwin Muir, and many more – Nietzsche's ideas had at last a chance of making an impact on literary practice and theory. The investigation of this impact is beyond the scope of the present enquiry; but the possibility of it being undertaken at all is due to Orage. He dared to make Nietzsche's name respected, and the *New Age* was the first to proclaim the importance of Nietzsche, as it was later to proclaim the importance of post-impressionism, Bergson, and Freudian psychoanalysis, when other sections of the English press found these subjects too unsavoury for serious consideration. It might even be said that Orage did more for the Nietzsche movement in England than any other man, not even excepting Levy: Levy, after all, had the easy privilege of preaching to the converted – Orage's sphere of influence was much more extensive. His personal magnetism was greater than Levy's, and his Nietzscheanism was never of the supererogatory, militant kind which tended to alienate rather than attract potential adherents. What Middleton Murry wrote in 1916 about Nietzsche is almost entirely applicable to Orage: "The memorable and true thing in Nietzsche's criticism is its incessant and fundamental humanism. It is the never-failing sympathy with the torments of the creative soul, and an almost unique understanding of them. He is therefore essentially self-guarded against the boorish insensitiveness of *soi-disant* disciples, Nietzscheans and *hoc genus omne*, for he has given us the touchstone to try his own achievements."[142] As we have seen, Orage's brand of Nietzscheanism was a mystical one, and it was against his mysticism, not its Nietzschean associations, that objections were lodged. Murry, for example, detects with some misgiving Orage's "obstinate substratum of belief that there was some secret of control over the universe: a key by which one could unlock all the doors, and be a master of Power."[143] And Herbert Read wrote: "He had a streak of mysticism in his make-up which personally I deplored: it rendered him ineffectual as a man of action, and in his particular situation action was needed."[144] But for Read, as for Edwin Muir, the discovery of Nietzsche, made through the instrumentality of Orage and the *New Age*, was nothing less than cataclysmic, and as the case of these two writers is the best documented, they will be taken as representatives of the first generation of English writers to approach Nietzsche in more than a fragmentary and piecemeal manner.

The work of Herbert Read was first published in the *New Age*, a review he read with such avidity that he had copies sent to him at the front in 1914. His discovery of Nietzsche dates from 1912, when at the age of nineteen he was a student at Leeds University and had access to the library copies of the new translations. He read all the volumes, and decided that *Zarathustra* and *Beyond Good and Evil* contained the essence of Nietzsche. This reading marked a crisis in his intellectual development:

> With Dostoevsky and Ibsen I was already partly acquainted, but Nietzsche was a new world, and since my discovery of Blake, the most cataclysmic. It was Nietzsche who first introduced me to philosophy – I read far more than I could understand in his pages, but I did not let my ignorance rest. From Nietzsche I passed to Schopenhauer, to Kant, Hegel, Hume, Pascal, Plato – in very much this indiscriminate order. It was as though I had tapped a central exchange of intellectual tendencies; from Nietzsche communications ran in every direction and for at least five years he, and none of my professors or friends, was my real teacher. ... He gave me vistas that were quite outside the range of formal education; he introduced me to the ferment of contemporary ideas. In his company I knew the excitement of an intellectual adventure, that highest exaltation which only comes when truth is conceived as a fleeting quarry in whose pursuit the whole mind must be engaged.[145]

And yet, Read adds, "my early enthusiasm for Nietzsche ... was purely intellectual: my life was unaffected – I never became a Nietzschean, either in thought or deed."* The substance of what he was to find most valuable

---

* *The Contrary Experience* (London, 1963), 187. Wyndham Lewis made a similar disclaimer (as, we recall, George Moore had earlier): "There is not the least taint of Uebermenschlichkeit anywhere in my mind." *Rude Assignment* (London, 1950), 188. But, nevertheless, he notes that Nietzsche was "the paramount influence" on many of his contemporaries before the First World War: "The other day I was interested, in listening to a broadcast by Herbert Read ... to find he had selected Nietzsche as the decisive influence, overshadowing the rest of his early reading. Germans of whom I saw a good deal in Paris as a student were very contemptuous: they called Nietzsche 'a salon-philosopher.' But for me Nietzsche was, with Schopenhauer, a thinker more immediately accessible to a Western mind than the other Germans, whose barbarous jargon was a great barrier – Hegel, for instance, I could never read. A majority of people, I daresay, found in the author of 'Zarathustra' a sort of titanic nourishment for the ego: treating in fact this great hysteric as a power-house. At present that is what I like least about Nietzsche: and I was reasonably immune then to Superman. The impulse to titanism and supernatural afflatus pervading German romanticism has never had any interest for me. On the other hand that side of his genius which expressed itself in 'La Gaya Scienza,' or those admirable maxims, rather resembling Butler's 'Notebooks,' which he wrote after the breakdown in his health, were among my favorite reading in those years." *Ibid.*, 120.

in Freud he had already found in certain passages on dreams in *Beyond Good and Evil*, and Nietzsche's attack on the state in *Zarathustra* contained a philosophy of anarchism which conflicted with the Christian or humanitarian anarchism of Tolstoy, Morris, and Carpenter in which he was simultaneously absorbed. This conflict was resolved by the discovery, in *Beyond Good and Evil*, of Nietzsche's doctrine of hardness, of self-discipline, of the creativity of suffering. Read quotes one passage which he thinks has never been equalled (part of this passage has already been quoted in connection with neo-classic theory, above, p. 258):

> Everything in the nature of freedom, elegance, boldness, dance, and masterly certainty, which exists or has existed, whether it be in thought itself, or in administration, or in speaking and persuading, in art as in conduct, has only developed by means of the tyranny of arbitrary law. ... Every artist knows how different from the state of letting oneself go, is his "most natural" condition, the free arranging, locating, disposing, and constructing in the moments of "inspiration" – and how strictly and delicately he then obeys a thousand laws, which by their very rigidity and precision, defy all formulation by means of ideas. ... The essential thing "in heaven and in earth" is, apparently ... that there should be long *obedience* in the same direction; and thereby results, and always had resulted in the long run, something which has made life worth living; for instance, virtue, art, music, dancing, reason, spirituality – anything whatever that is transfiguring, refined, foolish or divine.[146]

The ferment of Nietzsche's ideas continued to dictate the course of Read's thinking about democracy, culture, and the nature of man, as a diary, studiously kept up even during active service, sufficiently proves.[147] The germ of Read's later development is to be found in a small collection of poems *Songs of Chaos* (1915), which bears an epigraph from Nietzsche – "One must have chaos within oneself to give birth to a dancing star."

Edwin Muir tells us that he owed his introduction to Nietzsche to Orage's personal recommendation. The *New Age*, he says, stimulated his mind, sharpened his contempt for sentimentality, and gave him a ready access to contemporary politics and literature, "a thing I badly needed, and with a few vigorous blows shortened a process which would otherwise have taken a long time."[148] In 1912, three years after he had begun to read the *New Age*, he began to feel that his youthful illusions were crumbling around him, and sought Orage's advice by writing directly to him:

> He wrote me a long and kind letter describing his own intellectual struggles as a young man, and saying that he had been greatly helped by taking up some particular writer and studying everything he wrote, until he felt he knew the workings of a great mind. He had studied Plato for several years in this way, and he

was now studying the *Mahabharata*, which he tentatively recommended to me. I took his advice to study a particular writer, but after some hesitation I chose Nietzsche instead of the *Mahabharata*; it was the choice most likely to maintain me in my suspended brooding over the future and the least likely to lead me to wisdom.[149]

After a year's intensive study of Nietzsche, Muir confesses, he still refused to recognize that his socialism and his Nietzscheanism were incompatible, and that Nietzsche's last works were tinged with madness. He saw later that his Nietzscheanism was a compensation for his own psychological inadequacies: "I could not face my life as it was, and so I took refuge in the fantasy of the Superman": "Apart from all this Nietzsche had ruined my feeling for good English, for many of the volumes were badly translated. When I first began to write, some years later, what I produced was a sort of pinchbeck Nietzschean prose peppered with exclamation marks."[150] Muir is referring to a series of short notes and aphorisms which appeared weekly in the *New Age* under the heading of "We Moderns," afterwards published as *We Moderns: Enigma and Guesses* (1918) under the pseudonym of "Edward Moore." As imitations of Nietzsche, Orage thought these aphorisms were parody of a very high order, but Muir subsequently disowned them, and was relieved when the book went out of print: "In these notes I generalized in excited ignorance on creative love and the difference between it and pity, which I unhesitatingly condemned; I pointed out such facts as that humility is really inverted pride, and that the true antithesis of love is not hate but sympathy: whenever I hit upon a paradox which lay conveniently near the surface I took it for the final truth. My aphorisms, as they came from an inward excitement, excited some of the readers of the *New Age*; but the excitement was merely another escape, a lyrical refusal to come down to earth."*

This retrospective self-criticism suggests that Muir came to reject Nietzsche entirely, but this would be a misleading inference. He did reject

---

* *An Autobiography* (London, 1954), 151. Aldous Huxley has recommended Nietzsche's aphoristic works as ideal travel books: "Nietzsche's sayings have this in common with La Rochefoucauld's, that they are pregnant and expansive. His best aphorisms are long trains of thought, compressed. The mind can dwell on them at length because so much is implicit in them. It is in this way that good aphorisms differ from mere epigrams, in which the whole point consists in the felicity of expression. An epigram pleases by surprising; after the first moment the effect wears off and we are no further interested in it. One is not taken in twice by the same practical joke. But an aphorism does not depend on verbal wit. Its effect is not momentary, and the more we think of it, the more substance we find in it." *Along That Road* (London, 1925), 69.

the theory of morality in terms of the Will to Power, the idea that Christianity, because of Nietzsche, had sustained an irreparable reverse, and the concept of the superman, which was "no longer an ideal, but a character in fiction":

All this may freely be admitted. Yet how much poorer our vision of life to-day would be had Nietzsche never writen about Christianity, morality and the Superman. He brought a new atmosphere into European thought, an atmosphere cold, glittering and free; and any thinker in our time who has not breathed in it has, by that accident, some nuance of mediocrity and timidity which is displeasing. ... He has left us some criticism of the first rank; a body of observation on life, religion and morality which will be valid as long as men feel these things and think about them; an exercise in rhythmic prose which must continue to astonish and move, if it does not persuade, men of all habits of thought; and, above all, the spectacle of a passionate tragedy of thought, the like of which the human race will probably never see again.[151]

Muir believed that Nietzsche, along with Blake, belonged to a class of stimulating writers "who say more than they know they are saying [and who] incite us to complete what they have imperfectly said, and to make their thought our own."[152]

Orage agreed with this verdict, and despite all his controversies with the Nietzscheans, was able to maintain his admiration for their idol: "My respect for him increases with my knowledge of himself no less than of his works. It will be difficult, I venture to say, for any reader of Nietzsche's *Life*, by Daniel Halévy, to close the last chapter without tears. The spectacle is of a glorious being dashing his brains out against the bars of mortality and singing in his agony. The image, if you please, is monstrous, but so is the spectacle. It is pathos raised to tragedy."[153] The image of Nietzsche as the tragic martyr of thought is one to which Read, Muir, and Orage all subscribed. In Anne Sedgwick's novel *The Encounter* (1914), Nietzsche is the "piteous and splendid prototype" of the central figure, Ludwig Wehlitz. In 1912 the authoress wrote: "My new story turns on an episode taken from the life of poor, splendid, puerile Nietzsche; it struck my imagination so forcibly that I found it clothing itself in imaginary circumstances and imaginary characters (all but Nietzsche's, which I somewhat keep) and starting off on its own. I am extremely interested in it and only thankful to have it to do; but I foresee that it will be anything but popular."[154] It was an accurate forecast for at the vanguard of the reaction that set in at this time was the Bloomsbury Group, an élite assembly of Whig aristocrats who took their cue, not from Nietzsche, but from G. E. Moore and his Pateresque philosophy of the exquisite sensation. E. M. Forster's outburst in 1917 against the moral imperatives of the war demonstrated the Bloomsbury acceptance of modes of thinking and feeling which Nietzsche had decried: "Huysman's *A Rebours* is the book of that blessed period that I remember best. Oh, the relief of a world which lived for its sensations and ignored the will – the world of Des Esseintes! Was it decadent? Yes, and thank God. Yes; here again was a human being who had time to feel and experiment with his feelings, to taste and smell and arrange books and fabricate flowers, and be selfish and himself."*

One older member of the group, Desmond MacCarthy, wrote reviews of Nietzsche, praising his exultant courage, his buoyant scepticism and his ruthless honesty. Another, Rupert Brooke, ranked Nietzsche with Meredith, Shaw, and Wells as one of "our highest and clearest thinkers,"[155] and in 1910 read a paper called "Democracy and the Arts" to the Cambridge University Fabian Society in which Nietzsche is referred to as the Bible of modern man. But such interest was unusual; Leonard Woolf states that Nietzsche was "practically ignored by almost everyone known by me in the last seventy years, and I cannot remember even a discussion about him," and Duncan Grant believes that "Nietzsche's ideas were unsympathetic to my generation."† In his *Civilization* (1928), Clive Bell gleefully recounts the animus against Nietzsche at the outbreak of the First World War:

Down with Nietzsche! Ah, that was fun, drubbing the nasty blackguard, the man who presumed to sneer at liberals without admiring liberal-unionists. He was an epileptic, it seemed, a scrofulous fellow, and no gentleman. We told the working men about him, we told them about his being the prophet of German imperialism, the poet of Prussia and the lickspittle of the Junkers. And were anyone who had compromised himself by dabbling in German literature so unpatriotic as to

---

* *Abinger Harvest* (New York, 1947), 89. Through the character of Helen Schlegel in chapter XXVII of *Howard's End* (1910), Forster complains that the superman – Napoleon, Bluebeard, Pierpoint Morgan – has no personal identity: "If you could pierce through him," Helen says, "you'd find panic and emptiness in the middle."

† Unpublished letters from Leonard Woolf and Duncan Grant to the writer dated October 17, 1968 and November 9, 1968 respectively. A further portion of Duncan Grant's letter is worth quoting: "I seem to remember that Saxon Sidney Turner mentioned him rather casually with interest and admiration, but a little later I hardly remember him being talked of at all, except on one occasion when I was working on the Omega Workshop with Roger Fry, I remember his saying that Wyndham Lewis seemed to be influenced by his ideas and that Nietzsche's influence in his opinion had been detrimental as far as the Arts were concerned. He certainly otherwise was not a vital influence on the artists connected with Bloomsbury, if he was considered at all."

call our scholarship in question, we called him a traitor and shut him up. ... And yet this holding of the fort against Nietzsche was not wholly satisfying either. For one thing it seemed depressing to be on the defensive everywhere. For another Nietzsche was so difficult to pronounce; and besides it seemed odd to be fighting against someone of whose existence, six months earlier, not one in ten thousand had heard.[156]

Confounding Bloomsbury's ignorance of Nietzsche with ignorance at large is an example of in-group myopia – the attitude is fey, condescending, insular. Bloomsbury was an effort at mouth-to-mouth resuscitation on the cultural level, an effort to which we owe the novels of Forster and Virginia Woolf, Keynesian economics, Strachey's anti-Victoriana and the breakthrough in England of post-impressionist painting; but it was those whom Bloomsbury rejected, (not only Nietzsche but Joyce, Eliot, and Lawrence) who most clearly foresaw and helped to shape the modern world.

Bloomsbury apart, the whole tone of aesthetic discussion changes radically between 1890 and 1914. A new sense of social responsibility emerges which entails a more committed attitude to art and the role of the artist in society. Zarathustra asks: "Where is beauty? Where I must will with all my will; where I want to love and perish that an image may not remain a mere image."[157] This was the quasi-religious belief which inspired Orage in his editorship, attracted him to the study of Nietzsche, and motivated some of his followers and friends to do likewise. No wonder that in 1914 Levy, making public a plan to raise a monument on a hill near Weimar in commemoration of the seventieth anniversary of Nietzsche's birth, should have anticipated a good response from English readers: "A considerable fund has already been collected for the purpose, and any surplus that may accrue will be used for the support of the Nietzsche Archiv, which, under the guidance of Nietzsche's sister, Mrs. Foerster-Nietzsche, has done and is doing so much good work for the study of Nietzsche. It is likewise proposed that this latter institution shall be constituted an intellectual centre for securing that cultural unity of Europe which must precede its political and commercial union."[158] Nine weeks after this announcement was made, Nietzsche's "good Europeans" were mobilized for the most destructive and wasteful war in the history of the world.

CONCLUSION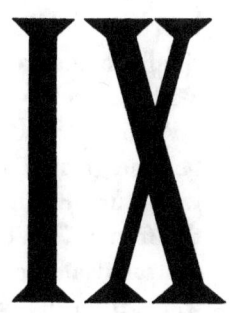

Whereas the *Mercure de France* and the *Revue des deux Mondes* had begun the task of translating Nietzsche and making him intellectually respectable by the end of the 1890s, England had to wait until 1907 for Dr. Levy, A. R. Orage, and the *New Age* to perform a similar function for the benefit of English readers. What is more, as Gide noted in his *Lettre à Angèle*, Nietzsche's influence in France had preceded the translations of his work, making it possible for his ideas to fall on ground which had been gradually prepared for them. Although Nietzschean motifs did appear in the work of some English writers (Davidson, Wells, Shaw, Moore, and Yeats, for example) before their first acquaintance with Nietzsche, they are hardly enough to indicate a strong advance infusion, as was the case in France.

"It is certainly astonishing," wrote Shaw, observing how slow the English were to appreciate the importance of Mozart, Ibsen, and Wagner, "how long English stupidity can stave off foreign genius."[1] His exasperation was shared by one of the Nietzscheans, who, rather ruefully, quoted Stendhal to the effect that "wit and genius lose twenty-five per cent of their value when imported into England."[2] It is true that the little island moored off Europe did manage to put up a sturdy resistance to the infiltration of Nietzsche's ideas, ideas which a vigorous fifth column of what were then regarded as "foreign interlopers" were trying to foist upon it. Not that the indigenous stupidity of the English can be held entirely responsible, for Max Nordau's *Degeneration* would not have pre-conditioned English opinion in the way it did if some discrimination had been exercised in the choice of works to be translated. *The Birth of Tragedy* would have made a better beginning than the violence of *The Antichrist*, the enigmas of *Zarathustra*, or the complexity of the anti-Wagner polemics, for these works immediately alienated the sympathies of Christians, philosophers, and Wagnerians, and made it acutely difficult to dispel the view of

Nietzsche as the mad preacher of egoism and anarchy. Nor did the simple-minded enthusiasm of some of Nietzsche's earlier disciples help matters much; yet, as Nietzsche saw, excess contains its own corrective: "Without blind disciples the influence of a man and his work has never yet become great. To help a doctrine to victory often means only so to mix it with stupidity that the weight of the latter carries off also the victory for the former."[3] What is more, for many years, partly as the result of the obstructiveness of the Nietzsche-Archiv, the English possessed only isolated works from the Nietzsche canon, and were consequently hard pressed to see in his work any sign of system or coherence. For twelve years (1896–1908) the few translations of Nietzsche which existed were both inadequate and expensive, yet they allowed many who read them to perceive that Nietzsche's writing was immensely provocative and stimulating, "full of thorns and secret spices"[4] as Nietzsche himself described it. Few writers were able to consider it with any degree of scholarly detachment.

Nietzsche writes from no settled vantage point. As a "perspectivist" philosopher, he wears a succession of masks which enable him to impersonate innumerable points of view and to speak with equal volubility on either side of a question; as he says in *Ecce Homo*, "I know both sides because I am both sides." Another difficulty in the way of comprehension was Nietzsche's tone – vehement, defiant, mocking by turns – which, much more than his meaning, so often defeats the purpose of his words. Thomas Mann believed that, in reading Nietzsche, literalness and straightforwardness are of no avail: "Rather cunning, irony, reserve are requisite. Anyone who takes Nietzsche 'as he is,' who believes him and takes him at his word, is lost. Seneca, Nietzsche said, is a man to whom we lend our ears but never our loyalty or belief. So it stands with Nietzsche."[5] Mann quotes a letter to show that Nietzsche would have approved of such an approach: "It is completely unnecessary, and even undesirable, to take my side. On the contrary, a dose of curiosity mingled with ironical resistance, as of someone confronted with a strange plant, would seem to be a far more intelligent attitude toward me."[6] Gradually the element of ubiquitous irony in Nietzsche's work became apparent, and readers were less prepared to seek in it any ready-made gospel. Nietzsche's symbol for self-referential irony, laughter, was even taken over by some creative writers like Davidson and Yeats and incorporated into their work.

Nietzsche's characteristic mode of expression, the aphoristic, can be justified as the only practical one for a man perpetually on the move, who preferred to compose while out walking and whose persistent migraines allowed him to concentrate only for short periods at a time, or even, as

Ludovici chose to see it, as the only possible one for a man of such inner riches: "It was the cheque-book of the wealthy man who cannot spare the time to count out separate coins."[7] Yet the aphoristic mode of expression, because it lent itself so readily to exaggeration, one-sidedness, paradox and ambivalence, explains not only why Nietzsche was thought to be self-contradictory, but also why his work gave rise to so many divergent interpretations: after all, aphorisms are, and perhaps ought to be, as enigmatic as the Delphic oracle.

His aphorisms, his apparent lack of system, his method of expression, and his tone constituted a stumbling-block to academic philosophers at the universities, but to poets and artists, who took their Nietzsche extramurally, they were a guarantee of intellectual and imaginative integrity.* Nietzsche's work, unlike that of "system-builders" like Spinoza and Hegel, did not demand a lifetime's study to understand: it offered an immediate stimulus at whatever point it was entered. His "ideality," because it consistently opposed abstraction, gave an impression of coiled energy, a dynamicism missing in the work of other nineteenth-century visionaries, Mill, Spencer, Carlyle, and Comte among them. Nietzsche's ideality was felt so strongly that it could be allied to many movements of an idealistic nature which he expressly denounced, such as socialism, imperialism, mysticism, and feminism, as well as to programmes for human betterment of which he approved, such as eugenics and the revitalization of society through art. The revolutionary role which Nietzsche assigned to art in the preservation of a healthy society appealed particularly to the artist. The idea that "only as an aesthetic phenomenon can life be justified," that art is the affirmation, blessing and deification of existence, although physiological in basis, was found to fit in very well with the symbolist and anti-realist view of art as the embodiment and manifestation of the infinite, something higher than ethics or philosophy, something which existed on the level of "being" rather than of "meaning." The cult of personality and of artistic impressionism which this generation had inherited from Pater,

---

* Auden (whose work shows the scope of Nietzsche's Europeanizing influence) may be taken as a spokesman for this attitude: "A poem must be a closed system, but there is something, in my opinion, lifeless, even false about systematic criticism. In going over my critical pieces, I have reduced them, when possible, to sets of notes because, as a reader, I prefer a critic's notebooks to his treatises." Foreword to *The Dyer's Hand* (New York, 1962). The aphorism incarnates this "unsystematic" approach to literature and philosophy, and in *The Faber Book of Aphorisms* (London, 1964), which Auden co-edited, Nietzsche is given more space than any other single author. Nietzsche belongs with Coleridge, Poe, Baudelaire, Mallarmé, Samuel Butler, Shaw, and Valéry in leading the attack on the merely voluminous.

Yeats came to suspect, was too passive and feminine, and had resulted in instability and disaster. It was in opposition to Pater, among other things, that Nietzsche was seen as "a mighty liberating force, a force making for sincerity and valour, for a clean hard way of living and of thinking."[8] This force was incarnated in the figure of the superman.

The advent of the *Übermensch* doctrine coincided, after the turn of the century, with an increased disenchantment with Christian belief, even with all religious belief, and with a persuasion among the politically minded that liberal democracy had failed to live up to the high hopes placed in it by earlier reformers. There was a conviction, too, that man was not standing on the threshold of a Spencerian heaven after all – man was a fast-degenerating species slithering about in the mire of mass mediocrity. The excited interest in a new science, that of Galtonian eugenics, testified to the degree of urgency with which a solution was sought: this was the atmosphere which enabled the *Übermensch* idea to exercise such a hypnotic fascination over men's minds in the first decade of the century, and to enjoy a vogue which, for various reasons, Nietzsche's philosophy as a whole did not achieve until later. One Nietzsche scholar who is not noted for a lack of caution has observed "a marked tendency to exalt *hardness*" in such writers as Shaw and Hofmannsthal: "It may even seem reasonable to attribute four-fifths of the reaction which has taken place, in literature and in life, against the nineteenth century, to the influence of the Superman and the Supermorality."[9]

Psychologically, the superman answered to feelings of personal inferiority, and to the desire, common in many writers of the time, to dissociate themselves from contemporary vulgarity and mediocrity by establishing a claim, however tenuous, to aristocratic descent – where this was not possible, writers tried to discover a time and place in the historic past which they could identify as their true spiritual home.* Existentially, the super-

---

* Eudo C. Mason sees this "psychological phenomenon" as an extension, appropriate to the aspirations and powers of genius, of the Freudian "Family Romance": "Thus Nietzsche attached great importance to his highly improbable Polish ancestry; D.H. Lawrence liked to think of himself as descended illegitimately from an emigrant French aristocrat; and Joyce dissociated himself from Celts and Sassenachs alike by assuming that he had a decisive Scandinavian streak in his blood." *Rilke, Europe and the English Speaking World* (Cambridge, 1961), 16. Other cases are not far to seek. Davidson liked to think of himself as an Englishman; George Moore believed that, by ancestry, he was a South Saxon – the very aspect of Sussex, he said, awakened in him "anti-natal instincts"; Yeats (heartened by the example of Carlyle, Stendhal, Balzac, Dostoevsky and Villiers de L'Isle Adam before him) laid claim to aristocratic descent, believing he had a right to be called the Duke of Ormonde.

man appealed to a generation in danger of being swamped by Darwinistic materialism, squalid urbanization, the "yellow" press, universal education, philanthropic sentimentality, and the democratic nonentity of "mass-man," all of which, together or separately, threatened to annul artistic activity and to bring the artist himself to self-contempt. Religiously, (and it must be remembered that Davidson, Ellis, Yeats, Shaw, and Orage were all trying to create, in Shaw's words, the iconography of a new religion), the superman was an acceptable substitute for a dispossessed deity, just as Nietzsche's Zarathustra was the new Moses, and his doctrines of eternal recurrence and the will to power the psychological equivalents of eternal life and heavenly grace: the superman was a knight-errant of the soul, who would reinstate the old religious values and reinvest man with the tragic dignity he had not known since the time of the Old Testament prophets. The superman stood as an assurance that man was not destined, in the words of Hermann Hesse, to be a "bourgeois compromise." The superman, unlike God, was not a transcendent being, and this recommended itself to the anthropomorphic vision exemplified, for example, in one of Yeats's "Two Songs from a Play": "Whatever flames upon the night / Man's own resinous heart has fed."

The superman was one of those myths which Sorel has called "not descriptions of things, but expressions of will"; and it was received by those who accepted it not in the intellectual sense, as a statement of belief, but symbolically, as an image of value. It is significant that Ellis, Yeats, Shaw, and Orage (Davidson having died in 1909) all sought different ways to maintain some hope in man's superhumanity even during and after the First World War: whereas those born in the shadow of that war, though their knowledge of Nietzsche was more extensive, were disillusioned enough to repudiate the superman as a panacea, and to welcome Nietzsche more for his searching diagnoses of the sick civilization in which he had so rightly predicted it would be their lot to live. The superman had begun to fade even before the outbreak of war, no longer exciting, in the words of T. W. Rolleston, "either reverence or revolt." Although Nietzsche, according to Rolleston, had been "a mighty prop and comfort to those who have felt that it is for great personalities to give law to the mob, not for the mob to give law to them,"[10] to sustain oneself on the superman after the war seemed, to many, to be squeezing blood from a stony fiction.

The aesthetics of Pater tended to assume an inevitable opposition between art and the way society was organized. Nietzsche, working in the tradition of Arnold, Ruskin, and Morris, broadened aesthetic enquiry, releasing it from the oppressively narrow confines which Pater, and later

Wilde, had imposed on it. Although Nietzsche granted art its own autonomy, he also stressed the vital relationship of art to life and society as a whole. He stood for civilization as opposed to aestheticism, and also, as Norman Douglas rightly saw, to socialism: "Progress is a centripetal movement, obliterating man in the mass. Civilisation is centrifugal: it permits, it postulates, the assertion of personality. The terms are therefore not synonymous. They stand for hostile and divergent movements. Progress subordinates. Civilisation co-ordinates. The individual emerges in civilisation. He is submerged in progress."[11] Nietzsche appealed to socialists because of his idealism, his vision of a new and better order of society, and because his emphasis on art reminded them of the dangers of Philistinism. This side of Nietzsche was also taken up by those who saw in socialism a development of nineteenth-century liberalism. The liberal possessed, in Yeats's words, "a levelling, rancorous, rational sort of mind,"[12] of which Bertrand Russell, with his "plebeian loquacity," was the detested epitome. Orage and Hulme had no difficulty in equating the social "anarchy" of liberal economic individualism with the stylistic "anarchy" of literary decadence.

In *The Reactionaries* (1966), John Harrison has discussed the anti-liberal, proto-fascist "tendencies" of Yeats, Lewis, Pound, Eliot, and Lawrence without laying sufficient stress on the extent to which their thinking derives from Nietzsche, particularly as it was presented in the *New Age*. The social, political, and cultural criticism of Ellis, Orage, Hulme, Lewis, and Eliot was indebted to Nietzsche for a workable definition of "decadence," not in terms of pathology, as in Nordau, but in terms of an "anarchy of atoms." What these later followers of Nietzsche sought to construct was a unity of style in every aspect of the national life. For these writers, an interest in politics was a by-product of the wish to find out what kind of society would best further the cause of learning and the arts. Political democracy had demonstrably resulted in a cultural decline. There was a new demand for authority on the cultural level, expressed by a re-emphasis, in criticism, on the value of "tradition," and by a swing in the literary theory and practice, towards the neo-classical virtues of coolness and precision. Whatever part Nietzsche may have played in the formulation of neo-classic doctrine, a part, it is suggested, that it would be unwise to underrate, his self-styled role of "physician of culture" certainly affected the tone of literary discussion between 1890 and 1914 – there is a great gulf between the impressionistic aestheticism of Pater and Wilde and the non-personal strictness of Eliot and Hulme. Under Nietzsche's influence the artist took it upon himself to act as the legislator of values for society, for the total cultural pattern; the superman, for example, tended during these years to lose a purely personal applicability and become, like the image of the dance, a sort of cultural and political ideogram, charged with hopes for the realization of a new "unity of being."

Ellis, Shaw, and Orage all sought, in various ways, to apply Nietzschean remedies to a sick culture and a sick society, to transvalue moribund values, to bring a heroic vision to an unheroic age. Of the creative writers, it was Yeats, and not Davidson or Shaw, who was most deeply affected by what he read, and he may be regarded as the chief beneficiary of the Nietzsche movement in England. As one of his critics has written: "It would be hard to think of any life which illustrates so strikingly as does Yeats's what Æ called the law of spiritual gravitation: the law according to which a personality attracts to itself the ideas, the symbols, and the experiences that it needs and is to need."[13] Yet all five writers, and others too, found in Nietzsche a wealth of materials with which to build, in Davidson's challenging words, "a new habitation for the imagination of man."

Notes & Bibliography

ABBREVIATIONS

CPBS *The Complete Prefaces of Bernard Shaw*, London: Paul Hamlyn, 1965.
CW   *The Complete Works of Friedrich Nietzsche*, edited by Dr. Oscar Levy. Translated by various hands. 18 vols. London: T. N. Foulis, 1909–13.
ES   *The Eagle and the Serpent*
EW   *Ethical World*
IJE   *International Journal of Ethics*
NA   *New Age*
NC   *Nietzsche as Critic, Philosopher, Poet and Prophet.* Compiled by Thomas Common. London: Grant Richards, 1901.
PN   *The Portable Nietzsche.* Edited and translated by Walter Kaufmann. New York: Viking Press, 1958.
TPW   *T.P.'s Weekly*
WBS   *The Works of Bernard Shaw*. 33 vols. London: Constable, 1930–38.

NOTES

I INTRODUCTION

1 *The Early H. G. Wells* (Manchester, 1961), 9.
2 *From Prophecy to Exorcism: The Premisses of Modern German Literature* (London, 1965), 28.
3 G. U. Ellis, *Twilight on Parnassus: A Survey of Post-War Fiction and Pre-War Criticism* (London, 1939), 226.
4 T. H. Gibbons, "Literary Criticism and the Intellectual Milieu: some aspects of the period 1880–1914 with particular reference to the literary and social criticism of Havelock Ellis and Alfred Orage," University of Cambridge dissertation, 1965, II, 11–12.
5 *Ibid.*, 15.
6 Leon Kellner, "Nietzsche in England," *Das literarische Echo* (June 1, 1914), 1174–6; Samuel Saenger, "Nietzsche in und über England," *Neue Rundschau* (Berlin), XXXV (1924), 1068–74; Gertrud von Petzold, "Nietzsche in englisch-americanischer Beurteilung bis zum Ausgang des Weltkrieges," *Anglia*, LIII (1929), 134–218, and *John Davidson und sein geistiges Werden unter dem Einflusse Nietzsches* (Leipzig, 1928); Paul Hultsch, "Das Denken Nietzsches in seiner Bedeutung für England," *Germanisch-Romanische Monatsschrift*, XXVI (September/October, 1938), 359–73. Hultsch states in a footnote that his article is only an extract from a more comprehensive study; a search for this study proved fruitless.
7 M. A. Morland, "Nietzsche and the Nineties," *Contemporary Review*, CXCIII (April, 1958), 209–12.
8 University of Michigan dissertation, 1962, iv.
9 LeRoy Culbertson Kauffmann, "The Influence of Friedrich Nietzsche on American Literature," University of Pennsylvania dissertation, 1963; Melvin Drimmer, "Nietzsche in American Thought, 1895–1925," University of Rochester dissertation, 1965.
10 Cf. Lionel Stevenson, *Darwin among the Poets* (Chicago, 1933), and Georg Roppen, *Evolution and Poetic Belief* (Oslo, 1956).

11 "Nature and Eternity," *Longman's Magazine*, XXVI (May, 1895), 48. This article was published posthumously.
12 E.g. Anna Balakian, "Influence and Literary Fortune: The Equivocal Junction of Two Methods," *Yearbook of Comparative and General Literature*, no. 11 (1962), 24–31.
13 George Brandes, *Friedrich Nietzsche* (London, 1914), 94. Nietzsche's letter is dated November 20, 1888.
14 André Morize, *Problems and Methods of Literary History* (Boston, 1922), 228.
15 Henri Peyre, "A Glance at Comparative Literature in America," *Yearbook of Comparative and General Literature*, I (1952), 8.
16 Balakian, "Influence and Literary Fortune," 29.
17 *Explorations* (London, 1962), 158.
18 "Reflections on Contemporary Poetry," *Egoist* (July, 1919), 59.
19 *The Journals of André Gide, 1889–1949* (New York, 1961), I, 326.
20 *Ibid.*, II, 30.
21 J. T. Shaw, "Literary Indebtedness and Comparative Literary Studies," in *Comparative Literature*, ed. Newton P. Stallknecht and Horst Frenz (Carbondale, 1961), 60.
22 "Nietzsche," *Albany Review*, III (April, 1908), 90.

II THE ENGLISH TRANSLATIONS OF NIETZSCHE

1 George Brandes, *Friedrich Nietzsche* (London, 1914), 64. Letter dated December 2, 1887.
2 Herman Scheffauer, "A Correspondence between Nietzsche and Strindberg," *North American Review*, CXCVIII (August, 1913), 198. Letter written November or December, 1888.
3 *Ibid.*, 203. Letter dated December 7, 1888.
4 "Some Recent Literature in France," *Contemporary Review*, LXXIV (December, 1898), 899.
5 "Friedrich Nietzsche," *To-morrow*, I (March, 1896), 161. Nietzsche's kinship to Bagehot is also noted (though perhaps not independently) by George Sampson, "Nietzsche," *Bookman*, XLVII (March, 1915), 173–5.
6 *PN*, 521.
7 *CW*, XII, 211.
8 *PN*, 474.
9 Cf. "Memories of Nietzsche," *Living Age*, CCCI (November 1, 1926), 272.
10 L. Huxley, *Life and Letters of Thomas Henry Huxley* (London, 1900), II, 360.
11 Quoted in advertisement in *To-morrow*, I (April, 1896).
12 "The Principles of Aesthetics," *To-morrow*, IV (December, 1897), 172–82; "The Old and New Nobility," *To-morrow*, IV (October, 1897), 29–35.
13 *The Case of Wagner*, transl. T. Common (London, 1896), xv–xvi.

14 *Ibid.*, xvii.
15 *Ibid.*, xix.
16 "The Case of Wagner," *Fortnightly Review*, LVIII (September, 1895), 367–79.
17 *Thus Spake Zarathustra*, transl. Alexander Tille (London, 1896), xiii–xiv.
18 *Ibid.*, xiv.
19 *Ibid.*, xvii.
20 *Ibid.*, xxii–xxiii.
21 *Ibid.*, xxiii.
22 *A Genealogy of Morals*, transl. W. Haussman (London, 1899), xiii.
23 *Ibid.*, xv.
24 *Ibid.*, xvi.
25 *Ibid.*, xvi–xvii.
26 *Degeneration* (London, 1913), 454.
27 *Ibid.*, 416.
28 *Ibid.*, 432.
29 *Ibid.*, 465.
30 *Ibid.*, 419.
31 *Ibid.*, 420.
32 Hugh E. M. Stutfield, "Tommyrotics," *Blackwood's Magazine*, CLVII (June, 1895), 838.
33 *Academy*, L (August 1, 1896), 75.
34 "The New Learning and Its Minor Prophets," *Saturday Review*, LXXXII (July 25, 1896), 89.
35 "A Philosophic 'Mr. Hyde,'" *Nation* (New York), LXII (June 11, 1896), 459.
36 "The Philosophy of Nietzsche," *Spectator*, LXXXII (June 17, 1899), 862.
37 *Academy*, L (August 1, 1896), 75.
38 "The New Learning and its Minor Prophets," 90.
39 "Nietzsche the Poet," *National Observer*, XVII (December 19, 1896), 134.
40 *Manchester Guardian* (July 14, 1896), 5.
41 "Nietzsche," *Times* (July 31, 1896), 3.
42 *Athenaeum* (November 7, 1896), 632.
43 *International Journal of Ethics*, VII (April, 1897), 369.
44 *Musical Studies* (London, 1905), 261, 277.
45 "Philosophy with the Hammer," *Academy*, LVII (July 8, 1899), 31.
46 "A Titanic Philosophy," *Pall Mall Gazette* (May 23, 1899), 4.
47 "Brimstone," *Pall Mall Gazette* (July 21, 1899), 4.
48 *Man's Place in the Cosmos* (London, 1902), 255. The articles originally appeared as "Friedrich Nietzsche: His Life and Works," *Blackwood's Magazine*, CLXII (October, 1897), 476–93; and "The Opinions of Friedrich Nietzsche," *Contemporary Review*, LXXIII (May, 1898), 727–50.
49 *Ibid.*, 254.
50 *Ibid.*, 278.
51 *Ibid.*, 278.

52 *Ibid.*, 276.
53 *Ibid.*, 285.
54 *Ibid.*, 319.
55 *Ibid.*, 254.
56 "Professor Seth's Attacks on Nietzsche," *University Magazine and Free Review*, XI (April, 1899), 49.
57 *Ibid.*, 50.
58 Bennet Hume, "Friedrich Nietzsche: His Life and Teaching," *London Quarterly Review*, XCIV (October, 1900), 338.
59 "Prof. Nietzsche," *Athenaeum* (September 1, 1900), 282.
60 "A Thinker and Poet," *Academy*, LXIV (February 21, 1903), 172.
61 "Nietzsche," *Academy*, LXIV (March 7, 1903), 234.
62 *Athenaeum* (March 7, 1903), 298.
63 "Nietzsche's Works in English," *Nation* (New York), LXXXII (March 29, 1906), 259.
64 "The Function of an Endowed Press," *Nation*, LXXXII (January 18, 1906), 50.
65 "Nietzsche's Works in English," 259.
66 "On Nietzsche Translations," *Nation*, LXXXII (April 26, 1906), 343.
67 *CW*, XVIII, x.
68 "Nietzsche," *Times Literary Supplement* (November 18, 1909), 433. The writer of this anonymous article was Mary Duclaux. A contributor to Oscar Wilde's *Woman's World*, Mary Duclaux was the friend of such "Nietzscheans" as George Moore, Vernon Lee, and Daniel Halévy. It was in her literary salon, according to Havelock Ellis, that he and Symons met Taine. See Ruth Van Z. Holmes, "Mary Duclaux (1856–1944): Primary and Secondary Checklists," *English Literature in Transition*, X, no. 1 (1967), 27–46.
69 *Saturday Review*, CVII (May 1, 1909), 568.
70 "Nietzsche and his Doctrine," *Westminster Gazette*, XXXIII (May 8, 1909), 4.
71 "Nietzsche," *Spectator*, CIII (December 4, 1909), 948.
72 "The Will to Power," *Nation*, IV (January 2, 1909), 547.
73 *CW*, XVIII, xx.
74 W. A. Ross, "Self-Assertion in Nietzsche," *Hibbert Journal*, VIII (January, 1910), 411.
75 Harold Brighouse, introduction to *The Works of Stanley Houghton* (London, 1914), xlv.
76 "The Genealogy of Morals," *English Review*, IX (August, 1911), 143.
77 "The Superman," *Times Literary Supplement* (May 23, 1912), 209.
78 *The Revival of Aristocracy* (London, 1906), xiii.
79 *CW*, XVIII, xiii.
80 *Ibid.*, xvi.
81 *Ibid.*, xvii.
82 *Ibid.*, xvii.

83 *Ibid.*, ix–x.
84 *Ibid.*, xx–xxi.
85 "Nietzsche Pioneers," *TPW*, XXI (June 6, 1913), 728.
86 "Nietzschean Business Blundering," *Good European Point of View*, no. 11 (Easter, 1914), 85.
87 "Uprightness or Unscrupulousness," *Good European Point of View*, no. 12 (Winter, 1915), 116.
88 H. Hamilton Fyfe, "The New Way of Life," *Daily Mail* (May 8, 1909), 8.
89 "The Philosophy of Friedrich Nietzsche," *Quarterly Review*, CCXVIII (January, 1913), 148–9.
90 *Ibid.*, 151.
91 *Ibid.*, 167.
92 "The Complete Nietzsche," *Bookman*, XLI (March, 1912), 310–11.
93 "The Literary Movement in Germany: Friedrich Nietzsche and His Influence," *Cosmopolis*, XII (October, 1898), 47.

III JOHN DAVIDSON

1 *A Leaf from the Yellow Book: The Correspondence of George Egerton*, ed. Terence de Vere White (London, 1958), 126.
2 Hugh E. M. Stutfield, "Tommyrotics," *Blackwood's Magazine*, CLVII (June, 1895), 838.
3 "The Tragedy of a Thinker," *Macmillan's Magazine*, LXXXI (December, 1899), 112–13.
4 "On Poetry," *Holiday and Other Poems* (London, 1906), 136.
5 *A Rosary* (London, 1903), 49, 50.
6 "Books in the Open," *Star* (March 10, 1898), 1.
7 *Self's the Man* (London, 1901), 79.
8 *The Testament of a Prime Minister* (London, 1904), 41–2.
9 "Without Compromise," *Westminster Gazette* (June 24, 1907), 2.
10 *ES*, no. 1 (February 15, 1898), 3.
11 *Ibid.*, 5.
12 *Ibid.*, 10.
13 *Academy*, LV (June 25, 1898), 687.
14 Quoted by George Woodcock and Ivan Avakomovic, *The Anarchist Prince: A Biographical Study of Peter Kropotkin* (London, 1950), 281.
15 *ES*, no. 1 (June 15, 1898), 48. Thomas Common discussed *Social Evolution* in the context of Nietzsche's work in "English Philosophers from Nietzsche's Standpoint: Benjamin Kidd," *To-morrow*, I (July, 1896), 40–8.
16 A series of articles, entitled "The Quintessence of Nietzsche's Antichrist," appeared in the *Secular Review and Secularist* in January and February, 1897, under the name of "Volcano"; an article by "E. MaCall" entitled "Nietzsche on Wagner and Bizet," *Musical Standard*, XI (June 10, 1899),

357–8, follows Barnhill's characteristic "enlightenment through quotation" method. The only bibliographical source for Barnhill is the letter "Friedrich Nietzsche in England," *TPW*, xxi (May 23, 1913), 662, which tells of his last illness in America.
17 Quoted by J. Benjamin Townsend, *John Davidson: Poet of Armageddon* (New Haven, 1961), 469. Davidson's letter (to Grant Richards) is dated December 13, 1903.
18 *A Rosary*, 132.
19 *ES*, no. 1 (September, 1898), 50–1.
20 *Darwin, Marx, Wagner* (Boston, 1941), 100–1.
21 Quoted by Townsend, *John Davidson*, 485. Letter dated December 24, 1900.
22 *The Last Ballad* (London, 1899), 105.
23 *Self's the Man*, 136.
24 *Holiday and Other Poems*, 155.
25 *Ibid.*, 73.
26 *The Testament of an Empire-Builder* (London, 1902), 80.
27 *Ibid.*, 61.
28 *PN*, 159.
29 *ES*, no. 11 (January–March, 1901), 23.
30 *Journal of the History of Ideas*, xviii (June, 1957), 411–29. For other studies relating Nietzsche to Davidson, see Lester, 411.
31 *Speaker* (November 28, 1891), 641. Brandes' lectures were, in fact, given in April and May, 1888.
32 *Ibid.*, 641.
33 "Littérature Étrangère: Frédéric Nietsche, le dernier métaphysicien," *Revue Bleue*, xlviii (November 7, 1891), 587.
34 "The New Sophist," *Speaker* (November 28, 1891), 642.
35 "Frédéric Nietsche," 592.
36 "The New Sophist," 642.
37 "Frederick Nietsche," *Glasgow Herald* (March 18, 1893), 4.
38 *Ibid.*, 4.
39 *Sentences and Paragraphs* (London, 1893), 84.
40 "Frédéric Nietsche," 586.
41 W. B. Yeats, *Autobiography* (New York, 1958), 212.
42 "On the Downs," *Speaker* (February 5, 1898), 179.
43 *A Rosary*, 182. Davidson insisted that he and Shaw (also supposedly influenced by Nietzsche) had no two ideas in common.
44 Quoted by Townsend, *John Davidson*, 373. Davidson's letter is dated June 9, 1906.
45 "A Poetic Disciple of Nietzsche," *Daily Chronicle* (May 23, 1902), 3. This letter also appeared in the *Academy*, lxii (June 14, 1902), 598.
46 *The Testament of an Empire-Builder*, 36–7.
47 *The Theatrocrat* (London, 1905), 29.

48 "On Poetry," *Holiday and Other Poems*, 137.
49 *Ibid.*, 143–4.
50 *A Rosary*, 60.
51 *The Theatrocrat*, 30–1.
52 *Ibid.*, 31.
53 *The Testament of a Vivisector* (London, 1901), 26–7.
54 *A Rosary*, 87.
55 *The Theatrocrat*, 35–6.
56 *Ibid.*, 27.
57 Quoted by Grant Richards, *Author Hunting: Memories of Years spent Mainly in Publishing* (London, 1960), 181. Shaw's letter to Richards is dated June 23, 1927.
58 *CPBS*, 532.
59 *CW*, XIII, 46.
60 *Ibid.*, VII, 99.
61 *Mammon and His Message* (London, 1908), 147.
62 "Poetry and the Something Behind Phenomena," *Speaker* (March 25, 1899), 346.
63 "Irony," *Speaker* (May 6, 1899), 523.
64 *A Rosary*, 88.
65 *The Triumph of Mammon* (London, 1907), 102, 103.
66 *The Testament of a Man Forbid* (London, 1901), 12.
67 *The Testament of a Prime Minister*, 86, 83.
68 *The Theatrocrat*, 166.
69 *The Triumph of Mammon*, 116.
70 *Mammon and His Message*, 149.
71 "On Poetry," *Holiday and Other Poems*, 136.
72 "Totnes and Salcombe," *Glasgow Herald* (May 11, 1907), 11.
73 "Tête-à-Tête; Froude, Carlyle," *Speaker* (June 17, 1899), 690.
74 *The Eighteen Nineties* (London, 1913), 230–1.
75 *Smith: A Tragic Farce* (London, 1888), 230.
76 *Diabolus Amans* (London, 1885), 139–40.
77 *Ballads and Songs* (London, 1894), 22.
78 *Fleet Street Eclogues* (London, 1896), 38.
79 *John Davidson*, 308.
80 *Self's the Man*, 177.
81 *The Triumph of Mammon*, 19.
82 *Ibid.*, 116.
83 *New Ballads* (London, 1896), 32–3.
84 *Fleet Street Eclogues*, 37. For Nietzsche's views on euthanasia, see *Human, All-Too-Human*, part I, aph. 80, and *The Wanderer and His Shadow*, aph. 185.
85 *Fleet Street Eclogues*, 41.

86 *The Testament of John Davidson* (London, 1908), 31.
87 *The Triumph of Mammon*, 120.
88 *Ibid.*, 99.
89 *The Theatrocrat*, 75–6.
90 "A Poetic Disciple of Nietzsche," 3.
91 *The Testament of John Davidson* (London, 1908), 12, 17–19.
92 Quoted by Townsend, *John Davidson*, 367. Davidson's letter is dated November 21, 1905.
93 *Ibid.*, 281.
94 "Autumnal London," *Glasgow Herald* (October 21, 1893), 7.
95 *The Triumph of Mammon*, 167.
96 *Ibid.*, 168.
97 *CW*, xiii, 56.
98 *The Testament of John Davidson*, 18–19.
99 Townsend, *John Davidson*, 9.
100 *The Theatrocrat*, 14–15.
101 *Ibid.*, 47.
102 "Tête-à-Tête: Froude, Carlyle," 690.
103 Lester, "Friedrich Nietzsche and John Davidson," 429.
104 *The Theatrocrat*, 5.
105 *The Island of Dr. Moreau* (London, 1927), 82.
106 See Davidson's letter to Archer, dated March 9, 1902, in Townsend, *John Davidson*, 303.
107 *The Sleeper Awakes* (London, 1927), 190.
108 *Ibid.*, 191.
109 Bernard Bergonzi, *The Early H. G. Wells* (Manchester, 1961), 152.
110 *Mankind in the Making* (London, 1903), 39.
111 *Star Begotten: A Biological Fantasia* (London, 1937), 184.
112 *Ibid.*, 87.
113 *New Ballads*, 40.
114 *Mammon and His Message*, 171.
115 *The Triumph of Mammon*, 151–2.
116 *Sentences and Paragraphs*, 16.
117 "A Poetic Disciple of Nietzsche," 3.
118 *The Theatrocrat*, 11.
119 "Through the Sieve," *Outlook* (February 25, 1905), 258.
120 *Mammon and His Message*, 148.
121 *Athenaeum* (August 30, 1902), 278.
122 "A Prophet of Nietzsche," *Academy*, lxii (June 7, 1902), 572. A thoroughly "Davidsonian" view of the superman is given by Heinrich Goebel and Ernst Antrim, "Friedrich Nietzsche's Übermensch," *Monist*, ix (July, 1898), 563–71.

123 *The Real Robert Louis Stevenson and Other Critical Essays* (New York, 1959), 106.
124 *Poets of the Younger Generation* (London, 1902), 143.
125 "The Supergod," *Academy*, LXXV (November 7, 1908), 440.
126 J. Kenneth Mozley, "Modern Attacks on Christian Ethics," *Contemporary Review*, XCIII (April, 1908), 432–3.
127 *Morning Leader* (November 24, 1905), 4.
128 *NA*, XIII (July 10, 1913), 297. Harris's essay on Davidson appeared in *Contemporary Studies: First Series* (New York, n.d.), 119–46.
129 *Athenaeum* (March 18, 1905), 329.
130 *Academy*, LXXII (April 27, 1907), 408.
131 *Times Literary Supplement* (May 14, 1908), 156.
132 Cf. "The Adoration of Matter," *Daily News* (December 21, 1905), 4.
133 "The Last Testament," *Daily News* (June 15, 1909), 4.
134 *CW*, XVIII, xxi.
135 *English Literature, 1880–1905* (London, 1912), 314.
136 "John Davidson," *Frankfurter Zeitung* (April 2, 1913), 1.
137 *Periods of European Literature*, XII: *The Later Nineteenth Century* (New York, 1907), 242.
138 *English Literature: An Illustrated Record* (London, 1903), II, 173.
139 Hayim Fineman, *John Davidson: A Study of the Relation of His Ideas to His Poetry* (Philadelphia, 1916), 32.
140 *Ibid.*, 31–2.
141 *Athenaeum* (August 22, 1908), 202.
142 Henry Bett, *Studies in Literature* (London, 1929), 163.
143 Townsend, *John Davidson*, 488.
144 Lester, "Friedrich Nietzsche and John Davidson," 428–9.
145 *The Theatrocrat*, 33.
146 *A Rosary*, 190.
147 *Ibid.*, 88.

IV HAVELOCK ELLIS

1 "The Soul of Man under Socialism," *Fortnightly Review*, XLIX (February, 1891), 293.
2 *The New Spirit* (London, 1890), 18.
3 *The Task of Social Hygiene* (London, 1912), 394. This chapter is reprinted from "Individualism and Socialism," *Contemporary Review*, CI (April, 1912), 519–28.
4 *The Task of Social Hygiene*, 393.
5 In particular, *International Journal of Ethics* (founded in 1890) and *Ethical World* (founded in 1898). Both reviewed translations of Nietzsche's work, and contained from time to time original articles about it. See Charles Bake-

well, "The Teachings of Friedrich Nietzsche," *IJE*, IX (April, 1899), 314–31; Alfred Fouillée, "The Ethics of Nietzsche and Guyau," *IJE*, XIII (October, 1902), 13–27; Mabel Atkinson, "The Struggle for Existence in Relation to Morals and Religion," *IJE*, XVIII (April, 1908), 291–311; A. C. Pigou, "The Ethics of Nietzsche," *IJE*, XVIII (April, 1908), 343–55; W. Libby, "Two Fictitious Ethical Types," *IJE*, XVIII (July, 1908), 466–75; Alfred W. Benn, "The Morals of an Immoralist – Friedrich Nietzsche," *IJE*, XIX (October, 1908), 1–23, and *IJE*, XIX (January, 1909), 192–211; Herbert Stewart, "Some Criticisms on the Nietzsche Revival," *IJE*, XIX (July, 1909), 427–43; "The Early Life and Teachings of Nietzsche," *EW*, II (November 11, 1899), 707–9; "Nietzsche's Doctrine of the 'Higher Man,' " *EW*, II (November 18, 1899), 724–5; "The Ethics of Nietzsche," *EW*, II (November 25, 1899), 742–3; "The Ideal of Human Excellence," *EW*, II (December 30, 1899), 820–1; and Thomas Common, "A Defence of Nietzsche," *EW*, III (January 27, 1900), 53–4.

6 "The Fabian Society," Fabian Tract no. 41 (London, 1892), 3.
7 Quoted by Houston Peterson, *Havelock Ellis: Philosopher of Love* (Boston, 1928), 139.
8 "Individualism in Masquerade," *Seedtime*, no. 4 (October, 1890), 11.
9 G. Harry Roberts, "Acts not Words," *Seedtime*, no. 19 (January, 1894), 3.
10 *Questions of Our Day* (London, 1936), 60.
11 "Morality under Socialism," *Albany Review*, I (September, 1907), 629. Reprinted under the title of "The New Morality" in Carpenter's *Civilisation: Its Cause and Cure* (London, 1921), 243–64.
12 *Three Modern Seers* (London, 1910), 7. The chapter on Nietzsche also appeared in *Forum* (New York), XLIV (October, 1910), 425–38.
13 Quoted by Havelock Ellis, *My Life* (London, 1940), 358. Letter dated September 7, 1909.
14 *Three Modern Seers*, 170. Three earlier references were to pp. 158, 170 and 167–8 respectively.
15 "The Ethics of Tolstoy and Nietzsche," *IJE*, XI (October, 1900), 93.
16 *Ibid.*, 105. Two earlier references were to pp. 98 and 102 respectively.
17 *Encyclopaedia of Religion and Ethics*, ed. J. M. Hastings (New York, 1917), IX, 370.
18 *Ibid.*, 370.
19 *The Task of Social Hygiene*, 404–5.
20 *The New Spirit*, 9.
21 *Affirmations* (London, 1898), 9. For a documented view that Nietzsche was not a Schopenhauerian misogynist, see H. Lichtenberger, "Quelques Lettres inédites de Nietzsche," *Cosmopolis*, VI (May, 1897), 460–74.
22 *Discords* (London, 1894), 241.
23 *Keynotes* (London, 1893), 23.
24 *Ibid.*, 63.

25 *Three Modern Seers*, 183–4.
26 *Ibid.*, 185.
27 Dora B. Montefiore, "Nietzsche's Teaching on Women and War," *Reformer*, v (February 15, 1901), 82. The two subsequent references are to pp. 83 and 85 respectively.
28 *My Life*, 75.
29 *Savoy*, no. 2 (April, 1896), 79–94; *Savoy*, no. 3 (July, 1896), 68–81; *Savoy*, no. 4 (August, 1896), 57–63. Advertisements of the Nietzsche translations accompanied the July and August numbers.
30 *Affirmations*, 1–2.
31 *Ibid.*, 14.
32 "Kultur," *New Statesman*, IV (January 2, 1915), 316.
33 *Affirmations*, 35.
34 *Ibid.*, 40.
35 *Ibid.*, 46.
36 *Ibid.*, 43–4.
37 *Ibid.*, 23.
38 *Ibid.*, 21.
39 *Ibid.*, 21.
40 *Ibid.*, 68.
41 *Ibid.*, 72.
42 *Ibid.*, 71.
43 *Ibid.*, 83.
44 *Ibid.*, 65.
45 *Ibid.*, 78.
46 *Impressions and Comments* (London, 1914), 81. Entry for February 8, 1913.
47 *Affirmations*, 69.
48 *Ibid.*, 85.
49 Quoted in *Savoy*, no. 3 (July, 1896), 106.
50 "Dogmatisms," *Academy*, LIII (February 26, 1898), 226.
51 "Nietzsche," *Academy*, LVI (August 27, 1898), 195. This brief outline is followed by "A Nietzsche Breviary," a selection of miscellaneous aphorisms which also appeared in the New York *Bookman*, VIII (October, 1898), 153.
52 *Athenaeum* (January 8, 1898), 44.
53 *IJE*, IX (October, 1898), 128.
54 J. G. Robertson, "Friedrich Nietzsche and His Influence," *Book Lover* (Winter, 1899), 144–51 – an article which appeared also in *Cosmopolis*, XII (October, 1898), 31–48; Oswald Crawfurd, "Nietzsche, an Appreciation," *Nineteenth Century*, XLVIII (October, 1900), 592–606.
55 M. A. Morland, "Nietzsche and the Nineties," *Contemporary Review*, CXCIII (April, 1958), 212.
56 *Nietzsche* (Cambridge, Mass., 1941), 191n.

57 *Views and Reviews, First Series: 1884–1919* (London, 1932), 148–9.
58 *Ibid.*, 152.
59 *Ibid.*, 153.
60 See Wilfred Scawen Blunt, *My Diaries* (London, 1932), 346–7, and The Earl of Lytton, *Wilfred Scawen Blunt* (London, 1961), 15; F. E. Hardy, *The Life of Thomas Hardy, 1840–1928* (Toronto, 1962), 315, 364, and E. Brennecke, *Life and Art by T. Hardy* (New York, 1925), 137–9; and William Archer, "Fighting a Philosophy," *North American Review*, CCI (January, 1915), 30–44. This last item also appeared as an Oxford pamphlet.
61 *Encyclopaedia of Religion and Ethics*, IX, 368.
62 *Ibid.*, 369.
63 *The New Spirit*, 33.
64 "The Making of the Superman," *Speaker*, IX (October 17, 1903), 61.
65 *Views and Reviews, First Series*, 207.
66 *Ibid.*, 206.
67 *Ibid.*, 209.
68 *The Dance of Life* (London, 1923), 88.
69 *Views and Reviews, First Series*, 194.
70 *Ibid.*, 200–1.
71 *Affirmations*, 65.
72 *Encyclopaedia of Religion and Ethics*, IX, 368–9.
73 Cf. *Human, All-Too-Human*, aph. 224; *The Gay Science*, aphs, 349, 357; *Beyond Good and Evil*, aph. 253; and *The Will to Power*, aphs. 647–51, 684–5.
74 "Gregariousness in Cattle and in Men," *MacMillan's Magazine*, XXIII (February, 1871), 357.
75 *The Problem of Race-Regeneration* (London, 1911), 63.
76 *Affirmations*, 79.
77 *Ibid.*, 47.
78 *CW*, XVIII, xxxv.
79 *The Grammar of Life* (London, 1908), 44.
80 "Eugenics and the Superman: A Racial Science, and a Racial Religion," *Eugenics Review*, I (October, 1909), 190.
81 *Ibid.*, 185.
82 J. A. Lindsay, "Eugenics and the Doctrine of the Super-Man," *Eugenics Review*, VII (January, 1916), 247–62.
83 *Views and Reviews, First Series*, 235–46.
84 *Affirmations*, 73–4.
85 *Ibid.*, 74.
86 *The Task of Social Hygiene*, 391–2.
87 *Ibid.*, 401.
88 *Ibid.*, 308.
89 *Ibid.*, 402–3.

90 *The Dance of Life*, 105.
91 *Ibid.*, 105.
92 "A New Aristocracy," *My Confessional* (London, 1934), 158.
93 *Encyclopaedia of Religion and Ethics*, ix, 369.
94 *Views and Reviews, Second Series: 1920–1932* (London, 1932), 111–12.
95 *The New Spirit* (London, 1926), vii–viii.
96 *The Dance of Life*, 261.
97 *Affirmations*, 62. Cf. *The Dawn of Day*, aph. 240.
98 *Views and Reviews, First Series*, 52.
99 *Affirmations*, 175.
100 *Ibid.*, 176.
101 *Ibid.*, 187.
102 *Ibid.*, 176–7.
103 *CW*, vi, 335.
104 Quoted by Isaac Goldberg, *Havelock Ellis: A Bibliographical and Critical Survey* (London, 1926), 135.
105 *Ibid.*, 71.
106 *Views and Reviews, Second Series*, 207.
107 *The Dance of Life*, x–xi.
108 *Ibid.*, 61.
109 *Vital Lies* (London, 1912), ii, 153. Vernon Lee's article, "Nietzsche and the Will to Power," *North American Review*, clxxix (December, 1904) 842–59, was reprinted in *Gospels of Anarchy* (London, 1908), 159–89.

V NIETZSCHE AND THE LITERARY MIND

1 *CW*, xviii, xxv–xxvi.
2 *Autobiography* (New York, 1958), 216.
3 *Ibid.*, 218.
4 *Affirmations* (London, 1898), 76.
5 *Ibid.*, 76.
6 *Thus Spake Zarathustra* (London, 1933), xvi.
7 *Letters from Aubrey Beardsley to Leonard Smithers*, ed. R. A. Walker (London, 1937), letter no. 67. Letter dated October 4, 1896.
8 *Last Letters of Aubrey Beardsley* (London, 1904), 22. Letter dated October 5, 1896.
9 "Nietzsche," *Outlook*, iii (July 8, 1899), 747. This review was reprinted in *Friday Nights: Literary Criticisms and Appreciations, First Series* (London, 1922), 3–12. In another review Garnett explains the reasons for English neglect of Nietzsche and the sources of Nietzsche's abiding value. "Nietzsche in English," *Daily News* (October 16, 1907), 4.
10 *Self-Portrait* (London, 1939), 43–4. See also the entry recording Ricketts' disillusionment over *Zarathustra*, 249.
11 *Flower o' the Thorn* (London, 1908), 130. For a later poem on Nietzsche,

see Auden's *New Year Letter* (London, 1941), 96.
12 Quoted from Payne's table talk in 1912 by Thomas Wright, *The Life of John Payne* (London, 1919), 242. George Gissing also read Nietzsche in German. Cf. *The Letters of George Gissing to Edouard Bertz, 1887–1903*, ed. A. C. Young (London, 1961), 228, 282–3.
13 *Letters from Edward Thomas to Gordon Bottomley*, ed. R. George Thomas (London, 1968), 152, 154. The letters are dated December 26, 1907 and January 15, 1908.
14 "Nietzsche," *Bookman* (June, 1909), 140.
15 *Ibid.*, 140.
16 *Periods of European Literature* (London, 1904–7), XII, 240.
17 Alfred W. Benn, "The Morals of an Immoralist," *IJE*, XIX (October, 1908), 8.
18 *Fortnightly Review*, LXV (March, 1899), 390–400.
19 *Oxford Lectures on Poetry* (London, 1909), 69.
20 *From Religion to Philosophy* (London, 1912), 111n.
21 F. J. Hoffman, Charles Allen, Carolyn F. Ulrich, *The Little Magazine: A History and a Bibliography* (Princeton, 1947), 73.
22 Quoted by R. H. Mottram, *For Some We Loved* (London, 1956), 69. From a letter dated May 5, 1905. Two pages later Mottram gives Galsworthy's considered view of Nietzsche. See also Galsworthy's defence of Nietzsche's individualism, "Second Thoughts on This War," *Scribner's Magazine*, LIX (January, 1916), 21.
23 *The Art of Reading* (New York, 1930), 205.
24 Margery M. Morgan, "Shaw, Yeats, Nietzsche, and the Religion of Art," *Komos*, I (March, 1967), 24–34.
25 F. N. Lees, "T. S. Eliot and Nietzsche," *Notes and Queries*, XI (September 9, 1964), 386–7. The Apollonian/Dionysian distinction has proved its usefulness in modern critical explorations. Cf. James Dresser Allen, "The Apollonian-Dionysian Conflict in the Works of Wyndham Lewis," *Dissertation Abstracts*, XXII (1961–2), 3196–7; Joseph N. Riddel, "A Streetcar Named Desire – Nietzsche Descending," *Modern Drama*, V (February, 1963), 421–30; R. E. Hughes, "Jane Eyre: The Unbaptized Dionysian," *Nineteenth Century Fiction*, XVIII (September, 1963), 347–64; and William R. Brashear, "Tennyson's Tragic Vitalism: *Idylls of the King*," *Victorian Poetry*, VI (Spring, 1968), 29–49. Its significance for philosophy was pointed out by Mary L. Coolidge, "Ethics – Apollonian and Dionysian," *Journal of Philosophy*, XXXVIII (August 14, 1941), 449–65.
26 Quoted by Anthony Rhodes, *The Poet as Superman: A Life of Gabriele D'Annunzio* (London, 1959), 48.
27 *Ibid.*, 77.
28 *Studies in Prose and Verse* (London, 1904), 174.
29 "Nietzsche on Tragedy," *Academy*, LXIII (August 30, 1902), 220.
30 *The New Spirit* (London, 1926), 4.

31 *Affirmations*, 77.
32 *Autobiography*, 201.
33 *Studies in Seven Arts* (London, 1924), 209.
34 *Athenaeum* (March 7, 1903), 298. Sections of this review were incorporated in the introduction to Symons' *William Blake*, which appeared in 1907.
35 Cf. Rémy de Gourmont, "Nietzsche sur la Montagne," *Revue du Nouveau Siècle* (March 15, 1902).
36 *The Letters of W. B. Yeats*, ed. Allan Wade (London, 1954), 93. Letter dated November 14, 1888.
37 *William Blake* (London, 1907), 1. This introduction, under the title of "Blake et Nietzsche," was reprinted in French in *Fontaine*, XI (May, 1947), 236–44, and French Nietzsche scholars soon took advantage of it. Cf. Albert Maillet, "Blake et Nietzsche," in *Nietzsche, 1844–1900: Etudes et témoignages du cinquantenaire* (Paris, 1950), 143–71.
38 *Confessions of a Young Man* (New York, 1959), 132.
39 *Ibid.*, 146.
40 E.g. "Nietzsche and Culture," *Contemporary Review*, CVI (November, 1914), 674–80; "Nietzsche, Wagner and Others," *New Statesman*, IV (February 20, 1915), 486–7; and "The Best Book on Nietzsche," *New Statesman*, XIII (June 28, 1919), 318–20. See also *The German Doctrine of Conquest* (London and Dublin, 1914), *passim*, and "Count Arthur of Gobineau: Race-Mystic," *Contemporary Review*, CIV (July, 1913), 94–103.
41 *Letters of George Moore to John Eglinton* (Bournemouth, 1942), 23–4. Letter dated July 27, 1914.
42 T. W. H. Rolleston in Charles H. Rolleston, *Portrait of an Irishman* (London, 1939), 39. Letter dated March 9, 1905.
43 *Hail and Farewell: Salve* (London, 1937), 122.
44 Malcolm Brown, *George Moore: A Reconsideration* (Seattle, 1955), 58.
45 Marvin Magalaner, "Joyce, Nietzsche, and Hauptmann in James Joyce's 'A Painful Case,'" *PMLA*, LXVIII (March, 1953), 95–102. Some of his ideas for "A Painful Case" were taken by Joyce from his brother's diary. See Stanislaus Joyce, *My Brother's Keeper* (London, 1958), 165–6.
46 *Anglo-Irish Essays* (Dublin, 1917), 91. Subsequent quotations are from this essay, which originally appeared in *Dana*, no. 6 (October, 1904), 182–8.

VI WILLIAM BUTLER YEATS

1 *Essays and Introductions* (London, 1960), 130.
2 *The Identity of Yeats* (London, 1954), 91, 92.
3 *The Letters of W. B. Yeats*, ed. Allan Wade (London, 1954), 402.
4 *Ibid.*, 403.
5 "A Canonical Book," *Bookman*, XXIV (May, 1903), 68.
6 Quoted by David H. Greene and Edward M. Stephens, *J. M. Synge: 1871–1909* (New York, 1961), 232. Letter dated January 21, 1907.

7 *Autobiography* (New York, 1958), 346. The idea is a common one in *Thus Spake Zarathustra.*
8 *Ibid.*, 321.
9 *Essays and Introductions*, 389. For the idea in Nietzsche, cf. *PN*, 230.
10 *Letters*, 650.
11 *W. B. Yeats and T. Sturge Moore: Their Correspondence 1901–1937*, ed. Ursula Bridge (New York, 1953), 103; and Yeats's essay on Bishop Berkeley, *Essays and Introductions*, 407.
12 *Explorations* (London, 1962), 247.
13 *Letters*, 773. Is Yeats confusing Rapallo with Mentone? Cf. Daniel Halévy, *The Life of Friedrich Nietzsche* (London, 1911), 288.
14 *Nietzsche as Critic, Philosopher, Poet and Prophet*, ed. Thomas Common (London, 1901), xx.
15 *Explorations*, 162.
16 *NC*, 109–10.
17 *Autobiography*, 334.
18 *NC*, 110.
19 *Ibid.*, 111.
20 *Autobiography*, 264.
21 *NC*, 129.
22 *Ibid.*, 111.
23 *Ibid.*, 130–1.
24 Sir Herbert Grierson, Preface to V. K. Narayana Menon, *The Development of W. B. Yeats* (Edinburgh, 1942), x.
25 *Autobiography*, 333.
26 Quoted by Joseph Hone, *The Life of W. B. Yeats* (London, 1942), 365.
27 *NC*, 132.
28 *Ibid.*, 133.
29 *Ibid.*, 133.
30 *Explorations*, 424.
31 *NC*, 133–4.
32 *Ibid.*, 134.
33 *Ibid.*, 135.
34 *Ibid.*, 135.
35 *Explorations*, 24.
36 *Letters*, 812.
37 *NC*, 193.
38 *Autobiography*, 99.
39 *Ibid.*, 100.
40 *Explorations*, 20–1.
41 *CW*, ix, 387.
42 *Ibid.*, xiii, 29.
43 A. Norman Jeffares, *W. B. Yeats, Man and Poet* (New Haven, 1949), 152.

44 *Yeats and the Heroic Ideal* (New York, 1965), 21.
45 *The Identity of Yeats*, 96.
46 *Yeats's Iconography* (London, 1960), 177.
47 Quoted by Richard J. Loftus, *Nationalism in Modern Anglo-Irish Poetry* (Madison and Milwaukee, 1964), 237.
48 *Letters*, 873.
49 *Autobiography*, 321.
50 *PN*, 139.
51 *Explorations*, 269.
52 *Ibid.*, 269.
53 Honoré de Balzac, *Catherine de Medici*, translated by Katharine Prescott Wormeley (Boston, 1894), 6.
54 *Ibid.*, 415.
55 *Ibid.*, 18.
56 *Explorations*, 162.
57 Richard Ellmann, *Yeats: The Man and the Masks* (London, 1949), 181.
58 *Letters to his Son W. B. Yeats, and Others, 1869–1922* (London, 1944), 97.
59 *Ibid.*, 41.
60 *Ibid.*, 117.
61 *Ibid.*, 135.
62 *Autobiography*, 306.
63 "A Canonical Book," 68.
64 *The Letters of Ezra Pound*, ed. D. D. Paige (New York, 1950), 172n.
65 *Explorations*, 392.
66 *PN*, 115.
67 *Ibid.*, 124.
68 *CW*, vii, 78.
69 *Autobiography*, 349, 350.
70 *Explorations*, 393. In *Samhain* for 1903 Yeats decks himself out in the Zarathustrian robes of the idol-smasher. See *Explorations*, 120–1.
71 *PN*, 170.
72 *Ibid.*, 226.
73 *NC*, 134.
74 *CW*, xv, 291.
75 *Ibid.*, xvi, 80–1.
76 *The Oxford Book of Modern Verse* (Oxford, 1936), xxxiv.
77 *Autobiography*, 132.
78 Quoted by Ellmann, *Yeats: The Man and the Masks*, 6.
79 *Essays and Introductions*, 321. But cf. the chapter on "War" in Ruskin's *The Crown of Wild Olive*.
80 *CW*, xvii, 25.
81 *Ibid.*, 134.
82 *Ibid.*, ix, 388.

83 *Ibid.*, xv, 222.
84 *Autobiography*, 340.
85 *A Vision* (New York, 1961), 127.
86 *Letters*, 402, 403.
87 Preface to *Poems, 1899–1905* (London, 1906), xii–xiii.
88 *Letters*, 469.
89 *CW*, vi, 70.
90 *Ibid.*, xii, 54–5. Cf. *The Wanderer and His Shadow*, aphs. 105, 175.
91 *Yeats: The Man and the Masks*, 93.
92 *CW*, xii, 141.
93 Quoted in *Scattering Branches*, ed. Stephen Gwynn (New York, 1940), 196.
94 *Autobiography*, 323. For an earlier use of the mirror image see *Explorations*, 149–50, 151.
95 *Autobiography*, 323.
96 *Mythologies* (London, 1959), 333–4.
97 *Explorations*, 376.
98 *Ibid.*, 436, 435, 412.
99 *CW*, v, 81.
100 *Explorations*, 441–2. Cf. *CW*, v, 19, 57.
101 *The Research Magnificent* (London, 1915), 109.
102 *Autobiography*, 333.
103 *CW*, xvii, 54.
104 *Letters on Poetry from W. B. Yeats to Dorothy Wellesley* (New York, 1940), 126.
105 *Essays* (New York, 1924), 399.
106 *CW*, xiii, 124.
107 Zwerdling, *Yeats and the Heroic Ideal*, 178.

VII GEORGE BERNARD SHAW

1 *English Literature, 1880–1905* (London, 1912), 201.
2 *The Philosophy of Nietzsche*, ed. Geoffrey Clive (New York, 1965), xx.
3 B. W. Downs, "Anglo-Norwegian Literary Relations, 1867–1900," *Modern Language Review*, xlvii (October, 1952), 480.
4 H. H. Boyesen, *Essays on Scandinavian Literature* (London, 1895), 214.
5 Preface to *Major Barbara*, CPBS (London, 1965), 117.
6 "Nietzsche in English," *Saturday Review*, lxxxi (April 11, 1896), 374.
7 "Giving the Devil His Due," supplement to the *Saturday Review*, lxxxvii (May 13, 1899), iii. These ideas reappear in the 1900 preface to *Three Plays for Puritans* in the section headed "On Diabolonian Ethics."
8 "The Quintessence of Ibsenism," WBS, xix, 45.
9 *Ibid.*, 159.
10 "The Position of Ibsen," *Literature*, ii (1898), 335.
11 "Music: *Der Ring des Nibelungen*," *Athenaeum* (August 12, 1876), 219.

12 "Nietzsche Unveiled," *Musical Times*, LVI (September 1, 1915), 525.
13 *Ibid.*, 528.
14 *Man's Place in the Cosmos* (London and Edinburgh, 1902), 265–6.
15 *A Study of Wagner* (London, 1899), 385. For a full discussion of Newman's views, see Roger Hollinrake, "Nietzsche, Wagner, and Ernest Newman," *Music and Letters*, XLI (July, 1960), 245–55.
16 "Wagner and Nietzsche," *Saturday Review*, XC (October 13, 1900), 457–8.
17 "Nietzsche and French Music," *Saturday Review*, CI (March 3, 1906), 266.
18 "Giving the Devil His Due," iii.
19 "Nietzsche in English," 374.
20 *The Perfect Wagnerite*, WBS, XIX, 225.
21 *Ibid.*, 212.
22 *Ibid.*, 227.
23 Arthur Johnstone, *Musical Criticisms* (Manchester, 1905), 213. This article, "Nietzsche and Wagner," originally appeared in 1896.
24 *Ibid.*, 215–16.
25 Maurice Todhunter, "Arthur Schopenhauer," *Westminster Review*, CXLIII (March, 1895), 364.
26 Michael Field, *Works and Days* (London, 1933), 93, 94.
27 W. Caldwell, "Schopenhauer and Present Tendencies," *New World*, IX (December, 1900), 643.
28 "Prof. Nietzsche," *Athenaeum* (September 1, 1900), 281–2.
29 "Wagner and Schopenhauer," *Fortnightly Review*, LXV (March, 1899), 413–32.
30 Respectively William Hirsch, *Genius and Degeneration* (London, 1897); and A. E. Hake, *Regeneration: A Reply to Max Nordau* (London, 1896).
31 Milton Foster, "The Reception of Max Nordau's *Degeneration* in England and America," University of Michigan dissertation, 1954, 279–80.
32 A. M. Ludovici, "The Case of Nietzsche," *NA*, VIII (March 30, 1911), 527.
33 *Degeneration* (London, 1913), 456.
34 "Nietzsche in English," 373. Subsequent references are to p. 374 of this article.
35 "Giving the Devil His Due," iii.
36 Preface to *Parents and Children*, *CPBS*, 100.
37 "Mr. Bernard Shaw Explains His Religion," *Freethinker*, XXVIII (October 1, 1908), 689.
38 *ES*, no. 2 (April 15, 1898), 21.
39 *Ibid.*, 27.
40 *NC*, lxv.
41 "Nietzsche's Works in English," *Nation* (New York), LXXXII (March 29, 1906), 259.
42 Archibald Henderson, *George Bernard Shaw: His Life and Works* (London, 1911), 477.

43 Preface to *Parents and Children*, CPBS, 69.
44 Preface to *Androcles and the Lion*, CPBS, 591.
45 Henderson, *Shaw*, 479.
46 "Our Book-shelf," *Fabian News*, xvii (April, 1907), 37.
47 Henderson, *Shaw*, 477–8.
48 Preface to *Back to Methuselah*, CPBS, 501. Cf. the epistle dedicatory to *Man and Superman*, WBS, x, ix–xl.
49 "The Quintessence of Ibsenism," 38n.
50 Quoted in Vincent H. Brome, *Six Studies in Quarreling* (London, 1958), 14.
51 C. Archer, *William Archer: Life, Work and Friendships* (London, 1931), 391.
52 Martin Ellehauge, *The Position of Bernard Shaw in European Philosophy and Art* (Copenhagen, 1931), 362.
53 *G.B.S. and Germany: The Major Aspects* (Ann Arbor, Michigan, 1957), 63. A recent attempt to parallel the two writers is Carl Levine's "Social Criticism of Shaw and Nietzsche," *Shaw Review*, x (1967), 9–17.
54 Preface to *Back to Methuselah*, CPBS, 527.
55 WBS, x, xxxi.
56 *Ibid.*, x.
57 CW, viii, 189.
58 *Ibid.*, xvii, 23.
59 Quoted by A. K. Rogers, "Mr. Bernard Shaw's Philosophy," *Hibbert Journal*, viii (July, 1910), 826.
60 WBS, x, 177–8.
61 Henderson, *Shaw*, 217.
62 Preface to *Back to Methuselah*, CPBS, 542.
63 Preface to *Three Plays for Puritans*, CPBS, 746.
64 Henrik Ibsen, *The Emperor and the Galilean* (London, 1876), 56.
65 CW, xv, 380.
66 Preface to *Three Plays for Puritans*, CPBS, 744.
67 "The Quintessence of Ibsenism," 59.
68 Shaw, *The Future of Religion* (Cambridge, 1911), 7–8.
69 WBS, ix, 212.
70 Preface to *The Sanity of Art*, CPBS, 802–3.
71 Preface to *Back to Methuselah*, CPBS, 520. Cf. Ludovici's similar attitude to Darwin in "Nietzsche and Science," *Spectator* (January 8, 1910), 52.
72 "The Perfect Wagnerite," 227.
73 Preface to *Back to Methuselah*, CPBS, 546.
74 WBS, x, 134–5.
75 *Ibid.*, xl.
76 *Ibid.*, 180.
77 *Ibid.*, 180.
78 *Ibid.*, 178.

79 *Ibid.*, 112.
80 Shaw, *Sixteen Self Sketches* (London, 1949), 115.
81 *CW*, XVI, 129.
82 *ES*, no. 18 (September, 1902), 69.
83 *WBS*, x, 188.
84 See Julian B. Kaye, *Bernard Shaw and the Nineteenth-Century Tradition* (Norman, 1958), 151. Kaye has some remarks on Nietzsche, 100–8, and *passim*.
85 *WBS*, x, 190.
86 *Ibid.*, 210.
87 Eric Bentley, *Bernard Shaw: A Reconsideration* (Norfolk, Conn., 1947), 56.
88 Preface to *Back to Methuselah*, *CPBS*, 536.
89 *CW*, XIII, 44.
90 Robert Brustein, *The Theatre of Revolt* (Boston, 1964), 202–3.
91 *CW*, XII, 220.
92 *Sixteen Self Sketches*, 78.
93 *WBS*, x, 181.
94 *Ibid.*, 181.
95 *CW*, XII, 209. I owe this observation to Kaye, *Bernard Shaw*, 103–4.
96 *Ibid.*, II, 22.
97 "A Spoke in Shaw's Wheel," *NA*, VII (July 7, 1910), 230.
98 Introduction to *Thus Spake Zarathustra* (London, 1933), xvii.
99 Stephen Graham, *Part of the Wonderful Scene: An Autobiography* (London, 1964), 13. A short, rather rapturous account of Nietzsche's attempts to reconcile the superman with the eternal recurrence will be found, under the title "The Phenomenon of Friedrich Nietzsche," in Graham's *The Death of Yesterday* (London, 1930), 147–51.
100 "Sham and Super-Sham," *Blackwood's Magazine*, CLXXXI (June, 1907), 827.
101 "Musings without Method," *Blackwood's Magazine*, CLXXIV (October, 1903), 533, 534.
102 *The Poetry and Philosophy of George Meredith* (London, 1906), 158.
103 Quoted by Eric Bentley, *Bernard Shaw* (London, 1950), 39–40.
104 G. Spiller, "Super-Man or Super-Society?" *Ethical World*, III (July 15, 1909), 100.
105 J. Kenneth Mozley, "Modern Attacks on Christian Ethics," *Contemporary Review*, XCIII (April, 1908), 435.
106 "Mr. Campbell's New Theology," *Westminster Gazette*, XXIX (March 20, 1907), 2.
107 *All Manner of Folk* (London, 1912), 206.
108 "The Making of the Superman," *In Peril of Change* (London, 1905), 196. In this same chapter there is a comment on the supermanly aspirations of H. G. Wells.
109 *WBS*, x, 214.

110 *The Condition of England* (London, 1960), 29.
111 *Ibid.*, 221.
112 *The Philosophy of Friedrich Nietzsche* (London, 1908), 272–9.
113 *Letters of James Gibbons Huneker* (London, 1922), 23–4. Letter dated June 4, 1904.
114 Anthony Ludovici, *Who Is to Be Master of the World?* (London, 1909), 158.
115 J. M. Kennedy, *The Quintessence of Nietzsche* (London, 1909), 79–80. St. Loe Strachey was the Tory editor of the *Spectator*.
116 "A Spoke in Shaw's Wheel," 230.
117 *Ibid.*, 230.
118 G. B. Edwards, "Shaw," *Adelphi*, IV (July, 1926), 31–2.
119 "Nietzsche," *Everyman* (May 16, 1913), 136.
120 *Autobiography* (London, 1936), 157.
121 *Heretics* (London, 1905), 37.
122 *Autobiography*, 176.
123 *George Bernard Shaw* (London, 1925), 203–4.
124 *Orthodoxy* (London, 1927), 66.
125 *George Bernard Shaw*, 205.
126 *Ibid.*, 206.
127 *Heretics*, 62.
128 *George Bernard Shaw*, 207.
129 "Unedited Opinions: On Drama," *NA*, IX (May 18, 1911), 58.
130 *A History of Ancient Greek Literature* (London, 1897), 250.
131 Louis Crompton, "Shaw's Challenge to Liberalism," *Prairie Schooner*, XXXVII (Autumn, 1963), 229–44.
132 *The Idea of a Theatre* (New York, 1949), 47.
133 *Autobiography* (New York, 1958), 195.
134 *Ibid.*, 188.
135 *CW*, II, 190.
136 *Ibid.*, IV, 198.
137 *Ibid.*, II, 170.
138 *Ibid.*, VII, 55.
139 Brustein, *The Theatre of Revolt*, 202.
140 "Mr. Shaw's Pom-Pom," *Daily Chronicle* (August 24, 1903), 7.
141 *Essays and Introductions* (London, 1960), 274.
142 *CW*, XVI, 212.
143 *WBS*, XV, 130.
144 *The Letters of T. E. Lawrence* (London, 1938), 669. Letter dated July 29, 1929.
145 *WBS*, X, xxxiv–xxxv.
146 *CW*, XVI, 210.
147 Kaye, *Bernard Shaw*, 104.

VIII A. R. ORAGE

1 "Readings and Re-Readings: *Zanoni*," *Theosophical Review*, XXXI (December 15, 1902), 343–4.
2 "The New Romanticism," *Theosophical Review*, XL (March, 1907), 51.
3 *Ibid.*, 55.
4 P. D. Ouspensky, *Tertium Organum* (New York, 1959), 295–6.
5 *Consciousness: Animal, Human, and Superman* (London, 1907), 22.
6 *Ibid.*, 68.
7 *Bernard Shaw* (London, 1907), 11–12.
8 *New English Weekly*, VI (November 15, 1934), 114.
9 Gerald Cumberland, *Set Down in Malice: A Book of Reminiscences* (New York, 1919), 91.
10 *The New God and Other Essays* (London, 1911), 188–9. This essay originally appeared as "Notes of the Month" in the *Occult Review*, XIII (January, 1911), 1–16.
11 *Fabian News*, VII (July, 1898), 17. A notorious philanderer, Bland credited himself also with sufficient philosophical endowment to write on "Nietzsche and the Woman," a dialogue published in the *Living Age*, CCLXXVIII (July 12, 1913), 122–4.
12 "Nietzsche: The Lyrical Bismarck," *NA*, VI (January 27, 1910), 305.
13 "Nietzsche v. Socialism," *NA*, V (June 3, 1909), 127.
14 *NA*, I (May 9, 1907), 19.
15 *NA*, VII (July 14, 1910), 261.
16 "Superman Consciousness," *NA*, I (June 6, 1907), 92.
17 "Towards Socialism," *NA*, I (October 3, 1907), 361.
18 *Ibid.*, 362.
19 "Towards Socialism," *NA*, II (October 31, 1907), 10.
20 *CW*, XV, 208–9.
21 "Readers and Writers," *NA*, XIV (February 19, 1914), 499.
22 "Readers and Writers," *NA*, XIV (January 22, 1914), 370.
23 Jackson, *Bernard Shaw*, 13.
24 "The Truth about Nietzsche," *TPW*, XXIV (October 31, 1914), 476. Concerned largely to demolish the idea that Nietzsche was the inspirer of German militarism, this article contains a lively, if brief, account of Jackson's connection with the Nietzsche movement in England.
25 "Fabian Arts Group," *Fabian News*, XVII (February, 1907), 20.
26 *Fabian News*, XVII (July, 1907), 55.
27 "The Future of the *New Age*," *NA*, I (May 2, 1907), 8.
28 Alfred Stead, "Bushido, the Japanese Ethical Code," *Monthly Review*, XIV (March, 1904), 62.
29 *Too Late to Lament* (London, 1955), 85.
30 "The Samurai Press," *NA*, I (June 6, 1907), 92–3.
31 P. V. Cohn, "Belloc and Nietzsche," *NA*, XII (January 2, 1913), 215.

32 *Friedrich Nietzsche: The Dionysian Spirit of the Age* (London, 1908), 18.
33 *Ibid.*, 11–12.
34 "On Largeness," *Daily News* (December 29, 1906), 6.
35 "Man and Super-Manikin," *NA*, xix (January 10, 1907), 230.
36 *Nietzsche in Outline and Aphorism* (London, 1907), 11–12.
37 *NA*, ii (November 30, 1907), 94.
38 "Nietzsche," *Albany Review*, iii (April, 1908), 90–4.
39 *The Eighteen Nineties* (London, 1913), 20.
40 "Marginalia," *NA*, i (July 18, 1907), 188.
41 *NA*, i (May 30, 1907), 74.
42 E[dwin] M[uir], "The Fire Signal," *NA*, i (September 26, 1907), 242; and "Fragments and Parables," *NA*, ii (November 14, 1907), 50. Other Nietzsche poems in translation: "In the South," *Nation*, v (April 17, 1909), 93; "A Dancing Song to the Mistral Wind," *Nation*, v (May 15, 1909), 249; "The Drunken Song," *Poet Lore*, xvi (Autumn, 1905), 91; and "The Seventh Solitude," *Poet Lore*, xxvii (March, 1916), 228.
43 Herbert Hughes, "The Salome Dance," *NA*, ii (December 7, 1907), 118. For a dissenting view see Gerald Cumberland, "The Nietzschean Spirit in Music," *Musical Times*, liv (September 1, 1913), 579–81.
44 The following items might be cited as samples of the range of this interest in Nietzsche: Angelo S. Rappoport, "Ibsen, Nietzsche, and Kierkegaard," *NA*, iii (September 19 and 26, 1908), 408–9, 428–9; Elisabeth Foerster-Nietzsche, "Friedrich Nietzsche and the Critics," *NA*, iv (December 10, 1908), 134; Karl Heckel, "Genius or Superman?" *NA*, v (May 20 and 27, 1909), 72–3, 95–6; Alfred E. Randall. "Neo-Nietzsche," *NA*, vi (February 3, 1910), 317; Francis Grierson, "Nietzsche and Wagner," *NA*, vi (April 14, 1910), 564–5; A. Messer, "Kant and Nietzsche," *NA*, x (February 29, 1912), 419; P. Selver, "Nietzsche and Strindberg," *NA*, xii (April 10, 1913), 559–60; Remy de Gourmont, "A French View of Nietzsche," *NA*, xiii (July 10, 1913), 300–1.
45 "Nietzsche in English," *Jewish Chronicle* (August 6, 1909), 17.
46 "Book of the Week," *NA*, iv (January 7, 1909), 225. Kennedy felt no qualms about proselytizing for Nietzsche in a review nominally devoted to Charles Lamb.
47 E.g. "Nietzsche: Who He Was and What He Thought," *Daily Dispatch* (May 31, 1909), 4; "The Superman in Embryo," *TPW*, xiii (June 4, 1909), 719.
48 W. Scott-King, "Friedrich Nietzsche and His Superman," *The Young Man* (February, 1909), 56.
49 Unpublished letter, undated.
50 Unpublished letter, dated November 24, 1910. Phillpotts made this praise of Ludovici public in an essay on Nietzsche in *Essays in Little* (London, [1931]), 172.

51 *New English Weekly*, VI (November 15, 1934), 115.
52 *NA*, XIV (January 8, 1914), 319. Lewis, by the way, professed himself a great admirer of the *New Age*.
53 Letter from Ludovici to the writer, dated November 26, 1966.
54 *My Confession of Faith in the Labour Alliance* (London, 1909), 14.
55 Quoted by S. Hobson, *Pilgrim to the Left* (London, 1938), 117.
56 "Book of the Week," *NA*, III (June 20, 1908), 153.
57 "Books and Persons," *NA*, V (October 7, 1909), 430.
58 "Correspondence between Friedrich Nietzsche and George Brandes," literary supplement to the *National Review*, XLIV (January, 1905), 31.
59 "Books and Persons," *NA*, IV (January 7, 1909), 224.
60 Prefatory note to Remy de Gourmont "A French View of Nietzsche," *NA*, XIII (July 10, 1913), 300.
61 "The Case of Nietzsche," *NA*, VIII (March 30, 1911), 527.
62 Herbert L. Stewart, *Questions of the Day in Philosophy and Psychology* (London, 1912), 255.
63 *Nietzsche: His Life and Works* (London, 1910), 99.
64 *NA*, VI (February 3, 1910), 333.
65 "Unedited Opinions, VI: Modern Novels," *NA*, VIII (December 29, 1910), 204.
66 *Tory Democracy* (London, 1911), 119.
67 *The Art of Reading* (New York, 1930), 134.
68 *Friedrich Nietzsche: The Dionysian Spirit of the Age*, 64.
69 *Ibid.*, 71–2.
70 *Ibid.*, 74–5.
71 *Consciousness*, 72. For an Indian mystic's view of the "beautiful doctrine of the Superman," see Ananda Coomaraswamy, "Cosmopolitan View of Nietzsche," *The Dance of Siva* (New York, 1924), 115–21. This chapter won the approval of Oscar Levy. Cf. "Open Letter to a Hindu Nietzschean," *New English Weekly*, V (September 6, 1934), 405–6.
72 *Consciousness*, 74.
73 *Ibid.*, 74–5.
74 *Ibid.*, 76.
75 *Ibid.*, 78.
76 *Ibid.*, 82. Nietzsche defined happiness as swiftness of thinking and feeling.
77 *Ibid.*, 82.
78 *Ibid.*, 85–6.
79 *Ibid.*, 79.
80 *Nietzsche in Outline and Aphorism*, 47–8.
81 *The Revival of Aristocracy* (London, 1906), 102–3.
82 "Towards Socialism, *NA*, II (November 21, 1907), 70.
83 "Towards Socialism," *NA*, II (November 30, 1907), 89.

84 "A Fourth Tale for Men Only," *NA*, xi (May 2, 1912), 13.
85 *The Art of Reading*, 210.
86 *Readers and Writers* (London, 1922), 106–7.
87 "Nietzsche, Culture and Plutocracy," *NA*, xiv (February 5, 1914), 446.
88 *The Art of Reading*, 211–12.
89 "Esprit de Corps in Elementary Schools," *Monthly Review*, xxv (December, 1906), 45–50.
90 *Nietzsche in Outline and Aphorism*, 43–4.
91 Letter to the *New English Weekly*, i (April 21, 1932), 21.
92 "A Commentary," *Criterion*, xiv (January, 1935), 261, 262.
93 "The Ruler Artist," *Daily News* (June 21, 1911), 4.
94 W. D. Martin, "The Literary Significance of *The New Age* under the Editorship of A. R. Orage, 1907–1922." University of London dissertation, 1961, 213.
95 *NA*, xiv (January 8, 1914), 307.
96 *CW*, xv, 263.
97 *NA*, xvii (May 6, 1915), 13.
98 *PN*, 518–9.
99 *Ibid.*, 517.
100 *PN*, 529.
101 *NA*, xxviii (November 18, 1920), 30.
102 *Nietzsche and Art* (London, 1911), vi–vii.
103 *NA*, iv (January 7, 1909), 225–6.
104 *Nietzsche and Art*, 137.
105 *Ibid.*, vi.
106 *CW*, viii, 19–20.
107 *NA*, xiv (November 27, 1913), 113.
108 *Ibid.*, xviii (November 25, 1915), 85.
109 *Ibid.*, xiii (October 23, 1913), 761.
110 *Ibid.*, xvii (June 10, 1915), 133.
111 *Ibid.*, xv (August 27, 1914), 397.
112 T. H. Gibbons, "Literary Criticism and the Intellectual Milieu," University of Cambridge dissertation, 1965, 251.
113 *Tory Democracy*, 55.
114 *Speculations* (London, 1949), 116, 117.
115 *Tory Democracy*, 58–9. Cf. Wells's attack on the "multitudinousness" of Liberalism, *The New Machiavelli* (London, 1911), 325–6.
116 "A Notebook," *NA*, xviii (December 9, 1915), 138.
117 *Speculations*, 118.
118 *Ibid.*, 62.
119 *CW*, viii, 135.
120 "A Tory Philosophy," reprinted in Alun R. Jones, *Life and Opinions of T. E. Hulme* (London, 1960), 190.

121 E.g. *Miscellaneous Maxims and Opinions*, aph. 173; *The Wanderer and His Shadow*, aphs. 122, 127, 135, 140; *The Gay Science*, aph. 370; *The Will to Power*, aphs. 826, 829, 847, 848.
122 *PN*, 557.
123 *CW*, vi, 199–200. Eliot has defined free verse as poetry which is ever on the point of settling into a form but never quite achieving it.
124 *Ibid.*, 202.
125 *Ibid.*, xii, 107. Cf. The *Twilight of the Idols*, aph. 47.
126 *Speculations*, 133.
127 *CW*, xvi, 283.
128 *Ibid.*, vi, 181, 182.
129 *Speculations*, xiv.
130 "Searchers after Reality; ii: Haldane," *NA*, v (August 19, 1909), 316.
131 *Speculations*, xv.
132 See, in particular, Nietzsche's essay "On Truth and Falsity in their Ultramoral Sense," *CW*, ii, 171–92.
133 *Speculations*, 263.
134 *Ibid.*, 17–18.
135 "A Tory Philosophy," *passim*.
136 F. J. Hoffman, Charles Allen, Carolyn F. Ulrich, *The Little Magazine: A History and a Bibliography* (Princeton, 1947); S. J. Kunitz, H. Haycraft, *Twentieth Century Authors* (New York, 1942); William Rose Benét, *The Reader's Encyclopaedia* (New York, 1948).
137 *New English Weekly*, vi (November 15, 1934), 110.
138 "The Truth about Nietzsche," *TPW*, xxiv (October 31, 1914), 476.
139 H. V. Routh, *Towards the Twentieth Century* (London, 1937), 359.
140 *Finishing Touches* (London, 1964), 117.
141 "A Shaker of Things," *Nation*, ii (March 7, 1908), 821.
142 *Between Two Worlds: An Autobiography* (London, 1935), 420.
143 *New English Weekly*, vi (November 15, 1934), 115.
144 *Ibid.*, 112.
145 *The Contrary Experience* (London, 1963), 165–6, 167.
146 Quoted in "On First Reading Nietzsche," *Tenth Muse* (London, 1957), 179.
147 *The Contrary Experience*, 59–146 *passim*. See also Read's review (written at Orage's request) of the Andler biography of Nietzsche, *NA*, xxx (December 29, 1921), 103. Orage, pleased with Read's work, invited him to take over as sub-editor of the *New Age* when, in the summer of 1922, he decided to study under Gurdjieff in Paris. Read declined.
148 *An Autobiography* (London, 1954), 123.
149 *Ibid.*, 126.
150 *Ibid.*, 127.
151 *Latitudes* (London, n.d.), 86, 93. The Nietzschean aspects of Muir's critical writing have been outlined by Charles Glicksberg, "Edwin Muir:

Zarathustra in Scotch Dress," *Arizona Quarterly*, xii (1956), 225–39. The Nietzschean motifs in Muir's poetry would repay extensive investigation. See Michael Hamburger, "Edwin Muir," *Encounter* xv (December, 1960), 46–53.
152 *Latitudes*, 293.
153 *The Art of Reading*, 205–6.
154 *Anne Douglas Sedgwick: A Portrait*, ed. Basil de Selincourt (London, 1936), 137.
155 *The Letters of Rupert Brooke*, ed. Geoffrey Keynes (London, 1968), 64. Letter dated October 4, 1906.
156 *Civilization* (London, 1938), 15–16. Osbert Sitwell put the following words into the mouths of the British Philistines he scorned: "It is tolerably clear to us/That the War/Was due to a German poet – All this Nietzsche and nonsense – We will not buy 'Art and Letters.'" "Te Deum," *Arts and Letters*, ii (Winter, 1918–19), 1.
157 PN, 235.
158 "Nietzsche," *New Weekly*, i (May 30, 1914), 341.

IX CONCLUSION

1 *Dramatic Opinions and Essays* (London, 1907), ii, 157.
2 J. M. Kennedy, *The Quintessence of Nietzsche* (London, 1909), x.
3 CW, vi, 127.
4 Ibid., xii, 263.
5 *Last Essays* (London, 1959), 173.
6 Ibid., 174.
7 *Who Is to Be Master of the World?* (London, 1910), 9.
8 T. W. Rolleston, "Modern Forces in German Literature," *Quarterly Review*, ccxxi (July, 1914), 42.
9 A. H. J. Knight, *Some Aspects of the Life and Work of Nietzsche* (Cambridge, 1933), 118. Knight is careful to point out that this influence was mostly "indirect."
10 "Modern Forces in German Literature," 42.
11 Quoted by G. U. Ellis, *Twilight on Parnassus* (London, 1939), 213. Douglas's book *How about Europe?* (1929), which is dedicated to Oscar Levy, shows how accurate Nietzsche's diagnoses about civilization were turning out to be.
12 *Collected Poems* (London, 1958), 272.
13 L. A. G. Strong, "William Butler Yeats," *Scattering Branches: Tributes to the Memory of W. B. Yeats*, ed. Stephen Gwynn (London, 1940), 193.

SELECTED BIBLIOGRAPHY

ADAMS, MAURICE "The Ethics of Tolstoy and Nietzsche," *International Journal of Ethics*, XI (October, 1900), 82–105.

ARCHER, WILLIAM *Fighting a Philosophy*. London: Oxford University Press, 1915.

AUDEN, W. H. *The Dyer's Hand*. New York: Random House, 1962.

BALAKIAN, ANNA "Influence and Literary Fortune: The Equivocal Junction of Two Methods," *Yearbook of Comparative and General Literature*, No. 11 (1962), 24–31.

BARRY, W. "The Ideals of Anarchy: Friedrich Nietzsche," *Quarterly Review*, CLXXXIV (October, 1896), 299–328.

— "Anarchy and Culture," *English Illustrated Magazine*, XXVI (November, 1901), 186–92.

BARZUN, JACQUES *Darwin, Marx, Wagner*. Boston: Little, Brown, 1941.

BEARDSLEY, AUBREY *Last Letters of Aubrey Beardsley*. Introduction by John Gray. London: Longmans, Green & Co., 1904.

— *Letters from Aubrey Beardsley to Leonard Smithers*. Edited by R. A. Walker. London: First Edition Club, 1937.

BENTLEY, ERIC *Bernard Shaw: A Reconsideration*. Norfolk, Conn.: New Directions, 1947.

— *Bernard Shaw*. London: Robert Hale, 1950.

— *The Cult of the Superman*. London: Robert Hale, 1957.

BENTON, RICHARD "The Aesthetics of Friedrich Nietzsche," Johns Hopkins University dissertation, 1955.

BERGONZI, BERNARD *The Early H. G. Wells*. Manchester: Manchester University Press, 1961.

BEYER, HAROLD *Nietzsche og Norden*. 2 vols. Bergen: Greig's, 1958, 1959.

BIANQUIS, GENEVIÈVE *Nietzsche en France*. Paris: Félix Alcan, 1929.

BRANDES, GEORGE *Friedrich Nietzsche*. Translated from the Danish by A. G. Chater. London: Heinemann [1914].

BRINTON, CRANE *Nietzsche*. Cambridge, Mass.: Harvard University Press, 1941.

BURDETT, OSBERT *The Beardsley Period*. London: John Lane, 1925.

CARPENTER, EDWARD *Civilisation: Its Cause and Cure*. London: G. Allen and Unwin, 1921.

CARUS, PAUL *Nietzsche and Other Exponents of Individualism*. London and Chicago: Open Court Publishing Co., 1914.

CHATTERTON-HILL, GEORGES *Heredity and Selection in Sociology*. London: Adam and Charles Black, 1907.

— *The Philosophy of Nietzsche: An Exposition and an Appreciation*. London: John Ouseley, 1912.

CHESTERTON, G. K. "The Adoration of Matter," *Daily News*, December 21, 1905, 4.

— *Heretics*. London: John Lane, 1905.

—"On Largeness," *Daily News*, December 29, 1906, 6.

— *Eugenics and Other Evils*. London: Cassell, 1922.

— *George Bernard Shaw*. London: John Lane, 1925.

— *Orthodoxy*. London: John Lane, 1927.

— *Autobiography*. London: Hutchinson, 1936.

CHILD, RUTH C. *The Aesthetics of Walter Pater*. New York: Macmillan, 1940.

COHN, PAUL V. "Belloc and Nietzsche," *New Age*, XII (January 2, 1913), 214–15.

CORNFORD, FRANCIS *From Religion to Philosophy*. London: Edward Arnold, 1912.

COMMON, THOMAS "Friedrich Nietzsche," *To-morrow*, I (March, 1896), 154–61.

—"Human Evolution according to Nietzsche," *Natural Science*, X (June, 1897), 393–4.

—"Professor Seth's Attacks on Nietzsche," *University Magazine and Free Review*, XI (April, 1899), 49–77.

—"A Defence of Nietzsche," *Ethical World*, III (January 27, 1900), 53–4.

—"Nietzsche's Works in English," *Nation* (New York), LXXXII (March 29, 1906), 259.

—"Nietzsche Pioneers," *T.P.'s Weekly*, XXI (June 6, 1913), 728.

—"Nietzschean Business Blundering," *Good European Point of View*, no. 11 (Easter, 1914), 83–7.

—"Uprightness or Unscrupulousness," *Good European Point of View*, no. 12 (Winter, 1915), 109–19.

COOMARASWAMY, ANANDA "Cosmopolitan View of Nietzsche," *The Dance of Siva*. New York: The Sunwise Turn, Inc., 1924, 115–21.

CRAWFURD, OSWALD "Nietzsche: an Appreciation," *Nineteenth Century*, XLVIII (October, 1900), 592–606.

DANTO, ARTHUR *Nietzsche as Philosopher*. New York and London: Macmillan, 1965.

DAVIDSON, JOHN "The New Sophist," *Speaker* (November 28, 1891), 641–2.

—"Frederick Nietsche," *Glasgow Herald* (March 18, 1893), 4.

— *Sentences and Paragraphs*. London: Lawrence and Bullen, 1893.

— *A Second Series of Fleet Street Eclogues*. London: John Lane, 1896.

— *New Ballads*. London: John Lane, 1897.

—"Tête-à-Tête; Froude, Carlyle," *Speaker* (June 17, 1899), 689–90.

— *Self's the Man*. London: Grant Richards, 1901.

—"A Poetic Disciple of Nietzsche," *Daily Chronicle* (May 23, 1902), 3.

— *Testament of a Vivisector; Testament of a Man Forbid; Testament of an Empire-Builder*. London: Grant Richards, 1902.

— *A Rosary*. London: Grant Richards, 1903.

— *The Theatrocrat*. London: Grant Richards, 1905.

— *Holiday and Other Poems*. London: Grant Richards, 1906.

— *The Triumph of Mammon*. London: Grant Richards, 1907.

— *Mammon and His Message*. London: Grant Richards, 1908.

— *The Testament of John Davidson*. London: Grant Richards, 1908.

— *The Man Forbid and Other Essays*. Edited by Edward J. O'Brien. Boston: Ball Publishing Co., 1910.

DOUGLAS, NORMAN *How About Europe?* London: Chatto and Windus, 1930.

DUKES, ASHLEY *The Scene is Changed*. London: Macmillan, 1942.

DUNCAN, ISADORA *My Life*. New York: Boni and Liveright, 1942.

EGERTON, GEORGE *Keynotes*. London: Elkin Mathews and John Lane, 1893.

— *Discords*. London: John Lane, 1894.

— *A Leaf from the Yellow Book: The Correspondence of George Egerton*. Edited by Terence de Vere White. London: The Richards Press, 1958.

EGLINTON, JOHN *Anglo-Irish Essays*. Dublin: Talbot Press, 1917.

ELIOT, T. S. Review of A. Wolf's *The Philosophy of Nietzsche*, *International Journal of Ethics*, XXVI (April, 1916), 425–6.

—"A Commentary," *Criterion*, XIV (January, 1935), 260–4.

ELLEHAUGE, MARTIN *The Position of Bernard Shaw in European Philosophy and Art*. Copenhagen: Levin and Munksgaard, 1931.

ELLIS, EDITH *Three Modern Seers*. London: Stanley Paul, 1910.

ELLIS, G. U. *Twilight on Parnassus: A Survey of Post-War Fiction and Pre-War Criticism*. London: Michael Joseph, 1939.

ELLIS, HAVELOCK *The New Spirit*. London: George Bell and Sons, 1890.

—"Friedrich Nietzsche," *Savoy*, no. 2 (April, 1896), 79–94; no. 3 (July, 1896), 68–81; no. 4 (August, 1896), 57–63.

— *The Problem of Race-Regeneration*. London: Cassell, 1911.

— *The Task of Social Hygiene*. London: Constable, 1912.

— *Impressions and Comments*. 3 vols. London: Constable, 1914.

—'Kultur," *New Statesman*, IV (January 2, 1915), 314–16.

— *Affirmations*. 2nd ed. London: Constable, 1915.

— *The Dance of Life*. Boston: Houghton Mifflin, 1923.

— *Views and Reviews, 1884–1932*. 2 vols. London: Desmond Harmsworth, 1932.

— *My Confessional*. London: John Lane, 1934.

— *My Life*. London: Heineman, 1940.

ELLIS, W. ASHTON "Wagner and Schopenhauer," *Fortnightly Review*, LXV (March, 1899), 413–32.

—"Nietzsche Unveiled," *Musical Times*, LVI (September 1, 1915), 525–9.

ELLMANN, RICHARD *Yeats: The Man and the Masks*. London: Macmillan, 1949.

— *The Identity of Yeats*. London: Macmillan, 1954.

"The English Nietzsche Completed," *New Statesman*, I (April 26, 1913), 91.

ENSOR, R. C. K. *England, 1870–1914*. Oxford: Clarendon Press, 1936.

FIELD, A. G. "Friedrich Nietzsche in England," *T. P.'s Weekly*, XXI (May 23, 1913), 662.

FÖRSTER-NIETZSCHE, ELISABETH "Correspondence between Friedrich Nietzsche and George Brandes," literary supplement to the *National Review*, XLIV (January, 1905), 1–32.

FOSTER, MILTON "The Reception of Max Nordau's Degeneration in England

and America." University of Michigan dissertation, 1954.

FRANC, MIRIAM ALICE *Ibsen in England*. Boston: Four Seas Co., 1919.

"The Function of an Endowed Press," *Nation* (New York), LXXXII (January 18, 1906), 49–50.

GARDNER, CHARLES *Vision and Vesture: A Study of William Blake in Modern Thought*. London: Dent, 1916.

GARNETT, EDWARD "Nietzsche," *Outlook*, III (July 8, 1899), 746–8.

—"Nietzsche in English," *Daily News*, October 16, 1907, 4.

—"The Ruler Artist," *Daily News*, June 21, 1911, 4.

— *Friday Nights*. London: Jonathan Cape, 1922.

GIBBONS, T. H. "Literary Criticism and the Intellectual Milieu: some aspects of the period 1880–1914, with particular reference to the literary and social criticism of Havelock Ellis and Alfred Orage." University of Cambridge dissertation, 1965.

GIDE, ANDRÉ *The Journals of André Gide, 1889–1949*. Edited by Justin O'Brien. 2 vols. New York: Vintage Books, 1961.

GISSING, GEORGE *The Letters of George Gissing to Edouard Bertz, 1887–1903*. Edited by A. C. Young. London: Constable, 1961.

GOURMONT, REMY DE "A French View of Nietzsche," translated by P. V. Cohn, *New Age*, XIII (July 10, 1913), 300–1.

GRAHAM, STEPHEN *Part of the Wonderful Scene: An Autobiography*. London: Collins, 1964.

GRAVES, ROBERT *The Crowning Privilege*. Harmondsworth: Penguin Books, 1959.

GROSHONG, JAMES W. *G.B.S. and Germany: The Major Aspects*. Ann Arbor, Michigan: University Microfilms, 1965.

HALÉVY, DANIEL *The Life of Friedrich Nietzsche*. Translated by J. M. Hone. London: T. Fisher Unwin, 1911.

HAMBURGER, MICHAEL *From Prophecy to Exorcism: The Premises of Modern German Literature*. London: Longman's, 1965.

HARRISON, JOHN R. *The Reactionaries*. London: Gollancz, 1966.

HELLER, ERICH *The Disinherited Mind*. Harmondsworth: Penguin Books, 1961.

HENDERSON, ARCHIBALD *Bernard Shaw: Playboy and Prophet*. New York: D. Appleton and Co., 1932.

HILLER, HAROLD "Nietzsche and Great Britain," *T.P.'s Weekly*, XXIV (November 7, 1914), 514.

HOFFMAN, FREDERICK J. *Freudianism and the Literary Mind.* Baton Rouge: Louisiana State University Press, 1957.

HOFFMAN, FREDERICK J., ALLEN, C., AND ULRICH, C. F. *The Little Magazine: A History and a Bibliography.* Princeton: Princeton University Press, 1946.

HONE, J. M. *The Life of George Moore.* London: Gollancz, 1936.

— *W. B. Yeats, 1865–1939.* London: Macmillan, 1942.

HULME, T. E. *Speculations.* Edited by Herbert Read. 2nd ed. London: Routledge and Kegan Paul, 1929.

HULTSCH, PAUL "Das Denken Nietzsches in seiner Bedeutung für England," *Germanisch-Romanische Monatsschrift,* XXVI (September/October, 1938), 359–73.

HUNEKER, JAMES *Overtones.* London: Isbister and Co., 1904.

— *The Pathos of Distance.* New York: Scribner's, 1913.

— *The Letters of James Gibbons Huneker.* London: T. Werner Laurie, 1922.

HYNES, SAMUEL *The Edwardian Turn of Mind.* Princeton: Princeton University Press, 1968.

JACKSON, HOLBROOK *Bernard Shaw.* London: Grant Richards, 1907.

—"What is a Superman?" *T.P.'s Magazine,* I (January, 1911), 435–40.

—"The Complete Nietzsche," *Bookman* (London), XLI (March, 1912), 310–11.

— *The Eighteen Nineties.* London: Grant Richards, 1913.

JOHNSTONE, ARTHUR *Musical Criticisms.* Manchester: Manchester University Press, 1905.

JOHNSTON, J. K. *The Bloomsbury Group.* New York: Noonday Press, 1954.

JONES, ALAN R. *The Life and Opinions of T. E. Hulme.* London: Gollancz, 1960.

KAUFFMAN, LEROY CULBERTSON "The Influence of Friedrich Nietzsche on American Literature." University of Pennsylvania dissertation, 1963.

KAUFMANN, WALTER *Nietzsche.* New York: Meridian Books, 1961.

KAYE, JULIAN B. *Bernard Shaw and the Nineteenth-Century Tradition.* Norman: Oklahoma University Press, 1958.

KELLNER, LEON "Nietzsche in England," *Das literarische Echo* (June 1, 1914), 1174–6.

KENNEDY, J. M. "The Prophet's Last Curse," *New Age,* III (October 24, 1908), 513–14.

— *The Quintessence of Nietzsche.* London: T. Werner Laurie, 1909.

—"A Friendly Letter," *New Age*, IX (July 20, 1911), 284.

— *Tory Democracy*. London: Stephen Swift, 1911.

— *English Literature, 1880–1905*. London: Stephen Swift, 1912.

KNIGHT, A. H. J. *Some Aspects of the Life and Work of Nietzsche*. Cambridge: Cambridge University Press, 1933.

KNIGHT, G. WILSON *The Golden Labyrinth*. London: Phoenix House, 1962.

LAVRIN, JANKO. *Nietzsche and Modern Consciousness*. London: Collins, 1922.

— *Aspects of Modernism*. London: Stanley Nott, 1935.

LEA, F. A. *The Tragic Philosopher*. London: Methuen, 1957.

LEE, VERNON *Gospels of Anarchy*. London: T. Fisher Unwin, 1908.

— *Vital Lies*. 2 vols. London: John Lane, 1912.

LEES, F. N. "T. S. Eliot and Nietzsche," *Notes and Queries*, XI (September 9, 1964), 386–7.

LESTER, JOHN "Friedrich Nietzsche and John Davidson: A Study in Influence," *Journal of the History of Ideas*, XVIII (1957), 411–29.

LEVY, OSCAR "A Spoke in Shaw's Wheel," *New Age*, VII (July 7, 1910), 229–32.

—"Mr. G. K. Chesterton and Christianity," *New Age*, X (April 18, 1912), 586–7.

—"Dr. Oscar Levy and Nietzsche Pioneers," *T.P.'s Weekly*, XXI (May 30, 1913), 694.

—"Nietzsche and Futurism," *New Age*, XIII (December 4, 1913), 157–8.

—"The Nietzsche Movement in England," *New Age*, XII (December 19, 1912), 157–8; XII (December 26, 1912), 181–3; and XII (January 2, 1913), 204–6.

—"Nietzsche," *New Weekly*, I (May 30, 1914), 341.

LEWIS, WYNDHAM *Rude Assignment*. London: Hutchinson, 1950.

LICHTENBERGER, HENRI *The Gospel of Superman*. Translated by J. M. Kennedy. London: T. N. Foulis, 1910.

LINDSAY, J. A. "Eugenics and the Doctrine of the Super-Man," *Eugenics Review*, VII (January, 1916), 247–62.

LUDOVICI, A. M. "Professor Saintsbury contra Nietzsche," *New Age*, I (October 10, 1908), 478–9.

—"Nietzsche and Science," *Spectator* (January 8, 1910), 52.

— *Who Is to Be Master of the World?* London: Constable, 1910.

— *Nietzsche: His Life and Works*. London: Constable, 1910.

— *Nietzsche and Art*. London: Constable, 1911.

—"Mr. Chesterton and Anarchy," *New Age*, XI (June 13, 1912), 166–7.

—"Dr. Oscar Levy," *New English Weekly*, XXX (November 14, 1946), 49–50.

MACCARTHY, DESMOND "Nietzsche," *Albany Review*, III (April, 1908), 90–4.

—"Nietzsche and the War," *New Statesman*, IV (October 10, 1914), 13–14.

MAGALANER, MARVIN "Joyce, Nietzsche and Hauptmann in James Joyce's 'A Painful Case,'" *PMLA*, LXVIII (1953), 95–102.

MAIRET, PHILIP *A. R. Orage: A Memoir*. Introduced by G. K. Chesterton. London: Dent, 1936.

MANN, THOMAS *Last Essays*. London: Secker and Warburg, 1959.

MARCUSE, L. "Nietzsche in America," *South Atlantic Quarterly*, L (July, 1951), 330–9.

MARSHALL, BEATRICE "Friedrich Nietzsche and Richard Wagner," *Fortnightly Review*, LXIX (June, 1898), 885–97.

—"Nietzsche," *Academy*, LXIV (March 7, 1903), 234.

MARTIN, W. D. "The Literary Significance of *The New Age* under the Editorship of A. R. Orage, 1907–1922." University of London dissertation, 1961.

MASON, EUDO C. *Rilke, Europe, and the English-Speaking World*. Cambridge: Cambridge University Press, 1961.

MASTERMAN, CHARLES *In Peril of Change*. London: T. Fisher Unwin, 1905.

— *The Condition of England*. London: Methuen, 1960.

MOORE, GEORGE *Confessions of a Young Man*. New York: Putnam, 1959.

— *Hail and Farewell*. 3 vols. Heinemann, 1933.

MONRO, HAROLD *Proposals for a Voluntary Nobility*. 2nd ed. Norwich: Samurai Press, 1907.

MORGAN, BAYARD QUINCY *A Critical Bibliography of German Literature in English Translation, 1481–1927*. 2nd. ed. Stanford: Stanford University Press, 1938.

MORGAN, MARGERY M. "Shaw, Yeats, Nietzsche, and the Religion of Art," *Komos*, I (March, 1967), 24–34.

MORLAND, M. A. "Nietzsche and the Nineties," *Contemporary Review*, CXCIII (April, 1958), 209–12.

MOSER, MAX *Richard Wagner in der englischen Literatur des XIX. Jahrhunderts*. Bern: Verlag A. Francke Ag., 1938.

MUEGGE, MAXIMILIAN *Friedrich Nietzsche: His Life and Work*. London: T. Fisher Unwin, 1908.

—"Eugenics and the Superman: A Racial Science, and a Racial Religion," *Eugenics Review*, I (October, 1909), 184–93.

MUIR, EDWIN *We Moderns: Enigmas and Guesses*. London: G. Allen and Unwin, 1918.

— *Latitudes*. London: Andrew Melrose, 1924.

— *An Autobiography*. London: Hogarth Press, 1954.

MURRY, J. MIDDLETON *Between Two Worlds: An Autobiography*. London: Jonathan Cape, 1935.

NETHERCOT, ARTHUR "Bernard Shaw, Philosopher," *PMLA*, LXIX (March, 1954), 57–75.

— *Men and Supermen*. Cambridge, Mass: Harvard University Press, 1954.
"The New Learning and its Minor Prophets," *Saturday Review*, LXXXII (July 25, 1896), 89–90.

NEWMAN, ERNEST "Friedrich Nietzsche," *University Magazine and Free Review*, VI (May, 1896), 117–22.

—"Nietzsche and Wagner," *University Magazine and Free Review*, VII (December, 1896), 268–75.

—"Nietzsche Once More," *Reformer*, III (January, 1899), 10–20.

— *A Study of Wagner*. London: Bertram Dobell, 1899.

NIETZSCHE, FRIEDRICH "The Case of Wagner," *Fortnightly Review*, LVIII (September, 1895), 367–79.

— *The Case of Wagner*. Translated by Thomas Common. Introduced by Alexander Tille. London: Henry & Co., 1896.

— *Thus Spake Zarathustra*. Translated and introduced by Alexander Tille. London: Henry & Co., 1896.

—"The Principles of Aesthetics," *To-morrow*, IV (December, 1897), 173–82.

—"The Old and the New Nobility," *To-morrow*, IV (October, 1897), 29–35.

— *A Genealogy of Morals*. Translated by W. A. Haussmann. Introduced by Alexander Tille. London: T. Fisher Unwin, 1899.

— *Nietzsche as Critic, Philosopher, Poet and Prophet*. Compiled by Thomas Common. London: Grant Richards, 1901.

— *The Dawn of Day*. Translated by Johanna Volz. London: T. Fisher Unwin, 1903.

— *The Complete Works of Friedrich Nietzsche*. Edited by Dr. Oscar Levy. Translated by various hands. 18 vols. London: T. N. Foulis, 1909–13.

— *Thus Spake Zarathustra*. Translated by Thomas Common. Introduction by Oscar Levy. London: G. Allen and Unwin, 1932.

— *Thus Spake Zarathustra*. Translated by Alexander Tille. Introduction by Ernest Rhys. London: Dent, 1933.

— *The Portable Nietzsche.* Edited and translated by Walter Kaufmann. New York: Viking Press, 1958.

— *The Philosophy of Nietzsche.* Edited and introduced by Geoffrey Clive. New York: Mentor Books, 1965.

"Nietzsche," *Times Literary Supplement* (November 18, 1909), 433–4.

"Nietzsche in England," *Nation* (New York), XCVI (1913), 589–90.

"Nietzsche in English," *Jewish Chronicle* (August 6, 1909), 17–18.

"Nietzsche's Criticism of Wagner," *Nation,* VII (July 9, 1910), 533–4.

NORDAU, MAX *Degeneration.* Popular ed. London: Heinemann, 1913.

NOWELL-SMITH, SIMON *Edwardian England, 1901–1914.* London: Oxford University Press, 1964.

ORAGE, A. R. *Friedrich Nietzsche: The Dionysian Spirit of the Age.* London: T. N. Foulis, 1906.

— Review of *Beyond Good and Evil, New Age,* I (October 17, 1907), 395.

— *Nietzsche in Outline and Aphorism.* London: T. N. Foulis, 1907.

— *Consciousness: Animal, Human, and Superman.* London: Theosophical Publishing Co., 1907.

— Review of *Thus Spake Zarathustra, New Age,* III (June 20, 1908), 153.

— "A Complete Nietzsche at Last," *New Age* (May 6, 1909), 38–9.

— *Readers and Writers.* London: Allen and Unwin, 1922.

— *The Art of Reading.* New York: Farrar and Rinehart, 1930.

— *Selected Essays and Critical Writings of A. R. Orage.* Edited by Herbert Read and Denis Saurat. London: Stanley Nott, 1935.

PETZOLD, GERTRUD *John Davidson und sein geistiges Werden unter dem Einflusse Nietzsches.* Leipzig: Bernhard Tauchnitz, 1928.

— "Nietzsche in english-amerikanischer Beurteilung bis zum Anfang des Weltkrieges," *Anglia,* LIII (1929), 134–218.

PHILLPOTTS, EDEN *Essays in Little.* London: Hutchinson, 1931.

PLATT, WILLIAM "Egoism, and the 'Eagle and the Serpent,'" *University Magazine and Free Review,* X (April, 1898), 96–102.

— "Nietzsche," *Reformer,* IV (November 15, 1900), 680–1.

PRINGLE-PATTISON, A. SETH *Man's Place in the Cosmos.* 2nd ed. London and Edinburgh: W. Blackwood and Sons, 1902.

QUINN, JOHN *Complete Catalogue of the Library of John Quinn Sold by Auction (12 November 1923–20 March 1924 etc.).* 2 vols. New York: Anderson Galleries, 1924.

RANSOME, ARTHUR *Portraits and Speculations*. London: Macmillan, 1913.

READ, HENRY *Anarchy and Order*. London: Faber and Faber, 1954.

— *Tenth Muse*. London: Routledge and Kegan Paul, 1957.

READ, HERBERT *The Contrary Experience: Autobiographies*. London: Faber and Faber, 1963.

REICHERT, HERBERT W., and SCHLECHTA, KARL, eds. *International Nietzsche Bibliography*. Chapel Hill: North Carolina University Press, 1960.

Review of *Nietzsche in Outline and Aphorism, New Age*, II (November 30, 1907), 94–5.

Review of Nietzsche translations, *English Review*, x (August, 1911), 184–6.

Review of *Thoughts out of Season, Westminster Review*, CIII (April, 1875), 501–3.

RICKETTS, CHARLES *Self-Portrait*. London: Peter Davies, 1939.

ROBERTSON, J. G. "The Literary Movement in Germany: Friedrich Nietzsche and His Influence," *Cosmopolis*, XII (October, 1898), 31–48.

ROBERTSON, JOHN M. "Nietzsche's Indictment of Christianity," *University Magazine and Free Review*, VIII (June 1, 1897), 225–37.

— *Essays in Sociology*, 2 vols. London: A. & H. B. Bonner, 1904.

ROLLESTON, T. W. "Modern Forces in German Literature," *Quarterly Review*, CCI (July, 1914), 27–50.

ROUTH, H. V. *Towards the Twentieth Century*. Cambridge: Cambridge University Press, 1937.

— *English Literature and Ideas in the Twentieth Century*. London: Methuen, 1946.

RUNCIMAN, J. "Wagner and Nietzsche," *Saturday Review*, xc (October 13, 1900), 457–8.

SAENGER, SAMUEL "Nietzsche in und über England," *Neue Rundschau* (Berlin), XXXV (1924), 1068–74.

SAINTSBURY, GEORGE *A History of Criticism and Literary Taste in Europe*. 3 vols. London and Edinburgh: William Blackwood, 1900–9.

— *The Later Nineteenth Century*. Vol. XII of *Periods of European Literature*. London and Edinburgh: William Blackwood, 1904–7.

SAMPSON, GEORGE "Nietzsche and Another," *Daily Chronicle* (May 14, 1909), 3.

—"Nietzsche," *Bookman*, XLVII (March, 1915), 173–5.

SAMUEL, HORACE BARNETT "The Genealogy of Morals," *English Review*, IX (August, 1911), 130–44.

— *Modernities*. London: Kegan Paul, 1913.

SAROLEA, CHARLES "Nietzsche," *Everyman* (May 16, 1913), 136–7.

SAUNDERS, T. BAILEY "Prof. Nietzsche," *Athenaeum* (September 1, 1900), 281–2.

SCHEFFAUER, HERMAN "A Correspondence between Nietzsche and Strindberg," *North American Review*, CXCVIII (August, 1913), 197–205.

SCHILLER, F. C. S. "Nietzsche and His Philosophy," *Book Buyer* (New York), XIII (1896), 407–9.

—"On Nietzsche Translations," *Nation* (New York), LXXXII (April 26, 1906), 343.

—"The Philosophy of Friedrich Nietzsche," *Quarterly Review*, CCXVIII (January, 1913), 148–67.

SELVER, PAUL *Orage and the New Age Circle: Reminiscences and Reflections*. London: George Allen and Unwin, 1959.

"A Shaker of Things," *Nation*, II (March 7, 1908), 820–1.

SHAW, G. B. "Nietzsche in English," *Saturday Review*, LXXXI (April 11, 1896), 373–4.

—"Giving the Devil His Due," supplement to the *Saturday Review*, LXXXVII (May 13, 1899), iii.

—"Our Book-shelf," *Fabian News*, XVII (April, 1907), 37–8.

—"Was ich der deutschen Kultur verdanke," *Neue Rundschau* (March, 1911), 335–49.

— *The Works of Bernard Shaw*. 33 vols. London: Constable, 1930–8.

— *Complete Prefaces*. London: Paul Hamlyn, 1965.

SHAW, J. T. "Literary Indebtedness and Comparative Literary Studies," in *Comparative Literature*. Edited by Newton P. Stallknecht and Horst Frenz. Carbondale: South Illinois University Press, 1961, 58–71.

SNIDER, NANCY VIOLA "An Annotated Bibliography of English Works on Friedrich Nietzsche." University of Michigan dissertation, 1962.

STEPHENSEN, P. R. "The Whirled Around," *London Aphrodite*, no. 5 (April, 1929), 338–41.

STEWART, HERBERT L. "Some Criticisms on the Nietzsche Revival," *International Journal of Ethics*, XIX (July, 1909), 427–43.

— *Questions of the Day in Philosophy and Psychology*. London: Edward Arnold, 1912.

— *Nietzsche and the Ideals of Modern Germany*. London: Edward Arnold, 1915.

STIRNER, MAX *The Ego and His Own.* Translated by Steven T. Byington. London: A. C. Fifield, 1912.

STUTFIELD, HUGH E. M. "Tommyrotics," *Blackwood's Magazine,* CLVII (June, 1895), 833–45.

"The Superman," *Times Literary Supplement* (May 23, 1912), 209–10.

SYMONS, ARTHUR "Nietzsche on Tragedy," *Academy,* LXIII (August 30, 1902), 220.

— Review of *The Dawn of Day, Athenaeum* (March 7, 1903), 298–300.

— *Plays, Acting and Music.* London: Duckworth, 1903.

— *Studies in Prose and Verse.* London: Dent, 1904.

— *William Blake.* London: Constable, 1907.

— *Figures of Several Centuries.* London: Constable, 1916.

— *Studies in Seven Arts.* London: Martin Secker, 1924.

THATCHER, DAVID S. "A Misdated Yeats Letter on Nietzsche," *Notes and Queries,* XV n.s. (August, 1968), 286–7.

"A Thinker and Poet," *Academy,* LXIV (February 21, 1903), 172–3.

TILLE, ALEXANDER, ED. *German Songs of Today and Tomorrow.* New York: Macmillan, 1896.

— Review of *Affirmations, International Journal of Ethics,* IX (October, 1898), 128–9.

TINDALL, W. Y. *Forces in Modern British Literature.* New York: Alfred A. Knopf, 1947.

TOWNSEND, J. BENJAMIN *John Davidson: Poet of Armageddon.* New Haven: Yale University Press, 1961.

WAGAR, W. WARREN *H. G. Wells and the World State.* New Haven: Yale University Press, 1961.

WALLACE, WILLIAM Review of *The Case of Wagner, Academy,* L (August 1, 1896), 75–7.

— *Lectures and Essays on Natural Theology and Ethics.* Edited by Edward Caird. Oxford: Clarendon Press, 1898.

WATTERSON, HELEN "Paragraphs from the German of Friedrich Nietzsche," *Century Magazine* (New York), XVI (May, 1889), 160.

WELLS, H. G. "Human Evolution," *Natural Science,* X (June, 1897), 244.

— *Mankind in the Making.* London: Chapman and Hall, 1903.

— *A Modern Utopia.* London: Thomas Nelson, n.d.

— *The Research Magnificent.* London: Macmillan, 1915.

— *The Sleeper Awakes*. London: Ernest Benn, 1927.

— *The Island of Dr. Moreau*. London: Ernest Benn, 1927.

— *Experiment in Autobiography*. 2 vols. London: Victor Gollancz and The Cresset Press, 1934.

— *You Can't Be Too Careful*. London: Secker and Warburg, 1941.

WENLEY, R. M. "Traffics and Discoveries," *Monist*, XXXI (January, 1921), 133–49.

WILDE, OSCAR *Essays*. London: Methuen, 1950.

WRENCH, G. T. *The Grammar of Life*. London: Heinemann, 1908.

— *The Mastery of Life*. London: Stephen Swift, 1911.

—"John Davidson," *Frankfurter Zeitung*, April 2, 1913, 1.

WYZEWA, THEODOR DE "Littérature Etrangère: Frédéric Nietsche, le dernier métaphysicien," *Revue Bleue*, XLVIII (November 7, 1891), 586–92.

YEATS, J. B. *Letters to His Son W. B. Yeats and Others, 1869–1922*. Edited by J. M. Hone. London: Faber, 1944.

YEATS, W. B. "A Canonical Book," *Bookman*, XXIV (May, 1903), 67–8.

— *The Letters of W. B. Yeats*. Edited by Allan Wade. London: Rupert Hart-Davis, 1954.

— *The Autobiography of W. B. Yeats*. New York: Doubleday, 1958.

— *Collected Poems*. London: Macmillan, 1958.

— *Mythologies*. London: Macmillan, 1959.

— *Essays and Introductions*. London: Macmillan, 1960.

— *Collected Plays*. London: Macmillan, 1960.

— *A Vision*. New York: Macmillan, 1961.

— *Explorations*. London: Macmillan, 1962.

ZWERDLING, ALEX *Yeats and the Heroic Ideal*. New York: New York University Press, 1965.

ADDENDA TO THE INTERNATIONAL NIETZSCHE BIBLIOGRAPHY

The following items have the same cut-off date (December, 1967) as those listed 4013–155 in the revised *INB*:

ALLEN, GAY WILSON "A Note on Comparing Whitman and Nietzsche," *Walt Whitman Review*, XI (1965), 74–6.

BERNDTSON, ARTHUR "Tragedy as Power: Beyond Nietzsche," *Bucknell Review*, XV, no. 3 (December, 1967), 97–107.

BOAS, GEORGE "The Romantic Self: An Historical Sketch," *Studies in Romanticism*, IV, no. 1 (Autumn, 1964), 1–16.

BUBER, MARTIN *The Philosophy of Martin Buber*. Edited by Paul Arthur Schilpp and Maurice Friedman. London: Cambridge University Press, 1967.

COLMAN, S. J. "Nietzsche as *politique et moraliste*," *Journal of the History of Ideas*, XXVII (October, 1966), 549–74.

CORDLE, THOMAS R. "Malraux and Nietzsche's *Birth of Tragedy*," *Bucknell Review*, VIII (1959), 89–104.

COULTER, JAMES A. "Nietzsche and Greek Studies," *Greek, Roman and Byzantine Studies*, III, no. 1 (Winter, 1960), 46–51.

FISCHER, KURT RUDOLPH "The Existentialism of Nietzsche's Zarathustra," *Daedalus*, XCII (1964), 998–1016.

FLACCUS, LOUIS WILLIAM *Artists and Thinkers*. New York: Books for Libraries Press, Inc., 1967 (a reprint of 329).

FRIEDMAN, MAURICE "Friedrich Nietzsche: Father of Atheistic Existentialism," *Journal of Existentialism*, VI, no. 23 (Spring, 1966), 269–77.

HAYES, DONNA GENE "Nietzsche's Eternal Recurrence: A Prelude to Heidegger," *Journal of Existentialism*, VI, no. 22 (Winter, 1965/6), 189–96.

HELLER, ERICH *The Artist's Journey into the Interior and Other Essays*. New York: Random House, 1965 (contains "Nietzsche and Wittingenstein" and 4066].

HELLER, PETER *Dialectics and Nihilism: Essays on Lessing, Nietzsche, Mann and Kafka*. Amherst: University of Massachussetts Press, 1966.

HENDERSON, ROBERT L. "Chopin and the Expressionists," *Music and Letters*, XLI (January, 1960), 38–45 [discusses 2728].

JUNG, C. G. *Psychological Types*. London: Kegan Paul, Trench, Trubner, 1923 (New York: Pantheon, 1959) [translation of 2143].

MURCHLAND, B. ED. *The Meaning of the Death of God*. New York: Random House, 1967.

PELZ, WERNER "Jesus and Nietzsche," *Listener*, LXVIII (July 5, 1962), 11–12.

ROSANTHAL (NÉE LEVY), MAUDE "Rediscovered Nietzsche," *Saturday Review of Literature*, XXXV (May 24, 1952), 28–9 [denies authenticity of *My Sister and I*, cf. 430].

SAMUEL, R. H. "Nietzsche Research in the Light of the Alleged Forgeries of His Works," *Proceedings of the Australasian Universities Language and Literature Association* (August, 1962), 65–7.

SCHIEDER, T. "Nietzsche and Bismarck," *Historian*, XXIX (August, 1967), 584–604.

SCHOENBERNER, FRANZ *Confessions of a European Intellectual*. New York: Macmillan, 1946.

SCOTT, NATHAN A. ED. *The Tragic Vision and the Christian Faith*. New York: New York Association Press, 1957.

SHEROVER, ERICA "Nietzsche: On Yea- and Nay-Saying," *Journal of Existentialism*, V, no. 20 (Summer, 1965), 423–7.

SPENGLER, OSWALD *Letters of Oswald Spengler*. Edited by Arthur Helps. New York: Alfred A. Knopf, 1966.

STACK, G. L. "Nietzsche and the Laws of Manu," *Sociology and Social Research*, LI (October, 1966), 94–106.

WEINBERG, KURT "Nietzsche's Paradox of Tragedy," *Yale French Studies*, no. 38 (1967), 251–66.

WEISSMANN, KARL "Nietzsche and the Anti-Maturism," *American Imago*, XX (1963), 315–29.

Index

INDEX

Italic figures refer to passages in which detailed treatment is given.

Abbott, G. F. 204
Adams, Morris 95, 96–7
Æ 154, 248, 275
Aeschylus 140n, 211, 243
Aldington, Richard 262
Alexander, S. 39
Allen, Grant 83
Andreas-Salomé, Lou 21, 247
Archer, William 36, 39, 61, 85, 124, 175, 190, 191, 214
Arnold, Matthew 249, 253, 273
Auden, W. H. 182n, 271n, 292n
Aurelius, Marcus 119

Bagehot, Walter 19
Bakunin, Michael 25, 181, 194
Balzac, Honoré de 132, 157–8, 272n
Barnhill, J. B. 58–60, 106
Barry, W. 128n, 237
Barzun, Jacques vii, 8, 60
Baudelaire, Charles 27, 271n
Beardsley, Aubrey 122
Beddoes, Thomas Lovell 12, 75n
Beer, Max 203
Beerbohm, Max 190
Beethoven, Ludwig van 80, 129
Bell, Clive 267
Belloc, Hilaire 228, 230
Benjamin, Judah 238
Bennett, Arnold 39, 188n, 228, 240, 241
Bentham, Jeremy 200, 212
Bergson, Henri 10, 50, 191, 201, 217, 255, 259, 260n, 262
Beyond-Man *see* Nietzsche, themes, superman
Bismarck 194, 203, 223, 243
Bizet 180, 186, 256, 283n

Blake, William 15, 90, 119, 130, 135, *139–41*, 142, 143, 144, 148, 157, 164, 177, 200, 231, 234, 244, 263, 266
Bland, Herbert 58, 94, 223, 227
Blavatsky, H. P. 29, 221
Bloomsbury Group 266–8
Boehme, Jakob 133n
Boer War 34, 61–2, 195
Borgia, Caesar 80, 89, 168, 246
Bourget, Paul 100, 118
Bradley, A. C. *125*
Bradley, F. H. 27
Brandes, George 13, 17, 18, 27, 40, 64, 108, 111, 76
Brooke, Rupert 267
Brown, Maurice 229, 261
Browning, Robert 12, 15, 21
Brutus 111
Buchanan, Robert 62
Bulwer-Lytton, Lord Edward 12, 219, 243
Bunyan, John 190, 200, 201, 211
Burns, Robert 69, 88n
Butcher, S. H. 39
Butler, Samuel 6, 190, 263n, 271n
Byron, Lord George Gordon 12, 19, 88n, 111, 197n

Caesar, Julius 80, 111, 112, 137, 168, *194*, 198
Carlyle, Thomas 12, 20, 54, 59, 74–5, 77, 79, 80–1, 114, 120, 169, 197n, 216, 217, 225, 271, 272n
Carpenter, Edward 58, 95–6, 221, 226, 264
Castiglione, B. 154, 160
Chamberlain, H. S. 133, 179
Chapman, George 103

Chatterton-Hill, Georges 114
Chesterton, G. K. 5, 7, 11, 188n, 207–10, 214, 215, 226, 228, 231, 232, 236, 237
Christianity 20, 26, 33, 36, 41, 45, 55, 62–3, 73–4, 88, 95, 97, 122, 129, 130, 134, 137, 140, 151, 168, 185, 194, 198, 203–4, 208, 209, 219, 223, 230, 233, 248, 266, 272, 273
Chubb, Percival 94
Cohn, Paul 235, 238, 241
Coleridge, S. T. 125, 128, 132n, 168, 271n
Collins, A. 235, 239
Common, Thomas 5, 22, 25, 36, 38, 39, 46–9, 57, 62, 63n, 64, 81n, 86n, 104, 106, 139, 143–4, 187–8, 189, 195, 205, 236
Comte, Auguste 12, 271
Cornford, Francis 125
Cousins, James 126
Croce, Benedetto 117
Cromwell, Oliver 79, 80, 81, 132, 246
Cunninghame-Graham, R. B. 58

D'Annunzio, Gabriele 105, 126–7
Dante 157
Darwin, Charles 10, 20, 21, 22, 24, 29, 60, 71, 76, 82n, 103, 112, 133, 154, 175, 183, 192, 195, 208, 232, 273, 279n, 298n
Davidson, John 4, 5, 6, 7, 8, 11, 15, 22, 31, 53–91, 93, 121, 122, 152, 155, 183, 190, 209, 234, 261, 269, 270, 272n, 273, 275
  discovery of Nietzsche 64–75; repudiation of discipleship 68–9, 84, 91; and anarchism 86n; on Carlyle 81; on Christianity 73–4; contemporary reaction to 85–9; on *The Eagle and the Serpent* 58–9; and egoism 53–5; materialism 70–2, 89n; Nietzscheans on 87–8; Orage on, 86; on poets 69–70, 84–5; and the superman 75–84, 85–6; on the will to power 69–70, 72, 89; compared with Wells 81–3
Davidson, Thomas 94
Da Vinci, Leonardo 115
decadence 102, 118, 122, 179, 254, 274
Degas, Edouard 132
De Gaultier, Jules 117
Delius, Frederick 42, 180
democracy 33, 114, 123, 127, 148, 170, 185, 199, 223, 267
De Quincey, Thomas 128
Dickinson, Lowes 227
Disraeli, Benjamin 243, 247

Dostoievsky, Feodor 10, 13, 15, 261, 263, 272n
Douglas, Norman 274
Duclaux, Mary 282n
Dujardin, Edouard 133, 179
Duncan, Isadora 120n

Eagle and the Serpent, The 5, 36, 55–63, 106, 186–7, 189, 221, 234
Egerton, George 53, 98–9
Eglinton, John 126, 133, 136–7, 159
egoism 53–63 *passim*
Einstein, Albert 119
Eliot, George 20, 103
Eliot, T. S. 10, 14, 15, 126, 249, 259, 260n, 262, 268, 274
Ellis, Edith 95, 96, 99
Ellis, Edwin 156
Ellis, Havelock 5, 8, 11, 27, 33, 36, 39, 58, 62, 93–120, 121, 122, 125, 126, 128, 129, 131, 183, 207, 209n, 221, 228, 231, 232, 273, 274, 275, 282n
  Savoy articles on Nietzsche 100–6, 108, 111, 120; other writing on Nietzsche 106–9; Nietzschean themes in 116–20; on art 117–8; on the dance 105, 118–20, 129; on decadence 118; on the eternal recurrence 108; on eugenics 112–3, 114–5; on Nietzsche's madness 106–7; on Shaw 109–11; on the superman 108–16; on Wells 109; on the will to power 107–8
Ellis, William Ashton 179, 183
Emerson, Ralph 55, 59, 94, 114, 120, 130, 231
Epicurus 111
Eugenics 112–5, 203–4, 208, 230, 271, 272
Euripides 127, 199, 211, 217

Fabianism 94, 152, 187, 203, 212, 221, 223–8, 267
Farr, Florence 167, 224, 231n
Fellowship of the New Life 94–8, 111, 122, 187, 223
Feminist Movement 98–100
Flaubert, Gustave 132, 252n
Förster-Nietzsche, Elisabeth 46–8, 49n, 101, 106, 241, 268, 302n
Forster, E. M. 266–7, 268
Freud, Sigmund 10, 100, 117, 262, 272n
Froude, J. A. 74–5, 81
Fry, Roger 267n

Galsworthy, John 7, 9, 125, 228
Galton, Sir Francis 112–13, 203, 272
Garnett, Edward 8, 36, 39, 46, 122, 250
Garnett, Richard 89
Gast, Peter 21, 62
Gautier, Theodore 27
George, Henry 238n
Gide, André 15, 251n
Gill, Eric 227
Gissing, George 88, 292n
Glennie, Stuart 26–7
Godwin, William 83, 222
Goethe, J. W. von 23, 25, 55, 79, 88n, 90, 101, 106, 111, 112, 168, 188n, 230, 246, 252n, 257
Goldman, Emma, 86
Good European Point of View 46, 63, 205
Gosse, Edmund 19, 36, 39, 89, 126, 175, 176
Gourmont, Rémy de 100, 126, 130, 160n, 255
Graham, Stephen 202
Grant, Duncan 267
Graves, Robert 10, 126
Gray, John 122
Gregory, Lady Augusta 139, 141, 142, 143n, 146, 147, 154, 155, 159–60
Grein, J. T. 23, 176
Grierson, Sir Herbert 148
Grove, Sir George 32, 235
Gurdjieff, G. 220, 245
Gwynn, Stephen 126

Halévy, Daniel 133, 134, 143n, 160, 266, 282n
Hamburger, Michael 3, 306n
Hamsun, Knut 53
Hansson, Ola 53
Hardie, Keir 239
Harris, Frank 86, 207
Harrison, Austin 237
Harrison, Jane 125
Hastings, Beatrice 233
Haussmann, W. A. 22, 26, 62
Hawthorne, Nathaniel 76
Hearn, Lafcadio 110n
Hegel, Friedrich 49, 125, 183, 263, 271
Heine, Heinrich 21, 25, 34, 100, 123, 182
Henley, William 60, 76, 77
Heraclitus 71, 163
Higgins, F. R. 156
Hinton, James 94, 96

Hitler, Adolf 216
Hobbes, Thomas 19, 83, 143
Hobhouse, L. T. 205
Hofmannsthal, Hugo von 272
Homer 151, 165
Hone, J. M. 133, 143
Horace 257
Hueffer, Franz 178, 183
Hulme, T. E. 3, 9, 10, 100, 238, 250, 255–61, 262, 274
Hume, David 50, 263
Huneker, James 106, 134, 205, 206
Husserl, E. 255, 260
Huxley, Aldous 10, 100, 265n
Huxley, Thomas Henry 22, 183
Huysmans, J. K. 118, 127, 267
Hyndman, H. M. 94

Ibsen, Henrik, 10, 12, 13, 23, 27, 54, 79, 86, 95, 99, 100, 105, 114, 121, 127n, 135, 181, 184, 187, 189, 190, 191, 193–4, 195, 201, 203, 208, 210, 217, 219, 223n, 226, 227, 231, 243, 244, 247n, 263, 269, 302n
    in England 175–8
Influence, concept of 12–6
International Nietzsche Bibliography 8, 10n, 321–2

Jackson, Holbrook 8, 14n, 50, 63, 75, 89, 204, 221, 226, 227, 228, 230, 234, 235, 241, 260n, 261
Jefferies, Richard 12
John, Augustus 261
Jordan, Wilhelm 25
Joyce, James 3, 7, 133, *134–6*, 268, 272n

Kafka, Franz 135n
Kant, Immanuel 12, 49, 50, 131, 183, 201, 302n
Kennedy, J. M. 41, 49, 88, 175, 224, 235, 236–7, 239, 241, 243, 250, 252, 253, 255–6, 260
Kidd, Benjamin 58
Kierkegaard 10, 302n
Kipling, Rudyard 60, 76
Kropotkin, P. 57, 86n

Lamarck, J. B. 199
Landor, Walter Savage 19
Lange, F. A. 117
Lasserre, Pierre 255
Lavrin, Janko 251

Lawrence, D. H. 6, 7, 10, 11, 14, 99, 207, 262, 268, 272n, 274
Lawrence, T. E. 7, 215
Leavis, F. R. 249
Lee, Vernon (Violet Paget) 120, 282n
Le Gallienne, Richard 83, 176n
Levy, Dr. Oscar 4, 23, *40–8*, 87, 100, 113, 121, 122, 202, 206–7, *235–6*, 237–43 *passim*, 246, 262, 268, 269, 303n, 306n
Lewis, P. B. Wyndham 3, 10, 100, 238, 262, 263n, 267n, 274, 292n
Lichtenberger, Henri 39, 62, 114n, 288n
Lindsay, Jack 8, 10
Lubbock, Sir John 110n
Lucretius 71, 88
Ludovici, A. M. 41, 42, 86n, 100, 188n, *235–8 passim*, 239, 242, 249n, 250, 252–3, 260, 260n, 298n
Lytton, Lord Edward Bulwer *see* Bulwer-Lytton

McCall, Erwin *see* Barnhill, J. B.
MacCarthy, Desmond 8, 16, 234, 267
McDougall, William 6
MacKenna, Stephen 126
Machiavelli 256
Maeterlinck 27
Mallock, W. H. 58
Manet, Edouard 132
Mann, Thomas 135n, 252n, 270
Marlowe, Christopher 79, 80, 89, 101
Marshall, Beatrice 37
Marx, Karl 13, 94, 197n, 203, 238n
Masterman, C. F. G. 205, 206
Maugham, W. Somerset vii
Mencken, H. L. 170n, 205, 206
Mendelsson, Felix 178
Meredith, George 12, 183, 203, 267
Michelangelo 193
Mill, John Stuart 20, 21, 103, 271
Milton, John 79, 81
Monro, Harold 229
Moore, G. E, 266
Moore, George 9, 126, *132–4*, 263n, 269, 272n, 282n
Morris, William 94, 122, 139, 152, 169, 264, 273
Muegge, M. A. 41, 113, 205
Muir, Edwin 5, 7, 10, 261, 262, *264–6*, 302n
Murray, Gilbert 163n, 211, 231
Murray, John 238n

Murry, J. Middleton 10, 207, 262
Mussolini 149, 216

Napoleon 72, 80, 90, 111, 112, 137, 147, 197, 198, 216, 246, 267
Neave, Adam 204
New Age 8, 40, 114, 160, 176, 184, 212n, *219–68 passim*, 269, 274
  foundation of 228; publicizing of Nietzsche 234–43
Newman, Ernest 5, 32, 32n, 58, 179
Nietzsche, Friedrich Wilhelm
  bibliographies of 8–11; earlier scholarship on 3–8; English translations of 4–5, *17–51*, 107, 235–6, 239, 240–1, 269–70; French translations of 18–9, 38, 39, 45, 269; Jewish interest in 21, 27, *235–6*, 243

  themes: *amor fati* 72, 89, 163, 172–3; as anarchist 33, 36, 86n, 105, 155, 183, 239, 262, 264; as aphorist 22, 28, 65, 102, 107, 129–30, 144, 185, 186, 192–3, 230, 231, 263n, 265n, 270–1; Apollonian and Dionysian 102, 118, *124–6*, 127, 129, 131n, 141, 166, 211, 213, 231, 233, 234, 247; eternal recurrence viii, 89, 106, 108, 133, 143, 161, 163, 171, 172, 207, 239, 299n; madness 25, 27, 28n, 41, 53, 66, 80, 101, 106–7, 241–2, 270; master morality 6, 28, 89, 104, 137, *145–52*, 169, 257; pragmatism 50; as prose writer 7, 18, 30–1, 34, 37, 65, 104, 108, 119, 124, 139n, 144, 182, 237; self-conquest 88n, 104, 113, 150, 157, 158, *161–73*, 246; superman viii, 4, 6, 12, 25, 28, 31–2, 36, 39, 43, 57, 62, 63n, 73, *75–84*, 87, 89, 90, 96, 97, 99, 103n, 104, 106, *108–16*, 122, 129, 131n, 134, 136, 137, 143n, 145, *152–61*, 161–73 *passim*, 177, 181, 192, *193–202*, 203–10 *passim*, 212–17 *passim*, 219–22 *passim*, 227, 230, 233 243–9, 253, 263n, 265–6, 267n, 272–3, 299n, 302n; transvaluation of values 3, 5, 50, 82, 84–5, 95, 99, 121, 142, 162, 173, 177, 194; will to power viii, 43, 69–70, 72, 89, 96, 107–8, 162, 192, 233, 246, 266

  views on: *amor fati* 172; art 66, 117, 163, 183, *249–61 passim*, 271, 273–4; Bagehot 19; Byron 19; Carlyle 20, 216; comedy 214n; convictions 216; the dance 21, 105, 119–20, 129, 173; Darwin 20, 21, 60, 112; decadence 4, 4n, 118, 254; democracy 148; disciples 270; Dostoievsky 13; England and the English 7, 19–21, 42, 103; English philosophy 19–21; eternal recurrence 108; euthanasia 285n; France 18–9; freedom 103, 225n; Germany 102; Horace 257; Landor 19; the mask 4n, 167–9, 270; master morality 145–51 passim; materialism 71–2; Mill 20, 21; Napoleon 80, 147; Pascal 13; pity 66, 115, 122, 131, 146–7; romanticism 4, 256–7; readers 17, 270; self-conquest 150, 161, 162, 163–4; Shakespeare 19; Socrates 213; Spencer 21; superman 152, 161, 169, 200, 213; transvaluation of values 84–5, 161–2; war 59, 107; women 66, 98–100, 201, 122, 247, 271, 301n

works: *Antichrist* 7n, 17n, 23, 73, 149, 185, 269; *Birth of Tragedy* 37, 39, 44, 48, 97, 101–2, 117, 119, 120n, *124–6*, 127, 129, 141, 143n, 163, 166, 182, 211, 212, 212n, 225, 231, 241, 248, 269; *Beyond Good and Evil* 18, 23, 27, 37, 38, 40, 42, 47, 48, 106, 115, 137, 145, 166n, 177, 185, 201, 231, 240, 244, 263, 264; *Case of Wagner* 23, 24, 30, 48, 139n, 143n, 179, 182, 253, 269; *Dawn of Day* 36, 37, 38, 39, 48, 63, 102, 106, 129–30, 141n, 143n, 153; *Ecce Homo* 18, 48, 142, 163, 241; *Gay Science* 7n, 37, 54, 102, 118, 133n, 188, 258n, 263n; *Genealogy of Morals* 23, 26, 27, 33, 43, 48, 69, 106, 123, 139n, 143n, 145, 153, 186, 202; *Human, All-Too-Human* 22, 48, 102, 260n; *Nietzsche contra Wagner* 23, 179, 180, 252, 269; *Poems* 24; *Thoughts out of Season* 19, 95, 101–2, 143n, 160n, 168, 169, 182; *Thus Spake Zarathustra* 6, 7n, 12, 17n, 18, 22, 23, 25, 26, 27, 30, 31, 33, 34, 39, 40, 41, 42, 44, 47, 48, 63, 65, 99, 106, 108, 110, 111, 117, 120n, 122, 129, 132, 135–6, 139n, 141n, 142, 145, 151n, 152n, 157, 160, 161, 164, 169, 178, 179, 185, 186, 191, 193, 201, 210n, 212n, 220, 221, 229n, 230, 231, 234n, 240, 244, 259, 263, 264, 268, 269, 291n, 294n; *Twilight of the Idols* 7n, 17n, 18, 23, 27, 253, 255; *Will to Power* 50, 82, 143n, 157, 160n, 163, 238

compared with: Bagehot 19, Balzac 157–8; Blake *130–1*, *139–41*, 157, 231, 234, 244, 266; Carlyle 169; Chapman 103; Emerson 130, 231; Goethe 66, 67; Ibsen 127n, 177–8, 231, 302n; Kant 302n; Kierkegaard 302n; Nordau 29–30; Pater 128; Schopenhauer 70, 98, 137, 183; Shaw 210–7; Stirner 62; Strindberg 19, 302n; Tolstoy 97–8, 130; Wagner 180, 302n

Nietzsche-Archiv 38, 40, 47–9, 268, 270
Nietzsche Society 57, 187, 223
Nietzscheans, English 41–2, 210, 229n, 235–9, 241–2, 246, 247, 248, 262, 266, 269
  and Davidson, 87–8; and Ellis 106; and eugenics 113–4; and Orage 235–9 passim; and Shaw 205–7
Nordau, Max 5, 27–9, 31, 34, 38, 53, 62, 100, 175, 180, 182, *184–5*, 242, 269, 274
Norregard, Julie 176n,
Notes for Good Europeans see *Good European Point of View*

Oneida Community 93
Orage, A. R. 3, 8, 11, 40, 100, 102, 106, 108, 125, 190, 192, 211, *219–68*, 269, 273, 274, 275
  books on Nietzsche 230–4; influence of 261–3; on Davidson 86; on Shaw 211; Shaw on 231–2; and socialism 223–6, 239; and the superman 219–21, 233, *243–9*
Ortega y Gasset 116
Overman see Nietzsche, themes, superman

Paget, Violet see Lee, Vernon
Pascal, Blaise 13, 104, 255, 263
Pater, W. 4, 88, 127, *128–9*, *131n*, 168, 266, 271, 272, 273, 274
Patmore, Coventry 143, 249
Payne, John 123
Pease, Edward 94, 227
Penty, A. J. 223, 226
Phillpotts, Eden 114, 188n, 237, 242
Plato 35, 199, 201, 220, 221, 224, 227, 228, 233, 238, 263
Platt, William 57
Plotinus 126n,
Podmore, Frank 94

Poe, Edgar Allan 127
Pound, Ezra 159, 160, 162, 164, 254, 262, 274
Powys, John Cowper 10
Pringle-Pattison, A. Seth 5, 8, 34–5, 64, 179
Prometheus 154, 193, 196, 213

Quinn, John 139, 141, 144

Racine, Jean 257
Rappoport, A. 235, 302n
Raven, Alexander 143n
Read, Herbert 10, 225n, 249, 259, 261, 262, 263–4, 266
Renan, Ernest 12, 111
Rhymers' Club 122
Rhys, Ernest 40, 122, 202
Richards, Grant 188
Richardson, Frederick 234
Richardson, Samuel 143
Ricketts, Charles 123
Rilke, Rainer Maria vii, 21, 272n
Rimbaud, Arthur 135
Robertson, J. G. 39, 51
Robertson, J. M. 5, 58, 106
Rodin, Auguste 238
Rolleston, T. W. 43, 122, 126, 273
Rousseau, Jean Jacques 107, 255, 256, 257
Runciman, J. F. 180
Ruskin, John 13, 81, 249, 273, 295n
Russell, George *see* Æ
Russell, Lord Bertrand vii, 154, 274

Saintsbury, George 64, 89, 124, 237
Salomé, Lou Andreas *see* Andreas-Salomé, Lou
Samuel, Horace B. 235
Samurai 170, 227, 228–9
Sarolea, Charles 64, 207
Saunders, T. Bailey 35–6, 183
Savoy 100, 101, 121, 122
Scheffauer, H. 239
Scheler, Max 255
Schiller, F. C. S. 6, 8, 10, 39, 49–50, 241n
Schopenhauer, Arthur 6, 10, 21, 35, 50, 70, 71, 80, 98, 102, 116, 120, 131, 133n, 135, 137, 144, 165, 175, 190, 197, 201, 230, 233, 263
   in England 182–4
Schwartz, George 235
Sedgwick, Anne 266

Seklew, Malfew 63n
Selver, Paul 160n, 238
Shakespeare, William 19, 88n, 69–70, 111, 125, 159, 201, 257, 258
   Richard III 79, 188
Shaw, George Bernard 5, 6, 6n, 7, 11, 13, 15, 26, 29, 33, 36, 39, 51, 59, 71, 86, 93, 94, 95, 99, 100, 108, 109–11, 126, 131n, 135, 143n, 144, 161, 171, *175–217*, 221, 223, 223n, 226, 227, 228, 229, 231, 236, 239, 243, 267, 269, 271n, 272, 273, 275, 284n
   reviews of Nietzsche translations 185–6; knowledge of Nietzsche 185–93; contemporary reaction to 202–10; on Davidson 71, 89n; Ellis on 109–11; and Ibsen, 175–8; Life Force 5, 6, 13, 110, 184, 194, 196, 198, 202, 215, 217, 228; Nietzscheans on 202, 205–7; and Nordau 184–5; on Orage 231–2; Orage on 211; and Schopenhauer 182–4; and the superman 177, 181, 192, *193–202*, 212–17 *passim*; and Wagner 178–82; compared with Carlyle 216; compared with Nietzsche 210–7; compared with Yeats 212–3
Shelley, Percy Bysshe 83, 140, 148, 154, 159, 160
Simons, L. 22, 49n
Sinnett, A. P. 219
Sitwell, Osbert 306n
Smart, Christopher 107
socialism 56, 74, 93–4, 97–8, 185, 190, 206, 223–6, 239, 265, 271
Socrates 13, 111, 127, 151, 165, 192, 211, 212, 213
Sophocles 211, 258
Sorel, Georges, 255, 273
Sorley, William 35n
Spencer, Herbert 21, 58, 59, 110n, 143, 154, 183, 190, 209
Stalin 216
Stendhal 168, 269, 272n
Stephen, Leslie 249
Stevenson, R. L. 59
Stirner, Max 25, 53n, 62, 74, 86, 86n, 93, 114, 234
Strauss, David 102, 168, 179, 180
Strauss, Richard 32, 129, 193, 235
Strindberg, August 18–9, 21, 53, 64, 99, 176, 190, 302n
superman *see* Nietzsche, themes

Swinburne, Algernon 155, 177
Symons, Arthur 37, 88, 100, 101, 114n, 118, 122, 125, *126–32*, 140, 282n
Synge, J. M. 111, 127, 142

Taine, Hippolyte 18, 40, 126, 282n
Tennyson, Lord Alfred 12
Theosophy 219–22 *passim*
Thomas, Edward 123–4
Thoreau, Henry David 55, 59, 94
Tille, Alexander 8, *23–7*, 30, 31, 32, 35, 36, 38, 61n, 64, 82n, 104, 106, 120, 143, 178, 195, 240
Tolstoy, Leo 19, 27, 94, 97, 99, 100, 120, 122, 127, 130, 143, 178, 208, 227, 229, 264
Trevelyan, G. M. 203
Turgenev, Ivan 19, 130
Turner, Saxon Sidney 267n
Twain, Mark 177
Tyndall, John 71, 183

Übermensch *see* Nietzsche, themes, superman
Upward, Allan 204

Vaihinger, Hans 50–1, 100, 110
Verlaine, Paul 132
Volz, Johanna 37, 48

Wagner, Richard 10, 26, 27, 28, 30, 33, 54, 116, 122, 129, 175, 177, 183, 184, 188n, 189, 190, 191, 193, 194, 195, 196, 197, 200, 201, 210, 216, 217, 219, 253–4, 269, 283n, 293n, 302n
  in England 178–82

Wallace, Alfred Russel 57, 133
Wallace, William 29, 30, 33, 33n, 182
Webb, Beatrice and Sidney 227
Wells, H. G. 6n, 7, 11, 33, *81–3*, 109, 143n, *170–1*, 190, 207, 209, 221, 227, 228, 229, 231, 267, 269, 299n, 304n
Whitman, Walt 27, 31, 43, 86, 86n, 100, 122, 231
Wilde, Oscar 27, 43, 96, 146, 168, 231, *251–2n*, 274
Woolf, Leonard 267
Worringer, W. 253, 255
Wrench, G. T. 88, 113, 235, 236, 239, 246
Wyzewa, Theodor de 31, *64–7 passim*, 133, 179, 185

Yeats, J. B. 159, 163
Yeats, W. B. 3, 6n, 7, 11, 14–5, 68, 88n, 100, 102, 108, 116, 117, 118, 119, 121, 122, 125, 126, 127, 128, 129, 130, 131n, 133n, 135, 136, 137, *139–73*, 176, 183, 207, 212, 219, 226n, 227, 229, 231, 246, 253, 269, 270, 272, 272n, 273, 274, 275
  references to Nietzsche in 139–43; annotations to Nietzsche 143–52; on the mask 167–9; on self-conquest 161–73; on the superman 152–61; compared with Shaw 212–13
Yellow Book, 121, 122

Zimmern, Helen 21, 22, 48, 182, 229n, 235, 237
Zola, Émile 27, 132, 178

www.ingramcontent.com/pod-product-compliance
Lightning Source LLC
Chambersburg PA
CBHW071148070526
44584CB00019B/2705